WITHDRAWN

by Steve Wiegand

U.S. History For Dummies®, 3rd Edition

Published by: **John Wiley & Sons, Inc.,** 111 River Street, Hoboken, NJ 07030-5774, www.wiley.com

Copyright © 2014 by John Wiley & Sons, Inc., Hoboken, New Jersey

Published simultaneously in Canada

No part of this publication may be reproduced, stored in a retrieval system or transmitted in any form or by any means, electronic, mechanical, photocopying, recording, scanning or otherwise, except as permitted under Sections 107 or 108 of the 1976 United States Copyright Act, without the prior written permission of the Publisher. Requests to the Publisher for permission should be addressed to the Permissions Department, John Wiley & Sons, Inc., 111 River Street, Hoboken, NJ 07030, (201) 748-6011, fax (201) 748-6008, or online at http://www.wiley.com/go/permissions.

Trademarks: Wiley, For Dummies, the Dummies Man logo, Dummies.com, Making Everything Easier, and related trade dress are trademarks or registered trademarks of John Wiley & Sons, Inc., and may not be used without written permission. All other trademarks are the property of their respective owners. John Wiley & Sons, Inc., is not associated with any product or vendor mentioned in this book.

LIMIT OF LIABILITY/DISCLAIMER OF WARRANTY: WHILE THE PUBLISHER AND AUTHOR HAVE USED THEIR BEST EFFORTS IN PREPARING THIS BOOK, THEY MAKE NO REPRESENTATIONS OR WARRANTIES WITH RESPECT TO THE ACCURACY OR COMPLETENESS OF THE CONTENTS OF THIS BOOK AND SPECIFICALLY DISCLAIM ANY IMPLIED WARRANTIES OF MERCHANTABILITY OR FITNESS FOR A PARTICULAR PURPOSE. NO WARRANTY MAY BE CREATED OR EXTENDED BY SALES REPRESENTATIVES OR WRITTEN SALES MATERIALS. THE ADVISE AND STRATEGIES CONTAINED HEREIN MAY NOT BE SUITABLE FOR YOUR SITUATION. YOU SHOULD CONSULT WITH A PROFESSIONAL WHERE APPROPRIATE. NEITHER THE PUBLISHER NOR THE AUTHOR SHALL BE LIABLE FOR DAMAGES ARISING HEREFROM.

For general information on our other products and services, please contact our Customer Care Department within the U.S. at 877-762-2974, outside the U.S. at 317-572-3993, or fax 317-572-4002. For technical support, please visit www.wiley.com/techsupport.

Wiley publishes in a variety of print and electronic formats and by print-on-demand. Some material included with standard print versions of this book may not be included in e-books or in print-on-demand. If this book refers to media such as a CD or DVD that is not included in the version you purchased, you may download this material at http://booksupport.wiley.com. For more information about Wiley products, visit www.wiley.com.

Library of Congress Control Number is available from the publisher.

ISBN 978-1-118-88898-8 (pbk); ISBN 978-1-118-88903-9 (ebk); ISBN 978-1-118-88907-7 (ebk);

Manufactured in the United States of America

10 9 8 7 6 5 4 3 2 1

Contents at a Glance

Introduction 1

Part I: Getting Started with U.S. History 5
Chapter 1: America: A Short Biography 7
Chapter 2: Native Americans and Explorers: 14,000 BC (?)–1607 21
Chapter 3: Pilgrims' Progress: The English Colonies, 1607–1700 39
Chapter 4: You Say You Want a Revolution: 1700–1775 53
Chapter 5: Yankee Doodlin': 1775–1783 69
Chapter 6: Blueprints and Birth Pains: 1783–1800 83

Part II: Growing Pains 95
Chapter 7: "Long Tom" and One Weird War: 1800–1815 97
Chapter 8: Pulling Together to Keep from Falling Apart: 1815–1844 115
Chapter 9: War, Gold, and a Gathering Storm: 1845–1860 137
Chapter 10: A Most Uncivil War: 1861–1865 151
Chapter 11: Putting the Country Back Together: 1865–1876 167

Part III: Coming of Age 179
Chapter 12: Growing Up: 1876–1898 181
Chapter 13: Growing into the 20th Century: 1899–1918 199
Chapter 14: Gin, Jazz, and Lucky Lindy: 1919–1929 215
Chapter 15: Uncle Sam's Depressed: 1930–1940 231
Chapter 16: The World at War: 1941–1945 247

Part IV: America in Adulthood 265
Chapter 17: TV, Elvis, and Reds under the Bed: 1946–1960 267
Chapter 18: Camelot to Watergate: 1961–1974 283
Chapter 19: Hold the Malaise, or, Ayatollah So: 1975–1992 299
Chapter 20: No Sex, Please, I'm the President: 1993–1999 313

Part V: Facing the New Millennium 325
Chapter 21: Terror Comes Home; America Goes to War(s) 327
Chapter 22: Recessions Can Be Really Depressing 341
Chapter 23: Reforming Healthcare Is No Tea Party 353
Chapter 24: This New America 367

Part VI: The Part of Tens 379
Chapter 25: Ten Events That Defined American Culture 381
Chapter 26: Ten Unfortunate Statements by U.S. Presidents 385

Part VII: The Appendixes 389
Appendix A: The Bill of Rights: Amendments 1–10 of the Constitution 391
Appendix B: The Declaration of Independence 393

Index 397

Table of Contents

Introduction 1
About This Book 1
Conventions Used in This Book 2
What You're Not to Read 2
Foolish Assumptions 3
Beyond the Book 3
Icons Used in This Book 3
Where to Go from Here 4

Part I: Getting Started with U.S. History 5

Chapter 1: America: A Short Biography 7
They Came, They Saw, They Stayed 7
    Catching up to the Spanish 8
    It's revolutionary! 9
Putting America on the Map 9
    Nationalizing a nation 10
    Dirty politics 11
    Fighting with a neighbor, finding gold, and heading for a breakup 11
    Fighting among ourselves 12
    Making up is hard to do 13
Struggling with Greatness 13
    Finding a place in the world 14
    Roaring through the '20s 14
    What's so great about a depression? 14
    The big one 15
A Cold War and a Brave New World 15
    From a Kennedy to a Ford 16
    Good intentions, mixed results 17
    Finishing out the century 17
America in the 21st Century 18
    Bursting economic bubbles 19
    Politics and healthcare are no tea party 19
    Changing technology, changing America 19

Chapter 2: Native Americans and Explorers: 14,000 BC (?)–1607....21

Coming to America 21
Exploring Early Civilizations 22
    The Anasazi 23
    The Mound Builders 23
Many Tribes, Not Many People..24
    In the Northwest 24
    In the Southwest 25
    On the Great Plains 25
    In the Northeast 25
    In the Southeast 26
De-stereotyping the Native Americans 26
Visiting by the Vikings 27
Spicing Up Life — and Other Reasons for Exploring 29
Discovering a Dozen Other People Who Dropped By.............................31
The Sword, the Cross, and the Measles..33
    Native American slavery 34
    The men in the brown robes 35
    Destruction through disease 35
Arriving Late for the Party...36
    France..37
    England..37

Chapter 3: Pilgrims' Progress: The English Colonies, 1607–1700....39

Seeing Potential in the New World 39
Settling in Jamestown 40
    Early troubles 40
    Making Native American friends..41
    Finding a cash crop 41
Instituting Slavery..42
Colonizing: Pilgrims and Puritans 43
    The Mayflower Compact: A Dutch pilgrimage 43
    The Massachusetts Bay colony: A pure haven 45
Bringing Religious Freedom: Dissidents, Catholics, and Quakers..........47
    Sneaking off to Rhode Island 48
    Condoning only Christianity in Maryland......................................48
    Promoting tolerance in Pennsylvania 49
Dealings of the Dutch...49
Coping with Native American Troubles..50
Rebelling — with Bacon 51

Chapter 4: You Say You Want a Revolution: 1700–1775............53

Looking at America in 1700 53
Colonizing New France 54

Fighting the First True World Wars...55
    King William's War...55
    Queen Anne's War 56
    King George's War 56
Awakening to Greater Religious Freedom 56
The French and Indian War 57
    Unifying the colonies 58
    Defeating British General Braddock...58
    Outfighting the French 59
Growing like a Weed...60
    Accounting for the population explosion 60
    Living the good life 61
Heading toward Divorce with Britain 62
    The Proclamation of 1763 63
    The Revenue Acts (1764) 63
    The Stamp Act (1765) 63
    The Townshend Act (1767) 64
    The Boston Massacre (1770) 65
    The Boston Tea Party (1773) 65
    The "Intolerable" Acts (1774) 66
Congressing over Cocktails 66
Mr. Revere, Your Horse Is Ready..67

Chapter 5: Yankee Doodlin': 1775–1783..69

In This Corner, the Brits. 69
In This Corner, the Yanks. 70
Mr. Washington Goes to War 71
    Finding faults in George 72
    Commanding a country..72
Declaring Independence 73
    Stirring up colonists' emotions 73
    Writing history 74
Kissing Up to the French 76
Undergoing Life Changes: The Loyalists and the Slaves 76
    Remaining loyal to the crown...76
    Confronting slavery issues 77
Winning a War...77
    Felling a British fort 78
    Battling it out on Bunker — make that Breed's — Hill..............79
    Losing the campaign in Canada 79
    Nixing plans to take New York 79
    Winnin' at Trenton and Princeton 79
    Making the Brits surrender at Saratoga 80
    Sparring at sea..80
    Losing big in Charleston 80
    Minimizing the damage at Guilford Courthouse.....................80
    Turning things around at Yorktown..81

Chapter 6: Blueprints and Birth Pains: 1783–1800 83

Making the Rules 83
    Going back to Philly 84
    Selling the Constitution to the states 86
Dishing Up Politics, American Style 87
    Washington the politician 87
    Family feuding: Jefferson vs. Hamilton 88
Raising the Dough 89
Earning Respect 90
    Shaking things up: Shays's Rebellion 90
    Taxing liquid corn: The Whiskey Rebellion 91
    Going "mad" over the Native Americans 91
    Attempting to censor the press 92
Finding Foreign Friction 93

Part II: Growing Pains 95

Chapter 7: "Long Tom" and One Weird War: 1800–1815 97

Jefferson Gets a Job 97
Disorder in the Court 99
Growing by Leaps and Bounds 101
    Capitalizing on Napoleon's going-out-of-business sale 102
    Lewis, Clark, and the woman on the dollar coin 104
Fighting Pirates, and a "Dambargo" 105
    "To the shores of Tripoli . . ." 106
    No one likes a bloodless war 107
"Little Jemmy" Takes the Helm 108
    New kids on the block 108
    Fighting the Native Americans — again 109
Why Not Invade Canada This Year? 110
Three Strikes and the Brits Are Out 112
Calling It Even 113
    Working on a settlement 114
    Squawking about things in New England 114

Chapter 8: Pulling Together to Keep from Falling Apart: 1815–1844 115

Embracing Nationalism . . . Sort Of 115
    Taking it to the bank 116
    A tariff-ic idea 116
    This land is my land, but for how much? 117
    Orders from the court 118
    Increasing industry 118
The Slavery Cancer Grows 119
    Cotton and sugar mean more slaves 119
    Opposing slavery 120

Compromising over Missouri... 121
Mind your own hemisphere: The Monroe Doctrine..................... 122
Mud-Wrestling to the White House 123
Adams wins, but Jackson isn't done 123
Old Hickory: The Jackson presidency.. 124
Nullify This 126
The nullification debate hits the Senate 127
A tarrible idea.. 128
Bringing down the Bank.. 128
Inventing a Better Life.. 130
Riding the train... 130
Reaping what you sow 131
Communicating across America 131
Staking Out New Land 132
Pushing out the Native Americans 132
Claiming independence for Texas 134
Changing it up at president 135

Chapter 9: War, Gold, and a Gathering Storm: 1845–1860 137

Wrenching Land from Mexico.. 137
Provoking a war 138
Capturing California and the Southwest... 138
Rushing for Gold 140
Risking life and limb to strike gold 140
Compromising on the slavery issue 141
Coming Over and Spreading Out 142
The Germans, the Irish, and the Know-Nothings
  who opposed them 143
Making waves: The Mormons... 144
Wagons ho!.. 145
Becoming aware of women's rights (or the lack thereof) 145
The Beginning of the End 146
Factoring a slave's life 146
Battling in Kansas 146
Making a "dredful" decision 148
Squaring Off for a Showdown: The Lincoln–Douglas Debate............. 149
Spark number 1: John Brown 149
Spark number 2: Lincoln's election 149

Chapter 10: A Most Uncivil War: 1861–1865 151

Introducing Abraham Lincoln.. 151
Presenting the 16th president.. 152
Understanding Lincoln's views on slavery and the Union 153
Bending the Constitution to preserve the Union —
  and win reelection.. 154
North versus South: Comparing Advantages and Action Plans 155

Freeing the Slaves 157
    Proclaiming emancipation 157
    Surveying the consequences of emancipation 158
Reviewing the Troops, the Generals, and the Major Battles 159
    The men at the top 160
    The war at sea 161
    The war on land 161
Two More Reasons Why the North Won 164
Losing a Leader 165

Chapter 11: Putting the Country Back Together: 1865–1876 167

A Southern-Fried Mess: Life in the South after the Civil War 167
    Starting a new life 168
    Becoming sharecroppers 169
Piecing the Union Back Together 169
    Demanding loyalty, legislating equality 170
    Using violence to keep blacks down 171
The Tailor-Made President: Andrew Johnson 172
Growing Corruption in Politics 175
    Riding the railroads to economic ruin 176
    Fixing a presidency (and not in a good way) 177

Part III: Coming of Age 179

Chapter 12: Growing Up: 1876–1898 181

Heading West in a Quest for Wealth 181
    Making money from minerals 181
    Making money from animals 182
    Making money from vegetables 184
Ousting "Undesirables" 185
    Putting up a fight 186
    Legalizing discrimination 186
Cramming into Cities 188
Inventing Big Business 190
    Building the railroads 190
    Manufacturing steel more efficiently 191
    Refining (and controlling) oil 192
    Getting wired for sound and light 192
    Forming trusts and striking against them 193
Electing a String of Forgettable Presidents 195
The Rise of Populism 196
"A Splendid Little War" 197

Table of Contents

Chapter 13: Growing into the 20th Century: 1899–1918 199
Here Today, Guam Tomorrow: Colonizing Spain's Lands 199
    Arguing about American imperialism 200
    Keeping a high profile in international affairs 201
Making a Lot of Noise and Carrying a Big Stick:
  Roosevelt Takes Office 201
Progressing toward Political and Social Reform 204
    The "muckrakers" expose evil and initiate change 204
    Improving working conditions — and
      other people's drinking habits 205
Contracting Labor Pains 206
    Struggling in a changing workforce 206
    Initiating improvements to working conditions 207
Transporting America 208
Suffering for Suffrage 208
Leaving the South: African Americans Migrate to Northern Cities 211
The War to End All Chapters 212

Chapter 14: Gin, Jazz, and Lucky Lindy: 1919–1929 215
Wilson Goes Out of His League for Peace 215
Restricting Immigration and Challenging the Natives 217
    Closing the gate 217
    Return of the Klan 218
Darwin versus God 218
Warren, Cal, and Herbert: Republicans in the White House 219
Good Times (Or Were They?) 221
    Helping the rich 221
    Increasing American spending habits 222
    Making it difficult on the poor 222
Ain't We Got Fun? 224
    Going to the movies 224
    Listening to the radio 225
    Listening to music and writing literature 225
    Playing games 226
Drying Out America: Prohibition Begins 226
Changing Morals 227
An Age of Heroes 229

Chapter 15: Uncle Sam's Depressed: 1930–1940 231
The Great Depression: Causes and Consequences 231
Shoving Aside Racial Minorities 234
Keeping Women at Home — or Work 236
Developing Organized Labor 237

  FDR: Making Alphabet Soup 238
    Electing a reformer 238
    Creating hope through a New Deal 239
    Packing the Supreme Court 241
    Assessing the New Deal 242
  Critics, Crooks, and Crime Fighters 243
    Huey Long 243
    Francis E. Townsend 243
    Charles E. Coughlin 244
    Bad guys and G-men 244

Chapter 16: The World at War: 1941–1945 247

  Trying to Avoid War — Again 247
    Playing the role of a good neighbor 248
    Sensing impending doom 249
  Gearing Up for War 251
    Getting industry and the economy in shape for World War II 251
    Working with labor unions during war times 252
    Employing women for the war effort 253
    Making strides — African Americans achieve greater equality 255
    Returning for work after being kicked out — Latinos 256
    Treating the Japanese Americans poorly 256
  Dealing with the War in Europe 257
    Meeting at Yalta 258
    Winning one step at a time 258
    Making the final push 259
    Discovering the war's greatest crime 259
    Ending the war in Europe, and the end of FDR 260
  Dealing with the War in the Pacific 261
    Fighting back 261
    Turning the tide 261
  Dropping the Bomb 263

Part IV: America in Adulthood 265

Chapter 17: TV, Elvis, and Reds under the Bed: 1946–1960 267

  A Cold War and a Hot "Police Action" 267
    Gauging the United Nations 268
    The world as a chessboard 268
    The Berlin airlift 269
    The "miracle of '48" 270
    The Korean War 270
    Uncle Sam's big stick 271
  Finding Commies under the Bed 272
    Casting suspicion on Hiss 273
    Leaking scientific secrets: The Rosenbergs 273

    Checking the loyalty of federal workers 274
    Telling tall tales: "Tail-Gunner Joe" 274
Having It All 275
    A booming economy 275
    Moving to the burbs 276
    Tuning in to the tube 277
    Rockin' 'n' rollin' 279
    An American king 279
Moving, Slowly, to the Front of the Bus 279
    Brown against the board 280
    Boycotting the bus 281

Chapter 18: Camelot to Watergate: 1961–1974 283

Electing an Icon 283
    The Bay of Pigs 284
    Facing the possibility of nuclear war 285
    A dark day in Dallas 286
Sending Troops to Vietnam 286
    Sinking deeper into a confusing war 287
    Taking a look at the Tet Offensive 287
Increasing Pressure in 'Nam and Escalating Fears at Home 288
Continuing the Fight for Civil Rights 290
    Enforcing their rights: African Americans 290
    Challenging the system: Latin Americans 292
    Maintaining their culture: Native Americans 293
Entering a Generation in Revolt 294
    Draft dodging, drugs, and demonstrations 294
    The rise of feminism 295
    Coming out of the closet 295
Weirdness in the White House 296
    Making strides: The Nixon administration 296
    Watching it all fall apart: Watergate 297

Chapter 19: Hold the Malaise, or, Ayatollah So: 1975–1992 299

Wearing Nixon's Shoes 299
    Doing the best he could 300
    Whipping inflation 301
Good Intentions, Bad Results 301
    Measuring misery 302
    Befriending the enemy 303
There's a First Time for Everything 304
    Buying into the "Reagan Revolution" 305
    Paying for "Reaganomics" 307
    Dealing with foreign affairs 307
Warming Up after the Cold War 309
    Engaging in the Gulf War 309
    Back on the home front 311

Chapter 20: No Sex, Please, I'm the President: 1993–1999 313

Bill, Newt, and Monica 313
    Treading lightly abroad... 314
    Pushing harder on the home front 314
    Pushing the "Contract with America" 315
    Judging a president 316
Homegrown Terrorism 317
    Rallying around Ruby Ridge 317
    Taking down a cult: Waco 318
    Bombings rock the nation 319
    Don't open that mail: The Unabomber 319
Making Ourselves Sick 320
    Suffering from AIDS 320
    Dealing with drugs 321
A World of Change 322
    You've got mail! 322
    Trading under a global economy 324

Part V: Facing the New Millennium 325

Chapter 21: Terror Comes Home; America Goes to War(s) 327

Whew! A Squeaker: Bush and Gore, 2000 327
    Hanging chads and butterfly ballots 328
    Post-election scrutinizing 329
A Nation Stunned 330
    al-Qaida and Osama bin Laden 331
    Taking on the Taliban 332
    Fighting terrorism on the home front 333
That Damn Saddam 335
    Toughening the stance against Iraq 335
    The U.S. invasion 336
Meanwhile, in the Rest of the World 337
Winds and Losses 338
    Big blow in the Big Easy 339
    Ike hits Texas 340

Chapter 22: Recessions Can Be Really Depressing 341

Ouch! The Economy Stubs Its Toe 341
    Dot-com dreams and investor nightmares 342
    The houses that went upside down 342
"We're from the Government; We're Here to Help . . ." 345
    Brand new president, same old problems 346
    Buying time by buying bonds 346
    Did government intervention work? 347

Brother, Can You Spare a Job? 348
  Looking for work. And looking 349
  Where the work went 350
Unspreading the Wealth 351
  The rich get richer 351
  The blame game 352

Chapter 23: Reforming Healthcare Is No Tea Party 353

The Great Presidential Race of 2008 353
  Obama versus McCain 354
  Obama's historic victory 354
  Calling the president a liar 355
Going to a Tea Party 356
  Taking over the House 357
  Cutting taxes by compromising 358
Lurching Toward Healthcare 359
  Courting the Supreme Court 360
  A stumbling start 362
Reelecting Obama 362
  The challenger 363
  The race 363
  The results 363
Meanwhile, Back at the Budget 364
  Hitting the debt ceiling 365
  Driving off the fiscal cliff 366
  Shutting down the government 366

Chapter 24: This New America 367

The Techno Revolution 367
  Getting news from new news sources 368
  Calling all cells 369
  Socializing on the web 369
  Entertaining ourselves, by ourselves 371
  Spying on web activities 372
Going Gray — but with More Variety 373
  Surfing the "silver tsunami" 374
  Stirring the melting pot 375
Redefining the American Family 377
  Changing with the times 377
  Legalizing gay marriage 378

Part VI: The Part of Tens 379

Chapter 25: Ten Events That Defined American Culture 381

The Publication of "Poor Richard's Almanack" (1732) 381
The Performance of "The Black Crook" (1866) 381
The Opening of the Home Insurance Building (1884) 382

The Advent of the Copyright Act (1909) 382
The Rise of Jazz (1920s) 382
The Birth of Talking Pictures (1927) 382
The Abstract Expressionism Movement (1950s) 383
The Establishment of the NEA (1965) 383
The Acceptance of "Deep Throat" (1972) 383
The Opening of Facebook (2004) 383

Chapter 26: Ten Unfortunate Statements by U.S. Presidents 385

I'm No Physicist, but 385
Uh, Are You Sure, Mr. President? 386
Yup, It'll Sure Come in Handy Some Day 386
Geography Was Not My Best Class 386
Well, Keep It in Your Pants 386
Uh, This Is Only a Test 387
Go Ahead and Read, but Don't Listen 387
I Shall Not Tell a Lie 387
They Were under Saddam's Bed 388
Geography Was Not My Best Class, Either 388

Part VII: The Appendixes 389

Appendix A: The Bill of Rights: Amendments 1–10 of the Constitution 391

Appendix B: The Declaration of Independence 393

Index 397

Introduction

"*T*hose who cannot remember the past," said American philosopher George Santayana, "are condemned to repeat it."

Generally in the 12th grade.

Lots of people think of learning U.S. history as a punishment. It's a subject you had to take in school. You memorized a bewildering array of dates, absorbed definitions for terms like *Manifest Destiny,* and wondered whether America really needed two presidents named Harrison. Historical figures were presented to you as if they were characters in a junior high school costume pageant. Their blemishes were airbrushed out, and their personalities were drained away.

Sure, you were taught George Washington warned the country about foreign entanglements in his "Farewell Address." But wouldn't it have been more interesting if you'd learned he never actually gave that speech? (It was printed in the newspapers. Washington didn't like giving speeches because of his false teeth, which were not made of wood but of hippopotamus ivory.)

Alas, textbooks often overlook the fascinating moments and details of history. They present U.S. history as something dry and distant — events, facts, trends, movements — and don't focus on what it really is: the story of Americans. It's the story of people: what they thought, did, and tried to do; what they ate, drank, and slept in and on; what made them angry and what made them laugh.

About This Book

This book is not a textbook, nor is it an exhaustive encyclopedia covering everything that happened in the United States in the past three or four centuries. Instead, it focuses on people: famous and infamous, well-known and obscure. It gives you a basic foundation of information about U.S. history. You can also use it as a handy reference. Haul it off the shelf to look up a fact, to settle an argument, or to store up ammunition for that next conversation with your know-it-all brother-in-law.

This book is also not completely objective. Although I've tried to stick to the facts — or at least the most widely accepted historical interpretations of the facts — the bottom line is that my own thoughts, biases, and interpretations may sneak in from time to time. Sorry. Just ignore them.

Because U.S. history hasn't always been bright and shining, especially when it comes to topics such as slavery, this book doesn't always deal with pleasant subjects. Some of what you read may anger you, sadden you, or even make you feel a little ashamed. But I think this book has a generally optimistic tone, and anyone who knows me will tell you it's not because I'm a naturally cheery guy. Thirty-five years as a journalist, most of which was spent covering politics, caused me to grow a pretty skeptical shell. But the truth is that overall, America's story is a positive one.

I've also included some things you may not find in most overviews of U.S. history. Although they may be of little importance in the long-term scheme of things, these facts are kind of fun to know about. Some examples: the Civil War general whose name helped to popularize a common term for prostitutes (Joseph Hooker); which canned meat product helped win World War II (Spam); and the major league baseball team that waited 86 years to lift the "Curse of the Bambino" (Boston Red Sox). And if you're a history purist, I think there's a mention of Manifest Destiny in here somewhere.

Conventions Used in This Book

To help you find your way around in the book, I use the following conventions:

- *Italics* are used both to emphasize a word to make a sentence clearer and to highlight a new word that's being defined.
- **Bold** highlights keywords in bulleted lists.

What You're Not to Read

As you ramble around the book, you'll encounter blocks of text in shaded boxes. They contain quotes; mini-profiles of both famous and semi-obscure people; the origins of things; factoids and numbers; and other historical debris. You don't need to read them to get what's going on. They're just there as little extras that I've thrown in at no additional charge. Feel free to read them as you find them, come back to them later, or save them for recitation at your next poker game.

Foolish Assumptions

I'm assuming you picked up this tome because you have some interest in U.S. history (which is why we chose the title). But it doesn't matter if you know a little or a lot about the subject. I think you may enjoy it either way, even if it's just to settle arguments about the Louisiana Purchase (Chapter 7) or how many states had casinos in 2013 (Chapter 20). There are enough facts in here to make this a good (if I do say so myself) basic U.S. history book and enough trivia to irritate dinner guests who won't go home.

Beyond the Book

You got more than you bargained for when you bought this book. You can access bonus material online at http://www.dummies.com:

- You can download the book's Cheat Sheet at www.dummies.com/cheatsheet/ushistory. It's a handy resource to keep on your computer, tablet, or smartphone.
- You can read interesting companion articles that supplement the book's content at www.dummies.com/extras/ushistory. There's even an extra top-ten list for your amusement.

Icons Used in This Book

Throughout the book, you can find icons in the margins or alongside boxed sidebars that alert you to particular aspects or features of history. Here's what they mean:

This icon calls your attention to mini-profiles of those people who made an impact on American history or who are just interesting to read about.

This icon points out quotes from letters, speeches, documents, advertisements, and such of the past.

You can find origins of customs, events, phrases, and other aspects of American life wherever this icon is located.

 The names, numbers, and other stats behind the news are the focus of this icon.

 This icon alerts you to a fact or idea that you may want to stash in your memory bank.

Where to Go from Here

Congratulations! By reading this far, you've already learned something about U.S. history: It doesn't bite, induce deep comas, or poke you in the eye with a sharp stick. Read a few more pages and you may get the itch to keep going even further.

As I said before, history is the story of people.

And people are the most interesting story of all.

Part I
Getting Started with U.S. History

getting started with
U.S.
history

Visit www.dummies.com for more great Dummies content online.

In this part...

- The early settlers make their way in a new land.
- The colonies establish themselves.
- The American Revolution leads to the creation of a new country.

Chapter 1
America: A Short Biography

In This Chapter
- Tracing America's roots
- Establishing a national identity
- Dealing with growing pains
- Fighting wars of a different kind
- Donning a new look for a new millennium

Long before it was a nation, America was an idea, a dream, a fanciful tale. For most of humankind's history, it didn't exist as anything but a blank slate, waiting to be filled.

Eventually it was filled, with people who came for all sorts of reasons and with all sorts of ideas on how best to assemble a country. Sometimes the ideas — and the people — clashed. But out of the clashes and struggles grew a country founded on a system of government that made it unique in the world.

America was lucky to have great leaders in bad times, when it most needed them. It had abundant natural resources, generally peaceable neighbors, and plenty of room to grow. And boy, did it grow. But before all this could happen, someone had to transform it from a fantasy to a very real place. This chapter gives you the lowdown on how that came about and directs you to the places in the book that give you the nitty-gritty in more detail.

They Came, They Saw, They Stayed

The first Americans probably wandered over from Asia about 14,000 years ago, which in geologic terms is an eye blink ago. Over the succeeding four or five millennia, they spread out over the North and South American continents.

There weren't a whole lot of these first Americans, at least not in what became known as the United States of America, but they were wildly diverse in their customs and culture. Many of the differences had to do with the environment in which they settled. Fast-forward to around AD 985. Northern Europeans popularly known as *Vikings* showed up on the North American continent but stuck around only long enough to irritate the Native Americans they encountered. Within about 40 years, the Vikings gave up trying to establish a permanent foothold on the continent.

But two things — greed and imagination — prodded other Europeans into taking their place. Looking for a new route to the riches of the East (particularly spices), explorers such as an Italian weaver's son named Christopher Columbus thought they might sail west around the globe until they hit Asia.

Of course, the Americas got in the way. Rather than reverse course, Columbus and his counterparts refocused their priorities to exploring and exploiting the New World.

The exploiting part of that plan included enslaving or killing off the native population. Sometimes the killing was deliberate; sometimes it was inadvertent, through the introduction of diseases for which the Native Americans had no defenses, for example. See Chapter 2 for more details on Native Americans and explorers.

Catching up to the Spanish

Spain got a head start in the Americas, mainly because the aforementioned Italian named Columbus was working for the Spanish and got them enthusiastic about exploring the Americas early on. But while the Spanish had a head start, other European countries eagerly sought to catch up. France split its efforts between colonizing and just carting off resources like fish and furs. But the English took steps to make their presence more permanent.

English settlements were founded for both economic and ecclesiastical reasons. In the South, colonists hoped to make money by growing tobacco, and later, cotton. To make their enterprises more profitable, they imported slaves from Africa. It was a practice that would prove far more costly in terms of human misery than the crops were ever worth.

In the North, settlers who had fled religious persecution established colonies based heavily on religious principles (although they weren't averse to making a buck). Like the Spanish, English settlers often found the easiest way to deal with those who had arrived first — the Native Americans — was to shove them aside or kill them. But the English colonists were a bit more tolerant to the arrival of other Europeans, and the American colonies grew rapidly. Chapter 3 has the stories of Pilgrims, Puritans, and entrepreneurs.

It's revolutionary!

It was probably of small comfort to the Native Americans, but the French and British also spent an inordinate amount of time killing each other. Throughout much of the 18th century, the two nations squared off in a series of wars that were fought in both Europe and the New World. When the dust settled, Britain had cemented its position as top dog among the European powers in North America. But a new power — whose members increasingly called themselves *Americans* — was beginning to assert itself.

Stung by slights both real and imagined from the mother country, American colonists grew restless under British control. In 1776, after a series of provocations and misunderstandings, the colonies declared themselves independent. Details about the pre-Revolution period are in Chapter 4.

The American Revolution took seven years for the colonists to win. To do so took a brilliant leader in George Washington, a timely ally in France, and healthy helpings of tenacity and luck. Chapter 5 has the details.

Making a country out of the victorious colonies also took tenacity, luck, and genius. Over the summer of 1787, a remarkable group of men gathered in Philadelphia to draw up the rules for the new nation. The United States of America promptly flashed its precocity by electing Washington as its first president, setting up a reasonable financial system, and avoiding war with European countries long enough to get itself established. Events surrounding the drafting of the Constitution are in Chapter 6.

Putting America on the Map

Remember what I said about America being lucky to have the right man show up at the right time? Well, Thomas Jefferson is a perfect example. The multitalented Jefferson helped the country make a smooth transition from one political party being in charge to another. Plus, he had the imagination to pull off a pretty big land deal.

It was during Jefferson's two terms that the U.S. Supreme Court asserted itself as a branch of government equal in importance to the executive and legislative branches. In a case known as *Marbury v. Madison,* the court first exercised its authority to decide whether acts of Congress and the president were constitutional.

While the various governmental branches were sorting themselves out, the country was filling up, and out. In 1803, U.S. negotiators worked out a deal to buy from France 828,000 square miles in the middle of the continent. The Louisiana Purchase doubled the size of America. Jefferson lost no time in sending people out west to size up the sizable new territory. See Chapter 7 for details about the Lewis and Clark expedition.

Meanwhile, in the other direction, the young country's ships were being strong-armed by pirate states in North Africa. American naval forces eventually succeeded in persuading the pirates to knock it off. But America had less success in preventing the British Navy from stopping U.S. ships and grabbing U.S. sailors for their own fleet. Jefferson responded by cutting off U.S. trade with both Britain and France.

But the embargo hurt the U.S. economy as much as the Europeans. By the time Jefferson's successor, James Madison, took office, a new group of congressmen were agitating for a shooting war. They got it, in 1812, with Britain.

For much of the war, American fortunes sagged. A U.S. invasion of Canada flopped. British troops invaded Washington, D.C., and burned the White House and other public buildings. But in late 1814 and early 1815, U.S. forces won key battles at Lake Champlain in New York and at New Orleans. Both sides basically agreed to call it a draw, and the war was over. All this is in Chapter 7 as well.

Nationalizing a nation

The end of the War of 1812 also marked the fading of the Revolution generation. People increasingly began to identify themselves as Americans rather than New Yorkers or Virginians. But it wasn't the end of tensions among sections of the country when their interests diverged.

One such area of interest was the idea of the country's central bank, which credit-dependent Westerners saw as a tool of Eastern financiers. Another bone of contention was the imposition of tariffs on imported goods. Northern manufacturing states thought tariffs were a swell idea because they helped make their products more attractive. Agricultural states in the West and South despised tariffs for driving up the cost of goods.

The biggest sectional difference, however, had its roots in cotton. The invention of the cotton gin made growing the fiber in the South quite profitable. Coupled with a surge in growing sugar, Southern agriculture became a labor-intensive concern — and slaves supplied most of the labor.

Many people in Northern states opposed slavery, for a variety of moral, political, and economic reasons. A fight over the question of allowing slavery to spread was averted in 1820, with a compromise that admitted one new slave state (Missouri) and one new free state (Maine) and drew a line of latitude — the Mason-Dixon line — above which slavery was prohibited.

Beyond its borders, the United States was nervously watching European nations who were avariciously watching former Spanish colonies in Latin America gain their independence. In 1823, Pres. James Monroe formally warned Europe to keep its hands off the Americas. See Chapter 8 for more info on nationalism, sectional differences, and the Monroe Doctrine.

Dirty politics

In 1824, a crusty military-man-turned-politician named Andrew Jackson lost a hotly contested and controversial election to John Quincy Adams. In 1828, Jackson avenged the loss after one of the sleaziest campaigns (by both sides) in U.S. history.

As president, Jackson found himself confronted by a theory — most eloquently championed by South Carolina Sen. John C. Calhoun — called *nullification*. It held that states could decide for themselves which federal laws they did and did not have to obey. The theory served to deepen the divide between North and South.

A confrontation over the theory arose in 1832, when South Carolina decided it wouldn't recognize a new federal tariff. Livid with anger, Jackson threatened to send federal troops to enforce the law. Fortunately, cooler heads prevailed, and a compromise postponed a showdown over the issue.

Reelected in 1832, Jackson tried to sink the country's only nationwide bank by ordering the withdrawal of all federal funds. Jackson viewed the bank as a tool of corrupt Eastern financiers. But sagging land sales and bank panics drove the national economy into recession.

Recession or not, Americans were busy coming up with ways to make life better. Improvements in equipment triggered a boom in railroad building. The development of steel plows and rolling harvesters greatly enhanced grain production. And the invention of the telegraph signaled the start of a national communications medium.

Down in Texas, meanwhile, American expatriates led a successful revolt against Mexico and then waited for nine years to become part of the United States. The annexation of Texas, in turn, helped start another war. It's all in Chapter 8.

Fighting with a neighbor, finding gold, and heading for a breakup

In 1844, America elected its first *dark horse,* or surprise, presidential candidate. He was a Tennessean named James K. Polk. Polk was a hard worker with a yen to expand the country to the Pacific Ocean by acquiring territory from Mexico. Polk saw it as the nation's *Manifest Destiny.*

Mexico, however, saw it as intolerable bullying. After the Mexican government refused to sell, Polk sent U.S. troops to the border. A fight was quickly provoked and just as quickly escalated into war. The Americans' quick and decisive victory resulted in their grabbing of about 500,000 square miles of Mexican territory, comprising much of what became the western United States.

These actions not only fulfilled Polk's vision of Manifest Destiny but also gave California to America. That addition proved to be particularly fortuitous when gold was discovered there in early 1848. By the end of 1849, the California gold rush had sparked a human stampede and given America all the elbowroom it would need for decades.

That was a good thing because immigration was again booming, particularly from Ireland and the European states that would become Germany. But the acquisition of Mexican territory also renewed the struggle to balance the interests of slave states and free states.

In 1850, Congress worked out a five-bill compromise. California was added as a free state. The free-or-slave question was postponed in other areas of the former Mexican lands. And Congress enacted a law that made it easier for slave owners to recover fugitive slaves.

While a movement to give women rights and opportunities equal to men's began to gather steam in the 1850s, the slavery issue overshadowed it. Violence broke out in Kansas and Virginia. An 1857 Supreme Court decision that held that slaves had no more rights than mules infuriated slavery opponents.

And in 1860, the badly divided country gave a plurality of its votes to a 51-year-old Illinois lawyer in a four-way race for the presidency. The election of Abraham Lincoln was the last straw for Southern states, which began leaving the Union. See Chapter 9 for accounts of the war with Mexico, the California gold rush, and America's divorce from itself.

Fighting among ourselves

Talk about timing: America had its best president at the worst time in its history — the Civil War. Underestimating Lincoln was easy, and many did. But he had a knack for getting the best out of most of the people around him and a self-deprecating sense of humor that disarmed others.

Lincoln was no fan of slavery, but even more important to him was repairing and preserving the Union. The North seemed well-equipped to accomplish that. It had a larger population, better manufacturing and transportation systems, and an established navy and central government. The South had the home-field advantage and better military leaders, and it only had to fight to a draw.

While the North was largely successful in establishing a naval blockade of Southern ports, the South won most of the early land battles. Its best general, Robert E. Lee, even succeeded in taking the fight to Northern territory for a while. But eventually, the North's superiority in numbers and supplies asserted itself, and the tide turned.

It took four years and 600,000 American lives for Northern forces to prevail, restore the Union, and end slavery. But less than a week after the surrender of the South's main army, Lincoln was assassinated. With him went the nation's best chance of healing its wounds. The details are in Chapter 10.

Making up is hard to do

The postwar South was a mess, and that's putting it mildly. The infrastructure was wrecked, the economy in shambles, and the best and brightest of its leaders gone. Millions of African Americans were free — with no education, no place to work, and nowhere to go.

With Lincoln gone, many of the North's leaders were more in the mood for revenge than for reconstruction. Andrew Johnson, Lincoln's successor, had few friends in Congress and fewer leadership skills. Such a climate resulted in the North imposing draconian laws on the South, which led, in turn, to economic and physically violent reprisals by white Southerners on black Southerners.

Reconstruction efforts suffered further when the great Northern general Ulysses S. Grant turned out to be a not-so-great president. Political corruption infected every level of government. The corruption peaked — or bottomed out — with a sleazy deal that gave the 1876 presidential election to a former Ohio governor named Rutherford B. Hayes. It's all there in Chapter 11.

Struggling with Greatness

With the North-South struggle over, America began stretching west in earnest. Great tracts of land were available to settle, and money could be made in mining, ranching, and farming.

Tragically, that meant pushing out or bumping off the original human residents. Most of America's surviving Native Americans were on the Great Plains. But by 1890, wars, murders, disease, starvation, and forced emigration had largely "solved" the "Indian problem."

Other minorities fared little better. In the South, the failures of Reconstruction led to a series of Jim Crow laws that sanctioned racial segregation. Immigration from China was temporarily banned in 1882, and the ban lasted six decades. Immigrants from other nations poured in, however, many of them populating vast slums in rapidly growing cities.

But Big Business boomed in what Mark Twain dubbed *The Gilded Age*. Railroads, steel, and oil were the objects of monopolistic cartels, and new industries sprang up around new inventions like the telephone and electric lighting.

With its frontier rapidly settled, America cast its eyes beyond its borders. In 1898, it went to war with Spain. The conflict lasted four months and resulted in Guam, Puerto Rico, and the Philippines becoming U.S. territories. See Chapter 12 for details.

Finding a place in the world

As the 20th century began, the nation marched along to the twin drums of *imperialism* — running other people's countries for America's benefit — and *progressivism* — improving the bad habits of Big Business and Big Politics. At the forefront of both was a human dynamo named Theodore Roosevelt.

The country was also undergoing labor pains, with unions striving, often violently and not very successfully, with business leaders. Women were also struggling to gain a place in the polling booth and in the pay line.

Chapter 13 winds up with America trying to stay out of World War I — and failing. America's participation in the war turned out to be a good thing for the rest of the world, as it helped the war get over with sooner.

Roaring through the '20s

After the war, America decided to mind its own business and restricted immigration to keep the rest of the world out. It also gave up drinking — at least legal drinking. Prohibition resulted in a lot of illegal drinking, which seemed in turn to lower the country's morals in other areas.

America also elected a string of rock-ribbed Republicans as president, all of whom did what they could to make the rich richer. Everyone else made do by buying things on installment plans and looking for ways to get rich themselves.

Americans also spent increasing amounts of leisure time going to the movies, listening to the radio, and paying homage to heroes like Babe Ruth and Charles Lindbergh. As Chapter 14 closes, the Roaring Twenties sputter to an end with a stock market crash, which makes for a depressing next chapter.

What's so great about a depression?

A whole fistful of factors helped cause the Great Depression: the stock market crash, a host of bank and farm failures, even terrible weather. It all added up to an economically catastrophic decade.

Unemployment and foreclosures soared. Tens of thousands of farm families migrated to the promise of better times in California. Minority groups were even worse off than usual. About the only groups to make progress were labor unions.

Trying to untangle the mess was a patrician New Yorker named Franklin D. Roosevelt. As president, FDR launched an alphabet's worth of federal programs to combat the Depression, with mixed results.

For Depression distractions, America had an array of demagogic politicians, dangerous criminals, and long-winded radio personalities. They're all right there in Chapter 15.

The big one

As the 1930s ended, most Americans were too preoccupied with their own problems to worry about problems in the rest of the world. As it turned out, however, the country couldn't get by indefinitely just selling war materials to friendly nations.

By the end of 1941, America was in another world war, and the country was up to the task. Industrial production ramped up. Women went to work, taking the place of men at war. Minority groups gained ground in the struggle for equality by making invaluable contributions to the effort.

American efforts overseas were even more valiant. After helping to secure North Africa, U.S. troops were at the vanguard of the allied invasions of Italy and France. In the Pacific, the military recovered quickly from the devastating attack on Pearl Harbor and began a methodical hopscotch across the Pacific. As Chapter 16 concludes, America ends the war by using nuclear weapons — and begins a very uneasy chapter in world history.

A Cold War and a Brave New World

After years of struggling with totalitarian regimes in other countries, America marked the end of World War II by beginning a period of years of struggling with different totalitarian regimes in other countries.

Instead of fascists, these were communists, especially those in the Soviet Union and, eventually, China. After helping get the United Nations off the ground, the United States began diplomatically — and sometimes not so diplomatically — dueling with communists who were trying to overthrow governments in other countries.

In 1950, UN troops, consisting mainly of U.S. troops, began what was termed a *police action,* trying to push back a Chinese-supported North Korean invasion of South Korea. It took until mid-1953, and 33,000 U.S. dead, to end the war in a stalemate.

At home, meanwhile, Americans' antipathy toward communism resulted in demagogic persecution of U.S. citizens. Commie hunting became something of a national pastime. It took until mid-1954 for a poison of innuendo and smear tactics spread by a Wisconsin senator named Joe McCarthy to run its course.

Communists aside, Americans were doing pretty well after the war. Returning veterans came home to plenty of jobs and government aid programs, and that meant a booming economy. People bought new houses and new cars in new suburban communities, where they watched a new cultural phenomenon called television and listened to a new kind of music called rock 'n' roll.

But not everyone was having fun. After helping win two world wars, African Americans decided it was past time to be treated as equals. A 1954 U.S. Supreme Court decision and a 1955 boycott of a bus company helped jump-start the civil rights movement. It's all in Chapter 17.

From a Kennedy to a Ford

After eight years of Dwight Eisenhower (a great general but a pretty dull president), America was ready for some charisma in the White House. It got it with the election of John F. Kennedy in 1960. Kennedy proved his leadership skills in 1962 when he pretty much pulled the country — and the rest of the world — back from the brink of nuclear war over the presence of Soviet missiles in Cuba. But his assassination the following year ended the promise of his presidency.

In Kennedy's place came Lyndon B. Johnson, a practiced politician. Johnson inherited a messy U.S. involvement in a civil war in Vietnam, which grew increasingly messier in his five years in office. Antiwar sentiment grew almost as fast and kept Johnson from seeking a second full term.

At home, the civil rights movement that began in the '50s picked up speed in the '60s, fueled by a confluence of Johnson-pushed federal legislation; nonviolent demonstrations led, most notably, by the Reverend Martin Luther King Jr.; and the violence of race riots in many U.S. cities.

African Americans weren't the only ones protesting. Latinos, women, and gay and lesbian Americans took their grievances to the streets. Young people embraced freer attitudes toward drugs, sex, and personal appearance. Their parents, meanwhile, elected Richard Nixon president — twice.

Except for Vietnam, Nixon enjoyed reasonable success in foreign policy, warming up relations with China and gingerly seeking middle ground with the Soviet Union. After expanding the U.S. role in Vietnam by bombing targets in neighboring Cambodia, Nixon administration officials decided it was time to exit and announced a peace settlement with North Vietnam in early 1973. At home, Nixon's paranoid fixation on getting even with political foes led to a spying-and-lying scandal that, in turn, led to him becoming the only U.S. president to resign his office. The dirt on Watergate is at the end of Chapter 18.

Good intentions, mixed results

After Nixon quit, the country had two very good men who were not very good presidents — Gerald R. Ford and Jimmy Carter. Ford angered many Americans by pardoning Nixon of any crimes connected with the Watergate scandal. Carter, who defeated Ford in the 1976 presidential race, angered many Americans by pardoning Vietnam War draft dodgers.

And both men had trouble with a national economy that suffered from runaway inflation and an embargo by oil-producing nations that resulted in long lines and high prices at gas stations. Carter did broker a peace deal between Egypt and Israel, but he also oversaw a mess in America's relations with Iran.

The successor to Ford and Carter was seemingly about as improbable a presidential choice as America ever made: a former B-movie actor who had served two unremarkable terms as governor of California. But Ronald Reagan turned out to have as much impact on the country as any president since FDR. He was charismatic, optimistic, stubborn, decisive, and lucky — all of which were just what the country needed to restore its self-confidence.

An ardent anti-communist, Reagan heated up the Cold War, in part by proposing an ambitious "Star Wars" military program based on laser-shooting satellites. But his tenacity, combined with tough economic and political times in the Soviet Union, pushed the Soviet bloc closer to its demise in the late '80s and early '90s.

Chapter 19 ends with the one-term presidency of George H. W. Bush, a short war with Iraq, the worst riot in a U.S. city in a century, and the election of a president whose hometown was Hope. Really.

Finishing out the century

A native of Hope, Arkansas, Bill Clinton was the nation's first president born after the end of World War II. Although he successfully pushed for a major trade agreement with Canada and Mexico and helped restore some order in the war-torn states of the former Yugoslavia, most of the Democratic president's energies were aimed at domestic issues.

A major effort to reform America's healthcare system failed, but he was more successful in working with a Republican majority in Congress to reform the welfare system. He also shone when it came to economic matters, turning a federal budget deficit into a surplus, and a 1993 tax hike into a 1997 tax cut, after he won reelection in 1996.

But in 1998, Clinton was caught lying about an affair with a White House intern. The GOP-controlled House impeached him, and he became just the second president to be tried by the Senate (Andrew Johnson was the first, in 1868). The Senate acquitted the president, mostly on the grounds that getting caught with his zipper down and trying to cover it up wasn't sufficient reason to throw him out of office.

Clinton's budgetary success was tied to the overall success of the U.S. economy in the '90s. That, in turn, was driven by technological advances (home computers, cellphones, the Internet) that helped foster tighter economic ties with the rest of the world.

But the '90s also saw the broadening of America's experience with a problem it heretofore had associated mostly with other countries: terrorism. Bombings of the World Trade Center in New York City, of a federal office complex in Oklahoma City, and at the 1996 Olympic Games in Atlanta brought home the chilling realization that America wasn't immune from horrific acts of sudden mass violence.

The country also battled the less sudden but more widespread problems of illicit drug use and the spread of AIDS. And as Chapter 20 (and the 20th century) ends, America and the rest of the world found themselves on the cusp of technological and economic changes that made a seemingly smaller planet spin at a faster pace.

America in the 21st Century

There's nothing like kicking off a new millennium with a nail-bitingly close presidential election, and that's where Chapter 21 begins. The contest between George W. Bush (the eventual winner) and Al Gore wasn't decided until seven weeks after the polls closed, and only then by a 5–4 U.S. Supreme Court decision. Over the eight years of the Bush presidency, America suffered the worst terrorist attack in modern times, fought two wars, toppled one dictator, and got hit with a couple of nasty hurricanes. All in all, it's one untidy chapter.

Bursting economic bubbles

As the biggest economic calamity to hit the country since the 1930s, the Great Recession seemed to warrant its own chapter, which is what Chapter 22 is all about. As America gradually got back on its fiscal feet, it found its economy had reshaped itself into a form that didn't fit all Americans the same.

Politics and healthcare are no tea party

In 2008, the country elected an African American as its president for the first time. Barack Obama faced a deeply divided nation when it came to choosing which political philosophy to be guided by, on issues that ranged from federal government spending to devising an efficient and broad-based healthcare system. Take a look at Chapter 23 to see how it worked out for him.

Changing technology, changing America

As the new century moved along, Americans found themselves riding a wave of technological innovation that upended old ways of communicating, socializing, and entertaining. At the same time, changes in both the demographics and cultural norms were dramatically reshaping the face of America. The new reflection is revealed in Chapter 24.

Of course, this wouldn't be a genuine *For Dummies* book without a Part of Tens or two — find those in Chapters 25 and 26. And don't forget the Bill of Rights and Declaration of Independence in the appendixes. They're worth the price of admission all by themselves.

Chapter 2

Native Americans and Explorers: 14,000 BC (?)–1607

In This Chapter
- Examining the early civilizations in the Americas
- Understanding Native American tribes
- Visiting by Viking ship
- Recounting the exploits of Columbus and other explorers

Because U.S. history is most often written about by the descendants of Europeans (me included), there has been a tendency to overemphasize the experiences of European settlers at the expense of others who dropped by the New World (Native Americans included).

But tracking what the Native Americans did can be difficult because they left no written records of their activities. In this chapter, I make some educated guesses and then get on with all those Europeans.

Coming to America

Once upon a time, about 14,000 years ago, some people from what is now Siberia walked across what was then a land bridge but is now the Bering Strait, and into what is now Alaska. They were hunters in search of ground sloths the size of hippopotamuses, armadillos the size of Volkswagens, mammoth-sized woolly mammoths, and other *really* big game.

They weren't in any kind of hurry. Their descendants kept walking south for 4,000 or 5,000 years — not stopping until they got to Patagonia, at the tip of South America. Along the way, they split up and spread out until people could be found in all parts of the continents and islands of North and South America. Maybe.

Actually, no one knows when humans first showed up in the New World. The most widely accepted view among scholars is the one told in the preceding paragraphs: People got to the Americas by walking across a land bridge during the Ice Age, when there was more ice and the water level of the world's oceans was lower than it is today.

Some obviously man-made artifacts were found among the bones of mammoths and other giant mammals. This finding proved that people got here during the late Ice Age or before all the animals died out. By estimating how long it might take a group of big-game hunters to walk that far from Alaska, scientists figured that no one was in the Americas until about 14,000 BC.

But recent discoveries have caused many scientists to think that Americans, in one form or another, have been around a lot longer than 14,000 years. Archaeological sites in Oregon, Pennsylvania, Peru, and other places have yielded clues — such as footprints, cooking fires, and artifacts — that indicate that humans may have been in the Americas for as long as 20,000 to even 40,000 years. If that's the case, they may very well have come some other way, such as by water, and from some place (or places) other than Siberia. But from where is anybody's guess.

The sites also yielded evidence that the first Americans didn't rely exclusively on hunting giant animals but also gathered and ate plants, small game, and even shellfish. Imagine being the first guy in your tribe to be talked into putting an oyster or a lobster into your mouth.

Other puzzles are popping up to cause scientists to look hard at the Bering Strait theory. One study of human blood types, for example, found that the predominant blood type in Asia is B, and the blood types of Native Americans are almost exclusively A or O. This finding seems to indicate that at least some of the Native Americans' ancestors came from somewhere other than Siberia.

Exploring Early Civilizations

Although it's unclear who got here first and when, it's known that the forerunners of Native Americans were beginning to settle down by about 1000 BC. They cultivated crops, most notably *maize,* a hearty variety of corn that takes less time to grow than other grains and can also grow in many different climates. Beans and squash made up the other two of the "three sisters" of early American agriculture.

Growing their own food enabled the groups to stay in one place for long periods of time. Consequently, they could make and acquire things and build settlements, which allowed them to trade with other groups. Trading resulted in groups becoming covetous of other groups' things, which eventually led to wars over these things. Ah, civilization.

Chapter 2: Native Americans and Explorers: 14,000 BC (?)–1607 | 23

> ### Getting the point
>
> In the early 1930s, researchers near Clovis, New Mexico, found long spearheads made of chert, obsidian, and other stone materials. The spearheads, which were found with the bones of dead animals, had grooves in their base, where they could be attached to wooden shafts and hurled with great force by using a throwing stick.
>
> These spearheads have since been found in a wide area of North America. Scientists call them *Clovis points* and offer them as proof that man was here during the Ice Age. Many scientists believe the point-chucking hunters were so efficient that they helped hasten the extinction of most of the period's great mammals.
>
> And they may have had some help from even older groups. In 2011, scientists in Texas announced the discovery of stone tools that predate the Clovis points by at least 2,500 years and may have been the basis for Clovis technology. Such as it was.

The Anasazi

One of the earliest cultures to emerge in what's now the United States was the *Anasazi.* The group's name comes from a Navajo word that has been translated to mean "ancient people" or "ancient enemies." Although they were around the southwestern United States for hundreds of years, they flourished from about AD 1100 to 1300.

At their peak, the Anasazi built adobe-walled towns in nearly inaccessible areas, which made the communities easy to defend. The towns featured apartment houses, community courts, and buildings for religious ceremonies. The Anasazi made highly artistic pottery and tightly woven baskets. The baskets were so good that the culture is sometimes referred to as the *Basket Makers.*

Because of the region's arid conditions, the Anasazi people couldn't support a large population and were never numerous. But just why their culture died out so suddenly around the beginning of the 14th century is a puzzle to archaeologists. One theory is that a prolonged drought simply made life unsustainable in the region. A more controversial theory is that marauding Indians from Mexico conquered the Anasazi or drove them off. However the Anasazi's demise came about, their culture was developed enough to continue, in many ways unchanged, and is evident in some of the Southwest tribes of today.

The Mound Builders

East of the Anasazi were groups of early Americans who became known as *Mound Builders,* after their habit of erecting large earthworks that served as tombs and foundations for temples and other public buildings. One group, known as the *Woodland Culture,* was centered in Ohio and spread east. Their mounds, which took decades to build, reached more than seven stories in height and were surrounded by earthwork walls as long as 500 yards. The largest of these mounds was near what's now the southern Ohio town of Hopewell.

The largest Mound Builder settlement was on the Illinois side of the Mississippi River, about 8 miles from what's now St. Louis. It was called *Cahokia.* At its zenith, around AD 1100, Cahokia covered 6 square miles and may have been home to as many as 30,000 people. To put that in perspective: Cahokia was about the same size as London was in 1100, and no other city in America grew to that size until Philadelphia did, 700 years later.

The residents of Cahokia had no written language, but they had a knack for astronomy and for building. Their largest mounds, like the pyramids of cultures in Mexico, were four-sided, had a flat top, and covered as much ground as the biggest pyramids of Egypt. The Cahokia Mound Builders also had a penchant for constructing stout, wooden stockades around their city. In doing so, however, they apparently cut down most of the trees in the area, which reduced the amount of game in the region and caused silt to build up in nearby waterways. The city also may have suffered from nasty air pollution because of the wood fires that were constantly burning.

By 1200, people were leaving Cahokia and its suburbs in large numbers. By 1400, the city was abandoned, an early victim of the ills of urban growth.

Many Tribes, Not Many People

Although what's now the United States didn't have a whole lot of Native Americans compared to the Americas as a whole — maybe 1 million to 1.5 million or so at the time of Christopher Columbus's arrival in 1492 — it certainly had a wide variety. Historians estimate that at least 250 different tribal groups lived in America at that time. Some estimates have put the number of distinct societies as high as 1,200. They spoke at least 300 languages, none of them written, and many of the languages were as different from each other as Chinese is from English.

In the Northwest

The Northwest Indians were avid traders. Acquisitions of material goods — including slaves — resulted in higher status, and gift-giving in ceremonies called *potlatches* marked public displays of wealth. Tribes such as the Chinook, the Salishan, and the Makah lived in well-organized, permanent villages of 100 or more. Abundant fish and a mild climate made many of the tribes relatively prosperous, especially because they dried fish to save for the times of year when food was less available. The Northwest cultures carved elaborate and intricate totem poles, which represented their ancestral heritage.

In the Southwest

Arid conditions made life tougher for tribes in the Southwest. Tribes such as the Apache were foragers, scrounging for everything from bison to grasshoppers, while tribes such as the Hopi scratched out an existence as farmers. In what's now California, most of the scores of different tribes were pretty laid-back. They lived in villages, as hunters and gatherers.

On the Great Plains

Game, especially bison, was plentiful on the plains, but few people hunted it. Hunting was pretty tough because the Plains Indians — who one day became expert horsemen — didn't have horses until the middle of the 16th century. Eventually, Plains tribes like the Cheyenne and Lakota domesticated the wild offspring of horses that Spanish soldiers and explorers brought over. In the meantime, the Plains tribes made do by stalking, ambushing, and occasionally stampeding a herd of bison over a cliff. The tribes were semi-nomadic; they packed up their teepees and moved on when the local food got scarce.

In the Northeast

Tribes fell into two large language groups in the Northeast: the Iroquoian and the Algonquian. Because history shows that human beings divided into two groups but living in the same area tend not to get along, guess what? The Iroquois and Algonquin tribes fought a lot. They often used tools and weapons made of copper or slate, which they traded back and forth when they weren't fighting. The Northeast Indians lived in communal longhouses and invented a light, maneuverable canoe made out of birch bark.

A remarkable event involving the Northeast tribes occurred around 1450, when five tribes — the Cayugas, Mohawks, Oneidas, Onondagas, and Senecas — formed the Iroquois League. The purpose of this league was to form an alliance against the Algonquin and settle disputes among themselves. Some scholars believe the uniting of individual tribes for a common cause may have been looked at by the country's founding fathers when they were putting together the federalist form of government after the American Revolution.

> ### Native American gifts
>
> Native American contributions to modern culture are plentiful, varied, and often overlooked. They include the names of 27 states and thousands of rivers, lakes, mountains, cities, and towns; foods such as potatoes, sweet potatoes, artichokes, squash, turkey, tomatoes, vanilla, cacao (which is used to make chocolate), and maple sugar; medicines like coca (used to make Novocain), quinine, curare, and ipecac; and other items such as hammocks, toboggans, parkas, ponchos, and snowshoes — oh yeah, and tobacco, too.

In the Southeast

The dominant tribes in the Southeast included the Cherokees, the Choctaws, the Chickasaws, the Creeks, and the Seminoles. These tribes got by through a mix of hunting, gathering, and farming. Europeans would later refer to them as the *Five Civilized Tribes,* in part because they developed codes of law and judicial systems but also because they readily adopted the European customs of running plantations, slaveholding, and raising cattle. They also often intermarried with Europeans. However, despite European admiration for the Southeast tribes' abilities to adapt, these Native Americans were still exploited, exterminated, or evacuated.

De-stereotyping the Native Americans

Both historians and Hollywood have often stereotyped pre-Colombian Native Americans as either noble people who lived in constant harmony with nature or mindless knuckleheads who sat around in the dirt when they weren't brutally killing one another. The truth is somewhere in between. Like people everywhere else, Native Americans had both virtues and faults. They showed remarkable ingenuity in areas like astronomy and architecture, yet lacked important cultural advances like the plow, the wheel, and sailing ships. Some tribes had no clue what a war was; others lived and died for little else.

Although different tribes and cultures sometimes traded with one another for necessities, they generally kept to themselves — unless they were fighting one another. Groups tended to refer to themselves as "human beings" or "the people" and referred to other groups as simply "others" or something less flattering.

Some Native Americans acted as environmental caretakers, at least to the extent that they took care not to overuse natural resources. Others engaged in environmentally tortuous acts such as clear-cutting forests or setting fires to catch game or clear land.

But it wasn't character traits, good or bad, that ultimately hurt Native Americans. Instead, it was a conspiracy of other elements: an unwillingness or inability to unite against the European invader, a sheer lack of numbers, a lack of biological defenses against European diseases, and the unfortunate tendency of many newcomers to see Native Americans not as human beings but as just another exotic species in a strange New World.

Visiting by the Vikings

Native Americans got their first look at what trouble was going to look like when Vikings showed up in North America. All Vikings were Norsemen, but not all Norsemen were Vikings. *Viking* meant to go raiding, pirating, or exploring. Although some of the Scandinavians of 1,000 years ago surely did all these things, most of them stayed in Scandinavia and fished or farmed.

For about 300 years, the Norsemen who were Vikings conquered or looted much of Western Europe and Russia. In the ninth and tenth centuries, sailing in ships was made speedy and stable by the addition of keels. Consequently, the Vikings journeyed west, not so much for loot as for new lands to settle.

Hopscotching from the British Isles to the Shetland Islands to the Faroe Islands, the Vikings arrived in Iceland about AD 870. But Iceland got crowded pretty quickly. Around 985, a colorful character known as Eric the Red discovered Greenland and led settlers there.

Like many things in human history, the Vikings' first visits to the North American continent were by accident. The first sighting of the New World by a European probably occurred around 987, when a Viking named Bjarni Herjolfsson sailed from Iceland to hook up with his dad and missed Greenland. Herjolfsson wasn't impressed by what he saw from the ship, and he never actually set foot on land before heading back to Greenland.

Herjolfsson was followed about 15 years later by the son of Eric the Red. His name was Leif Ericsson, also known as Leif the Lucky. Leif landed in what's now Labrador, a part of Newfoundland, Canada. Mistaking seasonal berries for grapes, Leif called the area Vinland. He spent the winter in the new land and then left to take over the family business, which was running colonies in Greenland that his dad had founded.

His brother Thorvald visited Vinland the next year. Thorvald got into a fight with the local inhabitants, and he thus gained the distinction of being the first European to be killed by the natives in North America. (Vikings called the natives *skraelings,* a contemptuous term meaning "dwarves.") After his death, Thorvald's crew went back to Greenland.

The next Viking visit was meant to be permanent. Led by a brother-in-law of Leif's named Thorfinn Karlsefni, an expedition of three ships, some cattle, and about 160 people — including some women — created a settlement.

The Karlsefni settlement lasted three years. Chronic troubles with the natives — who had a large numerical advantage, as well as weapons and fighting abilities that were equal to the Vikings' — and squabbles arising from too many males and not enough females in the settlement eventually wore the Vikings down. They sailed back to Greenland, and, by 1020, most scholars agree, the Vikings had given up on North America. Supply lines to the homelands were long, the voyages back and forth were dangerous, and the natives were unfriendly. The Norsemen apparently felt that the new land wasn't worth the trouble. By 1400, the Vikings were no longer even in Greenland; they fell victim to troubles with the Eskimos, the area's earlier residents, and a climate that became colder.

The Vikings' forays to the North American continent were relatively brief and had no lasting impact. The main evidence that they were even here is fairly limited: two long sagas written in the Middle Ages and the scattered ruins of three housing clusters and a forge at a place called L'Anse aux Meadows, on the northern tip of Newfoundland. But tales of their voyages were well reported around Europe, and they served to whet the exploration appetites of people in other places. Other nations, however, plagued by troubles like, well, plagues, weren't ready to follow them west for almost 500 years.

Freydis Eriksdottir

In a world of pretty macho guys, Freydis Eriksdottir stood out — and not just because she was Leif Ericsson's half-sister. According to Viking sagas, Freydis was part of the Karlsefni settlement. She reportedly stopped one Native American attack when "she pulled her breast from her dress and slapped her sword on it." She also allegedly ended a trading voyage to the New World by having her partners — who happened to be her brothers — murdered. Then she killed five women whom her men refused to do in. Her half-brother, Leif, however, declined to punish her. The Vikings were tough businessmen, especially when they were businesswomen!

Spicing Up Life — and Other Reasons for Exploring

For centuries, people in Europe had no way of preserving food other than salting it, which doesn't make it very palatable. When Europeans were fighting in the Middle East during the Crusades, however, they established overland trading routes that supplied a whole condiment shelf of spices: cinnamon from Ceylon, pepper from India, and cloves and nutmeg from the Moluccan Islands. They also developed a taste for silks from China and Japan, and they already liked the gold and precious metals of the East.

But in 1453, the Turkish Empire conquered Constantinople (now Istanbul), which had been the capital of the Eastern Roman Empire and the crossroads of the overland supply routes. The Turks closed the routes, and Europeans had to begin thinking about finding a sea route to reopen the trade.

Countries were also putting aside the feudal disputes of the Middle Ages and unifying. In Spain, for example, 700 years of war between the Spaniards and the Moors (Arabs from North Africa) were finally over in 1492. The marriage of Ferdinand of Castile and Isabella of Aragon had united the country's two major realms. And Europe was stepping briskly toward the Renaissance. People were beginning to believe in the power of the individual to change things and were more willing to take chances.

The Portuguese, the best navigators and sailors in the world at that time (except perhaps for the Polynesians), were pushing farther into the Atlantic and down the coast of Africa. When he reached what he named the Cape of Good Hope in 1488, Portuguese explorer Bartelmo Diaz verified that a sea route to India around the tip of Africa did exist.

Meanwhile, other explorers who knew the earth was a sphere were thinking about reaching the Indies and the East by sailing west across the Atlantic. One of them was named Columbus.

According to many accounts, Christopher Columbus was obsessive, religious, stubborn, arrogant, charming, and egotistical. He was physically striking, with reddish-blond hair that had turned white by the time he was 30, and he stood 6 feet tall at a time when most adult males were about 5 feet 6 inches. He was also one heck of a salesman.

Columbus was born in Genoa, Italy, in 1451, the son of a weaver. In addition to running a successful mapmaking business with his brother, Bartholomew, Columbus was a first-class sailor. He also became convinced that his ticket to fame and fortune depended on finding a western route to the Indies.

Starting in the 1470s, Columbus and his brother began making the rounds of European capitals, looking for ships and financial backing for his idea. His demands were exorbitant. In return for his services, Columbus wanted the title of Admiral of the Oceans, 10 percent of all the loot he found, and the ability to pass governorship of every country he discovered to his heirs.

The rulers of England and France said no thanks, as did some of the city-states that made up Italy. The king of Portugal also told him to take a hike. So in 1486, Columbus went to Spain. Queen Isabella listened to his pitch, and she, like the other European rulers, said no. But she did appoint a commission to look into the idea and decided to put Columbus on the payroll in the meantime.

The meantime stretched out for six years. Finally, convinced she wasn't really risking much because chances were that he wouldn't return, Isabella gave her approval in January 1492. Columbus was on his way.

Partly because of error and partly because of wishful thinking, Columbus estimated the distance to the Indies at approximately 2,500 miles, which was about 7,500 miles short. But after a voyage of about five weeks, he and his crews, totaling 90 men, did find land at around 2 a.m. on October 12, 1492. It was an island in the Bahamas, which he called San Salvador. The timing of the discovery was good; it came even as the crews of the *Nina, Pinta,* and *Santa Maria* were muttering about a mutiny.

Columbus next sailed to Cuba, where he found few spices and little gold. Sailing on to an island he called Hispaniola (today's Dominican Republic and Haiti), the *Santa Maria* hit a reef on Christmas Eve, 1492. Columbus abandoned the ship, set up a trading outpost he called Navidad, left some men to operate it, and sailed back to Spain in his other two ships.

A cigar a day keeps the doctor away

Of all the fabulous tales Columbus's men brought back to Europe, one of the strangest was about how many "Indians" had this weird habit of sticking dried leaves in a slingshot-shaped pipe called a *tabaco* and lighting it on fire. They then put the forked end of the pipe in their nostrils and inhaled. Another method was to roll the leaves into a big tube, light one end, put the other end in their mouths, and breathe in.

Columbus's men brought some of the plant's seeds, which they called *tobacco,* back to Spain with them, and they soon spread to other parts of Europe. (In France, a leading distributor was a guy named Jean Nicot — hence the word *nicotine* to describe the key ingredient in tobacco.) Europe marveled at the "miracle" herb, which was believed to help heal sword wounds, ward off plague, and help clear congested lungs.

Not everyone, however, was in love with the stuff. "Smoking tobacco is loathsome to the eye, hateful to the nose, harmful to the brain, dangerous to the lungs," fumed England's King James I in 1604. Forsooth! He knew whereof he spoke!

Chapter 2: Native Americans and Explorers: 14,000 BC (?)–1607

Could've been worse; could've been "Vespucci"

Amerigo Vespucci was an Italian who settled in Spain and helped supply Columbus's voyages. He then took several trips to South America under the command of one of Columbus's captains. In 1504, somewhat exaggerated letters by Vespucci about what he called Mundus Novus — the *New World* — were printed throughout Europe.

A German mapmaker read the letters, was impressed, and decided in 1507 to call the massive new lands on his maps *America,* in Vespucci's honor. Which is why we're not called the United States of Christopher.

So enthusiastically did people greet the news of his return that on his second voyage to Hispaniola, Columbus had 17 ships and more than 1,200 men. But this time he ran into more than a little disappointment. Natives had wiped out his trading post after his men became too grabby with the local gold and the local women. Worse, most of the men he brought with him had come only for gold and other riches, and they didn't care about setting up a permanent colony. Because of the lack of treasures, they soon wanted to go home. And the natives lost interest in the newcomers after the novelty of the Spanish trinkets wore off.

Consequently, Columbus took harsh measures. He demanded tribute in gold, which the Indians didn't have. He also divided up the land on Hispaniola and enslaved the natives, thousands of whom died. And he hanged some of the "settlers" for rebelling against his authority.

The third and fourth voyages by Columbus also failed to produce the fabulous riches he had hoped for. When he died in 1506, he was largely considered a failure. But even if Columbus was unaware that he never reached the Orient, he knew he had not failed.

"By the divine will," he said shortly before his death, "I have placed under the sovereignty of the king and queen an 'other world,' whereby Spain, which was considered poor, is to become the richest of all countries."

Discovering a Dozen Other People Who Dropped By

Remember in school when your history teacher would give you a sheet with a list of 15th-century explorers' names on one side and a list of their accomplishments on the other side, and you had to match them? Well, here's that list again. But before I sum up these people in a paragraph each, it may be a good idea to marvel at what they did. They sailed across unknown stretches of water in cramped, leaky ships no longer than a tennis court, were provisioned with food that would gag a starving pig, and had crews who were more than willing to cut the throats of their leaders if things went wrong.

When they reached the Americas, they wandered for months (sometimes years) through strange lands populated by people who, though not always hostile, were certainly unpredictable. And then they had to try to get home again to tell someone about what they'd found. Although their motives were rarely pure, they displayed a lot of courage and determination.

Here are a dozen of these daring explorers:

- **John Cabot (England):** An Italian, Cabot was commissioned by King Henry VII to explore the New World. Using the old Viking northern route, Cabot sailed to Newfoundland in 1497, saw lots of fish, and claimed the area for England. In 1498, he took a second trip with five ships, but only one ever returned to England. The other ships and their crews, including Cabot, disappeared. Even so, Cabot may have been the first non-Viking European to set foot on what's now the continental United States, and he gave England its first real claim on America.

- **Vasco Nunez de Balboa (Spain):** Balboa is credited with being the first European to see the South Seas from the New World. He named it the Pacific because it appeared to be so calm. He was later beheaded by his successor to the governorship of Panama.

- **Ferdinand Magellan (Spain):** Magellan, a Portuguese explorer who was one of the greatest sailors ever, led a Spanish expedition of five ships in 1519. He was looking for a quick passage to the East from Europe. He sailed around the tip of South America and into the Pacific. Magellan was killed by natives in the Philippines, but one of his five ships made it back to Spain in 1522 — the first to sail around the world.

- **Giovanni Verrazano (France):** Although born in Italy, Verrazano, an expert navigator, was hired by the French to find a quicker passage to the East than Magellan's. In 1524, he sailed along the East Coast of America from what's now the Carolinas to what's now Maine, and he decided that the landmass was probably just a narrow strip separating the Atlantic from the Pacific. On a second voyage to the Caribbean, Verrazano was killed and eaten by Indians.

- **Jacques Cartier (France):** He made two trips to the New World in 1534 and 1535, sailing up the St. Lawrence River. He went back in 1541 with a sizable expedition to look for gold and precious stones but returned to France with what turned out to be just a bunch of quartz. Still, his trips helped France establish a claim for much of what is now Canada.

- **Francisco Coronado (Spain):** This guy led an incredible expedition in 1540 that went looking for the "Seven Cities of Cibola," which were supposedly dripping with riches. Instead, in two years of looking for the elusive cities, Coronado's group explored Arizona, Texas, New Mexico, Kansas, and the Gulf of California, and discovered the Grand Canyon. But they never found gold.

- **Hernando de Soto (Spain):** He marched around what are now the Gulf states before discovering the Mississippi River in 1541. He died of a fever on its banks.

- **Sir Francis Drake (England):** One of the most famous swashbucklers in history, Drake sailed around the world from 1578 to 1580. During his trip, he explored the west coasts of South and North America as far up as present-day Washington State, stopping to claim present-day California before heading for the South Seas and eventually home to England. He returned with more than $9 million in gold and spices, most of it stolen from Spanish ships and cities. Queen Elizabeth I knighted him for it.

- **Sir Walter Raleigh (England):** Raleigh inherited the right to establish an English colony from Gilbert, his half-brother. In 1584, Raleigh established a colony in what's now Virginia, and he was knighted by Elizabeth I for his efforts. Unfortunately, 30 years later he was executed on the orders of Elizabeth's successor, James I, for disobeying royal orders.

- **Juan de Onate (Spain):** A *conquistador* (conqueror) who conquered the Pueblo tribes of the Southwest and established the territory of New Mexico in 1599, Onate was one cruel guy. In one conquered village, he ordered that a foot be cut off every male adult, and in others he required 25 years of "personal services" from all the inhabitants. But he did introduce the horse to the American Southwest: Mounts that escaped or were turned loose by his troops bred in the wild and were eventually domesticated by various Native American tribes.

- **Samuel de Champlain (France):** A mapmaker, Champlain landed in the New World in 1603 and explored extensively in the northeastern part of the continent. He founded the colony of Quebec in 1608.

- **Henry Hudson (Netherlands):** Hudson sailed up the bay and river that now bear his name in present-day New York in 1609. He was looking for a northwest passage to the Indies. Instead, he found an area rich in fur-bearing mammals and helped the Dutch lay claim to a piece of the continent. He was cast adrift by his crew in a mutiny in 1611 and was never heard from again.

The Sword, the Cross, and the Measles

One of the problems in "discovering" a new land that's already inhabited is figuring out what to do with the people who got there first. When it came to the Native American populations of the New World, the Europeans generally solved that problem by killing or enslaving them.

Native American slavery

It started with Columbus. By his second voyage to Hispaniola, he set up a system, called the *encomienda,* which amounted to slavery. Under it, a colonist who was given a piece of land had the right to the labor of all the natives who lived on that land — whether they were interested in a job or not. Columbus also imposed a gold tax on the Indians and sometimes cut the hands off of those who couldn't or wouldn't pay it. Between slavery, killings, and diseases, the population of Hispaniola's natives plummeted from an estimated 250,000 to 300,000 at the time of Columbus's arrival in 1492 to perhaps 60,000 by 1510, to near zero by 1550.

As the Indians on the main islands died off, the Spanish settlers in the Caribbean simply raided other, smaller islands and kidnapped the residents there. A historian at the time wrote that you could navigate among islands "without compass or chart . . . simply by following the trail of dead Indians who have been thrown from ships."

When even the populations of the little islands waned, the Spanish looked for other cheap labor sources. They found them in Africa. African slaves were first imported to the New World within a few years after Columbus's first trip. By 1513, King Carlos I of Spain had given his royal assent to the African slave trade. He made his decision in part, he said, to improve the lot of the Indians.

Of course, the fact that many Spanish landholders in the New World were beginning to prefer African slaves made his decision easier. They believed the Africans had better immunity to European diseases and were more used to hard agricultural labor because they came from agricultural cultures.

And for the serious sweet tooth . . .

On his second trip to the Americas in 1493, Columbus stopped by the Canary Islands and picked up some sugar cane cuttings. He planted them in Hispaniola, and they thrived. In 1516, the first sugar grown in the New World was presented to King Carlos I of Spain. By 1531, it was as commercially important to the Spanish colonial economy as gold.

Planters soon discovered a byproduct as well. The juice left over after the sugar was pressed out of the cane and crystallized was called *melasas* by the Spanish (and *molasses* by the English). Mixing this juice with water and leaving it out in the sun created a potent and tasty fermented drink. They called it *rum* — perhaps after the Latin word for sugar cane, *saccharum officinarum*. The stuff was great for long sea voyages because it didn't go bad.

Sugar and rum became so popular that sugar plantations mushroomed all over the Caribbean.

The men in the brown robes

Whatever his other motives, King Carlos I and his successors did have their consciences regularly pricked by some church leaders, as well as missionaries who accompanied the early voyagers. In 1514, Pope Leo X declared that "not only the Christian religion but Nature cries out against the slavery and the slave trade." In 1537, Pope Paul III declared Indians were not to be enslaved.

With 21st-century hindsight, it's tempting to shrug off the work of the early European missionaries as sort of a PR effort designed to make the nastier things the conquerors did look less nasty. Although the idea that the cross was used to justify bad treatment of the "heathens" has some truth (a 1513 proclamation required natives to convert or be enslaved or executed), most of the people who committed the worst atrocities apparently didn't much care who knew about their violent actions. Thus, they didn't need an excuse.

The horrendous actions of some of their fellow Europeans certainly didn't make the missionaries' jobs easier. One Native American chief, who was being burned at the stake — by government officials, not missionaries — for refusing to convert, reportedly replied that he feared if he did join the religion, he "might go to Heaven and meet only Christians."

Destruction through disease

If they managed to survive slavery, the sword, and the excesses committed in the name of the cross, the New World's natives were then likely candidates to die from the Europeans' most formidable weapon: disease. Because they had never been exposed to them as a culture, the Native Americans' immune systems had no defense when faced with diseases such as measles and smallpox.

The first major epidemic — smallpox — started in 1518 after the disease arrived at Hispaniola via a shipload of colonists. From there, it gradually and sporadically spread through North, Central, and South America by following the Native Americans' trade and travel routes. Sometimes, disease spread so fast that it decimated tribes before they ever saw a European.

Some historians believe that disease was spread less by the Europeans and more by the livestock they brought with them, particularly the pigs. The theory is that the pigs passed on microbes to the native wildlife, allowing disease to spread more quickly than it could have by mere human transmission.

What's certain is that over the next 400 years, smallpox, measles, whooping cough, typhus, and scarlet fever killed thousands of times more Native Americans than guns or swords did.

> ### A pox on the conquerors
>
> New World Native Americans may have gathered a measure of revenge in the disease department by giving Europeans syphilis. Many researchers believe that Columbus's sailors brought the disease back to Spain from the Americas, where it was relatively common among different Native American groups. The theory was bolstered in early 2008, when a study led by Emory University scientist Kristin Harper determined through molecular genetics that the sexually transmitted version of the disease originated in the New World.
>
> In 1495, after Columbus returned from his first voyage, the rulers of Spain and France sent large armies to besiege the Italian city of Naples. After the city was captured, the soldiers returned and helped to spread the new venereal disease. The French called it "the Neapolitan disease," and the Spanish called it "the French disease." They proved that there are some new things for which no nation wants credit.

Arriving Late for the Party

Spain's early explorations of the New World gave that country a great head start over its European rivals. Spanish conquerors defeated mighty empires in Mexico and Peru — the Aztecs and Incas. Both empires had huge caches of gold and silver and sophisticated cultures with built-in labor classes. All the Spanish had to do was kill the old bosses and become the new bosses, so they didn't have to import slaves as they had done in the Caribbean. Moreover, the conquests spawned a herd of *adelantadaos* (or "advancers"), who roamed all over the lower half of America in search of the next big empire.

But Spain's position of preeminence was short-lived. In 1588, Spanish plans to invade England with an armada of ships blew up when the fleet was scattered by the English navy and a fierce storm. Within 30 years, both England and France had established colonies in the New World.

Eventually, a growing spirit of independence would strip Spain of its New World empire. Early on, it was pretty clear that war-weary Europe would soon be fighting again over the spoils of the New World. In an effort to head that off — and also find a way to put his mark of authority over matters in the Americas — Pope Alexander VI divided the Americas between Spain and Portugal by drawing a line on the map.

This decision left Portugal with what's now Brazil, Spain with everything else, and the rest of Europe pretty peeved. King Henry VII of England declared that he would ignore the papal edict. King Francis I of France sniffed, "We fail to find this clause in Adam's will." Of course, the countries left empty-handed by the Pope's decree got over it in part by picking off Spanish ships laden with treasure on their way home.

France

Throughout much of the 16th century, France's efforts to get its share of the Americas were marred by civil wars and inept leadership. The French forays to the New World were limited to fishermen who came each year to mine the cod-rich banks off Newfoundland and explorations of areas that are now New England and eastern Canada.

Moreover, while the Spanish were in it for the loot and the English for the land, the French weren't quite sure what they wanted. They eventually settled on a little of both. Fur franchises were awarded private companies on the condition that they also start permanent colonies. But the companies didn't try very hard, and as the 1500s came to a close, the French had little more than a tenuous hold on its New World dominion.

England

Despite early explorations by John Cabot just on the heels of Columbus's voyages, England lagged behind Spain when it came to exploring and exploiting the New World. Part of the problem was that the English were broke, and part of it was that England feared Spain's military might.

By the end of the 16th century, however, the English were encouraged by the success of raids against Spanish-American cities and ships by *privateers* (a cross between patriots and pirates) such as John Hawkins and Francis Drake. The defeat of the Spanish Armada, the invasion fleet that met with disaster off the coast of England, encouraged England even more.

In 1587, Walter Raleigh, who had the royal right to colonize in the Americas, sent a group that consisted of 89 men, 7 women, and 11 children to what is now North Carolina. They called their colony Roanoke.

Unfortunately, the looming threat of the Spanish invasion meant the little colony got no support from the homeland. In 1590, when a relief expedition finally arrived, the colonists had vanished. They left behind only rotting and rummaged junk and a single word carved in a tree: *Croatoan*.

The word referred to an island about 100 miles south of Roanoke. No one knows the meaning behind the word. And no one knows exactly what happened to the first English colony in the New World.

Chapter 3

Pilgrims' Progress: The English Colonies, 1607–1700

In This Chapter

- Looking to the New World for a fresh start
- Settling and colonizing: Different strokes for different folks
- Setting slavery in motion
- Relating to the Native Americans, mostly negatively
- Planting the seeds of rebellion

With the defeat of the Spanish naval armada off the coast of England in 1588, Spain seemed to lose interest in expanding its empire in the New World. England, on the other hand, was eager to make up for lost time.

In this chapter, England establishes its colonies in the Americas, and two very different — and very key — elements of America's history are planted: slavery and the desire for independence from the Old World.

Seeing Potential in the New World

For most of the 16th century, England was too poor and too timid to do much about the opportunities presented by the opening of two new continents. By 1604, however, when England and Spain signed a tenuous peace treaty, the English had good reasons to think about branching out to the new lands of the West. Among them were

- **Economic incentive:** A middle class of merchants, speculators, and entrepreneurs had formed. By pooling their resources in "joint-stock companies," these capitalists could invest in schemes to make money in the New World by backing colonists who would produce goods England and the rest of Europe wanted. They could also harvest resources, such as timber, for which England had to depend on other Old World countries.

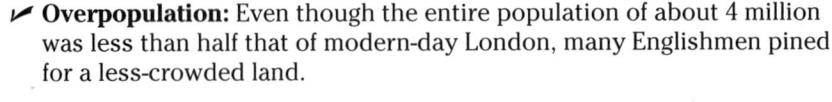

- **Overpopulation:** Even though the entire population of about 4 million was less than half that of modern-day London, many Englishmen pined for a less-crowded land.
- **Religious dissent:** Protestantism, a rival Christian religion to the one led by the Pope in Rome, had developed in the 16th century and become firmly rooted in England. Even though the country's own state church was Protestant, many English Protestants felt it wasn't different enough from the Roman Catholic faith they had left. Religiously restless, they looked to America as a place to plant the seeds of their own version of Christianity.
- **Wool:** England's woolen industry was booming in the late 1500s and early 1600s. Farms were turned into pastures for more and more sheep, and the tenant farmers on the former farms were forced off, with no particular place to go — except the New World.

Settling in Jamestown

It's pretty safe to say that the first permanent English colony in America was put together about as well as a soup sandwich. Those who set out to establish the colony weren't sure where they were going or what to do when they got there.

A group of investors known as the Virginia Company of London was given a charter by King James I to settle somewhere in the southern part of the New World area known as Virginia. After a voyage on which roughly 27 percent of the original 144 settlers died, three ships arrived at the mouth of a river they ingratiatingly named the James, after the king. On May 14, 1607, they began the settlement of Jamestown.

Early troubles

Some of the settlers were indentured servants who had traded seven years of their labor for passage to America. Others were upper-crust types who didn't have a clue how to farm, hunt, or do anything remotely useful in the wilderness. As one historian put it, "It was a colony of people who wouldn't work, or couldn't."

Worse, the site they had chosen for a settlement was in a malaria-ridden swamp, and the local inhabitants were both suspicious and unfriendly. In fact, the Native Americans launched their first attack against the newcomers within two weeks of their arrival. Within six months, half of the 105 settlers who had survived the trip were dead of disease or starvation.

Making Native American friends

Those who survived did so largely because of a character named John Smith. An experienced and courageous adventurer, Smith was also a shameless self-promoter and a world-class liar, with a knack for getting into trouble. On the voyage over, for example, he was charged with mutiny, although he was eventually acquitted.

But whatever his faults, Smith was both gutsy and diplomatic. He managed to make friends with Powhatan, the chief of the local Native Americans, and the tribe provided the colonists with enough food to hold on. Smith provided much-needed leadership, declaring, "He that will not work neither shall he eat." Without Smith, the colony may not have survived.

As it was, Jamestown came pretty close to disaster. In the winter of 1609, called "the starving time," conditions got so bad colonists resorted to eating anything they could get — including each other. One man was executed after eating the body of his dead wife. In 1610, the survivors were actually on a ship and ready to head home when a military relief expedition showed up and took charge.

Finding a cash crop

One of the biggest problems the colony faced was that the New World had nothing anyone in England wanted, so there was no basis for a profitable economy. But that began to change in 1613, when a fellow named John Rolfe came up with a variety of tobacco that was a huge hit in the mother country. Within a few years, Jamestown had a thriving cash crop.

In 1619, three things happened in the Virginia colony that had a large impact on the British in America. One was the arrival of 90 women, who became the brides of settlers who paid for their passage at a cost of 120 pounds of tobacco each.

The second was the meeting of the first legislative body of colonists on the continent. Known as the House of Burgesses, it met for about a week, passed laws against gambling and idleness, and decreed all colonists must attend two church services each Sunday — and bring their weapons with them. Then the legislators adjourned because it was too hot to keep meeting.

The third event — three weeks after the House of Burgesses had become a symbol of representative government in the New World — was the arrival of a Dutch ship. From its cargo, Jamestown settlers bought 20 human beings from Africa to work in the tobacco fields (see Figure 3-1).

Figure 3-1: The arrival of slaves in Jamestown: one of the key elements in America's history.

Courtesy of the Library of Congress, Prints & Photographs Division, LC-USZ62-53345

Instituting Slavery

While it was a Dutch ship that brought the first slaves to Virginia, no European nation had a monopoly on the practice. The Portuguese were the first Europeans to raid the African coast for slaves, in the mid-15th century. They were quickly followed by the Spanish, who used Africans to supplant the New World Indians who had either been killed or died of diseases. By the mid-16th century, the English sea dog John Hawkins was operating a thriving slave trade between Africa and the Caribbean.

Most slaves were seized from tribes in the interior of the continent and sold from ports in West Africa to the New World. Some were hunted down by European and Arab slave traders. Many were sold by rival tribes after being captured in wars or on raids. And some were sold by their own tribes when they failed to make good on personal debts or got on the wrong side of their leaders.

Although the use of African slaves in the tobacco fields proved successful and more slaves were gradually imported, the practice of slavery was by no means a strictly Southern colony phenomenon. While the Northern colonies had less use for slaves as agricultural workers, they put Africans to work as domestic servants.

Chapter 3: Pilgrims' Progress: The English Colonies, 1607–1700

REMEMBER

Not everyone in the colonies was enamored with slavery. In 1688, a radical Protestant group in Pennsylvania known as the Mennonites became the first American religious group to formally oppose the practice. In 1700, a New England judge named Samuel Sewall published a three-page tract called "The Selling of Joseph," in which he compared slavery to what Joseph's brothers did to him in the biblical story and called for the abolition of slavery in the colonies.

But voices such as Sewall's were few and far between. Although the total population of slaves was relatively low through most of the 1600s, colonial governments took steps to institutionalize slavery. In 1662, Virginia passed a law that automatically made slaves of slaves' children. In 1664, Maryland's assembly declared that all black people in the colony were slaves for life, whether they converted to Christianity or not. And in 1684, New York's legislators recognized slavery as a legitimate practice.

As the 17th century closed, it was clear that African slaves were a much better bargain, in terms of costs, than European servants, and the numbers of slaves began to swell. In 1670, Virginia had a population of about 2,000 slaves. By 1708, the number was 12,000. Slavery had not only taken root; it was sprouting.

Colonizing: Pilgrims and Puritans

While Virginia was being settled by gentlemen farmers, servants, slaves, and some people you wouldn't trust with your car keys, a very different kind of people were putting together England's second colony in America.

These people, who settled New England, came to America for wealth of another type. They were spurred by their deep religious beliefs and their zeal to find a haven for the freedom to practice their faith — although not necessarily for anyone else to practice theirs.

The Mayflower Compact: A Dutch pilgrimage

The Pilgrims (actually, they called themselves "the Saints" and everyone else "the Strangers," and they weren't dubbed *Pilgrims* until much later by one of their leaders) were mostly lower-class farmers and craftsmen who had decided the Church of England was still too Catholic for their tastes. So they separated themselves from the Church, thus resulting in everyone else calling them "Separatists." This didn't please King James I, who suggested rather forcefully that they rejoin or separate themselves from England.

The Separatists did just that, settling in Holland in 1608. But after a decade of watching their children become "Dutchified," the English expatriates longed for someplace they could live as English subjects and still worship the way they wanted. The answer was America.

After going back to England and negotiating a charter to establish a colony, taking out a few loans, and forming a company, a group of 102 men, women, and children left England on September 16, 1620, on a ship called the *Mayflower.* (A second ship, the *Speedwell,* also started out but sprang a leak and had to turn back.) The *Mayflower* was usually used for shipping wine between France and England. Its cargo for this trip was decidedly more varied than usual. Although the Pilgrims didn't really pack any smarter than had the Jamestown colonists, they did show some imagination. Among the things they took to the wilderness of North America were musical instruments, all kinds of furniture, and even books on the history of Turkey (the country, not the bird). One guy even brought 139 pairs of shoes and boots.

Despite a rough crossing that took 65 days, only one passenger and four crewmen died, and one child was born. After some preliminary scouting, they dropped anchor in a broad, shallow bay now known as Plymouth. (No evidence exists to indicate they landed on any kind of rock.)

Two important things happened on the way over. One was that the Pilgrims missed their turnoff and failed to land within the borders laid out by their charter. That meant they were essentially squatters and didn't fall under the direct governance of anyone in England. Secondly, concerned by mutterings from some members of the group that they should go home, the colony's leaders drew up a *compact,* or set of rules, by which they all agreed to abide. This became known as the Mayflower Compact.

Squanto

His real name was Tisquantum, and he was a member of the Pawtuxet tribe. In 1605, Squanto was taken to England, possibly as a slave, by a passing explorer named George Weymouth. In 1613, he returned to the New World as a guide for Capt. John Smith and remained there. A short time later, however, Squanto was abducted by yet another English expedition and sold as a slave in Spain. This time he escaped. He made his way to England and eventually onto a 1619 expedition to New England, only to find his tribe had been exterminated by disease, most probably brought by the white newcomers.

So, when the Pilgrims arrived, Squanto spoke fluent English, a little Spanish, and was essentially rootless. He was also apparently extremely tolerant. Until he died a little more than a year after their arrival, Squanto stayed with the Pilgrims, acting as their interpreter and advisor. Talk about a good sport!

Chapter 3: Pilgrims' Progress: The English Colonies, 1607–1700

> ### Thanks-a-drumstick
>
> When the first Thanksgiving feast took place is uncertain, but it was probably between September 21 and November 9, 1621. Under a decree by Gov. William Bradford, Chief Massasoit and his Wampanoag tribe were invited to share a few days' worth of wild fowl, venison, leeks, watercress, plums, berries, eels, oysters, corn bread, and "popped" corn. It was such a good idea that only 242 years later, Pres. Abraham Lincoln made it a national holiday.

The Mayflower Compact was remarkable in that it was drawn up by people who were essentially equal to one another and were looking for a way to establish laws they could all live under. Although it certainly left out equal rights for women, slaves, Native Americans, and indentured servants, it was still a key early step in the colonists' journey toward self-rule and independence from England.

Despite their planning, the Plymouth colony had a very rough first winter. Just like the Jamestown colonists, half the Plymouth settlers died in the first six months. But unlike many of the Jamestown colonists, the Pilgrims were hard workers. They had an extremely able leader in William Bradford, who was to be governor of the colony for more than 30 years, and an able, although diminutive, military leader in Miles Standish (his nickname was "Captain Shrimpe"). They were also extremely lucky because the local Native Americans proved not only to be great neighbors but also had one among them who spoke English.

The locals showed the newcomers some planting techniques and then traded the colonists' furs for corn, which gave the Pilgrims something to send back to England. By the fall of 1622, the Plymouth colonists had much to be thankful for.

The Plymouth colony never got all that big, and by 1691 it was absorbed by the larger Massachusetts Bay colony. But the impact of its approach to government and its effect on the American psyche far outstripped its size or longevity. Ever since (greatly aided by countless elementary school Thanksgiving pageants), the Pilgrims have dominated most Americans' images of the country's earliest settlers.

The Massachusetts Bay colony: A pure haven

It's easy to confuse the Pilgrims and the Puritans. Both groups were moved to journey to America for religious reasons. Both were remarkably intolerant of other people's religious beliefs. And neither was much fun at parties.

But they had differences. The Puritans were less radical and less interested in leaving the Church of England than in "purifying" it. Their leader was a well-to-do lawyer named John Winthrop. He had a lot of the qualities that came to be part of the stereotypical New England Yankee. He was deeply religious but a practical businessman. He advocated — and put into practice — such egalitarian principles as trial by jury, yet regarded democracy as "the meanest and worst" of all forms of government. He loved his fellow man, as long as his fellow man had exactly the same morals and beliefs as he did.

Armed with a charter that gave the colonists extraordinary independence in making their own rules, Winthrop led an impressive wave of about 500 Puritans to the Massachusetts Bay colony in New England in 1630, establishing the city of Boston later that year. An even larger group of Puritans had settled at Salem, in another part of the colony, the year before, and by 1642, as many as 20,000 Puritans had left England for America.

The Puritans established fur, fishing, and shipbuilding industries. They set up a system of compulsory free education, institutions of higher learning, and a model for what would eventually become a typical two-house state government in America. They developed crafts such as silversmithing and printed their own books.

They were also pretty puritanical. Religious dissidents, especially Quakers, were routinely banished and beaten, and sometimes hanged. "If they beat the gospel black and blue," one Puritan minister said in explaining this treatment, "it is but just to beat them black and blue." Adultery was punishable by death until 1632, when the penalty was reduced to a public whipping and the forced wearing of the letters "AD" sewed onto the clothing.

Which is witch?

Witch hunting in America started with three kids fooling around. It ended with 20 executions and a wave of hysteria that swept through New England. In early 1692, three young girls in Salem, Massachusetts, began to throw fits and claimed they had been bewitched by a West Indian slave and two other local women. The accusations begat more accusations as the girls and their friends basked in the attention they were getting. By the time they admitted they had made it up, however, no one was paying attention. Witchcraft accusations were used to settle all sorts of petty personal and political scores.

By the time Gov. William Phips (whose own wife was accused) had put an end to it, 150 people had been charged with consorting with Satan. Of that number, 28 were convicted: 5 confessed and were released, 2 escaped, 1 was pardoned, and 20 — 14 women and 6 men — were executed. All the women and 5 of the men were hanged. One man, who was particularly reluctant to speak at his trial, was pressed to death under heavy stones. Despite the widespread belief to the contrary, none of them was burned at the stake, the way witches were commonly dealt with in Europe.

Chapter 3: Pilgrims' Progress: The English Colonies, 1607–1700

REMEMBER: The impact of the Puritan society of New England was huge. In it were the roots of the modern corporate system, the representative form of state and federal government, the American legal system, and the moral conflict between wanting the freedom to think and act as you please and the authority to control how others think and act.

Bringing Religious Freedom: Dissidents, Catholics, and Quakers

The Massachusetts and Jamestown colonies were only the beginning. Throughout the rest of the 17th century, English settlers of all kinds moved to America. Some of those didn't like where they landed — or the place they landed didn't like them. But it was a big country, so they began the American tradition of moving on.

Some of the colonies — Maine, New Hampshire, Connecticut, North and South Carolina — were either privately founded or were offshoots of the Massachusetts and Virginia colonies (see Figure 3-2). But three of them had very different beginnings.

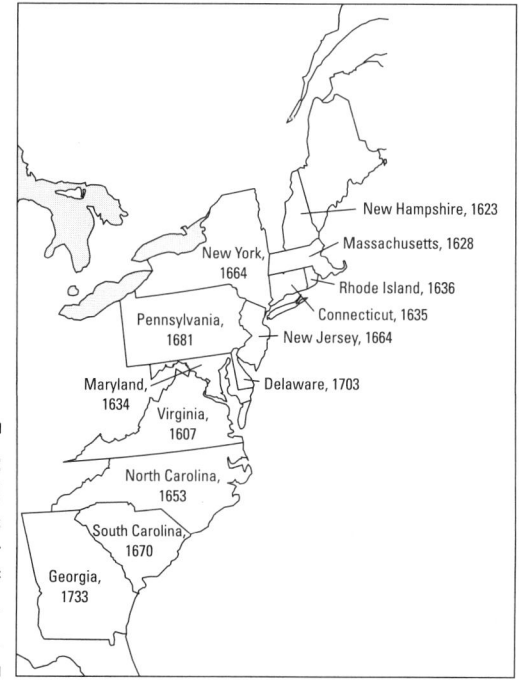

Figure 3-2: The original 13 colonies and their dates of establishment.

- New Hampshire, 1623
- Massachusetts, 1628
- New York, 1664
- Rhode Island, 1636
- Connecticut, 1635
- Pennsylvania, 1681
- New Jersey, 1664
- Maryland, 1634
- Delaware, 1703
- Virginia, 1607
- North Carolina, 1653
- South Carolina, 1670
- Georgia, 1733

© John Wiley & Sons, Inc.

Sneaking off to Rhode Island

In 1633, a smart and sociable guy named Roger Williams became a minister in Salem, Massachusetts. He also became an expert in Native American languages and was troubled by the way his fellow settlers treated the natives. His fellow settlers, meanwhile, were troubled by Williams's insistence that land shouldn't be taken from the Native Americans unless it had been the subject of valid treaty negotiations, and that there should be a separation between the institutions of church and state. So troubling was this latter idea to the governing Puritan leaders that they decided to ship the troublemaker back to England.

But Williams was tipped off to the plan by John Winthrop, and with the help of friendly Native Americans, Williams and his family slipped off in 1636 to an unsettled area. By 1644, it had become the colony of Rhode Island. Small and disliked by its neighbors, Rhode Island became a haven for those seeking religious freedom — or those who just plain didn't like life in the rest of Puritan New England.

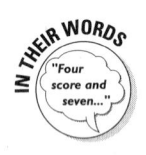

"No person in this country shall be molested or questioned for the matters of his conscience to God, so he be loyal and keep the civil peace," Williams said. "Forced worship stinks in God's nostrils."

Condoning only Christianity in Maryland

While the Puritans may have had some religious differences among themselves, they did agree on one thing: They didn't like Roman Catholics. Undaunted, Catholics established a colony north of Virginia in 1634. Called Maryland, it was the result of a grant given by King James I to his former secretary, George Calvert, who had converted to Catholicism.

Logging in

In 1638, a collection of Finnish and Swedish settlers, led by three Dutchmen who had left New Amsterdam, founded a new colony they called New Sweden (now called Delaware). The colony was soon taken over by the Dutch and after that the English. Perhaps the biggest contribution from the colony to the grand scheme of things was a new kind of housing the Finnish settlers gave the New World: a one-story cabin made of logs, caulked with clay or mud. It later became popular with the families of some future presidents.

The colony prospered as a tobacco exporter. But so many Protestants were allowed in that its Catholic founders were threatened with the prospect of being persecuted in their own colony. So they struck a compromise in 1649, which recognized all Christian religions — and decreed the death penalty for Jews and atheists.

Promoting tolerance in Pennsylvania

If Puritans didn't like Catholics, they *really* didn't like Quakers. Quakers (who referred to themselves as "Friends") were steadfast pacifists who had no paid clergy, refused to use titles or take oaths of allegiance, and were said to "quake" from deep religious emotion.

In 1681, a wealthy Quaker named William Penn got a charter to start a colony in America. He advertised it honestly and exhaustively, attracted a diverse group of settlers, and founded Pennsylvania. Penn treated the Native Americans fairly, set up a relatively liberal system of laws, and made it easy for just about anyone to settle in his colony. By 1700, Pennsylvania's leading city, Philadelphia, was, after Boston, the colonies' leading cultural center.

Penn died in poverty and in social and political disrepute. But more than any other colony, Pennsylvania was truly tolerant of differing religions, cultures, and national backgrounds.

Dealings of the Dutch

While the English, French, and Spanish were noisily tromping all over the New World, the Dutch were establishing themselves as the most successful maritime traders in the Old World. Intent on getting their share of the American trade, they formed the Dutch West India Company and in 1626 established a colony in the New World at the mouth of the Hudson River, calling it New Amsterdam. Three other settlements added up to a colony the Dutch called New Netherland.

New Amsterdam was different from the New England settlements in that it wasn't founded for religious reasons. So its attitude was more relaxed when it came to activities like drinking and gambling. In addition, land for the colonists wasn't an issue because New Amsterdam was basically a company town, run for the benefit of the Dutch West India stockholders.

After awhile, this began to chafe on the settlers. So in 1664, when English ships and troops showed up to attack the settlement, it surrendered without firing a shot. New Amsterdam became New York, named after its new owner, James, the Duke of York. The duke gave some of his new colony to a couple of friends, who thus began the colony of New Jersey. Despite its new English ownership, New York kept much of its Dutch flavor for decades.

> ### Fair trade?
>
> The chief purpose of the New Amsterdam colony was trade, and in one of the first such transactions, Dutch leader Peter Minuit gave the local Indians a couple of boxes containing stuff like hatchets and cooking pots and in return took title to the island of Manhattan, which the Indians didn't claim to own in the first place. The goods have since been estimated to have been worth 60 Dutch guilders, the equivalent of 2,400 English pennies. Hence, the idea that Manhattan was sold for $24.

Coping with Native American Troubles

When it came to the Native Americans, English colonists had varying opinions. Some thought they should be treated as pets; others as pests. Some thought the Native Americans should be treated with respect. Others thought they should be exterminated, and still others thought they should be tricked out of their lands and then exterminated.

For their part, the Native Americans weren't sure what to make of their uninvited guests. The newcomers had some pretty clever possessions, but they seemed awfully helpless at times. The English had a strange god, strange customs, and a fixation with other people's things.

In the Southern colonies, trouble between the two groups started almost as soon as the English got off the ships. In 1642, Native Americans under Chief Opechencanough attacked settlers over a large area of the Virginia colony and killed about 350 of them. The settlers counterattacked a few months later and killed hundreds of Native Americans. In New Netherland, the Dutch settlers treacherously murdered nearly 100 Native Americans in their sleep, cut off their heads, and kicked them around the streets of New Amsterdam. That launched a nasty war that ended when 150 Dutch soldiers killed about 700 Native Americans at a battle near present-day Stamford, Connecticut.

In New England, thanks in part to the good initial relations between the Pilgrims and local tribes, war was averted until 1634, when a rowdy pirate named John Stone and seven of his crew were murdered by Native Americans that the settlers decided were from a tribe called the Pequot. After an uneasy two-year truce, New Englanders went on the attack. In 1637, Puritan soldiers and their Native American allies attacked a Pequot fort near Mystic River, Connecticut. In about an hour, they burned the village and slaughtered 600 men, women, and children.

In September 1638, the Pequots surrendered. As many as 2,000 of them were sold as slaves in the West Indies or given to rival tribes. The Pequots were all but exterminated, and the Native American wars in New England were over for nearly 40 years.

In 1675, a Native American chief named Metacom but called King Philip by the settlers because he liked English customs and dress decided it was time to push the white invaders out once and for all. The result was King Philip's War.

This time, the Native Americans used guns and attacked everywhere. By the time the two-year war was over, half the settlements in New England had been destroyed, and the English were on the edge of being driven into the sea. Finally, however, the colonies united while the Native Americans did not, and the tide began to turn. King Philip was killed in August 1676, and the war finally ended. It would be 40 years before the area recovered enough to begin expanding its boundaries into the frontier again.

Rebelling — with Bacon

When they weren't fighting with the natives, some colonists weren't shy about fighting their own governments. One of these was a wealthy Virginian named Nathaniel Bacon. In 1675, troubles between whites and Native Americans were again on the rise in Virginia. Governor William Berkeley favored a defensive approach to the fighting. But Bacon and other settlers in the western part of the colony scorned that approach. They formed their own militia and took to the warpath, which led Berkeley to label them "rebels."

Bacon, in turn, accused the governor of "sucking up the public treasure" and for refusing to attack the Indians because Berkeley was in the fur-trading business with them. Bacon marched on Jamestown and burned it, and Berkeley fled. The rebel leader contended that all he wanted was a fair hearing of the settlers' grievances in London. But many of his early supporters grew nervous about going up against the king's representatives and quit the fight. Bacon died of dysentery in 1676, and 23 of his followers were hanged.

Although brief, Bacon's rebellion — and several others like it — were harbingers of things to come. They demonstrated that colonists who had been given a taste of liberties virtually unknown in Europe would rise up if they felt the "establishment" was threatening those liberties.

Chapter 4

You Say You Want a Revolution: 1700–1775

In This Chapter

▶ Engaging in the first world wars
▶ Relaxing religious views
▶ Fighting the French and the Native Americans — again
▶ Alienating the colonists with annoying acts
▶ Taking on the redcoats: The battle for independence begins

*B*y the beginning of the 18th century, European powers had been alternately exploring the New World and sparring over what they found. It was time for the main event: a showdown for control of the American continent. Actually, it was time for a series of main events. As this chapter unfolds, Europe engages in a succession of wars in which America is not only a pawn but also a battleground. Britain comes out on top, but her relationship with the American colonies is dramatically changed.

Britain views the colonies mainly as economic enterprises, whereas the colonists have a growing dislike for being told what to do by a distant government. The differing perspectives clash until, as the chapter ends, Britain gets popped in the snoot.

Looking at America in 1700

The English colonies in America had filled in the gaps between the first two settlements in Virginia and Massachusetts by 1700 and, in fact, had gone beyond them. They now stretched from Maine to South Carolina. But they were a pretty skinny bunch, as colonies go. Few settlers lived more than 75 miles from the Atlantic coast, and vast stretches of land lay unsettled by any nation, although claimed by more than one.

The population had reached 275,000 to 300,000, including 25,000 African slaves. Most people — as many as 90 percent — lived in small communities or farms. The population of New York City was about 5,000; Charles Towne (now Charleston) about 2,000.

Many of the newcomers weren't English but people from other Western European regions, such as Ireland, France, Scotland, and Germany, as well as the Scandinavian countries.

The colonies were maturing as they grew. Boston and Philadelphia were major publishing centers. Small manufacturing firms were turning out goods such as furniture and iron products that lessened the colonies' dependence on goods from England. And increasing secularism was loosening the hold of religious authority on everyday life. In fact, things were going along okay, except for all that fighting in Europe.

Colonizing New France

While New England was filling up with Puritans and the Southern colonies with tobacco growers, the area of North America dominated by the French was progressing more slowly.

By 1663, when Canada officially became a French crown colony, Quebec had only about 550 people, and the entire region had fewer than 80,000 Europeans by 1750. French officials did take steps to increase the population. Bachelors were censured, and fathers of unwed 16-year-old girls were fined. But the population remained low, especially compared to the English colonies.

One reason for the lack of settlers was that the colony was strictly Catholic, and Protestants from France were banned. Many French Protestants thus settled in the English colonies. Another reason was a looney-tunes system carried over from the Middle Ages that awarded vast tracts of the best land to just a few people. A third reason was the emphasis on fur trading — conducted by men called *courers de bois* (runners of the woods) — instead of on agriculture, for which people had to settle down.

Although few in number, the French were daring explorers, roaming as far south as present-day New Orleans and as far west as the Rocky Mountains. But the lack of permanent settlements by the French in the vast areas they explored, coupled with their small numbers, spelled trouble for their efforts to hold on to what they had when the wars in Europe spilled over to America.

Fighting the First True World Wars

Eighteenth-century royalty didn't need much of an excuse to start a war — they fought over everything from who should be the next king of Spain to the lopping off of a sea captain's ear. Their willingness to fight was based partly on greed for more territory and the wealth it could bring and partly on their fear that other countries would beat them to it and become more powerful.

What made these wars different from their predecessors was that they were global in scope, fought all over Europe, India, North and South America, and the Caribbean. The main combatants were the French and English, although the Spanish, Dutch, and Austrians did their share of fighting.

France and England were pretty even matches. England had a better navy, but France had a better army. In North America, England's colonies had a much larger population: 1.5 million compared to the French colonies' 80,000 in 1750. England's colonies had a much more varied economy, the protection of the English navy, and the support of the Iroquois Confederacy, a six-tribe alliance of Native Americans who hated the French. The French colonists, on the other hand, had better military leaders, did less quarreling among themselves than the English colonists, and had Native American allies of their own.

So, here's what happened in the first three true world wars.

King William's War

King William's War was the warm-up bout. After a revolution by Protestants in England, James II, a Catholic, was tossed out. Protestant William III and his wife Mary were brought in from the Netherlands and put on the throne in 1689. This didn't sit well with the French king, Louis XIV, a Catholic. After William III sided with other countries against France in a territorial dispute, a war was on in Europe that lasted until 1697.

In America, the war went back and forth. The French led Native American raiding parties into New York and practiced a kind of warfare that was to become known as *guerilla fighting:* ambushes and hit-and-run attacks. The English outlasted the attacks but botched attempts to conquer Quebec and Montreal. The war pretty much ended in a draw.

Queen Anne's War

After King William's War ended, Europe took all of four years to catch its breath. Then in 1701, Louis XIV of France tried to put his grandson on the throne of Spain. Queen Anne, who had succeeded William in England, objected, and they were back at it again.

This time the English colonists found themselves fighting the Spanish in the South and the French in the North. As with the previous war, there were few big battles and lots of raids and counter-raids, with both sides employing Native American allies.

When the war finally ended in 1713, Louis XIV got to put his grandson on the Spanish throne, but England got Nova Scotia, Newfoundland, and the Hudson River Valley, which put it in good position to take over even more of Canada in future wars.

King George's War

Most wars have more than one cause, but historians with a whimsical side like to start the story of King George's War with an English smuggler named Robert Jenkins. Spanish revenue agents caught Jenkins in 1731, and in the course of being interrogated, he involuntarily had one of his ears removed. "Take this back to the king, your master," a Spanish official was said to have said, "whom, if he were present, I would serve in the same fashion."

Jenkins did take his ear back to England, but he took his time about it and didn't actually tell his tale to Parliament until 1738. It didn't matter much, and a new war was on anyway. It eventually merged with a larger war that broke out in Europe. In America, the same kind of fighting that had taken place in the earlier wars was taking place again. The British colonists took a key port called Louisbourg, which commanded the Gulf of St. Lawrence, but they had to give it back as part of the 1748 treaty that settled the war.

Awakening to Greater Religious Freedom

Despite the nagging presence of almost-continual war, the American colonies were doing pretty well. And as the colonists did better economically, they began to loosen up in terms of their religious beliefs, too. "Pennsylvania," said a German observer, by way of example, "is heaven for farmers, paradise for artisans, and hell for officials and preachers."

It wasn't so much that Americans were becoming less devout, but more a function of their becoming less rigid and more likely to question the practice of most clergy to dictate exactly what they were to think and believe.

In the 1730s, a reaction to this shifting of religious attitudes resulted in what came to be known as the *Great Awakening*. Its catalyst was a genius named Jonathan Edwards. Tall and delicately built, Edwards entered Yale at the age of 13. By the time he was 21, he was the school's head tutor. He was a brilliant theologian and wrote papers on insects that are still respected in entomological circles.

He was also — excuse the expression — a hell of a public speaker. "The God that holds you over the pit of hell, much as one holds a spider or some loathsome insect over the fire, abhors you and is dreadfully provoked," he thundered in a sermon called "Sinners in the Hands of an Angry God."

But Edwards's message, preached to mass audiences throughout New England in the 1730s and 1740s, was not just fire-and-brimstone yelling. Edwards believed that God was to be loved and not just feared and that internal goodness was the best way to be happy on this earth.

Edwards was eventually surpassed on the revival circuit by a Georgia-based minister named George Whitefield. Called the *Great Itinerant* because of his constant traveling, Whitefield drew crowds in the thousands. On one crusade, he traveled 800 miles in 75 days and gave 175 sermons. Equipped with an amazing voice and a flair for the melodramatic, Whitefield quite literally made members of his crowds wild. He made seven continental tours from 1740 to 1770, and it's safe to say he was America's first superstar.

Although the Great Awakening had run its course by the time of the American Revolution, its impact was deep and lasting. It sparked widespread discussions about religion that in turn led to the development of new denominations, which in turn helped lead to more religious tolerance among the colonists. Several of the new or revitalized denominations were encouraged to start colleges, including Brown, Princeton, Dartmouth, and Columbia, to ensure a steady stream of trained ministers.

The Great Awakening also helped break down barriers among the colonies and unify them through their common experience with it. And as the first spontaneous mass movement in America, it heightened the individual's sense of power when it was combined with that of others.

The French and Indian War

Despite being filled with the divine spirit of the Great Awakening — or maybe because of it — American colonists were ready by 1750 to once more fight the French and Native Americans. The first to do so were led by a tall, 22-year-old Virginia militia captain named George Washington.

This time the world war, called the *Seven Years' War* in Europe and dubbed the *French and Indian War* in the New World, started in America. English speculators had secured the rights to 500,000 acres in the Ohio River valley.

At about the same time, the French had built a series of forts in the same area as a way to keep lines of communication and supply open between Canada and Louisiana.

In 1754, a year after he had conducted a diplomat/spy mission, Washington was sent to the Ohio Country with 150 men. They ran into a French detachment, the Virginians fired, and the French fled. "I heard the bullets whistle," Washington wrote later, "and, believe me, there is something charming in the sound."

The French set out to "charm" Washington by counterattacking a fort the young Virginian had hastily put up (and aptly named *Fort Necessity*) and by forcing Washington to surrender — on July 4. Then, in a stroke of luck for a nation yet unborn, the French let Washington lead his men home.

Unifying the colonies

While Washington was savoring his first taste of battle, representatives of 8 of the 13 colonies were meeting in Albany, New York, at the request of the British government. The purpose was to see whether the colonies could be more unified. The British wanted more unity because they figured it would make it easier to fight the French and also to govern the colonies.

But a few far-seeing colonists — most notably a Philadelphia printer, inventor, scientist, and man-about-town named Benjamin Franklin — saw the meeting as an opportunity to increase the colonies' economic and political clout.

Franklin engineered a sound plan for a colonial union, and the gathered representatives approved it. But the assemblies in the individual colonies rejected it, mostly because they felt they would give up too much of their independence.

Defeating British General Braddock

On the battlefield, meanwhile, the British had sent two of their worst regiments to the colonies and given command to a general named Edward Braddock. Though undeniably brave (he had five horses shot from under him in one battle), Braddock was arrogant and a plodding bozo when it came to military strategy. He was also contemptuous of the American militia under his command.

In 1755, Braddock and a force of about 1,400 men, including Washington, marched on French forts in the Ohio Country. A force of French and Native Americans surprised the British force. Braddock was killed, along with almost a thousand of his men.

Braddock's defeat was just one of a bunch of losses the British suffered over the next two years. The war in America merged with a war in Europe that involved all the major European powers. It went badly for the British in both theaters.

Pontiac and pox

Pontiac was a chief of the Ottawa tribe, which had historically sided with the French in the wars against the British. An able leader and outstanding orator, Pontiac realized early on that his tribe couldn't trust the French or the British, and he worked quietly to unite tribes in the area in a common cause. When British settlers hanged several Native Americans after a dispute among Native Americans that didn't involve white settlers, a war started.

The resultant fighting was nasty and prolonged, and eight British forts fell to Pontiac's troops. So in July 1763, when Col. Henry Boquet suggested distributing smallpox-infected blankets to the Native Americans, British military leader Jeffrey Amherst agreed, writing to Boquet that he should also "try every other method that can serve to extirpate [wipe out] this execrable race."

Whether this form of biological warfare was ever followed through is unclear. But smallpox did break out among the Native Americans. By 1765, decimated by disease, outnumbered, and running low on supplies, Pontiac and his allies sued for peace. The Native American leader was killed by another Native American in 1769 and eventually had a car named after him. Amherst lived to the ripe old age of 80. A Massachusetts town and a college were named after him.

Outfighting the French

In 1757, however, things began looking up. An able administrator named William Pitt became head of the London government. Pitt skillfully used the superior British navy and appointed good military leaders.

Among them were James Wolfe and Jeffrey Amherst. Wolfe and Amherst led a British force against the French fortress-city of Quebec in 1759. In one of the most important battles fought in North America, the British took the city. Montreal fell in the following year, and the French were finished in the New World.

The war was formally settled by the Treaty of Paris in 1763. The British got all of Canada, all of America east of the Mississippi, Florida, and some Caribbean islands.

The American colonists got rid of the decades-old threat from the French. More than in previous wars, men from different colonies fought alongside one another, lowering barriers among the colonies. Future leaders matured. And the animosity and friction that sprang up between British military leaders and the Americans lingered long after the war was over.

To see what land holdings that Britain, France, and Spain maintained in the mid-18th century, take a look at Figure 4-1.

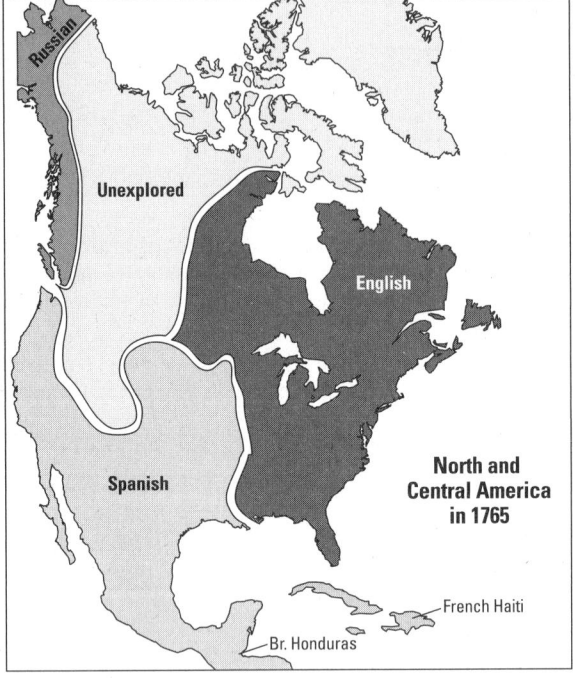

Figure 4-1: Map of North and Central America during the mid-18th century showing what belonged to Britain, France, and Spain.

© John Wiley & Sons, Inc.

Growing like a Weed

If there was one inarguable fact about the American colonies in the mid- to late 18th century, it was that they were growing like crazy. In 1730, the population of the 13 colonies was about 655,000. Boston was the biggest city, with a population of about 13,000, while New York and Philadelphia were home to about 8,500 people each.

By 1760, the population had reached 1.6 million, not including African slaves, and by 1775, the white population stood at 2.5 million. Philadelphia was the largest city in that year, with a population of about 34,000.

Accounting for the population explosion

The population explosion was caused by two things. One was the natural birthrate of the colonists. Partly because of the time-honored farm family tradition that large families meant more people to work (and maybe because there wasn't much else to do on those long winter nights in the country), the size of many American families was astounding. Benjamin Franklin wrote of a Philadelphia woman who had 14 children, 82 grandchildren, and 110 great-grandchildren by the time she died at the age of 100. The growth rate was

The "other" arrivals

One of the fastest-growing segments of the 18th-century American population didn't grow voluntarily. In 1725, an estimated 75,000 African slaves resided in the colonies. By 1790, the number was 700,000. The 1790 census reported that all but three states had slaves: Maine, Massachusetts, and Vermont. Forty-three percent of the people living in South Carolina belonged to other people; in Virginia, 39 percent were slaves.

More than a few colonists raised their voices in alarm at the increasing number of slaves. Some protested for humanitarian reasons. Benjamin Franklin argued the slave system didn't make sense from an economic perspective. Even the most ardent proslavery apostles had their doubts. Some were afraid of slave uprisings if the numbers continued to grow, while others wanted to stop the importation of slaves so the value of the ones already in America would increase. But the British government refused to allow bans on slave importation by the colonies for fear of damaging the lucrative trade. This refusal became a sore spot between Britain and America.

---

even more astounding when you consider the high infant mortality rate. One woman was reported to have lost 20 children at birth or soon thereafter.

But the growth was by no means all from within the colonies. Immigration was the second factor in the population explosion. It continued at a brisk pace, not only from England but also from other Western European countries. A 1909 population study estimated that at the time of the American Revolution, about 82 percent of the white population was from England and Wales; 5 percent from Scotland; 6 percent from the German states; and about 7 percent from Holland, Ireland, and other countries.

Despite a postwar recession after the fighting with the French stopped in 1763, the colonies were on a fairly sound economic foundation. About 90 percent of the colonists were involved in agriculture, with tobacco, corn, rice, indigo, and wheat being the main crops. Fishing and whaling were big in New England. Timber was the top manufacturing product, and because trees were plentiful and cheap, shipbuilding boomed. By the time of the American Revolution, one-third of the British navy had been built in America.

Living the good life

Although the colonists shared problems common to people all over the world in the 18th century, such as nasty epidemics, they generally ate better, lived longer, and were more prosperous than any of their European counterparts. Land was cheap and had to sustain fewer people because the population was smaller. Because labor was often in short supply, wages were higher, which raised the standard of living.

While enjoying the protections of the formidable British Empire's military, the average American colonist, if he paid any taxes at all, paid far less than his British cousin. The argument against British taxes, put forth by the eloquent Boston lawyer James Otis, that "taxation without representation is tyranny," was a bit hypocritical. After all, more than a few Americans had to pay taxes to American local governments and still couldn't vote or didn't have a representative in the colonial assemblies.

Moreover, for the most part, Britain didn't interfere in the colonies' internal affairs. Mostly, the mother country concerned itself with defense and trade issues, and many of the trade laws were mutually beneficial to both sides of the water (unless you happened to be a big-time smuggler like John Hancock, who later became the first to sign the Declaration of Independence and was Public Enemy Number One as far as the British were concerned).

So, most Americans in the 1760s and early 1770s had no interest in independence from Britain. What they wanted was what they had: protection by the world's mightiest navy, generally cozy trade rules, and freedoms and rights unequalled in the rest of the world.

Britain, however, couldn't afford to maintain the status quo.

Heading toward Divorce with Britain

After more than 60 years of almost continuous war, the British national debt had soared. Because a lot of the debt had come about by defending Americans from the French and Native Americans in America, the British government concluded that it was only fair that the Americans pay for part of it.

In addition, the British and the Americans fundamentally disagreed on what role Parliament, the British governing body, should play in the colonists' lives. For Britain, it was simple: Parliament made the rules for Britain and all its colonies. For America, however, the role of Parliament was negligible. The colonists wanted to come up with their own rules in their own mini parliaments and deal directly with the king. In the end, it came down to a fight over who should tell whom what to do.

Starting in 1763, Britain and her American colonies began to irritate each other almost incessantly. Like an impatient parent with an unruly child, Britain tried different methods to instill discipline. Only America wasn't such a kid anymore, or as Ben Franklin put it: "We have an old mother that peevish is grown / She snubs us like children that scarce walk alone / She forgets we're grown up and have sense of our own."

And as happens in family quarrels, incidents and issues that by themselves could be smoothed over began to pile up. In this case, the irritants helped lead to a revolution.

The Proclamation of 1763

One of the first things Britain wanted to do after finally whipping the French was to calm down the Native Americans, who were understandably upset by the generally pushy, and often genocidal, actions of the colonists. So King George III decided that as of October 7, 1763, no colonist could settle beyond the crest of the Appalachian Mountains. That decision meant America would remain basically a collection of coastal colonies.

The idea was to give everyone a sort of timeout after all the fighting. But even if it was well intentioned, it was impractical. For one thing, a bunch of colonials were already living west of the dividing line and weren't about to move just because some potentate thousands of miles away said so.

Worse, the decree was a slap in the face to those who had fought against the French and Native Americans with the expectation that winning meant they could move west to vast tracts of free land. In the end, it was an unenforceable law that did nothing but anger the colonists and vex British officials when it wasn't obeyed.

The Revenue Acts (1764)

On the other side of the sea, more than a few Brits were peeved that their colonial cousins paid relatively little in taxes, especially because the British were among the highest taxed people in the world. So British Prime Minister George Grenville pushed a bill through Parliament that was explicitly designed to raise money from the colonists to pay for their defense.

The law actually lowered the tax on molasses but raised or imposed taxes on other things like sugar, wine, linen, and silk. Colonists objected, asserting that Parliament had no right to impose taxes on them without their assent. They also organized boycotts of the taxed goods and increased their already booming smuggling enterprises.

The Stamp Act (1765)

Unsatisfied with the revenue from the Revenue Acts, Parliament imposed a new levy on 50 items, including dice, playing cards, newspapers, marriage licenses, college degrees, and just about every other kind of legal document. Some of the taxes doubled the cost of the item. Not only that, the items had to be stamped or have a stamped receipt on them, showing the tax had been paid.

British citizens had been paying similar taxes for years, at even higher rates. But American colonists saw the Stamp Act taxes as only the beginning. Paying anything, they argued, was an invitation to be milked dry later.

Samuel Adams

He was a flop at business and a crummy public speaker — and perhaps America's first truly great politician. More than any of his contemporaries, Samuel Adams kept the colonies on the road to independence. Born to a prosperous family, Adams graduated from Harvard. After failing at a business of his own, he took over a bustling family brewery and managed to run it into the ground. Then he became a tax collector and narrowly avoided jail for mismanaging funds.

But Adams was a success at backroom maneuvering. He helped organize the Sons of Liberty, the Boston Tea Party, and the minutemen. He wrote tirelessly for colonial newspapers on the urge to stand up to Britain, and his letters urging action were circulated throughout America. When the movement seemed to be sputtering, Adams kept it alive almost single-handedly with his writing and organizing.

He attended both Continental Congresses as a delegate and was a signer of the Declaration of Independence. But once independence was won, there was no need for a rabble-rouser. Although elected governor of Massachusetts for one four-year term in 1794, Adams had dropped from national prominence by the time of his death in 1803, at the age of 81.

In reaction to the tax, nine colonies sent 27 delegates to a meeting in New York City. The group drew up a petition and sent it to England, where it was ignored. But the colonies also began a boycott of British goods, which was not ignored. Groups calling themselves the *Sons of Liberty* encouraged and bullied their fellow colleagues to wear "homespun" clothing instead of British wool. They also tarred and feathered more than a few would-be tax collectors.

The boycott had its desired effect. In 1766, under pressure from British manufacturers, Parliament repealed the taxes. But it also tried to save face by declaring that henceforth it had the right to pass any laws it wanted to govern the colonies. Americans rejoiced at the tax repeal. They praised "Good King George." In New York, they even erected a statue of him in his honor. And they blithely ignored the warning from Parliament.

The Townshend Act (1767)

British Prime Minister William Pitt was a capable leader. But when he had a mental breakdown in 1766, he handed over the government to one of his lieutenants, Charles Townshend, also known as *Champagne Charley* because he was quite eloquent when drunk. A cocky sort, Townshend vowed to squeeze some money out of the obstinate American colonies, and he got Parliament to impose taxes on a number of goods, including glass, paper, paint, and tea. The revenues were to be used to pay the salaries of royal judges and governors in the colonies. To be fair, Townshend also dropped import duties on some American products entering England, thus making their export more profitable for the colonies.

It was too small a gesture as far as many colonists were concerned. For one thing, many of them had grown extremely fond of tea and were not keen on paying any tax on it. For another, they didn't like the idea of the money going to pay judges and governors. Up until that point, the officials' salaries had been controlled by colonial legislatures, which gave them a fair amount of influence over their policies.

Eager to show he meant business, Townshend sent two regiments of red-coated British troops — sneeringly dubbed *lobsterbacks* by the locals — to Boston in 1768. That set up the next confrontation.

The Boston Massacre (1770)

Because the soldiers sent to Boston were poorly paid, some of them tried to find part-time work, a practice that didn't sit well with many Bostonians. So it wasn't unusual for fights to break out between soldiers and groups of colonists.

On the night of March 5, a small mob of lowlifes began throwing rocks and snowballs at a British sentry outside the customs house. Another 20 British soldiers appeared with fixed bayonets, the crowd grew to as many as 300 boys and men, and after about 30 minutes of being taunted and pelted with rocks and sticks, one of the soldiers opened fire. A few minutes later, 11 members of the mob were dead or wounded.

At a subsequent trial, the soldiers were ably defended by a Boston lawyer named John Adams, and all but two were acquitted. The two soldiers found guilty were branded on the hand and then let go. But the radicals among the colonists milked the incident for all it was worth. A highly exaggerated engraving of the "massacre" was made by a silversmith named Paul Revere, and copies of it circulated all over the colonies.

Ironically, on the day of the incident, the Townshend Acts were repealed by Parliament — except for the tax on tea.

The Boston Tea Party (1773)

Despite the widespread publicity surrounding the tragedy in Boston, cooler heads prevailed for the next year or two. Moderates on both sides of the Atlantic argued that compromises could still be reached.

Then the powerful but poorly run British East India Company found it had 17 million pounds of surplus tea on its hands. So the British government gave the company a monopoly on the American tea business. With a monopoly, the company could lower its prices enough to undercut the smuggled tea the colonists drank instead of paying the British tax. But even with lower prices, the colonists still didn't like the arrangement. It was the principle of the tax itself, not the cost of the tea, that bothered them. Shipments of English tea were destroyed or prevented from being unloaded or sold.

On December 16, 1773, colonists poorly disguised as Native Americans boarded three ships in Boston Harbor, smashed in 342 chests of tea, and dumped the whole mess into the harbor, where, according to one eyewitness, "it piled up in the low tide like haystacks." No one was seriously hurt, although one colonist was reportedly roughed up a bit for trying to stuff some of the tea in his coat instead of throwing it overboard.

King George III wasn't amused. "The die is now cast," he wrote to his latest prime minister, Lord North, who had succeeded Townshend upon his sudden death. "The colonies must either submit or triumph."

The "Intolerable" Acts (1774)

In response to the tea party, Parliament passed a series of laws designed to teach the upstarts a thing or two. They were called the *Repressive Acts* in England, but to Americans, they were *Intolerable.* The new laws closed Boston Harbor until the colonists paid back the damage they had wrought, thus cutting the city off from sources of food, medical supplies, and other goods. The laws also installed a British general as governor of Massachusetts and repealed such liberties as the right to hold town meetings.

At the same time, the Brits passed the Quebec Act, a law that gave more freedom to conquered French subjects in Canada, including the right to continue customs such as nonjury trials in civil cases.

Though a sensible thing to do from a British perspective, the Quebec Act incensed Americans, especially at a time when they felt their own freedoms were being messed with. The act also pushed the borders of the Quebec province well into the Ohio River valley, which infuriated colonials who had fought several wars to keep the French out of that same valley.

The acts galvanized the colonies into a show of unity that had only occasionally been shown before. Food and supplies poured in by land to Boston from all over America. And in Virginia, the colonial legislature decided to try to get representatives from all the colonies together for a meeting.

Congressing over Cocktails

On September 5, 1774, leaders from all the colonies but Georgia gathered in Philadelphia to talk things over. There were 56 delegates, all of them men and about half of them lawyers. Some, such as New York's John Jay, were politically conservative. Others, such as Virginia's Patrick Henry, were fire-breathing radicals. Despite their differences and the serious state of events, all of them apparently managed to have a pretty good time over the seven-week meeting — except for Massachusetts's Samuel Adams, who had an ulcer and had to stick to bread and milk.

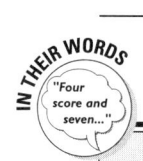

Chapter 4: You Say You Want a Revolution: 1700–1775

IN THEIR WORDS — "Four score and seven..."

Tough love and fighting words

"I love the Americans because they love liberty... but if they carry their notion of liberty too far, as I fear they do — if they will not be subject to the laws of this country... they have not a more determined opposer than me. This is the mother country, they are the children, they must obey." —William Pitt, member of the House of Lords, 1770.

"The gentlemen cry 'peace, peace,' but there is no peace! The war has actually begun!... Is life so dear or peace so sweet as to be purchased at the price of chains and slavery? Forbid it almighty God! I know not what course others may take, but as for me, give me liberty, or give me death!" —Patrick Henry, speech in the Virginia legislature, March 23, 1775.

His cousin John Adams had no such problem. He dined on "flummery [a sweet dessert], jellies, sweetmeats of 20 sorts, trifles and... [he] drank Madeira [a wine] at a great rate, and found no inconvenience in it."

But the delegates to what is called the *First Continental Congress* did more than party, even though they had no real powers. Several delegates wrote essays that suggested the colonies stay under the supervision of the king but have nothing to do with Parliament. They petitioned Parliament to rescind the offending laws. The group also proclaimed that colonists should have all the rights other British subjects had, such as electing representatives to make the laws they were governed by, and that all trade with Britain should cease until the "Intolerable" Acts were repealed.

The Congress also resolved that if one of the colonies was attacked, all the rest would defend it. And, probably much to the dismay of some members, the Congress resolved to abstain from tea and wine (but not rum) and to swear off recreational pursuits like horse racing and cock fighting until the troubles with England were resolved. The meeting served to draw the colonies closer together than ever before. "The distinctions between New Englanders and Virginians are no more," declared Patrick Henry. "I am not a Virginian, but an American."

The Congress adjourned on October 26, pledging to come back in May if things didn't get better by then. Things didn't.

Mr. Revere, Your Horse Is Ready

The Congress's decision to boycott all trade with Britain was embraced with enthusiasm almost everywhere. Lists of suspected traitors who continued to trade were published, and tar and feathers were vigorously applied to those who ignored the boycott.

While businessmen in England fretted, the colonists' actions were met with disdain by a majority of the members of Parliament. Lord North, the prime minister, resolved to isolate the troublemakers in Massachusetts and thus stifle dissent in other areas.

But some British knew better. Gen. Thomas Gage, the British commander in chief in America, reported that things were coming to a head. "If you think ten thousand men are enough," he wrote to North, "send twenty; if a million [pounds] is thought to be enough, give two. You will save both blood and treasure in the end."

In April 1775, Gage decided to make a surprise march from his headquarters in Boston to nearby Concord, where he hoped to seize a storehouse of rebel guns and ammunition and maybe arrest some of the rebels' leaders.

But the colonists knew he was coming, thanks to a network of spies and militia called the *minutemen,* aptly named because they were supposed to be ready to quickly spring into action. One of these was Paul Revere, the son of a French immigrant.

In addition to being a master silversmith, Revere made false teeth and surgical tools, and he was pretty good on a horse, too. So when word came on the night of April 18 that the British were marching on Concord, Revere and two other men, William Dawes and Doctor Samuel Prescott, rode out to warn that the British were coming. After rousing the town of Lexington, Revere and Dawes were captured and briefly detained. But Prescott escaped and made it to Concord. (Revere became the most famous of the three, however, because a poet named Henry Wadsworth Longfellow made him the star of a wildly popular poem in 1863.)

When the 700 British soldiers marched through Lexington on the morning of April 19 on their way to Concord, they encountered 77 colonials. "Don't fire unless fired upon," said the minutemen's leader, John Parker. "But if they mean to have a war, let it begin here."

Shots were fired, and eight of the minutemen were killed. By the time the British reached Concord, however, resistance had been better organized. At a bridge near one of the entrances to the town, British soldiers were attacked, and the fighting began in earnest.

Now facing hundreds of colonists who prudently stood behind trees and in houses and fired at the redcoats, the British soldiers beat a disorganized retreat to Boston. More than 250 British were dead, missing, or wounded, compared to about 90 Americans killed or wounded.

The war of words was over. The war of blood and death had begun.

Chapter 5
Yankee Doodlin': 1775–1783

In This Chapter
- Detailing the British and American forces
- Fueling and formalizing the desire for independence
- Getting a helping hand from the French
- Looking at ten key battles of the war

After blood was spilled at Lexington and Concord, war between Britain and her American colonies was inevitable, even though there were some efforts on both sides to avoid it. British leaders weren't too worried about quelling the disturbance. One British general suggested it wasn't anything that "a capable sheepherder" couldn't handle.

But there's an old saying that it's good to be good, better to be lucky, and best to be both. In this chapter, the American colonists are good when they need to be — and really lucky much of the rest of the time — and win their independence from Britain. They also lay out their reasons for doing so in a remarkable declaration.

In This Corner, the Brits....

The first thing the British had going for them when it came to fighting the Americans was a whole bunch of fighters. The British army consisted of about 50,000 men. They "rented" another 30,000 mercenary German soldiers. In addition, they had the best navy in the world. And the people the Brits were fighting, the colonists, had no regular army, no navy at all, and few real resources to assemble them.

But, as America itself was to find out about two centuries later in Vietnam, having the best army and navy doesn't always mean that much. For one thing, the British people were by no means united in a desire to rein in the colonies. When war broke out, several leading British military leaders refused to take part. Some British leaders also recognized the difficulty of winning a war by fighting on the enemy's turf thousands of miles from Britain, especially when the enemy was fighting for a cause.

"You may spread fire, sword, and desolation, but that will not be government," warned the Duke of Richmond. "No people can ever be made to submit to a form of government they say they will not receive."

Three factors contributed to Britain's ultimate downfall:

- **The British political leaders who did support the war were generally inept.** Lord North, the prime minister, was a decent bureaucrat but no leader, and he basically did what King George III wanted. And some of the British generals were nincompoops. One of them, leaving for duty in early 1777, boastfully bet a fair sum of money that he would be back in England "victorious from America by Christmas Day, 1777." By Christmas Day, he had surrendered his entire army.

- **Britain couldn't commit all its military resources to putting down the rebellion.** Because of unrest in Ireland and the potential for trouble with the French, who were still smarting from their defeats by the British in the New World, Britain had to keep many of its forces in Europe.

- **Because the Brits didn't take their opponents seriously, they had no real plan for winning the war.** That meant they fooled around long enough to give the Americans hope. And that gave the French a reason to believe the colonials just might win, so they provided the Americans with what proved to be indispensable arms, money, ships, and troops.

In This Corner, the Yanks. . . .

When you look at the problems the British had and then look at the dilemmas the Americans faced, it's no wonder the war took eight years.

In the early years at least, probably as few as a third of Americans supported the revolution. About 20 percent, called loyalists or Tories after the ruling political party in Britain, were loyal to the crown, and the rest didn't care much one way or another.

Because they weren't professional soldiers, many of those who fought in the American army had peculiar notions of soldiering. They often elected their officers, and when the officers gave orders they didn't like, they just elected new ones. The soldiers signed up for a year or two, and when their time was up, they simply went home, no matter how the war — or even the battle — was going. At one point, the colonial army under George Washington was down to 3,000 soldiers. They also weren't big on sticking around when faced with a British bayonet charge. Many, if not most, battles ended with the Americans running away, so often that Washington once observed in exasperation that "they run from their own shadows."

Regional jealousies often surfaced when soldiers from one colony were given orders by officers from another colony, and there was at least one mutiny that had to be put down by other American units. The American soldiers were ill-fed, ill-housed, and so poorly clothed that in some battles, colonial soldiers fought nearly naked. About 10,000 soldiers spent a bitter winter at Valley Forge, Pennsylvania, literally barefoot in the snow, and about 2,800 of them died. "The long and great sufferings of this army are unexampled in history," wrote the army's commander, George Washington.

They were also paid in currency called *continentals,* which became so worthless the phrase "not worth a continental" became a common American saying for decades after the Revolution. Because the money was so worthless, unpatriotic American merchants often sold their goods to the British army instead, even when American troops wore rags and starved. Others cornered the markets on goods such as food and clothing, stockpiling them until the prices rose higher and higher. As a result, desperate army leaders were forced to confiscate goods from private citizens to survive.

About the best thing the Americans had going for them was a cause, because men who are fighting for something often fight better. Indeed, as the war wore on, the American soldier became more competent. By the end of 1777, a British officer wrote home that "though it was once the tone of this [British] army to treat them in a most contemptible light, they are now become a formidable enemy."

The fact that there were 13 colonies was also an advantage because it meant there was no single nerve center for which the British could aim. They conquered New York, they took Philadelphia, and still the colonies fought on. America also had rapid growth in its favor. "Britain, at the expense of 3 million [pounds] has killed 150 Yankees in this campaign, which is 20,000 pounds a head," observed Ben Franklin early during the fighting. "During the same time, 60,000 children have been born in America."

But maybe most important, the Americans were lucky enough to choose an extraordinary leader and smart enough to stick with him. Not only that, he looks good on the dollar bill.

Mr. Washington Goes to War

George Washington has become so mythic a figure that some people think his importance has been blown out of proportion. That's too bad because Washington was truly one of the most remarkable people in American history.

At the time of the revolution, Washington was 43 years old. He was one of the wealthiest men in the colonies, having inherited a lot of land and money and married into more. Although he had been a soldier in the wars against the French and Native Americans, Washington had never commanded more than 1,200 men at any one time. There were other colonists who had more military command experience.

But the Second Continental Congress, which had convened in May 1775 and taken over the running of the Revolution (even though no one had actually asked it to), decided on Washington as the Continental army's commander in chief. Their choice was based more on political reasons than military ones. New England leaders figured that putting a Virginian in charge would increase the enthusiasm of the Southern colonies to fight; the Southern leaders agreed. Washington wasn't so sure. "I declare with the utmost sincerity, I do not think myself equal to the command I am honored with," he told Congress, and then refused to take any salary for the job.

Finding faults in George

Washington had his flaws. He wasn't a military genius, and he lost a lot more than he won on the battlefield. In fact, his greatest military gifts were in organizing retreats and avoiding devastating losses. He had no discernible sense of humor and was a snob when it came to mixing with what he considered the lower classes.

He also had a terrible temper. At one point, he was so angry with the lack of discipline and acts of cowardice in the American army that he unsuccessfully asked Congress to increase the allowable number of lashes for punishing soldiers from 39 to 500. Once he was so angry at a subordinate, he broke his personal rule against swearing. "He swore that day till the leaves shook on the trees," recalled an admiring onlooker. "Charming! Delightful! . . . sir, on that memorable day, he swore like an angel from heaven."

Commanding a country

In spite of his flaws, Washington was a born leader, one of those men who raised spirits and expectations simply by showing up. He was tall and athletic, an expert horseman and a good dancer. He wasn't particularly handsome — his teeth were bad, and he wasn't proud of his hippopotamus ivory and gold dentures, so he seldom smiled. But he had a commanding presence, and his troops felt they could depend on him. He was also a bit of an actor. Once while reading something to his troops, he donned his spectacles, and then apologized, explaining his eyes had grown dim in the service of his country. Some of his audience wept.

He also had an indomitable spirit. His army was ragged, undisciplined, and undependable, with a staggering average desertion rate of 20 percent. His bosses in Congress were often indecisive, quarrelsome, and indifferent. But Washington simply refused to give up. Just as important, he refused the temptation to try to become a military dictator, which he may easily have done.

One of the reasons men loved him was that Washington was personally brave, often on the battle's front lines, and always among the last to retreat. He was also very lucky: In one battle, Washington rode unexpectedly into a group of British soldiers, most of whom fired at him at short range. They all missed.

Declaring Independence

Despite the fact that fighting had actually started, many in the Continental Congress and throughout the colonies still weren't all that keen on breaking away completely from Britain. The radicals who were ready for a break needed a spark to light a fire under those who were still reluctant to act. Not only did they get the spark they needed, but they also got it in writing with the Declaration of Independence.

Stirring up colonists' emotions

The first motivator was a political blunder by the British government. The Brits needed more fighters, but British citizens didn't fall all over themselves trying to sign up. Being a British soldier often meant brutal treatment, poor pay and food, and the chance that someone would kill you. So British officials hired the services of soldiers who worked for a half-dozen German princes. Eventually, they rented about 30,000 of these *Hessians,* named after the principality of Hesse-Kassal, from which many of them came.

The Americans were outraged at this. It was one thing for the mother country and her daughters to fight, but it was a real affront for Mom to go out and hire foreigners to do her killing for her. (Eventually, about 12,000 Hessians deserted and remained after the war as citizens of the new country.)

The second spark came from the pen of a 38-year-old, tomato-faced Englishman with a big nose. Thomas Paine arrived in the colonies in November 1774. He had been a seaman, a schoolmaster, a corset maker, and a customs officer, and he wasn't successful at any of these jobs. But with the help of Benjamin Franklin, Paine was hired as editor of a Philadelphia magazine.

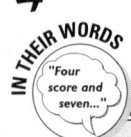

> ### Wanted: Freedom asylum
>
> "O ye that love mankind! Ye that dare oppose not only the tyranny, but the tyrant, stand forth! Every spot of the Old World is overrun with oppression. Freedom hath been hunted around the globe... O receive the fugitive, and prepare in time an asylum for mankind." —Thomas Paine in "Common Sense," 1776.

On January 10, 1776, Paine anonymously published a little pamphlet in which he set forth his views on the need for American independence from Britain. He called it "Common Sense."

This pamphlet was straightforward, clear, and simple in its prose. Basically, it said the king was a brute, with no reasonable mandate to rule in Britain, let alone America; that Britain was a leech feeding off the back of American enterprise; and that it was time for the colonies to stand up on their own and become a beacon of freedom for the world.

The pamphlet electrified the country. Within a short time, 120,000 copies were sold, and the number eventually rose to a staggering 500,000 copies, or one for every five people in America, including slaves. (Paine never made a dime, having patriotically signed over royalties to Congress.) It was read by soldiers and politicians alike, and it shifted the emphasis of the fight to a struggle for independence and not just for a new relationship with Britain.

Writing history

On June 7, 1776, Congress began to deal with the issue of independence in earnest. A delegate from Virginia, Richard Henry Lee, prepared a resolution that stated the colonies "are, and of a right ought to be, free and independent states." A few days later, the representatives appointed a committee of five to draft a formal declaration backing Lee's resolution, just in case Congress decided to adopt it.

The committee consisted of Benjamin Franklin, John Adams, a Connecticut lawyer named Roger Sherman, a New York iron mine owner named Robert Livingston, and a 33-year-old, red-haired lawyer from Virginia named Thomas Jefferson. (The committee got on well, although Sherman had a habit of picking his teeth, which provoked Franklin into warning that if he didn't stop, Franklin would play his harmonica.)

REMEMBER

Jefferson set to work at a portable desk he had designed himself, and a few weeks later he produced a document that has come to be regarded as one of the most eloquent political statements in human history. True, he exaggerated some of the grievances the colonists had against the king. True, he rather hypocritically declared that "all men are created equal," ignoring the fact that he and hundreds of other Americans owned slaves, whom they certainly didn't regard as having been created equal.

Overall though, it was a magnificent document that set forth all the reasons America wanted to go its own way — and why all people who wanted to do the same thing should be allowed to do so. After a bit of tinkering by Franklin, the document was presented to Congress on June 28. (See Appendix B for the full text.)

At the demand of some Southern representatives, a section blaming the king for American slavery was taken out. Then, on July 2, Congress adopted the resolution submitted by Lee. "The second day of July, 1776, will be the most memorable epoch [instant of time] in the history of America," predicted John Adams. He missed it by two days because America chose to remember July 4 instead — the day Congress formally adopted the Declaration of Independence, or as one member put it, "Mr. Jefferson's explanation of Mr. Lee's resolution."

With independence declared, Congress now had to find a substitute form of government. Starting in August 1776 and continuing into 1777, members finally came up with something they called the Articles of Confederation. Basically, it called for a weak central government with a virtually powerless president and congress. The power to do most key things, such as impose taxes, was left to the states. Even so, it took the states until 1781 to finish ratifying the articles, so reluctant were they to give up any of their power. It was a poor excuse for a new government, but it was a start. In the meantime, the new country was looking for a few foreign friends.

Patriots with accents

There were a lot of unemployed European soldiers at the time of the American Revolution, and some of them came to America looking for a job. There were military gems among them: Baron Johann de Kalb, a German soldier of fortune who was an able commander; Count Casimir Pulaski, a Polish cavalryman; and Baron Frederick Von Steuben, a Prussian army expert who helped Washington reorganize the army into more efficient fighting units.

But the most famous was a 19-year-old French aristocrat named Marie Joseph Paul, the Marquis de Lafayette. Lafayette was a godsend to the Americans. He not only contributed about $200,000 of his own money to the cause but also helped convince the French government to aid America and proved to be an able battlefield leader and one of Washington's most trusted aides. After the war, Lafayette helped smooth over sometimes-rocky relations between France and America and remained America's favorite Frenchman for decades.

Kissing Up to the French

Still smarting from its defeats by Britain in a series of wars, France was more than a little happy when war broke out between its archenemy and the American colonies and almost immediately started sending the rebels supplies and money. By the end of the war, France had provided nearly $20 million in aid of various kinds, and it's estimated as much as 90 percent of the gunpowder used by the Americans in the first part of the Revolution was supplied or paid for by the French.

In December 1776, Congress sent Benjamin Franklin to Paris to see whether he could entice even more aid from the French. Personally, he was a big hit with most of France, especially the ladies. But King Louis XVI wasn't overly impressed (he is reported to have given one of Franklin's lady friends a chamber pot with Franklin's picture on the bottom), and the king took a wait-and-see attitude before committing the country to a more entangling alliance.

News of a great American victory at the Battle of Saratoga, however, caused Louis and his ministers to think the rebels just might win. On February 6, 1778, France formally recognized America as an independent nation and agreed to a military alliance. Two different fleets and thousands of French soldiers were sent to the war and played key roles in the deciding battles. The French entry also caused Britain to have to worry about being invaded by a French army and about having to fight the French navy in the West Indies — or wherever else they encountered it.

Undergoing Life Changes: The Loyalists and the Slaves

Before I get to who fought whom where and how it all came out, it's worth taking a look at the war's impact on two very different parts of the American population: the Loyalists and the slaves.

Remaining loyal to the crown

Slightly less than one of every three white colonists didn't side with the Revolution and remained loyal to the crown. Many, but by no means all, were from the aristocracy or had jobs they owed to the British government. Some of these Loyalists, or *Tories* as they were also called, kept quiet about their allegiances, but many acted as spies or guides for the British forces. As many as 30,000 actually fought against their rebel neighbors, and some battles were purely American versus American affairs. One of the Tories, Banastre Tarleton, rose to a major command in the British army and was feared and hated for his savagery and reputation for executing prisoners.

In some areas, such as New York City and parts of North and South Carolina, Loyalists were dominant, but in areas where they weren't, they paid a heavy price for their loyalty. Their taxes were sometimes doubled, their property trashed, and their businesses shunned.

When the war ended, things got even worse. A new verse was added to "Yankee Doodle" by victorious rebels: "Now Tories all what can you say / Come — is this not a griper? / That while your hopes are drained away / 'Tis you must pay the piper." Tory property was confiscated, and as many as 80,000 Loyalists eventually left America for Canada, England, and the West Indies.

Confronting slavery issues

One of the thorniest — and most embarrassing — problems Congress was confronted with during the Revolutionary War was what to do about slaves. At first, Congress declared that no Africans, freed or not, could fight in the Continental army. But when Washington pointed out that they might end up fighting for the British, who were offering freedom in exchange for fighting the rebels, Congress relented and allowed freed slaves to enlist.

More than a few American leaders were also red-faced about fighting for freedom while owning slaves — a hypocrisy not lost on their critics. In the end, some slaves fought for the American cause, and some fled to the British side. The issue of slavery, meanwhile, grew as a divisive issue between North and South. In most of the Northern states during the war, the slave trade was outlawed. In the South, the number of slaves actually grew, mostly because of the birthrates among slaves already there. And slavery spread as Southerners moved west, into Kentucky and Tennessee.

Winning a War

Okay, here's pretty much how the actual fighting unfolded: The Americans started off pretty promisingly — winning an early battle in New York and holding their own at a big battle outside Boston — mostly because the British were slow to recognize they had a real war on their hands. But then the Americans launched an invasion of Canada, which proved to be a really bad idea. Shortly after the Canada failure, Washington got his tail kicked in New York and escaped total disaster only through great luck.

But Washington learned a valuable lesson: He couldn't possibly win by fighting the British in a series of open-field, European-style major battles. The trick, the Continental army learned, was to be a moving target. "We fight, get beat, rise, and fight again," noted Gen. Nathanael Greene.

Washington did win a couple of smaller victories, which were great for morale, but he also suffered through a couple of hideous winters at Valley Forge, Pennsylvania, and Morristown, New Jersey, which were bad for morale.

But the British made a series of tactical blunders and lost an entire army in upstate New York. Then they turned their attentions to the South, made more blunders, and lost another entire army in Virginia. Having apparently run out of mistakes, they quit, and America won. Figure 5-1 shows the highlights of ten key battles or campaigns in the American Revolution.

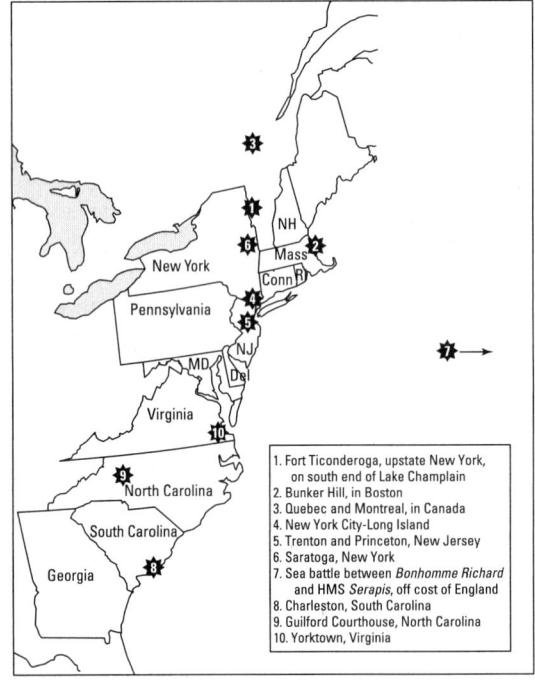

Figure 5-1: Ten key battles of the American Revolution.

1. Fort Ticonderoga, upstate New York, on south end of Lake Champlain
2. Bunker Hill, in Boston
3. Quebec and Montreal, in Canada
4. New York City-Long Island
5. Trenton and Princeton, New Jersey
6. Saratoga, New York
7. Sea battle between *Bonhomme Richard* and HMS *Serapis*, off cost of England
8. Charleston, South Carolina
9. Guilford Courthouse, North Carolina
10. Yorktown, Virginia

© John Wiley & Sons, Inc.

Felling a British fort

Less than a month after Lexington and Concord, American troops under Vermont frontiersman Ethan Allen surprised and captured a British fort — Fort Ticonderoga — on the shores of Lake Champlain in New York. They captured 60 cannons and mortars, which they eventually used to drive the British out of Boston. The victory was a big confidence booster.

Battling it out on Bunker — make that Breed's — Hill

This battle, on June 17, 1775, was actually fought on Breed's Hill, which is next to Bunker Hill, just outside Boston. About 1,400 Americans held the hill. About 2,500 British troops attacked them in a frontal assault rather than by surrounding them. The Brits won after two charges, but they paid a heavy toll. About 1,000, or 40 percent, of their troops were killed or wounded, while the Americans suffered about 400 killed or wounded. The carnage shook British commander William Howe so much he became overly cautious and conservative in future battles.

Losing the campaign in Canada

In late 1775, American leaders Richard Montgomery and Benedict Arnold launched an invasion of Canada. The Yanks thought the Canadians wouldn't put up much of a fight. Bad thought. Americans lost battles at Quebec and Montreal and were forced to retreat. The losses left Canada firmly in British hands and gave the Brits a good base from which to launch attacks on New York and New England.

Nixing plans to take New York

In mid-1776, Washington and his entire army of about 18,000 men moved to the area around New York City, hoping to hem in and defeat a British army of about 25,000. But many of the American troops were raw recruits, who panicked and ran in a series of battles in the area. By the fall, it was Washington who was nearly trapped. Under protection of a heavy fog that materialized at just the right time, the American army slipped away into New Jersey and then to Pennsylvania. It was a major defeat for the American army, but it could've been a lot worse.

Winnin' at Trenton and Princeton

Smarting from about six months of running away, Washington moved his army across the ice-choked Delaware River on Christmas Eve 1776 and surprised a Hessian brigade in Trenton, New Jersey. The result was that Washington captured more than 900 Hessian troops and 1,200 weapons without losing a single man. Washington then followed up with a victory over the British a few days later at Princeton, New Jersey. The victories were smashing morale boosters for the Yanks.

Making the Brits surrender at Saratoga

In 1777, British General "Gentleman Johnny" Burgoyne proposed to lead a British army into New York and New England from Canada, while the British army already in New York City sailed down to capture Philadelphia. It turned out to be a disaster for the Brits. Burgoyne had no concept of a march through enemy-infested wilderness and took along officers' wives and children. Continually harassed by American troops and running low on food and supplies, Burgoyne's army lost two battles near Saratoga. On October 17, 1777, the British army of nearly 6,000 men surrendered. News of the American victory helped convince France to enter the war on the American side.

Sparring at sea

On September 23, 1779, an American navy ship named the *Bonhomme Richard* took on the British warship *Serapis* off the coast of England. The American captain, John Paul Jones, saw two of his major guns explode on the first discharge. Undismayed, he pulled alongside the *Serapis* and the two ships pounded each other for more than two hours. At one point, when asked if he would surrender, Jones replied, "I have not yet begun to fight!" Finally, faced with the arrival of another American ship, the *Serapis* surrendered. Jones's own ship was so badly damaged it had to be abandoned, and he transferred his flag to the British ship. But the victory was the greatest single naval feat of the war and shook British confidence in its navy.

Losing big in Charleston

This was the worst American defeat of the war, which is saying something. In the spring of 1780, about 8,500 British and Loyalist troops and 14 ships surrounded the city of Charleston, South Carolina, trapping an American army under the command of Gen. Benjamin Lincoln. On May 12, Lincoln surrendered his entire army of 5,500 men, along with huge amounts of weapons.

Minimizing the damage at Guilford Courthouse

Most of the war in the South consisted of British troops beating American troops, chasing them, and then beating them again. In December 1780, Congress finally put a competent general in charge of the American forces in the South while Washington fought in the North. He was 38-year-old Nathanael Greene, who was probably the only American general to consistently out-strategize his opposition. After a couple of victories at the battles of Cowpens and Eutaw Springs, Greene faced British Gen. Charles Cornwallis at Guilford Courthouse in North Carolina. The British won what was one of the bloodiest and most bitter battles of the war, but they suffered almost 30 percent casualties, while Greene's losses were light. Cornwallis was forced to withdraw out of the Carolinas and back to Virginia, taking his troops to Yorktown.

Turning things around at Yorktown

Washington had been trying for months to coordinate his own troops with the French troops and ships that were supposedly ready to aid the American cause. On top of that, Congress had failed to supply him with desperately needed reinforcements and supplies.

Finally, in May 1781, things began to fall into place with his French allies. Together with two French fleets, French and American armies converged on Yorktown and hemmed in the British army under Cornwallis. The British, meanwhile, mishandled two fleets of their own and were unable to come to Cornwallis's rescue.

On October 19, 1781, Cornwallis surrendered his entire army of 8,000 men. The British band played a tune called "The World Turned Upside Down," and a band hired by the French played "Yankee Doodle." In London, when Lord North, the British prime minister, heard the news, he cried out "O God! It is all over!"

Actually, it wasn't over for more than a year. The British army still held New York, and there were some small battles until the formal peace treaty was signed on February 3, 1783.

The British were gracious losers, mainly because they wanted to drive a wedge between America and France. They gave up rights to all the land from the Atlantic Coast to the Mississippi River and from Canada to Florida, which was far more than the Americans actually controlled. In return, the Americans promised to treat the Loyalists in their midst fairly and set up fair rules so that British creditors could collect prewar debts. (Neither of those promises was kept.)

American independence had been won. The question now was what to do with it.

Chapter 6

Blueprints and Birth Pains: 1783–1800

In This Chapter
- Bringing order to the colonies
- Electing the first president
- Establishing an economy
- Increasing troubles at home and overseas

After winning its independence from Britain, America felt a little like a kid who has just moved out of his parents' house and isn't sure what step comes next in growing up. The country had no real government, no sound financing system, and no true foreign friends.

Fortunately, it did have a group of extraordinary individuals — some of whom had helped lead it through the Revolution — who were willing to try to find a form of government that would fit. Putting aside most of their personal differences and aspirations (at least at first), they came up with a system of governing the new country that became a true wonder of the world.

Making the Rules

America limped through the Revolutionary War guided by the Continental Congress, a group of men selected by colonial legislatures. The Congress, in turn, came up with something called the Articles of Confederation.

Drafted in 1777 but not ratified by all the states until 1781, the Articles were based on the idea that the individual states would be friendly with one another and cooperate when it was in their mutual interest. Each state had one vote in Congress, and it took 9 of the 13 states to ratify any decision.

Congress ran matters of war and peace, operated the post office, coined money, and dealt with Native Americans when the states didn't want to. It had no power to tax or to establish a federal judicial system, and it lacked any real power to make the individual states pay attention to its legal authority to make postal, coin, or war-and-peace decisions.

It wasn't an awful system, but it guaranteed a continual stream of squabbles among the states. Making things worse were schemes by agents of Spain, France, and Britain. They tried to get Americans who lived in the western parts of the new country to break away. War hero Ethan Allen, for example, met with British agents to discuss making his beloved Vermont a British province and narrowly escaped being tried for treason.

Still, at least two good bits of legislation came out of the loose-knit confederation. The first was the Land Ordinance of 1785, which set up the way land owned by the federal government — which basically was territory won from Britain that wasn't claimed by one of the states — would be divided and sold. The ordinance called for the land to be surveyed into square townships, which were six miles on each side. Each township was then surveyed into 36 areas of one square mile each (640 acres). The parcels were then listed for sale at public auction and could, in turn, be subdivided by the owner into smaller parcels for sale. Part of the revenue went to the establishment of public schools.

The second piece of legislation was enacted in 1787. Called the Northwest Ordinance, it stated that as new states were admitted to the country, they would be equal in every way to the original 13. It also banned slavery in the new territories, although this was later changed. Both laws were good starts to stabilizing the new country. But ongoing troubles in trying to regulate commerce among the states and in trying to raise money for the federal government still plagued the nation, especially because every state had its own currency and assigned it its own value.

Going back to Philly

By 1787, it was apparent to many leaders that the Articles of Confederation needed an overhaul or the union of states would eventually fall apart. So Congress agreed to call a convention of delegates from each state to try to fix things. The first of the delegates (selected by state legislatures) to arrive in Philadelphia in May 1787 was James Madison, a 36-year-old scholar and politician from Virginia who was so frail he couldn't serve in the army during the Revolution. Madison had so many ideas on how to fix things he couldn't wait to get started.

Not everyone else was in such a hurry. Although the convention was supposed to begin May 15, it wasn't until May 25 that enough of the delegates chosen by the state legislatures showed up to have a quorum. Rhode Island never did send anyone.

Eventually, 55 delegates took part. Notable by their absence were some of the leading figures of the recent rebellion against England: Thomas Jefferson was in France, Thomas Paine was in England, Sam Adams and John Hancock weren't selected to go, and Patrick Henry refused.

But those who did show up were hardly second-stringers. George Washington was there and was unanimously selected the convention's president. Benjamin Franklin, at 81 the oldest delegate, was there. But Madison and a handsome 32-year-old, self-made success story from New York named Alexander Hamilton were the true stars of the group.

Half of the group's members were lawyers and 29 were college-educated. Many were wealthy and thus had a bigger-than-most stake in straightening out the country's financial mess. Their average age was 42.

They met in long and highly secret sessions, with armed guards at the doors. Their reasoning was that their task was so difficult that any leaks about what they were doing would only increase outside pressures. They studied other forms of government; they debated. And after 17 weeks, on September 17, 1787, they voted 39 to 3, with 13 absent, to approve a ten-page document that became the United States Constitution. Then most of them adjourned to a local tavern and hoisted a few.

The document the delegates created was a masterpiece of compromises. Big states gained more clout when it was decided that representation in the House of Representatives would be based on population, while small states got protection from being bullied when it was decided that each state would have the same number of members (two) in the Senate. The South won the right to count slaves as three-fifths of a person when determining population for representation in the House; the North got a promise that the slave trade would end for good in 1807. Actually, the South didn't mind this compromise all that much because it didn't mean slavery itself would end — just the practice of importing more slaves from overseas. In fact, it ensured that the value of slaves already here would increase, thus making their owners richer.

The Constitution gave Congress the power to regulate commerce among states as well as with foreign nations and to pass laws with a simple majority of its members. It gave the presidency a powerful role. It created a federal judicial system, with the Supreme Court at the top. And it left the individual states with a fair amount of independence to make their own laws on most matters. No one thought it was perfect, but most of the delegates thought it was a pretty good blueprint from which to build.

While the last members of the convention were signing the document, Franklin pointed to a sun painted on the chair in which Washington was sitting. "I have often . . . looked at that behind the president, without being able to tell whether it was rising or setting," he said. "But now, at length, I have the happiness to know that it is a rising, and not a setting sun."

But they still had to sell the blueprint to the rest of the country.

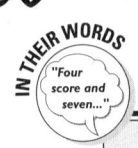

Stand up and be heard...

"A standing army is like an erect penis — an excellent assurance of domestic tranquility but a dangerous temptation to foreign adventure."

—Elbridge Gerry, a convention delegate from Massachusetts, arguing against a provision that would allow for a full-time military organization.

Selling the Constitution to the states

The convention submitted its work to the Congress that was still laboring under the old Articles of Confederation, and Congress accepted it after three days of sometimes-intense debate. But because of the enormity of the issue, Congress also didn't want to be totally responsible if things went wrong (proving that some things never change).

So Congress sent the proposal to the states for ratification. Each state had to elect delegates who would consider the proposed Constitution, and when nine states had approved it, it would become the law of the land.

It was a gamble because if any of the big states — Virginia, New York, Massachusetts, or Pennsylvania — rejected it and went its own way, the whole deal might fall apart. In addition, a lot of people who hadn't thought much about the need for a central government (which was probably the majority of Americans) weren't sold on the idea at all. But the idea of letting "ordinary" people have a say (actually, only about one-fourth of the population was eligible to vote) led to a great deal of spirited debate on the subject, which allowed pro-Constitution forces a chance to make their case.

They did. In a brilliant series of 85 newspaper essays that became known as the Federalist Papers, Hamilton, Madison, and John Jay argued eloquently for adoption of the Constitution. Much more important was the public support of the two most popular men in America: Franklin and Washington. Anti-Constitution forces also made powerful public arguments, but their efforts were not as well organized and lacked star appeal.

The first five states to ratify did so by January 1788. The following month, Massachusetts agreed — but only on the condition that a list of specific individual rights be added to the Constitution as soon as possible (see the sidebar "Giving weight to the Bill of Rights"). By July, all but North Carolina and Rhode Island had ratified it, and they fell in line by May 1790.

"Our constitution is in actual operation," Franklin wrote, "and everything appears to promise that it will last. But in this world, nothing can be certain but death and taxes."

> ### Giving weight to the Bill of Rights
>
> The first 10 amendments to the Constitution were added mainly because a lot of Americans believed in the saying "get it in writing." The drafters of the original Constitution didn't spell out specific rights mainly because they didn't think it was necessary. The document defined the powers of Congress, and, thus, its creators assumed that everything left over belonged to individuals and the states.
>
> But some states insisted the specific rights be spelled out as soon as possible after the Constitution was ratified. So James Madison, at the urging of Thomas Jefferson, came up with a list of 12 amendments, only 10 of which were ratified by 11 of the states in 1791. The two amendments left out had to do with the number of members of the House of Representatives and prohibiting Congress from setting its own salaries. For some reason, Connecticut and Georgia didn't get around to ratifying the remaining 10 until 1941. See Appendix A for the list of the 10 amendments that made it.

Dishing Up Politics, American Style

Now that it had rules, America needed a president, and the choice was a no-brainer. George Washington was unanimously elected in April 1789 by the Electoral College, which had been established by the Constitution and was composed of men elected either by popular vote or by state legislatures. Washington set out from his home in Virginia for the temporary capital at New York (which soon moved to Philadelphia, where it stayed until the federal district that is now Washington, D.C., was completed in 1800). Everywhere he went, Washington was greeted by parades and cheering crowds.

Washington the politician

Washington wasn't a great politician, although he did know enough to buy 47 gallons of beer, 35 gallons of wine, and 3 barrels of rum for potential voters in his first campaign for the Virginia legislature. Still, he wasn't a good public speaker and he wasn't a great innovator.

But he was perfect for the new country. He was enormously popular with the public, even those who didn't like his policies. Because of that, other political leaders were wise to defer to him. (At least publicly: Behind his back, John Adams referred to Washington as "Old Muttonhead," and Alexander Hamilton called him "the Great Booby.")

Washington was also good at assembling competent people around him and playing to their strengths while ignoring their faults. And he assembled a heck of a group: Adams was his vice president, Hamilton his treasurer,

Thomas Jefferson his secretary of state, old Revolutionary War buddy Henry Knox his secretary of war, and sharp-tongued Edmund Randolph of Virginia his attorney general.

Family feuding: Jefferson vs. Hamilton

But it wasn't exactly one big happy family. Hamilton and Adams disliked each other even though they shared many of the same political views — Adams once referred to Hamilton as "the bastard brat of a Scotch peddler." And Jefferson and Hamilton were different in a host of ways. Hamilton was short but impeccable in his dress and manners. Jefferson was tall and often looked like an unmade bed. Hamilton grew up poor in New York and was illegitimate; Jefferson grew up wealthy in a leading family in Virginia. Hamilton had a deeply abiding distrust of the common man and a deep affection for wealth. Jefferson disliked the upper classes and professed that the farmer was nature's greatest creation. And although Jefferson was a relatively pleasant guy to be around, Hamilton could be arrogant and snotty.

Given their differences, it shouldn't be surprising that the two men were at opposite ends of the political spectrum. And given their abilities and stature, it shouldn't be surprising that people who thought the same way began to form political parties around them. At the time, most politicians repudiated the idea of political parties — at least publicly. "If I could not go to heaven but with a [political] party," Jefferson said, "I would not go at all." But people being people, and politicians being politicians, the formation of parties revolving around a certain philosophy of governing was probably inevitable.

The Hamiltonians were called *Federalists*. In essence, they supported a strong central government, a powerful central bank, government support of business, a loose interpretation of the Constitution, and restrictions on public speech and the press. They opposed the expansion of democratic elections and were generally pro-British when it came to foreign affairs. "Those who own the country," said Federalist John Jay, "ought to govern it."

The Jeffersonians were first called *Democratic Republicans,* then just *Republicans.* They favored more power to individual states and state-chartered banks, no special favors for business, a strict reading of the Constitution, giving more people the vote and relatively free speech and a free press. They were generally pro-French. It's too simplistic to say today's Republicans are yesterday's Federalists and today's Democrats are descended from Jefferson's party. Hamilton, for example, supported big federal government programs, which today would make him more of a Democrat, while Jefferson wanted to minimize government, which sounds like the modern Republican. But the dominance of just two parties, Federalists and Republicans, foreshadowed the two-party system that America has pretty much stuck with throughout its history.

By 1796, Washington had had enough of fathering a country. He declined a third term and went home to his plantation in Mount Vernon, Virginia. Hamilton, who was born in St. Croix and therefore under the Constitution couldn't be president, hoped someone he could control would be elected, and he backed a guy named Thomas Pinckney of South Carolina, who was Washington's minister to England. But his plans were thwarted, and Vice President John Adams won.

Jefferson was the Republican candidate, and because he came in second, he became vice president, per the Constitution. (It soon became clear that this wasn't a great idea. So in 1804, the states amended the Constitution to allow candidates to run for either president or vice president, but not both.)

Raising the Dough

Every country needs a sound financial plan (at least every successful country does), and it fell to Hamilton to devise one for America.

The first thing he had to do was establish the new nation's credit. To do that, he had to clean up its existing debts, such as the $54 million the federal government owed foreign and domestic creditors. Hamilton proposed the debt be paid off in full, rather than at a discount as creditors had feared. Hamilton argued that if America didn't make good on what it already owed, no one would want to lend it money in the future.

In addition, he proposed that the federal government also pay off about $21 million in debts the individual states had run up. The old debts would be paid off by issuing bonds. But states like Virginia, which had paid off much of its Revolutionary War debts, were peeved at the thought of the federal government picking up other states' tabs and then sticking all U.S. residents with the bill. So they engaged in a little horse-trading. Virginia withdrew its objections to the plan, and in return, Hamilton and the Washington administration agreed to locate the new federal district next door to Virginia on the Potomac. Whatever advantage Virginia thought that would give it has certainly evaporated by now.

Many members of Congress supported Hamilton's plan to pay off the debts dollar for dollar, especially because many of them either held the old bonds or had snapped them up for next to nothing and stood to make enormous profits. Hamilton himself was accused of using his office to make money off the bonds, but if he was guilty, he didn't do a very good job, because he died broke.

To raise money to pay off the bonds, the federal government established taxes, called *tariffs,* on goods imported into America. It also slapped a tax of 7 cents a gallon on whiskey, which was pretty steep considering whiskey in many of the southern and western states sold for only 25 cents a gallon.

Finally, Hamilton proposed a nationally chartered bank that would print paper money backed by the federal government and in which the government would be the minority stockholder and deposit its revenues. To be located in Philadelphia, the bank would be chartered for 21 years. Jefferson howled that the whole idea would cripple state banks and was unconstitutional, but Hamilton, with the backing of Washington, prevailed. The bank's stock sold out within four hours after going on sale.

Hamilton's plan worked, in large part because the American economy kicked into high gear in the 1790s. Another war between France and England helped increase America's share of the world market; trade in the West Indies that had been stunted by the Revolutionary War was revived; and industry, particularly in the North, began to develop. America, the new kid on the block, now had some change in its pockets.

Earning Respect

A government is only as good as the respect it commands from its citizens, and respect for the new U.S. government wasn't universal. Whiskey makers, former soldiers, Native Americans, and people who thought some politicians were jerks — and said so publicly — were among the groups whose respect the new government had to earn.

Shaking things up: Shays's Rebellion

Daniel Shays needed $12 and couldn't get it. Shays was a Massachusetts farmer and Revolutionary War veteran who, like many of his fellow veterans, found himself broke and in debt after the war. Moreover, the state constitution Massachusetts adopted in 1780 was drafted mostly by businessmen who lived along the coast, and the state's inland farmers got the short end of the stick when it came to things like paying taxes but not being able to vote.

When taxes couldn't be paid, homes, farms, livestock, and personal possessions were seized, and debtors were sometimes thrown into prison. So in 1786, Shays found himself at the head of an "army" of about 1,000 men who were fed up. They marched on Springfield, forced the state Supreme Court to flee, and paraded around town. In January 1787, Shays's group tried to take a military arsenal at Springfield. But the state militia routed them, and after a few weeks of skirmishing, they dispersed and abandoned the fight. Several of the group's members were hanged. Shays fled to Vermont and was eventually pardoned, but he died the next year.

> IN THEIR WORDS
> "Four score and seven..."

The whole thing wasn't in vain, however. Some of the reforms they wanted — such as lower court costs, an exemption on workmen's tools from debt seizures, and changes in the tax laws — were adopted. Jefferson noted "a little rebellion now and then is a good thing . . . the tree of liberty must be refreshed from time to time with the blood of patriots and tyrants." Washington, however, despaired that the rebellion illustrated how too much democracy would lead to anarchy.

But the biggest impact of Shays's Rebellion may have been that it helped convince some of the delegates to the Constitutional Convention that the country needed a strong central government to handle such things.

Taxing liquid corn: The Whiskey Rebellion

This is how important whiskey was on the American frontier: Americans often used it in place of cash for commercial transactions. It was also the cheapest way to market some of the surplus corn crop. So it's easy to understand why people got upset when the new federal government announced it was slapping what amounted to a 25 percent tax on the drink.

Distillers in western Pennsylvania organized a revolt in 1794, roughing up tax collectors and threatening distilleries that tried to pay the tax. When the state's governor refused to intervene for fear of losing votes, President Washington himself led a massive force of about 13,000 men — a larger army than he had during most of the Revolutionary War — and the rebels scattered.

The short-lived rebellion didn't amount to much, but it provided an early test of the federal government's willingness to enforce federal laws.

Going "mad" over the Native Americans

Despite their loss in the Revolution and subsequent peace treaty, the British still had a string of forts in the American Northwest, which was then defined as the area northwest of the Ohio River, east of the Mississippi, and south of the Great Lakes. The Brits said they were there to protect their interests in Canada, but many Americans suspected they were there to stir up the Native

Americans. Because the Native Americans had been lied to, stolen from, pushed off their lands, and murdered in large numbers, they didn't need a lot of stirring up.

In 1791, a U.S. army of about 2,000 troops under Gen. Arthur St. Clair marched into what is now Indiana to counter the British/Native American threat. But St. Clair was surprised and routed by a Native American force, and he suffered nearly 50 percent casualties.

In 1793, another force of 2,000 U.S. troops tried again, this time led by Gen. "Mad Anthony" Wayne. A Revolutionary War hero, Wayne got his nickname not from being nuts but from being daring and a bit reckless in battle (which may be the same thing). Anyway, in August 1794, Wayne's troops attacked a Native American force of about the same size at a site called Fallen Timbers in Indiana. Wayne's army rolled over the Native Americans, burning their villages and destroying their crops. The victory ended the Native American threat and restored much confidence in the U.S. Army.

Attempting to censor the press

American newspapers had been used as a political weapon almost as long as there had been American newspapers. But the rise of the two-party system in the 1790s greatly increased their use and their sting. Pro-Jefferson editors, such as Phillip Freneau and Benjamin Bache, squared off against pro-Hamilton scribes, such as John Fenno and William Cobbett.

These were nasty fellows with a quill in their hands. Bache once wrote that "if ever a nation was debauched by a man, the American nation has been debauched by Washington," and Cobbett opined that America would be truly free only "when Jefferson's head will be rotting cheek-to-jowl with that of some toil-killed Negro slave."

By 1798, the Federalist-controlled Congress had had enough. It narrowly approved the Alien and Sedition Acts. The acts extended the naturalization period from 5 to 14 years, to keep out the foreign riff-raff. And Congress also made it a crime to publish "any false, scandalous and malicious writing" about the president, Congress, or the government in general.

Hundreds were indicted under the Sedition Act, but only ten — all of them Republicans — were convicted. Among them was Congressman Matthew Lyon of Vermont, who had already gained a reputation of sorts by spitting in the face of Federalist Congressman Roger Griswold on the floor of Congress (see Figure 6-1). Lyon was sentenced to four months in jail for writing about President Adams's "unbounded thirst for ridiculous pomp, foolish adulation and selfish avarice." Lyon was reelected to Congress while in jail.

ation was so one-sided, the Sedition Act's popularity
e end probably hurt the Federalist cause much more
xpired on March 3, 1801, a day before Republican
residency. It wasn't renewed, and American politicians
better to develop a thick hide when it came to the
a muzzle on the First Amendment.

Finding Foreign Friction

Most Americans applauded when the French Revolution, which eventually overthrew the French monarchy and did away with a feudalistic system of government ruled by an aristocracy, began in 1789. Americans even continued to support it after the revolution was usurped by radical rebels, who turned it into the Reign of Terror. Thousands of French aristocrats, including King Louis XVI, had their heads lopped off by the guillotine. But many Americans shrugged off the excesses and focused on the French revolutionaries' goals of "liberté, égalité, fraternité" (French for "liberty, equality, brotherhood").

But when the revolt spread to once again engulf Europe in war, more sober Americans started to worry. The Federalists, led by Hamilton, didn't want to take the French side against the British. For one thing, they detested the excesses of the French "mobocracy," or mob rule. For another, they realized that England was America's best customer, and most of the revenues from tariffs paid on imports came from English ships.

The Jefferson-led Republicans, on the other hand, didn't want to side with the British. They reasoned that the French had backed them in their revolution, so they should do the same.

But America's first two presidents, Washington and Adams, didn't want to side with anyone. Both men saw that the longer America could stay out of the European mess, the stronger the country would become, and thus the more able it would be to control its own destiny rather than rely on the fortunes of an alliance.

Staying neutral wasn't easy. British naval ships routinely stopped American merchant ships and forced American sailors into service aboard British ships, a practice called *impressments.* French ships also attacked American merchants with England-bound cargoes.

But luck and skillful negotiating kept America out of the Anglo-Franco fracas for a generation. In 1794, Washington sent diplomat John Jay to England. Jay eventually negotiated a treaty with the British in which the British agreed to give up their forts in the American Northwest and pay for damages caused by seizures of American ships. But the British didn't agree to stop impressing American sailors, and Jay agreed the United States would repay pre-Revolutionary War debts it still owed. The Jay treaty was greeted with widespread howls of rage in America, but it cooled things down with the British for more than a decade.

The Jay treaty also angered the French, who stepped up their attacks on U.S. ships. In 1797, President Adams sent U.S. envoys to Paris to meet with the French foreign minister, Charles Talleyrand. But upon their arrival, the Americans were met by three go-betweens known publicly only as "X, Y, and Z," who tried to get a $250,000 bribe from the Americans just for the chance to meet with Talleyrand. The U.S. envoys told X, Y, and Z to stick it and returned home.

So for about two years, France and the United States waged an undeclared war on the seas. The newly created U.S. Navy captured about 80 French ships, and the French continued to prey on American vessels. Then Adams did a remarkable thing. Ignoring the fact that war fever was raging and declaring war on France could help him win a second term as president, Adams sent another peace team back to Paris in 1800. This time, the two countries made a deal. Adams kept the United States out of war, but he also lost reelection to the presidency and sealed the doom of the Federalist Party in doing so.

Part II
Growing Pains

Five Key Battles of the Civil War

- **Fort Sumter:** After the first Southern states seceded, they began seizing federal forts and shipyards inside their borders. Maj. Robert Anderson, commander of the fort in Charleston Harbor, South Carolina, agreed to surrender as soon as the food ran out. But Southern forces wouldn't wait, and at dawn on April 12, 1861, they fired the first shots of the Civil War.

- **Bull Run:** The first large fight of the war took place near Manassas Junction, Virginia, on July 21, 1861. Neither army was trained or prepared, and for most of the day utter confusion reigned. Then Confederate forces got the upper hand, and Union forces panicked and ran. The rebel army was too tired to chase them.

- **Gettysburg:** Robert E. Lee again pushed into Northern territory in early June 1863, this time into Pennsylvania. In a massive battle (a total of more than 50,000 casualties) from July 1 to July 3, Lee's army hurled itself at Union forces led by Gen. George Meade. But the South's effort failed, and Lee was once again forced to withdraw.

- **Chickamauga and Chattanooga:** These confrontations, which ran from August to November 1863, led to William T. Sherman's march across Georgia. At Chickamauga, Union Gen. George H. Thomas withstood a furious attack and saved the Union Army from a rout. After the Union Army was surrounded at Chattanooga, Ulysses S. Grant led a rescue effort and drove off the Confederate forces.

- **Appomattox Courthouse:** This wasn't a battle, but it was the site in Virginia where on April 12, 1865, Lee formally surrendered to Grant. The Southern Army was exhausted, outnumbered, and half-starved. Grant generously fed the defeated Southerners and allowed them to go home, taking their horses and mules with them.

Visit www.dummies.com/extras/ushistory for an additional article on U.S. history in the mid 1800s.

In this part...

- The people of the United States march westward.
- A Civil War divides the country.
- The U.S. reconstructs the South and rebuilds the Union.

Chapter 7

"Long Tom" and One Weird War: 1800–1815

In This Chapter

▶ Getting the deal of the century — the Louisiana Purchase

▶ Paving the way to the Pacific — the Lewis and Clark expedition

▶ Being stuck in the middle between Great Britain and France

▶ Struggling through the War of 1812

The turn of the century brought what has been called the *Revolution of 1800*. The term, first used by Thomas Jefferson, refers to the fact that for the first time in the young country's history, America saw one political party give up power to another.

In this chapter, you see how well it worked, look at the development of the U.S. Supreme Court in the grand scheme of things, sit in on a big land sale, and fight some pirates. I wrap it up with a pretty weird war with the British.

Jefferson Gets a Job

President John F. Kennedy once hosted a dinner party at the White House and invited a guest list so impressive that he joked it was the finest group of genius and talent to sit at the table "since Thomas Jefferson dined alone."

Kennedy's quip held as much truth as humor. A tall, loose-limbed man who was said to amble more than walk and was thus nicknamed *Long Tom*, Jefferson was a statesman, a writer, an inventor, a farmer, an architect, a musician, a scientist, and a philosopher.

Thus, it may not be surprising that he was also a bundle of contradictions. Jefferson was

- An idealist who could bend the rules when he needed to accomplish something
- A slave owner who hated slavery
- A man who believed Africans were naturally inferior, yet for years had one of his slaves as his mistress
- A believer in sticking to the letter of the Constitution who ignored it on at least one major issue during his presidency
- A guy who preached frugality for the country, yet died $100,000 in debt

But Jefferson's contradictory nature made him flexible, and flexibility in a president can be a very valuable asset. In addition, Jefferson was a true man of the people, much more so than his predecessors George Washington and John Adams. He did away with the imperial trappings that had built up around the office, sometimes greeting visitors to the White House in his robe and slippers. That kind of informality added to the popularity he already enjoyed as author of the Declaration of Independence.

But public popularity meant pretty much diddly-squat in the election of 1800 because of the screwy way the Constitution's drafters had set up the presidential election process. Republican Jefferson received the votes of 73 members of the Electoral College, while Federalist incumbent John Adams snagged 65. But the electors were required by the Constitution to list two names (with the second-highest vote-getter becoming vice president). And as it happened, the 73 electors who voted for Jefferson also listed a New York politician named Aaron Burr, who had helped deliver New York to the Republican side. That meant a tie between Jefferson and Burr, and the winner had to be decided by the House of Representatives, which was still controlled by the Federalists. (The goofy system was done away with by the 12th Amendment to the Constitution, which was added before the next presidential election in 1804.)

The Federalists took their cues mainly from Alexander Hamilton. Hamilton disliked Jefferson, but he detested Burr, with good reason. To call Burr a reptile is a slur to cold-blooded creatures everywhere. Born to a wealthy New Jersey family and well-educated, Burr established the first true political machine in the United States. He was a power-hungry schemer and a dangerous opportunist.

But even with Hamilton's grudging support, it took 35 ballots before the House gave the presidency to Jefferson, with Burr becoming vice president. In return, Jefferson privately promised not to oust all the Federalist officeholders in the government — a promise he mostly kept.

> ### Sally and Tom
>
> When Jefferson ran for reelection in 1804, the nastiest bit of campaigning against him was a claim that he had an affair with one of his slaves, a woman named Sally Hemmings, beginning while he was U.S. envoy to France. Moreover, the story was that he had fathered children by her. Jefferson ignored the charges and easily won reelection.
>
> The issue seemingly died with Jefferson and was largely ignored by historians until the 1970s, when two books revived the rumor and claimed it was true. Jefferson apologists howled, and their arguments ranged from the lack of concrete evidence to back up the assertion to the idea that Jefferson's nephews were the fathers to the contention that Jefferson was impotent.
>
> But in 1998, some pretty concrete evidence did surface, in the form of DNA samples taken from the descendants of Jefferson and Hemmings. The conclusion: Jefferson and Hemmings had children together. In 2000, a commission formed by the Thomas Jefferson Foundation concluded that the weight of all evidence "indicated a high probability" that Jefferson and Hemmings had been more than friends.

As president, Jefferson played to his supporters, who were mainly in the South and West. He pushed bills through Congress that changed the time required to become a citizen from 14 to 5 years and repealed the tax on whiskey. Because he wasn't very good at finances, he left the government's financial fortunes in the hands of his Swiss-born secretary of the treasury, Albert Gallatin, and Gallatin managed to cut the national debt almost in half.

Disorder in the Court

One of the last things the Federalist-controlled Congress did before giving way to the Jeffersonian Republicans in early 1801 was to create 16 new federal circuit court judgeships. Federalist Pres. John Adams then spent until 9 p.m. the last day of his term filling the judgeships — with Federalists.

But when the Republicans took over, they promptly repealed the law creating the judgeships, and the judges were out of a job, along with a few dozen other judicial appointees made by Adams in his last days as president. One of them, a guy named William Marbury, didn't take it gracefully. Marbury sued Jefferson's secretary of state, James Madison, for refusing to give him his judicial commission, and the case went to the U.S. Supreme Court.

Part II: Growing Pains

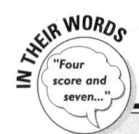

Void this, Mr. President

"The particular phraseology of the Constitution of the United States confirms and strengthens the principle, supported to be essential in all written constitutions, that a law repugnant to the constitution is void." —Chief Justice John Marshall, *Marbury v. Madison*, 1803.

In 1803, the court made a historic ruling. The justices said that though Marbury's appointment was legal, another section of the 1789 law that created the federal judiciary in the first place was unconstitutional because it gave powers to the judiciary that weren't spelled out in the Constitution and weren't within the power of Congress to create.

The ruling marked the first time the Supreme Court ruled an action taken by Congress to be unconstitutional. The result was that the Court asserted its place as a co-equal with the legislative (congressional) and executive (presidential) branches.

John Marshall: A memorable man

John Marshall quite possibly represented the most important accomplishment of the John Adams administration, becoming the patron saint of the U.S. Supreme Court.

A distant cousin of Thomas Jefferson, Marshall was born in 1835 in a log cabin in Virginia, where his father was active in politics. After serving in the Continental army — including the winter at Valley Forge — Marshall earned his law degree and entered politics. In 1799, he went to Congress; in 1800, he became Adams's secretary of state; and in January 1801, Adams appointed him chief justice of the Supreme Court.

It was a job Marshall held until his death, 34 years later. During his tenure as chief justice, he led a series of landmark decisions that established the court's role as a key player in American government and strengthened the power of the federal government. But he also had a good time.

According to one story, Marshall suggested to his fellow justices that on days they were considering a case, they should only drink hard spirits if it was raining. When the sun continued to shine in Washington, however, Marshall decided that because the court had jurisdiction over the entire nation, justices should drink only when it rained somewhere in America.

But the Republicans weren't done. A Supreme Court justice named Samuel Chase, a signer of the Declaration of Independence, so irritated the Jeffersonians with his harangues from the bench that they took to naming vicious dogs after him. Then in 1804, the Republican-controlled Congress took it a step further by impeaching him.

Chase was tried by the Senate, but because he really hadn't done anything that would warrant removing him from the court, he was acquitted. It was the last attempt by one political party to reshape the Supreme Court by directly pushing judges appointed by another party off the bench, although there were efforts to block nominees from being confirmed by the Senate. Free from becoming partisan political puppets, justices were also free to make decisions based on the law as they saw it.

Growing by Leaps and Bounds

The young United States was a restless rascal. And like most kids, it was growing so fast, you couldn't keep it in shoes. The census of 1800 reported a population of 5.3 million (including about 900,000 slaves), a whopping 35 percent increase over 1790. About eight in ten Americans lived and worked on farms.

The largest states were still Virginia, Pennsylvania, and New York. More significantly, the fastest-growing were Tennessee and Kentucky, which had nearly tripled in population since 1790. Americans were moving west.

One of the reasons for this move was that in some areas, they had literally worn out their welcome. Tobacco can be as tough on soil as it is on lungs, and the crop had depleted a lot of land in the South. In the North, the growing population helped drive up the price of land to $14 to $50 an acre.

But in the West — which in 1800 was what was or would become Michigan, Ohio, Kentucky, Tennessee, Indiana, and Illinois — federal government land could be bought for less than $2 an acre. Of course, Native Americans occupied some of it, but in the first few years of the 19th century, government officials such as Indiana Territory Gov. William Henry Harrison were more willing to buy the land than steal it.

So thousands of Americans began to do something they would do for most of the rest of the century — move west. "Out west" was more an idea than a location, the latter of which changed as the country's borders changed. And the borders changed big time, in large part because of a slave revolt in Haiti.

John Jacob Astor

He was the founder of America's first great fortune, and he did it the old-fashioned way: through brains, hard work, and political string-pulling.

Astor was born in Germany in 1763 and came to New York at the age of 20. He parlayed a music store business into real estate, and after 1800, he got into fur trading and importing goods from China. When U.S. companies were barred from foreign trade in 1807, Astor had a clerk pretend to be a Chinese VIP who wanted to go to China for his grandfather's funeral. The trip was approved, and of course the ship came back with a fortune in Chinese goods.

During the War of 1812, Astor lost his trading post in Oregon — the first American post on the Pacific coast — to the British. But after helping to finance the U.S. war effort, Astor got Congress to pass a law banning "foreigners" from the U.S. fur trade. That allowed him to buy out his Canadian partners cheaply and establish a lucrative monopoly.

By the time he died in 1848, Astor had amassed a $30 million fortune, some of which went to establish the New York Public Library. *Astor* became synonymous with wealth in America. Oh, the name of that Oregon trading post? *Astoria*, of course.

Capitalizing on Napoleon's going-out-of-business sale

Napoleon Bonaparte, emperor of France, scourge of Europe, and namesake of a good dessert pastry, was in kind of a jam. In 1800, Spain had reluctantly transferred its control of the vast territory of Louisiana, including the key city of New Orleans and the Mississippi River, to France. Napoleon took it with plans to create a vast new French empire on the North American continent.

The following year, Spanish and French officials clamped down on the rights of Americans to use the Mississippi to float their goods and produce to New Orleans for overseas shipment. U.S. farmers and traders howled, and Jefferson considered siding with the British against France. "The day France takes possession of New Orleans," he wrote, "we must marry ourselves to the British fleet and nation."

Instead, he decided to try to buy a way out first. So he sent his friend James Monroe to France in 1803 and instructed Monroe and Robert Livingston, the U.S. ambassador to France, to offer up to $10 million for New Orleans and Florida, or $7.5 million for New Orleans alone.

Chapter 7: "Long Tom" and One Weird War: 1800–1815

But by 1803, Napoleon's plans for an American empire had hit a snag on what is now the island of Haiti. Napoleon had sent 35,000 crack French troops to the island to crush a rebellion led by a brilliant former slave named Toussaint L'Ouverture, and it proved to be a very bad idea. More than 24,000 of the French soldiers were wiped out by the Haitians or yellow fever, and the disaster soured the French dictator on the whole subject.

So when the Americans made their pitch, the French flabbergasted them with a counteroffer: Why not buy all of Louisiana? After some dickering, they struck a deal. For 60 million francs (about $15 million), the Louisiana Purchase gave the United States an area that stretched from New Orleans to Canada and from the Mississippi River to what is now Colorado and Idaho (see Figure 7-1). That's 828,000 square miles for about three cents an acre, surely one of the best real-estate bargains in history.

But there was a problem. Under the Constitution, Jefferson had no legal power to make such a deal without congressional approval first. And he knew it, confessing privately that he had "stretched the Constitution till it cracked." Undaunted, he pushed a treaty ratifying the sale through the Senate, and America doubled in size almost overnight. Now it was time to go see what the new half looked like.

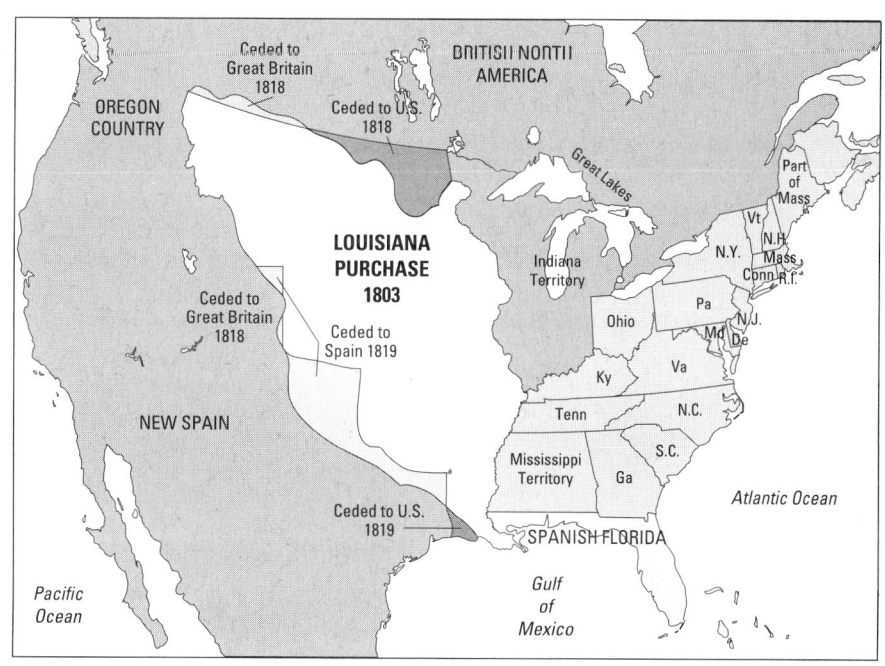

Figure 7-1: Territory gained by the Louisiana Purchase.

© John Wiley & Sons, Inc.

Duel to the death

Vice President Aaron Burr was a sore loser. So when he lost a bid to become governor of New York in April 1804, he was more than a little angry at his old enemy, Alexander Hamilton, who had helped engineer his defeat. In June, Burr sent a letter to Hamilton demanding an apology for slurs on Burr's character in the newspapers, which had been attributed to Hamilton. When the former treasury secretary refused, Burr challenged him to a duel.

The two met on July 12, on the bluffs above the Hudson River near Weehawken, New Jersey. Hamilton, who detested dueling and who had lost a son in a duel a few years earlier, reportedly fired into the air. But Burr aimed at his rival and shot him. Hamilton died the next day.

Burr continued to be a slimeball. In 1807, he was charged with treason for plotting to overthrow the government, and, failing that, to create a new country in the West. He was acquitted because of a lack of witnesses and then spent the next few years in Europe, trying to find support for an invasion of Mexico. He died in 1836, largely, and deservedly, despised.

Lewis, Clark, and the woman on the dollar coin

Even before the purchase of the Louisiana territory was a done deal, Jefferson had a hankering to send an expedition west. So in late 1803, he appointed a 29-year-old army officer named Meriwether Lewis to lead a group to the Pacific Ocean. Lewis, who was Jefferson's former private secretary, enlisted a friend and former army colleague named William Clark as his co-captain (see Figure 7-2). Their mission was to find a good route to the Pacific through the mountains, open the area to American fur trading, and gather as much scientific information as they could. Accompanied by a force of 34 soldiers, 10 civilians, and Seaman, Lewis's big Newfoundland dog, the expedition left St. Louis in 1804.

One of the civilians was a French trapper named Toussaint Charbonneau, who served as an interpreter with the Native Americans. Another was Charbonneau's wife, a Shoshone Indian named Sacajawea. Sacajawea, who was also known as *Birdwoman,* gave birth to a son on the expedition and ended up carrying him on her back much of the way. She was the star of the trip. Not only did she know many of the tribes' customs, but her presence with an otherwise all-male group also helped convince Native Americans that the tourists' goals were peaceful. For her efforts, 196 years later, Sacajawea's image was chosen for the U.S. dollar coin that was first issued in early 2000.

Figure 7-2: Lewis and Clark on expedition.

© Bettmann/CORBIS

The expedition trekked up the Missouri River through what are now the Dakotas and then took a left turn through Montana, Idaho, and Oregon. Traveling by boat, foot, and horseback, the group reached the Pacific near the mouth of the Columbia River in late 1805. After wintering there, they returned to St. Louis in the fall of 1806, having traveled a distance of nearly 7,000 miles in a bit less than three years.

The trip cost $2,500, and it was a smashing success. Only one man died, of a burst appendix. Trouble with the Native Americans was kept to a minimum, and a vast storehouse of knowledge was gained, from information on plants and animals to whether there was land suitable for farming (there was) to whether it was possible to get there and back. Much of the country was thrilled by the stories of a strange new land just waiting to be Americanized.

Fighting Pirates, and a "Dambargo"

Things were going so well for the country in 1804 that Jefferson was reelected in a landslide. But while everyone was excited about what was going on in the West, there was trouble over the eastern horizon.

> ### America gets bookish
>
> On April 24, 1800, Congress passed a resolution creating the Library of Congress, even though it didn't have any books or papers to put in it yet or any building in which to put them. But there were books out there. According to the 1800 census, the country had 50 public libraries, with a total collection of 80,000 books. In 1803, the first tax-supported library opened in Salisbury, Connecticut.
>
> The Library of Congress eventually got settled in Washington and began building a collection under John James Beckley, who was appointed its first chief librarian by Jefferson. Ironically, Jefferson had probably the largest private library in America — some 15,000 volumes. They ended up in the Library of Congress because Jefferson was forced to sell them to the government in later years to pay his private debts.

"To the shores of Tripoli..."

For several years, America — as well as other countries — had been paying a yearly tribute to the Barbary States of Algiers, Morocco, Tunis, and Tripoli in North Africa as protection insurance against pirates. But in 1800, the dey (or leader) of Algiers humiliated the U.S. ship that brought the tribute by forcing it to fly the flag of the Ottoman Empire while in Algiers Harbor. The action angered American officials and hastened the building of naval ships that the penny-pinching Jefferson administration had only reluctantly supported.

The following year, the pasha (or leader) of Tripoli declared war on the United States because it wouldn't increase its tribute. Over the next four years, the fledgling American navy dueled with the pasha and his pirates with mixed success. Then in 1805, William Eaton, the former U.S. counsel to Tunis, led a motley force of about 200 Greek and Arab mercenaries — and 9 U.S. Marines (which is where the "to the shores of Tripoli" line in the "Marines' Hymn" comes from) — on a 600-mile desert march. Eaton's force captured the city of Derna. Coupled with the presence of American warships off its harbors, Tripoli was forced to sign a peace treaty, free the American prisoners it was holding, and stop exacting tribute.

Although fighting with other pirates continued off and on for another six or seven years, the victory was a huge shot in the arm for American morale. But the real foreign threat about to surface was from a more familiar source.

No one likes a bloodless war

Britain and France were at war again, and the United States was trying to stay out of it — again. One reason for staying out of it was that it was hard to figure out which side to like less. Both countries decided to blockade the other, and that meant French naval ships stopped American ships bound for Britain and seized their cargoes, and the British navy did the same to U.S. ships bound for France or its allies.

But the British also had the maddening habit of *impressments* — pressing Americans into British naval service. Britain relied on its navy for its very survival. But it treated its sailors so poorly that they deserted by the hundreds and sometimes took refuge in the American merchant fleet, where treatment and pay were better. So British warships often stopped American ships and inspected their crews for deserters. And just as often, they helped themselves to American citizens when they couldn't find deserters.

In one particularly galling case in June 1807, the British frigate *Leopard* fired on the U.S. frigate *Chesapeake,* forced the *Chesapeake* to lower its flag, took four "deserters" — including a Native American and an African American — and hanged one of them. The incident infuriated much of the country, and the louder members of Congress called for war.

But Jefferson wanted to avoid that. Instead, he decided to put pressure on Britain economically. In late 1807, he prodded Congress into passing the Embargo Act, which essentially ended all American commerce with foreign countries. The idea was to hurt Britain — and France too — in the wallet and force them to ease off American shipping.

Bad idea. While smuggling made up some of the loss, American commerce plunged. U.S. harbors were awash in empty ships, and farmers watched crops once bound for overseas markets rot. Jefferson received hundreds of letters from Americans denouncing the *dambargo,* including one purportedly sent on behalf of 4,000 unemployed seamen. Meanwhile, France and Britain continued to slug it out.

Finally, in early 1809, just before leaving office, Jefferson relented, and Congress passed a milder version of an embargo. But the damage had been done, and the bloodless war was on its way to being replaced with a real one.

"Little Jemmy" Takes the Helm

If James Madison were alive today, he might well be a computer nerd. He was extremely intelligent, conscientious, and focused on the task at hand. A neat dresser who was slight of build (5 feet 4 inches, but he had a big head) and shy in public settings, Madison was referred to by both friend and foe as *Little Jemmy*. He could also be very stubborn.

Madison was easily elected president in 1808, mostly because

- He was well regarded as the father of the U.S. Constitution.
- Thomas Jefferson, who believed two terms was enough for anyone to be president, handpicked Madison to be his successor.
- The opposing Federalist Party was so disorganized it would have had a hard time organizing a one-coach funeral.

Madison inherited a messy foreign situation. France and Britain were still at war, and both countries had continually raided American ships. Jefferson's efforts to stop this practice by cutting off all U.S. trade with foreign countries had nearly sunk a previously buoyant U.S. economy.

So Madison and Congress tried a different approach. In 1809, Congress passed a law that allowed U.S. ships to go wherever they wanted but banned French and British ships from U.S. ports. The following year, Congress lifted all restrictions but gave the president the power to cut off trade with any country that failed to recognize America's neutrality.

The French dictator Napoleon then announced the French would stop their raids if the British agreed to end their blockades of European ports. The British, quite correctly, didn't trust Napoleon and refused. But Madison decided the French despot was sincere and re-imposed the U.S. trade ban on Britain. American merchants, especially in New England, moaned, and the British seethed, but Madison refused to change his mind.

New kids on the block

Madison's decision was cheered by a new group of congressmen who took office in 1811. They were led by the new speaker of the House of Representatives, a 34-year-old Kentuckian named Henry Clay and a 29-year-old lawyer from South Carolina named John C. Calhoun. This new Washington brat pack had missed a chance to participate in the American Revolution, and because so many of them wanted their own chance to fight the British, they became known as the *War Hawks*.

Dolley Madison: Proof that opposites attract

If James Madison was kind of a nerd, his wife was anything but. Born in 1768 to a poor Quaker family in Philadelphia, Dolley Payne Todd's marriage to Madison was her second. After her first husband died in 1793, Aaron Burr introduced her to Madison. Within a few months, she was married to "the great little Madison," as she called him.

She took to being First Lady like a duck to water. After all, she had practiced for the job for eight years as the White House's unofficial hostess while Thomas Jefferson, a widower, was president. When Madison took over, Dolley assumed the task of decorating the great house. Her charm also made her a great political asset to her husband. "She is a fine, portly, buxom woman who has a smile and a pleasant welcome for everybody," observed the writer Washington Irving.

Dolley also showed her pluck when the British army invaded Washington and burned the White House. With British soldiers less than a rifle shot away, Dolley stubbornly refused to flee until a portrait of George Washington by the famous artist Gilbert Stuart could be saved. Dolley died in 1849 at the age of 81, 13 years after her husband's death.

But there was more to the War Hawks' desire for war than just a chance to kick some British butt. Canada belonged to the British Empire, and more than a few land-hungry Americans thought it should belong to the United States. A war with Britain would provide the perfect reason to conquer the neighboring northern nation.

Fighting the Native Americans — again

There was also the perennial vexing issue of what to do about the Native Americans. For the first decade of the century, the American policy had been to buy, coerce, bully, and swindle Native Americans out of their land in the Northwest rather than go to war.

By 1811, an inspirational Shawnee chief named Tecumseh had had enough. Aided by his religious fanatic brother Tenskwatawa, who was also known as the *Prophet* and who urged a holy war against the whites, Tecumseh rallied tribe after tribe to join his confederacy and stop the white men's invasion. He urged the Native Americans to give up everything white — their clothes, their tools, and especially their alcohol.

By late 1811, Tecumseh had put together a force of several thousand Native Americans. An army of about 1,000 U.S. soldiers, led by Gen. William Henry Harrison, marched to the edge of the territory claimed by Tecumseh at Tippecanoe Creek, Indiana. While Tecumseh was away, his brother led an attack against Harrison. The result of the battle was a draw, but Tecumseh's confederacy began to fall apart.

IN THEIR WORDS: "Four score and seven..."

> ### No deal
>
> "Sell our country? Why not sell the air, the clouds, and the great sea? Did not the Great Spirit make them all for the use of his children?" —Chief Tecumseh, speaking to Gen. William Henry Harrison, 1810.

Why Not Invade Canada This Year?

In Britain, the long war with Napoleon and the trade fights with America had caused hard times, and a lot of British wanted to drop the squabbling with the former colonies and focus on the French. On June 16, 1812, the British government decided to stop raiding American ships. But there was no quick way to get the news to America, which was too bad, because two days later, Congress declared war on England under the rallying cry of "Free Trade and Sailors' Rights."

War was a bold — and foolhardy — move for a country with such a shabby military system. The U.S. Army had about 7,000 men and very few competent officers. Many of the top officers were antiques from the Revolutionary War 30 years before. One army official, Maj. Gen. Henry Dearborn, was so fat he had to travel in a specially designed cart. The U.S. Navy consisted of 16 ships and a bunch of little gunboats that had been a pet project of Jefferson's and proved to be completely useless. And a fair-sized segment of the population was against the war, particularly in New England.

It took about a month to demonstrate just how unready America was. A U.S. command of about 1,500 troops marched to Detroit as a staging ground for an invasion of Canada. When a Canadian army showed up to contest the idea, the American general, William Hull, surrendered without firing a shot.

It was the first of several failed U.S. efforts to conquer Canada, which had looked so easy on paper. After all, the U.S. population was more than 7 million by 1810, while there were fewer than 500,000 white Canadians, many of whom were former Americans. The British army had about 5,000 soldiers in Canada, but there wasn't much chance of them being reinforced because the English were busy fighting Napoleon.

Everyone's relative

Sam Wilson was a nice guy. He was born in Arlington, Massachusetts, in 1766; served as a drummer boy and then a soldier in the American Revolution; and in 1789 moved to Troy, New York, to start a meatpacking company. Everyone liked him for his good humor and fair business practices.

In 1812, Wilson's solid reputation landed him a contract to supply meat to the American army. He began the practice of stamping "U.S." on the crates destined for the troops. Because the term "United States" still wasn't often used, federal meat inspectors asked one of Wilson's employees what it stood for. The guy didn't know, so he joked "Uncle Sam," referring to Wilson.

Soon troops began referring to rations as coming from "Uncle Sam," and by 1820, illustrations of Uncle Sam as a national symbol were appearing in newspapers. Wilson died in 1854 at the age of 88. In 1961, Congress recognized his claim to be the original Uncle Sam.

Still, the U.S. efforts managed to fail. After Hull's defeat at Detroit, another U.S. force tried to invade from Fort Niagara. It flopped when many of the New York militia declined to fight outside their own state and refused to cross the river into Canada. A third army set out from Plattsburgh, New York, bound for Montreal, and marched 20 miles to the border, only to quit and march back to Plattsburgh.

In September 1813, a U.S. Navy flotilla built and commanded by Capt. Oliver Hazard Perry destroyed a British fleet on Lake Erie. Perry's victory was notable not only for the famous saying that came from it — "We have met the enemy and they are ours" — but also because it forced the British out of Detroit and gave Gen. William Henry Harrison a chance to beat them at the Battle of the Thames River. Tecumseh, the Native American leader who was now a brigadier general in the British army, was killed and, thus, the Native American–Britain alliance was squelched.

The victories of Perry and Harrison kept the British from invading the United States through Canada, but the American efforts to conquer Canada were over.

Things were a little better at sea. With most of Britain's navy tied up in Europe, U.S. warships like the *Constitution, United States,* and *President* won several one-on-one battles with British ships and so cheered Congress that it decided to build more ships. But none of the naval engagements were very important from a military standpoint, and after the rest of the formidable British fleet showed up and bottled most of the U.S. Navy up in American ports, the victories at sea ceased.

Three Strikes and the Brits Are Out

By mid-1814, the British had finally defeated Napoleon and sent him into exile. Now they could turn their full attention to the war in America — and unlike the first war with Britain, America wouldn't be getting any help.

Britain's first big effort came in August 1814, when a force of about 4,000 veteran British troops landed in the Chesapeake Bay area east of Washington, D.C. At the village of Bladensburg, the Brits encountered a hastily organized force of 6,000 American militiamen who quickly showed they had no stomach for a fight. Almost as soon as the shooting started, the militia ran like scalded dogs, and the British army easily strolled into America's capital.

The government officials fled, and the British burned every public building in the city (see Figure 7-3). The burnings were partially to avenge the American torching of the Canadian city of York and partially to take the heart out of the Yanks. Instead, they enflamed U.S. anger and delayed the British advance on Baltimore, which was the real military target.

Figure 7-3: The British army burns the White House.

© Bettmann/CORBIS

REMEMBER

By the time the British forces got to Baltimore, the city's Fort McHenry had been fortified. An all-night bombardment of the fort accomplished nothing, except to inspire a Washington lawyer who watched it from the deck of a British ship, where he was temporarily a prisoner. Francis Scott Key jotted down his impressions in the form of a poem, on the back of a letter. After the battle, he revised it a bit and showed it to his brother-in-law, who set it to the tune of an old English drinking song called "To Anacreon in Heaven." It was published in a Baltimore newspaper as "Defense of Fort McHenry" but was later renamed "The Star-Spangled Banner." Soon soldiers were singing it all over the country. Meanwhile, the British efforts to invade Baltimore ended.

A second, even larger British force attempted an invasion of the United States via a land-water route through New York. In September 1814, a British fleet sailed against an American fleet on Lake Champlain, near Plattsburgh. The U.S. fleet, under the command of Lieutenant Thomas Macdonough, was anchored, and Macdonough rigged his ships so they could be turned around to use the guns on both sides. After a savage battle, the American fleet prevailed thanks to Macdonough's trick, and the shaken British force retired to Canada.

The third and last major British effort took place at New Orleans. A 20-ship British fleet and 10,000 soldiers squared off against an army of about 5,000 American soldiers, backwoods riflemen, and local pirates who disliked the British more than they disliked the Americans.

The American force was under the command of a tall, gaunt Tennessee general named Andrew Jackson. Jackson had already made a name for himself as a great military leader by defeating the Creek Indians earlier in the war. After a few fights to feel each other out, the two sides tangled in earnest on January 8, 1815.

Actually, it was more of a slaughter than a fight. The British charged directly at Jackson's well-built fortifications, and U.S. cannon and rifles mowed them down. In less than an hour, more than 2,000 British were killed, wounded, or missing, compared to American losses of 71. The British retreated. It was a smashing victory for the United States. Unfortunately for those killed and wounded, it came two weeks after the war had formally ended.

Calling It Even

Almost as soon as the war started, Czar Alexander I of Russia offered to mediate between Britain and America, mostly because he wanted to see Britain concentrate its military efforts against Napoleon. But nothing came of the offer.

Working on a settlement

Early in 1814, both sides agreed to seek a settlement. A few months later, America sent a team of negotiators to Ghent, Belgium, led by its minister to Russia, John Quincy Adams, and House Speaker Henry Clay.

At first, the British negotiators dragged things out while waiting to see how their country's offensive efforts worked out on the battlefield. England then demanded America turn over loads of land in the Northwest Territory and refused to promise to stop kidnapping American sailors off U.S. ships. But when news of the defeats at Plattsburgh and Baltimore reached Ghent, the British tune changed.

They dropped their demands for territory, agreed to set up four commissions to settle boundary disputes, and agreed to stop the habit of impressing American seamen. On December 24, 1814, both sides signed a treaty that basically just declared the war over.

"I hope," said John Quincy Adams in toasting the treaty, "it will be the last treaty of peace between Great Britain and the United States." It was — the countries have never gone to war against each other since.

Squawking about things in New England

In New England, meanwhile, Federalist Party officials had been chafing for a while about the dominance of the Democratic-Republican Party and the waning influence of the region as the country moved west. In late 1814, representatives from five New England states sent delegates to Hartford, Connecticut.

They met for about three weeks and came up with some proposed amendments to the Constitution, including requiring approval by two-thirds of the states before any future embargoes could be set, before war could be declared, or before any new states could be admitted.

There was even some talk about states leaving the Union. (Although it didn't amount to much, it was a chilling harbinger of things to come.) Eventually, three of the delegates were sent to Washington with the demands. They got there just in time to hear about the victory at New Orleans and the treaty at Ghent. They left town quietly.

Thus did a goofy war end. Fewer than 2,000 U.S. soldiers and sailors were killed. No great changes came immediately from it. But the War of 1812 did serve to establish America firmly in the world's eye as a country not to be taken lightly. It may not always choose its fights wisely or fight with a great deal of intelligence. But it would fight.

Chapter 8

Pulling Together to Keep from Falling Apart: 1815–1844

In This Chapter
- Trying to hold on to nationalism
- Bolstering slavery in the South with new crops and inventions
- Setting the foundations for dirty politics and land expansion
- Debating states' rights
- Making travel, farming, and communication easier with technological advances

Fresh from a "victory" over England in the War of 1812 (it was really a draw), America was feeling pretty full of itself in 1815. The country made big strides in pulling together. But like any adolescent, America was subject to wild mood swings. As this chapter unfolds, the country suffers an attack of the economic blahs, encounters some pretty sick politicking, and sees one of the most tragic aspects of its national character, slavery, take firm hold.

There's also the election of Andrew Jackson, which begins a Democratic dynasty; a speech from Daniel Webster that helps get the North ready to fight the Civil War; the coming of the railroad; and more shameful treatment of Native Americans. Oh, and don't forget the Alamo.

Embracing Nationalism . . . Sort Of

By 1815, the generation that had brought on — and fought through — the American Revolution was fading away. James Monroe, who was elected president in 1816, was the last chief executive to have actually fought in the Revolutionary War. And as the revolutionary crowd faded, so did many of the memories of what it had been like to be individual colonies before uniting to become a single country.

More people began to think of themselves as Americans first and Virginians or Vermonters second. The rising tide of nationalism showed itself in the beginnings of a truly American literature and art. The District of Columbia, rebuilt on the ashes of the capital the British had burned in 1814, became a source of national pride.

But these nationalist feelings were sorely tested by several issues that different sections of the country viewed with different perspectives. These included the banking system, tariffs, public land sales, and Supreme Court decisions on the powers of the central government versus individual states.

Taking it to the bank

The first Bank of the United States, whose majority stockholder was the federal government and which had helped the nation get a grip on its finances, had been created at the urging of Alexander Hamilton in 1790. But it had been allowed to expire in 1811, and a horde of state-chartered banks swarmed to take its place. In 1811, there were 88 state banks; by 1813, the number was 208, and by 1819, 392. Most of them extended credit and printed currency far in excess of their reserves; when the war with Britain came, most of them couldn't redeem their paper for a tenth of its worth.

In 1816, Congress chartered a second Bank of the United States, with capital of $35 million. The idea was to provide stability to the economic system by having a large bank that would serve as the federal government's financial agent. But the new bank's managers were corrupt, stupid, or both, and they lent money like mad to land-crazed Americans flocking to the West.

In 1819, land prices dropped, manufacturing and crop prices collapsed, and scores of overextended banks failed. The yahoos who were first put in charge of the second Bank of the United States finally got the boot; new management stepped in, clamped down hard on credit, and foreclosed on its debtors.

But the Panic of 1819, the nation's first widespread financial crisis, triggered strong resentment toward the Bank, which was nicknamed "the Monster." The Bank was particularly hated in the credit-dependent West, which saw it as a creature of rich financiers and speculators in New York and New England. The West's antipathy toward the bank drove a wedge between the regions.

A tariff-ic idea

The largest source of income for the federal government came from *tariffs*, the taxes collected on goods imported into the United States. During the War of 1812, the average tariff doubled, to about 25 percent. In 1816, Congress voted to keep tariffs at those levels.

The idea was that higher tariffs would not only generate money for the government but also drive up prices on foreign goods and thus encourage Americans to buy U.S.-made products. Most sections of the country liked the idea at first, especially the North, where manufacturing of goods from furniture to textiles had developed during the war.

But as time passed, the South and much of the West came to hate tariffs because those regions had little manufacturing to protect, and the taxes just drove up the cost of goods they had to get from somewhere else.

This land is my land, but for how much?

Nothing attracts a crowd like a new country, and America was certainly doing that. In 1810, the census counted 7.2 million Americans. By 1820, that number shot up to 9.6 million, a 33 percent increase. Much of that was the result of an astonishing birthrate, but an upswing in the number of European immigrants crossing the Atlantic helped as well. The crossing was relatively cheap (maybe $25 from London). No customs, no immigration, no passport. You got off the ship and you looked for a job. By 1820, an estimated 30,000 people a year were doing just that. Although some immigrant-bashing surfaced when economic times got tough, most of the newcomers were greeted with a big yawn.

"The American Republic invites nobody to come," wrote Secretary of State John Quincy Adams. "We will keep out nobody. Arrivals will suffer no disadvantages as aliens. But they can expect no advantages either . . . what happens to them depends entirely on their individual ability and exertions, and on good fortune."

One of the reasons for this attitude was that the country had plenty of room. Between 1815 and 1821, six new states joined the Union, bringing the total number to 24. And federal land was cheap and plentiful: $2 an acre for a minimum of 160 acres, with only $80 down and the rest paid over four years.

But when hard times hit in 1819, even those lenient terms were too much. Many folks lost their land to banks when they couldn't pay the mortgage. The banks themselves weren't immune, either: Many failed, taking the settlers' savings with them.

In 1820, Congress lowered the minimum amount of land that could be bought to 80 acres, at $1.25 an acre. The West supported the move, but the North and East, which saw public land as a cash cow to be milked for every dollar that could be squeezed out, were less enthusiastic. Public land thus became another sore point between regions.

Orders from the court

One place where nationalism was secure was in the U.S. Supreme Court. Under Chief Justice John Marshall, the court consistently ruled in favor of a strong central government over the rights of individual states.

In an 1819 case, for example, the court ruled that Maryland had no legal right to try to run the Bank of the United States out of the state by heavily taxing it. "The power to tax is the power to destroy," Marshall wrote, and states had no power to destroy federal institutions. In an 1821 case involving Virginia and an illegal lottery, the court asserted its right to review the decisions of state supreme courts in cases involving powers of the federal government. And the court ruled in 1824 that New York had the power to regulate steamboat commerce only within itself, not between states.

Increasing industry

America was basically a country of farmers for much of the 19th century, but the War of 1812 had cut off the supply of many manufactured goods from Europe and encouraged the growth of domestic industry.

The rise of factories

In 1790, the first factory devoted to spinning cotton into thread opened in New England, and by 1815, there were 213 such factories.

Most goods were still produced and sold by individuals or small companies. But strides in manufacturing parts that could be interchanged to make assembling objects easier, the use of water- and steam-powered machinery, and increases in demands for American-made goods all helped foster growth in the nonagricultural segment of the economy.

Transportation gets rolling (well, floating)

As the market for goods increased, the need for a sound transportation system also grew. Congressional leaders such as Henry Clay and John C. Calhoun were eager for the federal government to lead the development of roads and waterways.

But Presidents Madison and Monroe balked, claiming that the Constitution limited the federal government's public works efforts to projects that crossed state boundaries and not projects that were contained within a single state. Because most states didn't have the money for big road-building projects, traveling or shipping by road remained a real pain in the back pocket.

On the water, however, things were a little different. One of the advantages of moving goods by water is that you can move a lot more with less effort — if you can get the water to go where you want to go and move in the direction you want. The development of the steamboat opened two-way traffic on rivers, particularly the Mississippi, because cargo could go upstream against the current. And construction began in New York in 1817 on a remarkable engineering feat: the 363-mile-long Erie Canal, linking Lake Erie at Buffalo with the Hudson River and Atlantic Ocean. Completed in 1825, the $7 million canal soon repaid its costs through tolls and brought prosperity to the entire region. It also sparked a nationwide canal-building boom as areas raced to link up major natural waterways with man-made ditches.

The Slavery Cancer Grows

In the South, no one was digging canals or building factories. Tobacco, once the major crop, had worn out the soil in many areas, and many Southern planters were looking for a substitute. Cotton was a possibility because of the big demand for it, especially in England. But the variety of cotton that grew well in most of the South was difficult to de-seed.

Cotton and sugar mean more slaves

In 1793, a teacher and inventor from Massachusetts named Eli Whitney visited a plantation in Georgia. Fascinated with the cottonseed problem, Whitney fiddled around and came up with a simple machine that rotated thin wire teeth through the slots of a metal grill. The teeth picked up the cotton fibers and pulled them through the slots, leaving the seeds behind.

Whitney's *cotton gin* (short for "engine") could do the work of 50 men. The result was a cotton boom. In 1793, the South produced about 10,000 bales of cotton. By 1820, that amount rose to more than 400,000. In 1794, a Frenchman in New Orleans named Jean Etienne Bore came up with a method of boiling off sugar cane until it turned into crystals, and the cultivation of sugar spread over the Southeast.

But growing cotton and sugar were labor-intensive activities, and that labor was supplied almost exclusively by slaves. Until the cultivation of cotton and sugar took off, slavery had appeared to be on the decline. A federal constitutional provision had outlawed the importation of any more slaves in 1808, but all the individual states had already banned the practice five years earlier. And the prices of slaves had been steadily dropping, a sign that the economics of the system were too unfavorable to continue it.

Noneconomic reasons also factored in. A religious revival that swept the country in the late 18th and early 19th centuries did much to raise the level of opposition to slavery. In addition, many whites were fearful that an increase in the number of slaves could lead to a massive rebellion such as the one that had happened in Haiti in the 1790s. But the rise of the cotton and sugar crops and the spread of tobacco to new areas increased the dependence of the South on slave labor. Ten to 20 slaves worked every 100 acres of cotton, and they became valuable "commodities." In 1800, the average cost of a slave was about $50; by 1850, it was more than $1,000.

As the need for slaves increased, owners were anxious to increase their holdings through births. But as their value rose, slaves were sold from state to state as the market dictated, often breaking up families. In 1800, the number of slaves in America was put at about 900,000; by 1860, on the eve of the Civil War, the number was 4 million.

In summary, slave owners had a labor force they could force to work at no wages, and keep, sell, rape, or kill as they saw fit. To defend the system, the owners often fell back on the rationale that slavery was good for the slave and frequently mentioned in the Bible as a normal human condition.

Opposing slavery

Many Northerners felt compelled to attack the system. Some of the opposition was on moral grounds, but much of it was based on politics. The Constitution allowed slaves to be counted as ⅗ of a person when deciding how many members each state could have in the House of Representatives, and non-slave states (those that specifically prohibited slavery) resented slave states (those that allowed it) for gaining more political clout through their nonvoting slaves. In the West, much of the anti-slave sentiment stemmed from free laborers not wanting to have to compete with slave labor.

The truth was that African Americans were discriminated against in the North, too. In most situations, they couldn't vote, testify at trials, marry outside their race, join labor unions, live in "white" areas, or go to school. Free African Americans in the North, especially children, were also at risk of being kidnapped and taken to the South to be sold.

With even well-intentioned antislavery advocates convinced that the two races may not be able to live together, many people supported sending former slaves to Africa. President Monroe, a Virginia slave owner, pushed in 1819 for the establishment of a colony in Africa where freed American slaves could go. In 1824, the colony of Liberia was established, with its capital of Monrovia named after Monroe. But many American-born freed slaves had no interest in going to a strange country. They preferred to take their chances on staking a claim to their birthrights as American citizens.

Compromising over Missouri

In February 1819, the territory of Missouri petitioned Congress to be admitted as a state. At the time, America consisted of 11 slave and 11 free states, so the question was whether Missouri, with 10,000 slaves, should be admitted as a slave state or be forced to free its slaves before it was allowed into the fold. Debate on the issue raged across the country. Finally, Henry Clay crafted a compromise in March 1820. Under the aptly named *Missouri Compromise,* Missouri was admitted as a slave state, and the territory of Maine came in as a free state, keeping a balance of 12 slave and 12 free. Figure 8-1 shows a breakdown of the slave/free arrangement created by the compromise. Congress also deemed that slavery would be excluded from any new states or territories above latitude 36 degrees, 30 minutes.

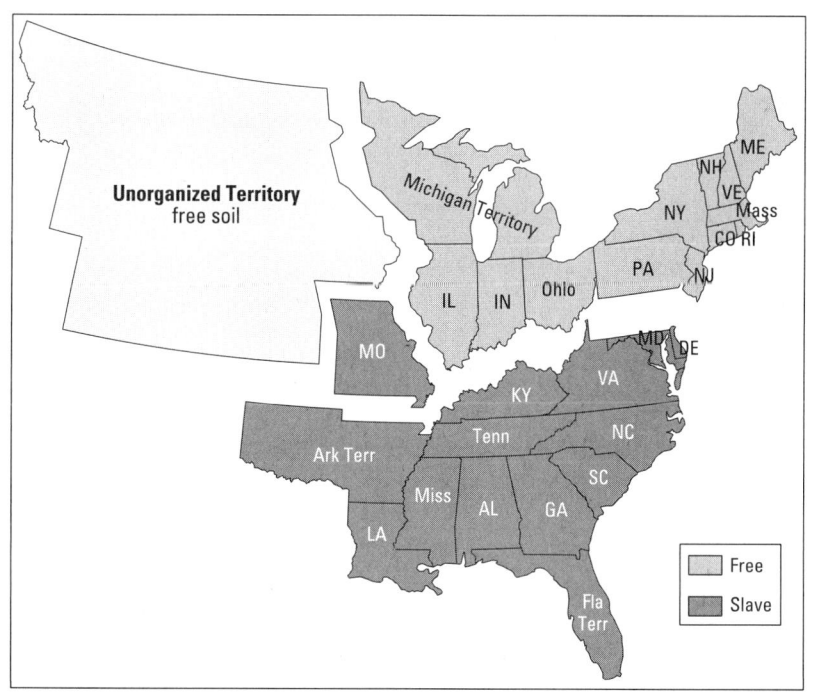

Figure 8-1:
Results of the Missouri Compromise.

© John Wiley & Sons, Inc.

Proslavery forces grumbled that Congress had no constitutional right to say where slavery could and couldn't occur; antislavery forces complained that the compromise was an admission that slavery was acceptable. But the compromise held for the next three decades, giving the country a little more time to seek a better solution it would not find.

"[T]his momentous question [the spread of slavery], like a fire bell in the night, awakened and filled me with terror. I considered it at once as the knell of the Union, noted slaveholder Thomas Jefferson. "(W)e have the wolf by the ears, and we can neither hold him, nor safely let him go."

Mind your own hemisphere: The Monroe Doctrine

While the issue of slavery was growing at home, big events were happening elsewhere in the Americas. Spain's Latin American colonies were struggling for their independence, and U.S. citizens generally supported the struggles as being like their own with the British. As several colonies broke free, Washington clamored to recognize their independence.

In 1819, after Spain had sold Florida to America for $5 million and a promise that the United States would keep its hands off Texas, President Monroe promptly urged Congress to formally recognize the newly independent Latin American countries, including Mexico.

In Europe, meanwhile, a group of monarchs known as the Holy Alliance was scheming to pick off Spain's former colonies. And on the Pacific Coast, the Russians claimed an area from present-day Washington State to Alaska.

Declining an offer from the English to go in as partners against the Holy Alliance's plans, Monroe and his secretary of state, John Quincy Adams, decided to issue what became known as the *Monroe Doctrine*, which amounted to a hands-off warning in the Western Hemisphere. In December 1823, Monroe told Congress that America wouldn't tolerate further attempts by European powers to colonize in the New World. What they had, they could keep, he said. Everything else was off limits.

"The American continents, by the free and independent condition which they have assumed and maintained, are henceforth not to be considered as subjects for future colonization by any European powers," Monroe wrote.

Although it probably had little to do with Monroe's warning, the Russians did agree in 1824 to pull back to what is now the southern border of Alaska and stay there. In fact, Monroe's statements didn't really have much to back them up, because American military might was slight. But the Monroe Doctrine has been interpreted and employed by many presidents since to justify interfering in, or staying out of, the affairs of neighboring countries.

Mud-Wrestling to the White House

In the space of 12 years — from 1817 to 1828 — presidential politics went from dignified to disgusting. In March 1817, James Monroe assumed the office. Monroe, who had easily beaten Rufus King, the last candidate the Federalist Party would ever nominate, wasn't a brilliant man. But he had a good deal of common sense, and he was so honest Thomas Jefferson said, "[T]urn his soul wrong side outwards, and there is not a speck on it."

Monroe was also immensely popular, so much so that he won reelection in 1820 with all but one electoral vote. In 1824, however, he followed the tradition started by Washington and didn't seek a third term. With no need to unite behind one candidate because the Federalist Party was extinct, plenty of Republicans decided to run. They included Monroe's secretary of state, John Quincy Adams; House Speaker Henry Clay; Treasury Secretary William Crawford; Secretary of War John C. Calhoun; and war hero General Andrew Jackson.

Adams wins, but Jackson isn't done

By the 1824 election, Calhoun had dropped out in favor of running (successfully) for vice president, and Crawford had suffered a stroke that left him unable to serve. Despite a bitter, nasty campaign and the crowded field, voter turnout was only 27 percent.

When the electoral votes were counted, Jackson had 99, Adams 84, Crawford 41, and Clay 37. Because no one had a majority, the Constitution required that the House of Representatives pick the winner. Clay had no love for Adams but even less for Jackson, so he threw his support to Adams, who was thus elected.

The son of former president John Adams, Adams was an intelligent and disciplined visionary — and a lousy politician. He refused to use his appointment powers to win support and then appointed Clay as his secretary of state despite their well-known personal differences. Clay's appointment set off howls of protest — many viewed it as a political payoff for Clay's support in the House showdown for the presidency — and it became known as "the Corrupt Bargain." It marred Adams's time in office almost from the start.

Jackson, meanwhile, never stopped running in what turned out to be one of the sleaziest presidential campaigns in American history. His supporters attacked Adams as an aristocrat who had lived his entire life at the public trough. When Adams bought a billiard table and chess set with his own funds, they accused him of turning the White House into "a den of gambling." And Adams was charged with supplying a young American girl for the pleasure of the Russian tsar while he was U.S. minister to Russia.

The Adams camp counterattacked. Jackson, they said, was a murderer, a slave-trader, and a bigamist. A pro-Adams newspaper claimed Jackson's mother was a prostitute brought to America by British soldiers. Posters were distributed listing 18 people Jackson had supposedly killed.

The mudslinging may have been sleazy, but it sure brought out the vote. The turnout in 1828 was 58 percent, more than twice as high as it was in 1824. It was also the first truly democratic presidential election because in 22 of the 24 states, the popular vote determined how many electoral votes went to each candidate. When the votes were tallied, Jackson had 178 electoral votes to Adams's 83. Adams returned to Massachusetts, was elected to Congress (the first president ever to do so after his presidency), and served until his death in 1848. Jackson went to Washington and ushered in a new American era.

Old Hickory: The Jackson presidency

Andrew Jackson wasn't in a good mood when he arrived in Washington in early 1829 to become president. His beloved wife, Rachel, had died two months before, shortly after discovering that she had been the target of vicious personal attacks during the 1828 election. Jackson was sure the discovery contributed to her death, and he was bitterly angry.

But if Jackson was angry, the thousands of his supporters who came to see him take the oath of office were jubilant. Jackson was the first Westerner to win the office and the first to come from humble beginnings. Though some came just to cheer their hero, many came hoping for a cushy government job.

More than 20,000 people surrounded the Capitol for the inauguration. Jackson gave a speech that hardly anyone heard and then fought his way through the crowd and went off to a reception at the White House. So did almost everyone else. Hordes of people crowded into the place, drinking, eating, and stealing souvenirs. Jackson escaped through a back window and spent the first night of his presidency in a nearby hotel.

Jackson's supporters were referred to as "the mob" by Washington onlookers used to more refinement and less tobacco-spitting, but the mob also reflected a growing sense of democracy in America.

More people had the vote and were using it. The turnout of eligible voters for the presidential election of 1824 had been 27 percent. In 1828, it was 58 percent, and in 1840 it was 78 percent. Cheap newspapers and magazines were flourishing, giving the common man access to ideas and information.

And a fight for providing free public schools had begun, eventually spreading to every state in the West and North. The average guy was finding his voice, and in Jackson, a focus for his admiration.

Jackson was the first president since Washington who hadn't been to college. He was tall and thin (6 feet 1 inch, 145 pounds) with a full mane of silver-gray hair and hawklike features. His father died before he was born, and the family was so poor they couldn't afford a headstone. Jackson's mother became a housekeeper, and the family went to live with a brother-in-law.

As a boy, Jackson received a sword cut on his head from a British officer who thought the boy hadn't been humble enough, and Jackson learned never to let a slight or insult go unanswered. He had a violent temper, although he often pretended to be angry just to get his way. Like many military men, he was often inflexible when he made up his mind. His friends called him "Old Hickory" or "Gineral;" his foes called him "King Andrew."

As a Western lawyer and politician, Jackson had seen firsthand how the West was often at the mercy of financial interests in the East, and he had a Westerner's distrust of banks. But as a wealthy man by the time he became president, he wasn't a champion of the idea that all men are equal. Instead, he believed that every man should have an equal chance to succeed, and that no one's rights were more important than another's — unless you were a woman, a Native American, or an African American.

Jackson was also a believer in an adage offered by a New York politician at the time: "To the victors belong the spoils of the enemy." That meant replacing federal officeholders who had been appointed by previous administrations with his own appointees in what became known as the *spoils system.* Jackson's theory was that most government jobs weren't very tough and that personnel should be changed up to bring in new ideas.

Jackson didn't actually invent this idea; all the presidents since Washington had done it to some degree. In fact, in his eight years in office, Jackson only turned out about 20 percent of the 1,100-member federal bureaucracy. And many of them needed turning out because they were inept or corrupt.

But the spoils system did much harm, too. It changed qualifications to hold a federal post from being able or experienced to being a campaign worker or contributor. It gave rise to political machines by giving them something to reward supporters with, and it reduced the efficiency of government. Jackson's efforts to democratize the government created problems that took decades to fix.

> ### Kill or cure
>
> By 1810, America had five formal medical schools in operation. Still, most "doctors" received their training by spending an apprenticeship with someone who had been trained the same way.
>
> Many doctors followed the teachings of Benjamin Rush, a Philadelphia physician and medical professor. Rush advocated bleeding, purging, blistering, sweating, and puking as ways of relieving disease symptoms. He also believed Africans had dark skin from a form of leprosy. Rush's ideas were popular through the middle of the 19th century. But he wasn't all bad: He did advocate the humane treatment of the mentally ill.
>
> Medicine was so riddled with quacks and so unregulated that distrust of physicians was rampant, and many Americans turned to home remedies, like these described in an 1828 book of household hints: "A good quantity of old cheese is the best thing to eat when distressed by eating too much fruit, or oppressed with any kind of food ... honey and milk is very good for worms; so is strong salt water ... for a sudden attack of quincy or croup, bathe the neck with bear's grease, and pour it down the throat."

Nullify This

John C. Calhoun had waited a long time to be president. Intelligent but humorless, the South Carolinian had served as vice president under John Quincy Adams and was now vice president under Jackson. Then, as now, the best part about being vice president was that it made becoming president easier, and Calhoun figured to follow Jackson into the White House. But two relatively trivial things happened to throw him off-course and, in a way, helped push the country toward civil war. The first involved the wife of Jackson's old friend and secretary of war, John Eaton. Peggy Eaton had a reputation of being something of a slut, which she may or may not have deserved. But Washington society's leading females — led by Calhoun's wife — snubbed her.

Jackson, whose own wife had been the target of scandalous gossip, was enraged at the snubs. At one point he called an evening Cabinet meeting to defend Mrs. Eaton. The issue, dubbed "Eaton Malaria" by Washington wags, dominated the first months of Jackson's presidency and drove a wedge between Jackson and Calhoun. The second incident involved a letter Jackson received from Calhoun's enemies suggesting that while he was a member of James Monroe's cabinet, Calhoun had called for Jackson to be court-martialed for invading Florida when it was still owned by Spain. When confronted, Calhoun could provide only vague half-answers. The rift between the two men grew wider, and Jackson turned his successor-favor to Secretary of State Martin Van Buren, a wily New Yorker who had helped get him elected.

Calhoun eventually resigned as vice president and was immediately elected a senator from South Carolina. When it was clear he wouldn't become president, Calhoun abandoned his support of a strong central government and became a champion of the rights of states to pick and choose what federal laws they would obey, a theory of government called *nullification*.

The nullification debate hits the Senate

Calhoun's embrace of states' rights and nullification further pushed him away from Jackson. Even though he was a Westerner and a slave owner, Jackson was an ardent nationalist. At a White House dinner, when nullification proponents tried to test his loyalties by offering a series of toasts about states' rights, Jackson responded, "Our Federal Union: It must be preserved!" (To which Calhoun replied, "The Union — next to our liberty, the most dear!")

Despite Jackson's support, nationalism was having a tough time. In the Senate, a January 26, 1830, debate on whether to stop selling public land in the West gradually turned into a debate on nullification. Senator Robert Hayne of South Carolina gave a long, impassioned, eloquent speech in favor of the idea, pointing out that it was the only way a state could safeguard its interests and not be dominated by other areas.

Then Daniel Webster of Massachusetts took the floor. Webster was one of the greatest orators in American history. Dark and imposing, with eyes that glowed like coals and a deep but pleasing voice, Webster spoke for hours. The people, not the states, had ratified the Constitution, he said, and if the states were allowed to decide which sections they would or wouldn't subscribe to, the country would be held together by nothing but "a rope of sand."

"While the Union lasts we have high, exciting, gratifying prospects spread out before us, for us and our children," he exclaimed. "When my eyes shall be turned to behold for the last time the sun in heaven . . . [l]et their last feeble and lingering glance rather behold the gorgeous ensign of the republic . . . and in every wind under the whole heavens, that other sentiment dear to every true American heart — liberty and union, now and forever, one and inseparable!"

Webster's speech had a spectacular effect. Within three months, 40,000 copies had been published, and within a few years, parts of it were standard reading in textbooks throughout the North and West. Hundreds of thousands of young Northerners and Westerners were exposed to its sentiments — including a 21-year-old man on his way to Illinois named Abraham Lincoln. For many of them, the speech's message became words worth fighting for.

A tarrible idea

In 1828, Congress had passed a bill that set high tariffs (taxes) on a bunch of imported goods. The tariffs were favored in the North because they drove up prices of imported goods and, thus, made goods produced in Northern factories more attractive. The West was okay with the bill because revenues from the tariffs were supposed to pay for public works projects the region needed. But the South, without factories and with less need for roads and canals, hated them.

In 1832, Congress passed a new tariff schedule that was lower than the 1828 rates. But it wasn't enough for the South Carolina legislature. Legislators called for a special convention, which decided that not only was the tariff null and void in South Carolina, but the state would also militarily defend its right to nullify the law.

The move infuriated Jackson, and he sent some army and navy units to the state while he prepared a larger force "to crush the rebellion." Fortunately, cooler heads prevailed. Henry Clay, the great negotiator, came up with a compromise tariff that reduced the rates over a decade. The South decided it could live with that without losing face. Both sides claimed victory, and a bloody civil clash was once again delayed.

Bringing down the Bank

With South Carolina back in the fold, Jackson was easily reelected in 1832, despite his ill health and his earlier statements that he would serve only one term. Part of the reason he sought a second term was to thrash his old foe, Henry Clay, who was the first nominee of the new National Republican Party (which would soon take the name of the opposition party to the English king and become the Whigs). Another factor was that Jackson had some unfinished business with a bank.

The charter of the country's only nationwide bank, the Bank of the United States, was set to expire in 1836, and Clay pushed a bill through Congress in 1832 to extend it. But Jackson vetoed the bill, contending the Bank was a private monopoly that fed off the little banks and benefited only a handful of rich American and foreign investors.

The Bank's stock was, in fact, controlled by a relatively few men, and the charge of corruption also had its truth. Bank president Nicholas Biddle was a brilliant but arrogant aristocrat who often loaned money at no or low interest to the "right people" — including dozens of members of Congress — while clamping down hard on banks in the West. But since 1819, the Bank had provided stability to the economy by requiring local banks to keep adequate gold and silver reserves to back up the currency they issued and to be careful about making loans.

> ## Nat Turner's rebellion
>
> Despite all the rhetoric about how well they treated their slaves and how happy the slaves were, Southern slave owners' deepest fear was that the humans they so degraded would some day rise up to seek freedom — and revenge. Slave rebellions, in fact, had occurred in both Northern and Southern states and had been responded to with harsh brutality.
>
> In 1822, for example, just the rumor of a possible uprising resulted in the execution of 37 slaves in South Carolina. In August 1831, however, a preacher/slave named Nat Turner led 70 followers on a murderous rampage around Southampton, Virginia. Before the uprising was over, Turner's group had murdered 57 white men, women, and children. The rebellion was broken up quickly, and after two months in hiding, Turner was captured and hanged, along with 19 others.
>
> But the rebellion sent shock waves through the South. In retaliation, about 100 slaves were slain at random. New laws were passed to make it harder for owners to free slaves, to restrict the ability of slaves to travel without supervision, and to censor antislavery material. Any serious talk of the South voluntarily freeing its slaves ceased.

After his veto, Jackson decided to kill the Bank off rather than wait until 1836. So in 1832, he ordered that all federal funds be withdrawn from it and deposited in smaller banks. When his treasury secretary balked, he got a new one, and when that one also balked, he got a third who agreed to go along.

At first, the plan worked pretty well, mostly because the economy was sailing along. The federal government's budget deficit dropped to zero for the first time in history; the budget even had a surplus, which was shared with the states for projects like road building and education. But then the boom busted.

In 1836, Jackson ordered that all public land could be sold only for silver or gold, not paper currency. Land sales sagged from 22 million acres to 6 million in one year. Local banks held mortgages that weren't being paid, and they couldn't foreclose because the land was worth little and no one could buy it anyway.

In 1837, after a bank panic, the country sank into a four-year recession. But by that time, Jackson was out of office, and it was someone else's problem.

Horace Mann

Of all the reform movements in the 1830s and 1840s — including temperance, the abolition of slavery, and women's suffrage — the most effective was the *common school* movement, an effort to provide compulsory free education to children.

Its leader, Horace Mann, was anything but common. Born in 1793, Mann became a Massachusetts legislator; in 1837, he drafted a bill that created the state's school board and then he became the board's secretary. Mann advocated tax-supported schools that would bring together kids from all economic, cultural, and ethnic backgrounds. He fought for higher salaries for teachers and better schoolhouses, established the first American teacher training school, and encouraged women to become teachers.

Mann's exuberance and persistence spread, and by the 1850s, every state outside the South had free elementary schools and teacher-training institutions. Mann died in 1859, having lived up to his own advice: "Be ashamed to die until you have won some victory for humanity."

Inventing a Better Life

While politicians were debating lofty issues like nullification and national banks, other people were creating better ways to get around, get something to eat, and get their points across.

Riding the train

On September 18, 1830, a nine-mile race on the outskirts of Baltimore pitted a horse pulling a carriage against a noisy contraption on wooden wheels called a steam locomotive engine. The horse won after the engine broke down, but it was a relatively short-lived victory for Old Paint, because the railroad had arrived in America.

Although trains had been operating in England for some years, the Baltimore & Ohio (B&O) line's Tom Thumb was the first in the United States. By the end of 1830, the B&O had carried 80,000 passengers along a 13-mile track. In South Carolina, a 136-mile line between Charleston and Hamburg opened in 1833. By 1840, 409 railroads had laid 3,300 miles of track, and by 1860, America had close to 30,000 miles of rail.

Early trains had their flaws. Sparks caused fires along the tracks and in the rail cars, and the rails themselves had a nasty habit of coming up through the bottoms of the cars. Trains were also subject to the occasional explosion, which hardly ever happened with horses.

Chapter 8: Pulling Together to Keep from Falling Apart: 1815–1844

But trains had an enormous impact. The demands for labor to build tracks encouraged immigration, and the demand for capital to finance the lines attracted foreign investment. The ability to transport large amounts of goods and agricultural products opened new markets and linked old ones. Communications improved vastly, and going from here to there got a whole lot easier. Even philosopher Henry David Thoreau conceded, "When I hear the iron horse make the hills echo with his snort, like thunder, shaking the earth with his feet and breathing fire and smoke . . . it seems the earth had got a race now worthy to inhabit it."

Reaping what you sow

As the nation grew, so did its appetite. Steel plows, most notably the kind developed by Illinois blacksmith John Deere, had made it easier to plant crops. But harvesting, especially grain, was still a laborious process that involved men swinging heavy scythes all day long and then going back and picking up the threshed grain.

In 1831, a Pennsylvanian named Cyrus McCormick came up with a rolling machine that both cut down the grain and threw it onto a platform. McCormick's machine could do the work of 15 men, and more quickly. By 1860, he was making 4,000 harvesters a year and selling them on an installment (financing) plan so farmers could afford them. America's breadbasket got much bigger because of it.

Communicating across America

In New York, meanwhile, a painter named Samuel F.B. Morse was tinkering with a device (the *telegraph*) that could send messages using electricity. After he patented the telegraph in 1841, Morse got Congress to put up $30,000 so he could string electric wire between Washington and Baltimore. On March 24, 1844, the first message — "What hath God wrought?" — was sent. In 1856, the Western Union Company was formed, and by 1866, a transatlantic telegraph cable had been laid between America and Europe.

On tonight's menu . . .

One thing you can say about 19th-century Americans is that they didn't waste much when it came to chow. Some samples from an 1836 book called *The Frugal Housewife:* "A bullock's heart is very profitable to use as a steak, broiled just like beef. There are usually five pounds in a heart, and it can be bought for 25 cents. . . . Calf's head should be cleansed with very great care. . . . The brains, after being thoroughly washed, should be put in a little bag, with one pounded cracker, or as much crumbled bread, seasoned with sifted sage and tied up and boiled one hour. After the brains are boiled, they should be well broken up with a knife, and peppered, salted and buttered."

> ### The great moon hoax
>
> In 1833, a four-page newspaper appeared on the streets of New York City, called the *Sun.* It was different from other American newspapers in that it favored sensational crime over ponderous politics, was hawked on the streets by newsboys, cost only a penny — and it sometimes made up wild stories that were printed as fact.
>
> In August 1835, the *Sun* published a series of stories it said were reprinted from the *Edinburgh Journal of Science.* They "revealed" the discovery by British astronomer Sir John Herschel of life on the moon. The life included bison, trees, and four-foot-tall furry winged bat men.
>
> The stories electrified the city. The *Sun's* circulation grew to 19,360, the largest of any newspaper in the world. Rival editors frantically tried to match the stories, and when they couldn't, stole them. In September, *Sun* publisher Benjamin Day admitted it was all a hoax. But rather than be angry, most readers were amused, and the *Sun's* popularity shone on.

The telegraph was the first true mass communication medium. By the end of the century, there were few places in the world that couldn't send and receive messages. Not everyone, however, was impressed. When someone remarked that, with the telegraph, Maine could now talk to Florida, writer Ralph Waldo Emerson reportedly observed, "Yes, but has Maine anything to *say* to Florida?"

Staking Out New Land

When not busy inventing things, Americans were on the move, mostly in a westerly direction. That movement was unfortunate for the Native Americans already there. It also proved unfortunate for the Mexican government, which was determined to hold onto an area known as "Tejas" in Spanish. Americans called it Texas.

Pushing out the Native Americans

A Native American name for Andrew Jackson was "Long Knife," and not because they considered him a swell guy. For his part, Jackson contended he didn't hate the Native Americans despite the fact that as a soldier he had killed them and burned their villages. He just didn't want them where they would be in the way.

Therefore, Jackson wholeheartedly supported a policy (actually started by Pres. James Monroe) to systematically move all the Native Americans east of the Mississippi River to west of the Mississippi, or off the fertile acreage of the river valley and onto the dusty prairies of what is now Oklahoma.

In 1830, Congress passed the Indian Removal Act and set aside $500,000 for the task. By the time the odious job was done in the 1840s, more than 100,000 natives had been moved off more than 200 million acres of real estate. Proponents contended the forced exodus was a humane gesture, because the only practical alternative was to exterminate them. This conveniently ignored the fact that thousands of Native Americans did die — of disease, hunger, and exposure — on the forced marches, giving rise to the term *Trail of Tears.* Of all the nation's leaders, only Henry Clay spoke out against the policy.

Two tribes, in particular, didn't go easily. The Sauk and Fox tribe, led by Chief Black Hawk, originally crossed the Mississippi and then came back. Met by a large U.S. military force that included an Illinois militia volunteer named Abe Lincoln, the tribe surrendered after bloody fights in which women and children were slaughtered along with the native warriors. In Florida, the Seminoles under Chief Osceola used the swamps and Everglades to fight for a decade before ultimately surrendering. The war with the Seminoles cost the U.S. military $20 million and 1,500 lives.

In the Southeast, the so-called civilized tribes of the Cherokee, Creek, Choctaw, and Chickasaw had actually been pretty adaptable to the encroaching white man's ways. They built roads and houses, raised cattle, and farmed. Some even owned slaves. When the state of Georgia tried to force the Cherokee off their land, they appealed to the U.S. Supreme Court, which ruled in their favor. But the ruling didn't help; what the state couldn't do, the federal government could. By the end of the 1840s, most of the Native Americans in the eastern United States were gone.

Sequoyah

If the Cherokee, or any other Native Americans for that matter, wanted to jot down their thoughts, they had to do it in English because none of the tribes had a written language. Sequoyah, a Tennessee-born Cherokee trader, hunter, diplomat, and genius, changed that.

In 1809, Sequoyah began work on an 86-letter alphabet for the Cherokee language, using symbols from an English grammar book and then adding to them as needed to reproduce the sounds of Cherokee. By 1821, the language could be read and written, and the Cherokee could now preserve their ancient traditions and culture on paper. *Sequoyah,* by the way, means "hog's foot" in Cherokee.

Later in his life, Sequoyah acted as a mediator with federal officials when the Cherokee were forced off their lands in the Southeast and moved to the Indian Territory in present-day Oklahoma. He died in 1843 but left a version of his name behind in the giant sequoia trees of California and Sequoia National Park.

Claiming independence for Texas

Everyone wanted Texas. Pres. John Quincy Adams offered $1 million for it; Andrew Jackson upped the offer to $5 million. But the newly independent country of Mexico wasn't interested in selling, even though it was sparsely settled and Mexico had no firm plans for the area. But for some unexplained reason, Mexico did allow Americans to settle there.

Growing the American base

In 1821, a Connecticut man named Moses Austin contracted with Mexico to bring 300 American families to an area near San Antonio. Austin died shortly afterwards, but his son Stephen took over and led settlers to the area in 1823.

By 1834, Austin's colony had 20,000 white colonists and 2,000 slaves. That was four times the number of Mexicans in Texas. Slavery was abolished in Mexico in 1831, but Austin ignored the law, as well as the one requiring the settlers to convert to Roman Catholicism. The settlers began thinking of themselves less as Mexican subjects and more as a cross between Mexicans and Texans — or *Texians,* as they called themselves.

The area began to attract restless and sometimes lawless Americans who weren't as peaceful as the Austin bunch. These folks included Sam Houston, a soldier and good friend of Andrew Jackson's; the Bowie brothers, Louisiana slave smugglers who had designed an impressive long knife that bore their name; and Davy Crockett, a Tennessee ex-congressman and daredevil backwoodsman with a flair for self-promotion.

Remembering the Alamo

In 1835, Mexican Pres. Antonio López de Santa Anna proclaimed a new constitution that eliminated any special privileges for Texas, and the Texians declared their independence. They kicked the Mexican soldiers out of the garrison at San Antonio, and a motley force of 187 Texians and American volunteers set up a fort in an old mission called the Alamo.

On March 6, 1836, after a 13-day siege and a brief predawn battle, Santa Anna's army of about 5,000 overran the Alamo, despite heavy Mexican losses, and killed all its defenders. (Figure 8-2 shows a depiction of the battle at the Alamo.) The victory accomplished little for Santa Anna, but "Remember the Alamo" became a rallying cry for Texians. Six weeks after the Alamo fell, an army led by Sam Houston surprised, defeated, and captured Santa Anna at the San Jacinto River.

Chapter 8: Pulling Together to Keep from Falling Apart: 1815–1844

Figure 8-2: Battle of the Alamo.
© Bettmann/CORBIS

Becoming a state

Texas ratified a constitution that included slavery and waited to be annexed to the United States. But Jackson was in no hurry. He didn't want a war with Mexico that could ruin the election chances of his handpicked successor, Martin Van Buren. And the fact that Texas was proslavery would upset the delicate balance between free and slave states.

Jackson did formally recognize Texas on his last day in office in March 1841, after Van Buren had been elected. But it wasn't until December 1845 that the Lone Star Republic became the Lone Star State.

Changing it up at president

In the 16 years between 1820 and 1836, America had three presidents. In the eight years between 1836 and 1844, it also had three.

"The Little Magician"

The first was Martin Van Buren, who was the first president born under the U.S. flag. Van Buren was a New York lawyer and governor whose political machine had helped elect Jackson. Dubbed "the Little Magician" for his political skills, Van Buren snuggled up to Jackson, serving as secretary of state and vice president and winning Jackson's considerable support in beating Whig candidate William Henry Harrison.

Unfortunately for him, Van Buren took office just as the Panic of 1837 and its subsequent economic recession hit the country. The recession lasted most of his term, and he was blamed for it. But he did manage to strike a blow for labor while in office, agreeing to lower the working day for federal employees to ten hours.

"Old Tippecanoe"

Despite his vast political skills, Van Buren was outfoxed by the Whigs when he ran for reelection. It began when a Democratic newspaper reporter sneered at Harrison, who was again Van Buren's opponent: "Give him [Harrison] a barrel of hard cider and settle a pension of two thousand a year on him, and . . . he will sit the remainder of his days in a log cabin."

That image didn't sound like a bad idea to a lot of voters. Harrison, an old Native-American fighter who had defeated Tecumseh at the Battle of Tippecanoe Creek in 1811, was actually a moderately wealthy Virginia farmer. But the Whigs seized on the chance to present him as a tough frontiersman. Rallies were held featuring log cabins and plenty of hard cider, and "Old Tippecanoe" squashed Van Buren in the election.

At his inauguration on March 4, 1841, a hatless 68-year-old Harrison gave a long and pointless speech in a pouring rainstorm. He fell ill with pneumonia and died a month later, making him the first president to die in office.

And Tyler too

His successor was the newly elected vice president: John Tyler, a stubborn slave owner from Virginia who had only become a Whig because he had a falling out with the Democrats and Jackson over the issue of nullification and states' rights.

Tyler earned the distinction of being the only sitting president thrown out of his own political party when he refused to go along with Whig policies in Congress and vetoed many Whig bills. In 1844, Tyler started his own party, the Democratic-Republicans, so he could run again, but he gave up after Jackson asked him to step aside.

In 1844, the Whigs put up Henry Clay, who had been running unsuccessfully for president for 20 years. The Democrats, after a long and heated convention, nominated a *dark horse,* or surprise candidate in James K. Polk of Tennessee. Polk was such an ardent follower of Jackson that he was called "Young Hickory."

It was a very close election, but Polk squeaked through. He made few promises during his campaign, among them: to acquire California from Mexico, to settle a dispute with England over the Oregon border, to lower the tariff, and not to seek a second term. When he took over the presidency in March 1845, he kept all of them.

Chapter 9

War, Gold, and a Gathering Storm: 1845–1860

In This Chapter
- Picking a fight with a neighbor
- Getting gold fever
- Diversifying the populace
- Dividing a country

*I*n the 1840s, it seemed America had an unscratchable itch for elbowroom. It annexed Texas, quarreled with England over Oregon, and took half a million square miles of real estate away from Mexico. A good part of the nation — and the world, for that matter — came down with gold fever, too.

In the 1850s, however, much of the country's attention was on trying to cure the seemingly incurable disease of slavery without amputating the Union.

Wrenching Land from Mexico

Pres. James K. Polk was a hard worker with a thick hide, which are good traits in a president. He worked 18-hour days, didn't miss many days at work, and was also a goal-oriented guy. One of his goals was to buy California, which would give America a base on two oceans and fulfill its *Manifest Destiny* to stretch from sea to sea.

But Mexico wasn't in a selling mood. Mexican leaders were furious at the admission of Texas as a state in December 1845, even though it had been independent from Mexico for almost ten years. So when Polk sent diplomat James Slidell to Mexico City in late 1845 with an offer to buy California for around $25 million, Mexican leaders refused to even meet with Slidell.

Provoking a war

IN THEIR WORDS *"Four score and seven..."*

Polk then decided to take California by force, pushing America into its first war whose primary purpose was simply to gain territory. A young Army lieutenant named Ulysses S. Grant called it "one of the most unjust [wars] ever waged by a stronger against a weaker nation."

It took a little prompting to get it started without firing the first shot. Polk sent an "army of observation," under the command of Gen. Zachary Taylor, to the banks of the Rio Grande River, an area that Mexico considered its territory. The army was gradually built up until there were about 4,000 U.S. troops there in April 1846. Taylor's soldiers managed to provoke a small attack by Mexican troops, and the war was on.

It wasn't much of a war. The United States lost 13,000 men, 11,000 of them to disease, and won every major battle. The Mexican army was badly led, badly equipped, and badly trained. The American army, while sometimes short on supplies because Polk was a penny pincher, was very well led, chiefly by Taylor and Gen. Winfield Scott.

Taylor, whose men called him "Old Rough and Ready" because he was tough (and something of a slob), was a career soldier. So was Scott, whose nickname was "Old Fuss and Feathers" because he had a taste for pomp and showy uniforms. Scott and Taylor were ably supported by West Point-trained officers such as Grant and Capt. Robert E. Lee, as well as others to whom the Mexican War would prove a training ground for the Civil War 15 years later.

The first major battle, at Palo Alto, gave a taste of what was to come. Taylor led 2,300 soldiers against a Mexican army of 4,500 and routed them. In a follow-up fight, a U.S. force of 1,700 scattered a Mexican force of 7,500. American losses totaled less than 50 men for the two fights; the Mexicans lost more than 1,000.

In fact, the biggest American worry was that it might have to fight Britain at the same time over a dispute in the Northwest. American officials insisted that a boundary line between America and Canada be drawn at latitude 54 degrees, 40 minutes (which would have given the United States Vancouver, British Columbia). A slogan from Polk's campaign, "54-40 or fight," became popular with some of the more pugnacious members of Congress. But in July 1846, the two sides agreed to compromise at 49 degrees.

Capturing California and the Southwest

The United States then turned its full attention to acquiring California, which was rather easily captured. Many of the Mexicans in California considered themselves "Californios" first and weren't overly concerned about a U.S. takeover.

Chapter 9: War, Gold, and a Gathering Storm: 1845–1860

In Mexico, meanwhile, U.S. forces kept their undefeated streak going. Mexican forces were now commanded by Gen. Antonio López de Santa Anna of Alamo infamy. Santa Anna, who had been in exile in Cuba, talked U.S. officials into helping him sneak back into Mexico, where he promised he would sell his country out. Once there, he promptly took over command of the army and vowed to crush the hated Yankees.

In September 1846, Taylor's troops took the city of Monterrey, Mexico. In March 1847, Scott captured the fortified seaport of Vera Cruz after a three-week siege. And in September 1847, his forces captured Mexico City, all but ending the war.

The formalities were contained in the Treaty of Guadalupe Hidalgo. It gave America more than 500,000 square miles of Mexican territory (see Figure 9-1), including California, Nevada, Utah, Arizona, and parts of New Mexico, Wyoming, and Colorado. Mexico dropped claims to Texas. Perhaps to soothe a guilty conscience, Polk agreed to pay Mexico $18.25 million, about 80 percent of what he offered before the war.

Not everyone was thrilled. In Congress, a gangly representative from Illinois named Abe Lincoln attacked the war as unjust aggression. In Massachusetts, the iconoclastic writer Henry David Thoreau refused to pay his poll tax because the money might be used to support the war. His aunt paid it for him after he spent only one night in jail, but the essay that came out of it, "Civil Disobedience," became a handbook for non-violent protestors and passive resistance demonstrators around the world well into the next century.

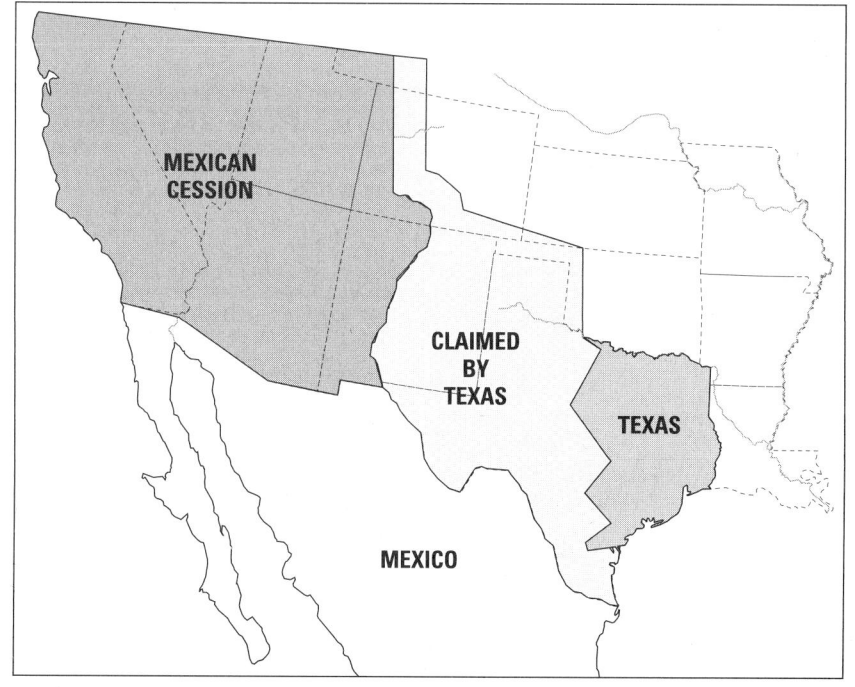

Figure 9-1: Territory won from Mexico.

Much of the dissent about the war stemmed not just from being uncomfortable about picking on Mexico, but also from fears that the war was designed to acquire more territory for the spread of slavery. "They just want Californy / So's to lug new slave states in / To abuse ye and to scorn ye / And to plunder ye like sin," wrote poet James Russell Lowell in 1848. But even as Lowell wrote, another, richer reason was lying on the bottom of a California river.

Rushing for Gold

On the chilly morning of January 24, 1848, a man looked down into a sawmill ditch off the American River, about 40 miles east of Sacramento, California (or 120 miles east of Yerba Buena, which soon became known as San Francisco). The man, a dour carpenter from New Jersey named James Marshall, saw a pea-shaped dollop of yellow metal glinting in the gravel.

"Boys," Marshall told the group of laborers who were helping build the sawmill, "by God, I believe I have found a gold mine."

What he had really found was the ignition switch for one of the most massive migrations in human history: the California gold rush. It was quite literally a rush, as soon as the news got out. That took awhile. Although rumors of the find surfaced in the East not long after Marshall's discovery, no one paid much attention. Then President Polk announced in December 1848 that there looked to be enough gold in California to pay for the costs of the Mexican War many times over. That made people sit up and take notice.

Risking life and limb to strike gold

More than 90,000 people made their way to California in the two years following the first discovery and more than 300,000 by 1854 — or 1 of about every 90 people then living in the United States. The stampede ripped families apart and stripped towns of a large percentage of their young men. Not all the prospectors were American. An 1850 census found that 25 percent of those counted were from countries as far away as Australia and China.

It wasn't easy getting there. From the East Coast, one could take a 15,000-mile, five-month voyage around the tip of South America. More than 500 ships made the voyage in 1849 alone. You could also cut across the Isthmus of Panama and take two months off the trip, if you were willing to risk cholera and malaria. By land, the 2,200-mile journey from trailheads in Missouri or Iowa might take three or four months — with a lot of luck.

History recalls them as the 49ers, because the first big year of the gold rush was 1849. They called themselves Argonauts, after the mythical Greek heroes who sailed in the Argo with Jason to search for the Golden Fleece. Most of them found nothing but disappointment, and many found death.

With few women to add a touch of civilization and balance, and no government, it was a pretty rough place. In just one July week in 1850 in a town called Sonora, two Massachusetts men had their throats slit, a Chilean was shot to death in a gunfight, and a Frenchman stabbed a Mexican to death. The town of Marysville had 17 murders in one week, and at the height of the gold rush, San Francisco averaged 2 murders a day.

A miner making $8 a day (about $217 in 2012 dollars) was doing eight times better than his coal-mining counterpart in the East. But prices were outrageous, too. A loaf of bread that cost 4 cents in New York cost 75 cents in the goldfields. All in all, most gold seekers weren't any better off than laborers in the rest of the country. But there was gold, and plenty of it. During the Civil War alone, California produced more than $170 million worth of bullion, which helped prop up wartime Union currency.

The gold rush had other impacts as well. Although many of the 49ers came and left after a relatively short stay, many of them stuck around. From a non-Native American population of about 18,000 in January 1848, California grew to a resident population of 165,000 within three years. San Francisco became a booming U.S. port and doorway to the Pacific. The growth and importance of the state also helped spur long-delayed congressional approval of the proposal for a transcontinental railroad.

Eventually the state was to become a magnet for different kinds of gold rushes. The beginning of the aerospace industry, Hollywood, the beginnings of the computer age in Silicon Valley, and the birth of the biotechnology industry all had California roots. But before all that could happen, it had to become a state.

Compromising on the slavery issue

Zachary Taylor was probably the least political of all American presidents. He served 40 years in the U.S. Army but never held any other office before being elected president. In fact, he had never even voted in a presidential election. But the popularity of "Old Rough and Ready" carried him to the White House in the 1848 election after Polk lived up to his promise not to seek a second term.

Taylor had expressed no opinions during the campaign about the hottest issue of the time, slavery, and had no plans for what to do about all that land he had just helped take from Mexico. At the time, the country was equally, if uneasily, divided into 15 free and 15 slave states. So when California asked to be admitted as a state, the debate raged on which side it should fall. Its own constitution banned slavery, mostly on the practical grounds that gold miners didn't want to compete with slaves digging for their masters. Those aging giants of Congress, Henry Clay of Kentucky and Daniel Webster of Massachusetts, urged yet another compromise approach, which eventually became the Compromise of 1850. But Taylor was adamant that California be admitted without delay as a free state. Southerners, led by their own aging giant, John C. Calhoun of South Carolina, were just as adamantly opposed. Representatives from nine southern states met in Nashville in June 1850 to consider leaving the Union if California was made a free state.

Fortunately for everyone but himself, Taylor helped solve the problem by suddenly dying of typhoid fever. His successor, a pliable fellow from New York named Millard Fillmore, was more agreeable to compromise. Pushed by the last great speeches by Clay and Webster, and with the help of a U.S. Senate newcomer from Illinois named Stephen Douglas, a deal was reached.

The Compromise of 1850 consisted of a series of five bills. California was admitted as a free state; New Mexico and Utah were admitted as territories, with the slavery question to be settled later; Texas received $10 million for land it gave the new territory of New Mexico; the slave trade was abolished in Washington, D.C.; and a fugitive slave law was approved that made it much easier for slave owners to recapture escaped slaves by getting federal help.

The Fugitive Slave Law put all African Americans at risk, because all a slave owner had to do was sign a paper saying the person was an escaped slave, show it to a federal magistrate, and slap the chains on. Although only a few hundred African Americans were victims of the law, it outraged many Northerners, and anti-slavery resentment grew. But talk of dissolving the Union died down. For the last time, a compromise worked. Clay, Calhoun, and Webster would all be dead before it fell apart.

Coming Over and Spreading Out

One thing you could say with certainty in the middle of the 19th century was that there were a lot more Americans than there were when the century started. The country's population in 1860 was 31.4 million, four times more than it had been a half-century before. Of the world's predominantly white nations, only France, Russia, and Austria had larger populations.

Many of the new Americans had been born elsewhere. The number of immigrants to America in 1830 was about 25,000. In 1855, the number was closer to 450,000. They came from as close as Mexico and Canada and as far away as China and Japan. When they got here, they tended to stay with their fellow expatriates, where the language, food, and culture were more familiar, creating mini-nations.

They also increasingly stayed in cities, even if they had come from a farm background. In 1840, there were 10 Americans living on farms to every 1 that lived in a town. By 1850, that ratio was 5 to 1, and many of the new city dwellers were from foreign shores.

The Germans, the Irish, and the Know-Nothings who opposed them

The parts of the cities they dwelled in were usually like something from a horror movie: dark, smelly, filthy, and violent. Many of the immigrants were so appalled that reality didn't match their glittering visions of America that they went back home.

Because of the glut of people wanting any kind of a job when they got here, wages in the largest cities were pitifully low. In 1851, New York newspaperman Horace Greeley estimated it took a minimum of $10.37 a week to support a family of five, and that didn't include money for medical needs or recreation. The average factory worker, laboring six days a week for 10 or 11 hours a day, might make $5 a week, which meant everyone in the family had to do something to make ends meet.

Because they were newcomers and because most native-born Americans still lived in smaller towns or on farms, there was little appetite for reforms or cleaning up the cities. That wouldn't come until the number of immigrants got even larger and middle-class Americans became more affected by it.

And still they came, from 600,000 immigrants in the 1830s to 1.7 million in the 1840s to 2.6 million in the 1850s. More than 70 percent of the immigrants between 1840 and 1860 were from just two areas in Europe: Ireland and the German states.

For the Irish, it was come or starve. A fungus all but wiped out Ireland's potato crop in 1845, and there was a widespread famine. So more than 1.5 million Irish scraped up the $10 or $12 one-way fare and piled into America-bound ships for an often hellish two-week trip in a cargo hold. Many of the ships had brought Southern cotton to Britain, and in a way they were bringing back the North's cash crop — cheap labor to work in factories and build railroads. Many of the Irish settled in New York City or Boston. Politically savvy, they served first as soldiers for the big-city political machines and then as bosses. Even so, they were harshly discriminated against in many places, and "N.I.N.A." signs hung in many employers' windows. It stood for "No Irish Need Apply."

Almost as many Germans as Irish came during this period, although they were more likely to spread out. The Germans also came because of food shortages or other tough economic conditions. But many decided to come after efforts failed to throw off despotic rule in the various German states in the late 1840s. Generally better off financially and better educated than other immigrant groups (they brought the idea of "kindergarten," or "children's garden," with them), many Germans pushed away from the Eastern cities to the Midwest, especially Wisconsin.

The rise in immigration also increased anti-immigrant feeling, especially in areas where the newcomers were competing with people born in America for jobs. In 1849, an organization surfaced called the *Nativists*. They were better known as the *Know-Nothing Party,* because members supposedly replied, "I know nothing" when asked by outsiders what was going on at their meetings. The Know-Nothings demanded an end to immigration, a prohibition on non-natives voting or holding office, and restrictions on Roman Catholics.

The Know-Nothings made a lot of noise for awhile. Renamed the American Party, they attracted more than 1 million members by 1855 and managed to elect several governors and scores of congressmen. Their 1856 presidential candidate, Millard Fillmore, who as a Whig had been vice president under Taylor and served as president from 1850 to 1853 after Taylor died in office, even managed to carry one state, Maryland. But the Know-Nothings faded away as the Civil War approached, torn apart by differences between the party's Northern and Southern members over the dividing issue of slavery.

Making waves: The Mormons

Although one of the Know-Nothings' chief targets had been Roman Catholics, Americans in the mid-19th century were generally a pretty tolerant bunch when it came to religion. About three-fourths of them were regular churchgoers, and there were so many denominations that no one church dominated. By 1860, almost every state had repealed laws against Jews or Catholics holding public office, and the question "What can you do?" was more prevalent than "How do you worship?"

Of course, try telling that to a Mormon in 1846. The Church of Jesus Christ of Latter Day Saints began in 1830 with the publication of the Book of Mormon by a New York man named Joseph Smith. To escape persecutions, Smith moved his headquarters to Ohio, and then Missouri and then to Nauvoo, Illinois, on the banks of the Mississippi. Nauvoo became one of the most thriving cities in the state.

But the Mormons' habits of working hard, sticking to themselves, and having more than one wife at a time seemed to irk outsiders, and the persecutions began again. This time Smith and his brother were killed by a mob, and Mormon leaders decided they needed some distance between themselves and the rest of America.

Led by a strong and capable lieutenant of Smith's, Brigham Young, the Mormons moved west, many of them pushing two-wheeled carts for hundreds of miles. Finally, they settled in the Great Salt Lake Basin, a forbidding region in Utah that most other people thought of as uninhabitable. Establishing a rather rigidly run society and economic system, the Mormons thrived. By 1848, there were 5,000 living in the area, many of them Europeans who had been converted by Mormon missionaries.

Many of the Mormons fought in the Mexican War as a way of "earning" what had been Mexican territory. In 1850, Utah became a territory. But its statehood was delayed for almost 50 years, in part because of the Mormons' refusal until then to drop their practice of multiple wives, or *polygamy*.

Wagons ho!

Although it's often attributed to Horace Greeley, it was actually Indiana journalist John B. Soule who advised in 1850, "Go west, young man, go west!"

He was a little late. Even before the gold rush, Americans in ever-increasing numbers were moving west. Despite the awesome dangers and hardships, settlers piled their belongings into fortified farm wagons and started out, mostly from St. Joseph or Independence in Missouri.

Some of them stopped on the Great Plains of Kansas and Nebraska, while others pushed on to the West Coast. By 1846, 5,000 Americans had settled in the Willamette Valley in the Oregon Territory, and by 1859, the territory had become a state. America's Manifest Destiny was being achieved.

Becoming aware of women's rights (or the lack thereof)

As more and more women got involved in the fight over slavery, many of them came to resent how, in many ways, they were also second-class Americans. Like slaves, women couldn't vote, couldn't retain their property when they got married, and could legally be beaten by their husbands.

Leaders, such as Lucretia Mott, Elizabeth Cady Stanton, and Susan B. Anthony, began to publicly demand more rights. In 1848, feminists met at Seneca Falls, New York, at a women's rights convention. Stanton read a *declaration of sentiments* that paraphrased the declaration Thomas Jefferson had written 72 years before: "All men *and women* are created equal."

Although some states began allowing women to keep their own property after marriage and some colleges began admitting women in the 1840s, the feminist crusade was overshadowed by the fight over slavery. For many of their rights, women would have to wait.

The Beginning of the End

The issue of slavery not only overshadowed the women's movement, it overshadowed virtually every part of American life. The Methodist and Baptist churches split into North–South factions because of it. Families with branches in the North and South stopped speaking to each other. It even strained business relations in a country where hardly anything got in the way of making a dollar.

And it was showing no signs of going away by itself. Despite a federal ban on importing slaves, the slave population grew from 3.2 million in 1850 to almost 4 million in 1860, almost all of it through childbirths. Adult slaves who could put in a full day's work had become so expensive that some Southerners began calling for ending the ban on new slaves from Africa.

Factoring a slave's life

Actually, about 75 percent of Southern families didn't even own any slaves. But even nonslave owners defended slavery. Slaves, they said, received the benefits of being exposed to the Christian religion, of having cradle-to-grave shelter and food, and of being a contributing part of Southern society. That was more, they said, than many Northern factory workers could say. (Of course, that ignored the fact that even the most miserable factory worker could still make his own choices as to where he worked, didn't have to submit to beatings from his employer, and wasn't likely to see his wife and children taken from him and sold off to some other state.)

Proslavery forces also pointed out that slaves were actually well treated if they behaved. "Negroes are too high [priced] in proportion to the price of cotton," explained a slave owner in 1849, "and it behooves those who own them to make them last as long as possible." And, slavery's defenders said, what would the nation do with them if all the slaves were freed?

That was a question that stopped many Northerners who did oppose slavery but did not agree with the abolitionists' demand for an immediate end to it. In 1854, Abraham Lincoln, who was then in private practice as a lawyer, admitted, "If all earthly power were given me, I should not know what to do as to the existing situation." But Lincoln and others balked at the idea of slavery being allowed to spread, and that's what the fighting was about.

Battling in Kansas

The South wanted a railroad, Kansas and Nebraska wanted to be states, and the combination of wants caused even more troubles. Spurred by the California gold rush and westward expansion, Congress was getting ready to decide on a route for a transcontinental railroad.

The route that made the most sense, and the route the South wanted, started in New Orleans and moved across Texas before ending up in San Diego. It was the shortest route and went most of the way through already organized states or territories. But Sen. Stephen A. Douglas of Illinois was pressing hard for a central route, starting in Chicago. Douglas owned a lot of real estate in the area and stood to make a sizeable chunk of cash if the trains ran through his property. Trouble was his route went through land that had been given to the Native Americans. (See Chapter 12 for more on the railroads.)

So Douglas pushed a bill through Congress that organized the area into the Kansas and Nebraska territories. To win Southern support, his bill also repealed the Missouri Compromise of 1820, which prevented slavery in the new territories. Instead, it said people in Kansas and Nebraska should decide for themselves, a process he called *popular sovereignty*.

The North seethed with anger. Douglas was burned in effigy all around the North and ripped in the press. Nebraska proved to be too far north for crops that would attract much proslavery interest. But Kansas became a warm-up for the Civil War. Antislavery forces clashed with proslavery forces, and both sides were guilty of terrorism and guerilla warfare.

One of the effects of Douglas's bill was to kill the Whig Party, whose leaders were wishy-washy on the subject. In its place came the Republican Party, which was strongly against the spread of slavery. In 1856, the Republicans ran John C. Fremont, a famous explorer and soldier, against the Democrats' James Buchanan, a former Pennsylvania congressman and secretary of state, who had Southern sympathies. Buchanan, a heavy man with tiny feet and almost no backbone, won. He proved to be worthless as president.

The little lady and the big book

Harriet Beecher Stowe was a diminutive Connecticut woman who dabbled in writing from time to time to bring in a little extra money. But when the Fugitive Slave Law was passed, it ticked her off enough to write a novel about slavery. She called it *Uncle Tom's Cabin*.

The book was published in Boston in 1852 — and it was a sensation. It sold 10,000 copies in one week, 300,000 copies in its first year and more than 1.5 million copies worldwide. Its chief effect was to put human (if painfully stereotypical) faces on an issue that many Northerners had thought about only in political terms. It outraged Southerners, who felt it was grossly unfair.

Stowe was hailed as a saint; she was also mailed the ear of a "disobedient slave." Stung by accusations that her book exaggerated the plight of slaves, Stowe wrote a second book called *A Key to Uncle Tom's Cabin,* in which she documented all the abuses in the first book. *Uncle Tom's Cabin* became one of the most powerful propaganda pieces ever written. In 1862, Stowe was introduced to Abraham Lincoln. "So," Lincoln reportedly said to her, "you're the little woman that wrote the book that made this great war."

> ### Canes and congressmen
>
> This is how emotional the issue of slavery was: In the Spring of 1856, Massachusetts Senator Charles Sumner, an acid-tongued abolitionist, launched a long and personal attack on South Carolina Senator Andrew P. Butler, an elderly man who had the unfortunate habit of drooling. So nasty was Sumner's attack on Butler, who was not there at the time, that Sen. Stephen Douglas warned "That damn fool will get himself killed by some other damn fool."
>
> The "other damn fool" turned out to be Butler's nephew, a congressman named Preston Brooks.
>
> Two days after Sumner's speech, Brooks approached him as he sat at his desk on the Senate floor and began beating Sumner with a cane until he fell bloody and unconscious to the floor. "I gave him about 30 first-rate stripes," Brooks later bragged. Sumner was so badly shaken he could not return to Congress for three years. Brooks resigned his House seat, and then was reelected. The North got a martyr out of the deal, the South a hero.

Making a "dredful" decision

Dred Scott was a slave who was temporarily taken by his master to Illinois, which was a free state. When they returned to Missouri, Scott sued for his freedom, claiming that his time in Illinois, on free soil, made him an ex-slave.

But the seven Southern members of the U.S. Supreme Court, led by Chief Justice Roger Taney, found against Scott in 1857. The court decided that as an African American, Scott wasn't a U.S. citizen and, thus, had no right to sue; that as a Missouri resident, Illinois laws didn't apply to him; and that as a slave, he was property, just like a mule, and the government had no right to deprive his master of property without a good reason. The decision absolutely infuriated people in the North. The court's contention that Scott had no more rights than a mule caused many moderate Northerners to take a harder look at the true injustice of slavery.

The decision, along with the Fugitive Slave Law of 1850, also added greatly to business on the *Underground Railroad,* the name given to a network of abolitionists in the North and South who worked together to get escaped slaves to freedom, often in Canada. It's estimated that the system, which involved "conductors" and "stations," or hiding places, helped from 50,000 to 100,000 people with their escape.

Squaring Off for a Showdown: The Lincoln–Douglas Debate

In 1858, Lincoln challenged Douglas to a series of seven debates as part of their race for a U.S. Senate seat in Illinois. It was a classic confrontation. Douglas, the incumbent, was barely 5 feet tall, with a big head made larger by his pompadour hairstyle. He was resplendent in finely tailored suits and arrived for the debates in a private railroad car. Lincoln was 6 feet 4 inches, with a homely face topped by a shock of unruly hair. He wore ill-fitting suits that stopped well short of his wrists and ankles and arrived for the debates on whatever passenger train was available.

Their debate strategies were simple. Douglas tried to make Lincoln look like an abolitionist, which he wasn't, and Lincoln tried to make Douglas look like he was proslavery, which he wasn't. But they did have a fundamental disagreement on what the eventual outcome of slavery would be.

Douglas won the election, but Lincoln won a national reputation. In the meantime, the country edged closer to a final showdown, needing only a spark to set off the firestorm. It got two.

Spark number 1: John Brown

John Brown was an Ohio abolitionist who was crazier than an outhouse rat. He believed he had been commanded by God to free the slaves, and he went about it by killing people in the Kansas fighting. On October 16, 1859, Brown led a group of 18 white and black men on a raid on the federal arsenal at Harpers Ferry, Virginia. After killing the mayor and taking some hostages, Brown's gang was surrounded by militia and U.S. troops under the command of Capt. Robert E. Lee. Brown and five others were captured, and the rest killed. After a trial, Brown was hanged. Many Southerners were convinced Brown had done what a lot of Northerners wanted to do; many Northerners considered him a martyr to a noble cause.

Spark number 2: Lincoln's election

Lincoln, now a national figure, was nominated by the young Republican Party as its 1860 presidential candidate, mostly because they thought he would appeal to the North and the West. But the Democrats were split by the slavery issue. Douglas was the official nominee, but a splinter group supported Buchanan's vice president, John Breckenridge of Tennessee. And a fourth group of moderates, called the Union Party, supported John Bell of Kentucky.

When the votes were in, Lincoln had won less than a majority of the popular vote, but easily won the electoral vote and was the new president. Before he could take office, however, seven Southern states had already pulled out of the Union. Buchanan did nothing to try to stop them, and once the fighting started, they were followed by four more.

As the sun rose on April 12, 1861, secessionist guns fired on Fort Sumter, in Charleston Harbor, South Carolina. America's Civil War had begun.

Chapter 10

A Most Uncivil War: 1861–1865

In This Chapter

▶ Welcoming Lincoln to the White House

▶ Assessing the respective strengths and strategies of the North and the South

▶ Ending slavery, or at least starting the process

▶ Surveying the Civil War's key events and analyzing the North's victory

*I*t pitted brother against brother and killed more American soldiers than any other war in U.S. history. But from this terrible struggle emerged a country that had fought its toughest enemy — itself — and won.

This chapter is a guide to the key aspects of the Civil War, from the man who struggled to reunite a torn nation to the beginning of the end of slavery to who won which battle where. (For a closer look at the Civil War, check out *The Civil War For Dummies,* written by Keith D. Dickson and published by Wiley.)

Introducing Abraham Lincoln

Abraham Lincoln began his presidency by sneaking into Washington, D.C. Because of a suspected assassination plot in Baltimore, Maryland, Lincoln's railroad car was rerouted so he arrived at a different time than what was publicly announced.

It was an inauspicious beginning to a very tough job. Within a few months of Lincoln taking office, 11 states — Alabama, Arkansas, Florida, Georgia, Louisiana, Mississippi, North Carolina, South Carolina, Tennessee, Texas, and Virginia — had left the Union, and 4 more — Delaware, Kentucky, Maryland, and Missouri — were thinking about leaving. The man in charge of sorting out the whole mess had received only about 40 percent of the popular vote. Although he's now considered one of the most extraordinary men in American — and world — history, Lincoln was more of a puzzle than a leader to most Americans at the time.

Presenting the 16th president

Lincoln was an enormously complex person. He had a great sense of humor but also an air of deep sorrow and melancholy about him (likely exacerbated by the fact that two of his four sons died before him and his wife suffered from various mental illnesses). He was fiercely ambitious and firm of purpose, but he was also modest and cheerfully ready to poke fun at himself. Lincoln didn't drink at a time when many men drank to excess, was skeptical when it came to organized religion (although he professed a belief in God), and delighted in telling racy stories.

He was also at ease with his ungainly appearance (6 feet, 4 inches tall and weighing 180 pounds, with large hands and feet) and usually just smiled when his enemies referred to him as "an ape." He often dressed all in black and wore a stovepipe hat in which he sometimes stored his correspondence. Lincoln spoke with a high squeak, which may have been why he kept his speeches short. One popular and perhaps apocryphal story about Lincoln is that when a young girl suggested he grow a beard to improve his appearance, he whimsically did so between the election and his inauguration.

Lincoln's greatest gift may have been his ability to use people, in the best sense of the term. He could overlook people's faults — and even their dislike of him — if he thought they had something to offer, and he did so with humor and grace. Case in point: When a troublemaker reported to him that his secretary of war, Edwin Stanton, had called the president a "damned fool," Lincoln replied, "Then I must be one, for Stanton is generally right, and he always says what he means."

He had plenty of need and opportunity to use his gift of getting the most out of people. Throughout his presidency, Lincoln had few close friends or advisors. His cabinet (notably William Seward, secretary of state; Salmon P. Chase, secretary of the treasury; and Stanton, secretary of war) represented a wide range of political philosophies. The biggest thing the men had in common was their low opinion of their boss. For many of them, that opinion rose considerably in succeeding years.

Fortunately, Lincoln had a talent for making his point without being confrontational. For example, he was often exasperated at the reluctance of his leading generals to fight, particularly Gen. George B. McClellan. However, Lincoln didn't want to be seen as micromanaging the war. So instead, he once drolly observed, "If General McClellan does not want to use the army, I would like to borrow it."

Ultimately, Lincoln was able to use his many gifts and unique personality to rally people in the North to keep fighting, first for the cause of preserving the Union and later for the cause of ending slavery.

Jefferson Davis

As president of the Confederate States of America, Jefferson Davis may have been Lincoln's counterpart, but he was in no way his equal. Davis was stiff, unyielding, narrow-minded, and humorless. In fact, he may have been the anti-Lincoln. Born in 1808, Davis was a West Point graduate who was wounded and decorated for bravery in the Mexican War. He was also a U.S. senator and served as secretary of war under Pres. Franklin Pierce. With his brother, Davis owned a Mississippi plantation and believed in good treatment of slaves. But he also firmly believed in the institution of slavery.

After Lincoln's election, Davis resigned his Senate seat. Although he first opposed secession, he accepted the presidency of the Confederate states as a compromise candidate. His presidency was plagued by mediocre cabinet members, quarreling among the rebel states, and his own inability to think anyone could possibly be right if they didn't agree with him.

When the South's major armies surrendered, Davis fled with what was left of the government's treasury and vowed to fight on. He was soon captured, however, and thrown in a prison cell for almost two years without a trial. Upon his release, he went to Canada before returning to Mississippi. Davis spent his remaining years writing about how the war's outcome was everyone else's fault. He died in 1889. More than 250,000 people attended his funeral, many of them nostalgic for the "Old South" he represented.

Understanding Lincoln's views on slavery and the Union

Lincoln's views and values were influenced heavily by his upbringing. Born in Kentucky in 1809, Lincoln lost his mother when he was 9 and moved with his father (an unsuccessful farmer) to Indiana and then to Illinois. Lincoln had almost no formal schooling. After leaving home, he took a flatboat trip down the Mississippi, worked in a store, studied law, and was elected to the state legislature at the age of 25. In 1846 he was elected to Congress, but by 1850 he had given up on politics. But as the slavery debate grew hotter, Lincoln decided to reenter the political arena in 1854 and fight the spread of slavery.

That Lincoln opposed slavery is clear. "If slavery is not wrong, then nothing is wrong," he once wrote. "I cannot remember when I did not so think and feel." But like most white Americans, he thought black Americans were inferior, and he wasn't in favor of immediate freedom for slaves. He also didn't think blacks and whites could live together: "My first impulse would be to free all the slaves and send them to Liberia, to their own native land," he once said. "But a moment's reflection would convince me, that whatever high hope (as I think there is) there may be in this, in the long run, its sudden execution would be impossible."

As president of the United States, Lincoln put a higher value on preserving the Union than on ending slavery: "If I could save the Union without freeing any slaves," he wrote, "I would do it; and if I could save it by freeing all the slaves, I would do it; and if I could save it by freeing some and leaving others alone, I would also do that."

He was also adamant that no states would be allowed to leave the Union without a fight: "A husband and wife may be divorced," he said, "but the different parts of our country cannot . . . . Intercourse, either amicable or hostile, must continue between them."

Bending the Constitution to preserve the Union — and win reelection

Not everyone in the North felt the same way. As the war progressed, opposition to it formed around *Peace Democrats,* who called for negotiating a way to let the "wayward sisters go in peace." The more radical of these Peace Democrats, who actually called for disloyalty to the federal government, were dubbed *Copperheads* after the poisonous snake that strikes without warning.

The generally patient Lincoln had no patience with the Copperheads. In some areas, he suspended their rights to have a speedy trial and be charged with a specific crime when arrested. More than 13,000 people were arrested and held without trial during the Civil War. By taking these actions, Lincoln disregarded the Constitution in his drive to preserve the Union. (In fact, several of Lincoln's actions were declared unconstitutional by the Supreme Court — but only after the war ended.)

In 1864, Lincoln was up for reelection. He feared he might lose to someone not as devoted to preserving the Union. So he again bent some rules, suspending voting rights in some anti-Union areas of the border states and arranging for Union soldiers to get leave so they could go home and vote, presumably for him.

In addition, the Republican Party formed a temporary alliance with Democrats who favored the war, thereby creating the Union Party. The Democrats against the war put up George McClellan, a general whom Lincoln had twice removed from command. Despite his fears about not being reelected, Lincoln won 55 percent of the popular vote and held a comfortable 212–21 margin in the Electoral College.

IN THEIR WORDS
"Four score and seven..."

Fortunately for the country, the war remained Lincoln's responsibility to the end. "With malice to none, with charity to all, with firmness in the right, as God gives us to see the right, let us strive on to finish the work we are in to bind up the nation's wounds," he said in his second inaugural address.

Uh, thanks for coming Abe

One of the most famous speeches in American history is Lincoln's Gettysburg Address. But the speech wasn't exactly a big hit when he delivered it on November 19, 1863. The occasion was the dedication of the national cemetery at the site of the Battle of Gettysburg in Pennsylvania. The cemetery had been ordered because many of the 8,000 bodies that fell there had been so hastily buried after the battle that they'd become exposed again.

Lincoln wasn't even the featured speaker. That honor fell to Edward Everett, a famous orator who'd been a U.S. senator and president of Harvard University. Everett spoke for nearly two hours and delivered some 1,500 long and windy sentences before he finally sat down.

Lincoln, who, contrary to myth, didn't write his 268-word speech on the back of an envelope during the train trip to Gettysburg, spoke for about three minutes. He was interrupted several times by applause. When he was done, a Philadelphia newspaper reporter on the stage leaned over and whispered to Lincoln, "Is that all?" Lincoln replied, "Yes, for the present."

Although some newspapers commended the speech, others said it stunk. The Harrisburg, Pennsylvania *Patriot-News,* for instance, dismissed Lincoln's words at the time as "silly remarks." But the paper reconsidered: In November 2013, *Patriot-News* editors apologized for "a judgment so flawed . . . it cannot remain unaddressed in our archives."

Actually, Lincoln shared the newspaper's original opinion about his remarks. "I failed, I failed, and that is all that can be said about it," he reflected after the speech. Seldom was he more wrong.

North versus South: Comparing Advantages and Action Plans

If London bookies had been taking bets on the outcome of the American Civil War, they may have set the odds a little in favor of the South based on the Confederacy's advantages. Sure, the North had some big pluses, including the following:

- A population of about 22 million, compared to about 9 million in the South (of which 3.5 million were slaves); in addition, immigration during the war added thousands of new recruits for the Union Army
- Seven times as much manufacturing, which meant the Union Army was always better supplied
- A far better railroad system (75 percent of all the track in America), which greatly aided the transport of troops and supplies
- Control of the U.S. Navy and the merchant fleet
- A central government already in place, and a more diverse economy
- Lincoln

The South, however, had a number of its own advantages:

- **The benefit of history:** The Southern secessionists were in good company. Secession by determined regions had previously succeeded in Latin America, the original 13 American colonies, the Netherlands, and Greece, just to name a few well-known places.

- **A defensive stance:** The Confederacy didn't have to conquer the North or even win a lot of big battles; it only had to fight long enough for the North to give up its quest to bring the Southern states back into the Union. A defensive war is much cheaper to fight than an offensive one in terms of both men and materials. Although the South's population was smaller overall, it still had about 200,000 men available to fight within a short time of the war's start.

- **Home-field advantage:** Much of the fighting was on the South's territory because the North had to conquer the South to get it back into the Union. Southerners not only knew the terrain better but also had the incentive of defending their homes and farms. (Of course, as the war progressed, they found that fighting on the home field wasn't all it was cracked up to be.) Although the idea of letting slaves fight was out of the question for most Southerners (and most slaves), the slaves' presence at home meant the South's farms and plantations could keep running.

- **Strong military leadership:** The South had much better luck finding able military leaders right from the start, particularly a courtly and brilliant Virginian named Robert E. Lee and his right-hand man, a former military school instructor who liked to suck on lemons named Thomas "Stonewall" Jackson.

To win, reasoned Gen. Winfield Scott (the top Northern general, who was 75 and so fat he couldn't get on a horse), the first step was to suffocate the South by blockading its coast. Next, cut the South in half by seizing the Mississippi River. Then chop it up by cutting across Georgia and then up through the Carolinas. Finally, capture the Confederate capital of Richmond, Virginia.

Many Northern newspapers sneered at Scott's strategy as too timid. They suggested abandoning his *anaconda plan* (so-called because it envisioned encircling the South and squeezing the life out of it like a giant snake) in favor of marching directly on Richmond and getting the whole thing over with. But Lincoln recognized the worth of Scott's approach.

Confederate Pres. Jefferson Davis, meanwhile, favored a simpler plan for the South: Make the Northern armies press the fight, whip them, and push them back North, thereby breaking the morale of the Northern people. General Lee concurred at first but then realized that the South's limited resources might be better used in a quick and decisive strike to take the heart out of the North. Twice he tried to take the fight to the Union; twice his limited resources forced him to go home.

> ### Hell no, we won't go
>
> Although most men who fought in the Civil War were volunteers, both sides resorted to drafting troops as well. The Confederacy was first, in 1862. A year later, the North followed — but not without some serious opposition. One of the causes of the opposition was the fact that draftees who put up $300 or hired someone to go in their place could get out of the service. Men who took advantage of the exemption included tycoons, or soon-to-be tycoons, such as J. P. Morgan and Andrew Carnegie, and future president Grover Cleveland. Another sore point was the dislike of many Irish immigrants for African Americans, whom they feared would compete with them for jobs.
>
> The worst anti-draft troubles occurred in New York City. In July 1863, mostly Irish anti-draft mobs, chanting "to hell with the draft and the war," terrorized the city for four days. They burned homes, churches, saloons, police stations, and factories. More than 400 people were killed, and $5 million worth of damage was done. The riots weren't stopped until federal troops — fresh from the carnage at Gettysburg — showed up. The draft was subsequently suspended in the city for the duration of the war.

Freeing the Slaves

One of Lincoln's most pressing problems was what to do about slaves. As soon as the Northern troops first moved into Southern territory, escaped slaves began pouring into Union Army camps. One general declared the slaves as "seized" property and put them to work in labor battalions so they could earn their keep. But other generals who favored the abolition of slavery immediately declared them freed.

Lincoln was forced to rescind the orders because, as president, he felt that freeing slaves was solely his responsibility and because he had to be careful not to antagonize the slave-holding states that had stayed loyal to the Union: Delaware, Kentucky, Maryland, and Missouri, and later, West Virginia, which broke away from Virginia during the war. What Lincoln really hoped for was that each state would abolish slavery on its own and compensate slave owners so that federal funds could be used to send freed slaves to Africa. Eventually, however, circumstances forced Lincoln to take action.

Proclaiming emancipation

In June 1862, members of Congress who were impatient with Lincoln's caution mustered enough votes to abolish slavery in the District of Columbia and the U.S. territories. Congress also authorized Lincoln to allow the Union Army to enlist African Americans who wanted to fight. Prodded by these

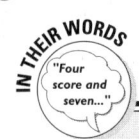

> ### An all right guy
>
> "I took the [Emancipation] proclamation for a little more than it purported, and saw in its spirit a life and power far beyond its letter... Lincoln was not... either our man or our model. In his interests, in his associations, in his habits of thought, and in his prejudices, he was a white man. [But] he was one whom I could love, honor, and trust without reserve or doubt." —abolition leader and former slave Frederick Douglass.

congressional actions, Lincoln then told his cabinet in July that he intended to proclaim freedom for slaves as of January 1, 1863. But he wanted to wait until the Union Army had won a big battle before making the announcement.

On September 22, five days after the Union gained what was more of a tie than a win at Antietam Creek, Maryland, Lincoln made his *Emancipation Proclamation* public. As of January 1, he announced, all slaves in any state still in rebellion "shall be, then, thenceforth and forever free."

Surveying the consequences of emancipation

In reality, Lincoln's proclamation didn't free a single slave. It didn't apply to slaves in the border states, where Union forces could have enforced it, and slave owners in the Confederacy certainly didn't obey it. But it did have effects Lincoln hadn't intended.

- In the South, the Emancipation Proclamation reinforced the will of the proslavery forces to fight on because it was clear that if they lost, slavery would end.
- In the North, it angered people who were comfortable with fighting to preserve the Union but not to free people who might then come north and compete with them for jobs. Union Army desertions increased, and enlistments decreased after the announcement.
- Abolitionists thought the Emancipation Proclamation didn't go far enough, and other people thought the government had no right to take away the Southern slave owner's "property."

But many Northerners gradually came to embrace the idea of abolishing slavery as a moral cause, and Lincoln's move added another reason for the North to continue to fight. Just as important, working people in England and France cheered the emancipation of slaves. At one point, a letter of support was sent to Lincoln that supposedly came from 20,000 laborers in England. Such support helped ensure that European leaders wouldn't risk the wrath of public opinion by aiding the South.

Reviewing the Troops, the Generals, and the Major Battles

The Civil War was mostly a young man's fight. Most of the enlisted men were under the age of 21, and more than a few were in their early teens. The Civil War was also truly "a brothers' war," with families and friends divided by their allegiances. Mary Lincoln, the president's wife, lost three brothers in the war — they all fought for the South. The Confederacy's leading general, Robert E. Lee, had a nephew who was an officer in the Union Navy. And if you want to talk about a house that was truly divided, consider the situation of Sen. John Crittenden of Kentucky: He had a son who was a major general in the Confederate Army and another son who was a major general in the Union Army.

Because of the fraternal flavor of the two armies, it wasn't unusual for them to engage in friendly banter between battles, sometimes even getting together for a game of baseball or to trade tobacco for coffee during truces.

The friendliness didn't stop the carnage: More than 600,000 American soldiers died during the Civil War. That's more than the number who died in World War I, World War II, and the Korean War combined. About two-thirds of that number died from diseases rather than battle wounds, and it's estimated that the average soldier ended up in the hospital at least once or twice a year. If the soldier ever left the hospital, he was lucky. Sanitary conditions were awful, and 75 percent of the operations consisted of amputations, many of them needless.

Northern forces almost always outnumbered their Southern opponents. At the end of the war, the Union Army had about 960,000 men in uniform compared to the Confederates' 445,000. In addition to having a larger population to draw from, the North's forces also included thousands of European immigrants who took up a rifle almost as soon as they got off the boat.

Additionally, thousands of African Americans fought for the North after being allowed to join the army in 1863. They were paid $7 a month (about a third of what white soldiers got), and they fought well under white officers, earning the grudging respect of those they fought against and alongside.

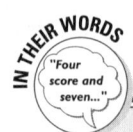

A scene from hell

"Eleven hundred dead bodies . . . swollen to twice the natural size . . . lying in every conceivable posture — some on their backs with gaping jaws — some with eyes as large as walnuts, protruding with a glassy stare — some doubled up like a contortionist — here one without a head — there one without legs — yonder a head and legs without a trunk — everywhere horrible expressions." —from an eyewitness account after the Battle of Chancellorsville, May 1863.

The men at the top

What each side did have, at least by the close of the war, was a great general at the head of its army. In the South, that man was Robert E. Lee, the son of a Revolutionary War general. A West Point graduate, Lee was actually asked by Lincoln to take over the Union Army before the war began. But Lee's loyalties were to his native state of Virginia. He was honorable, courteous, skillful, and not afraid to take a chance.

Lee's Northern counterpart was Ulysses S. Grant, the shy and sloppy son of a storekeeper. Grant was also a West Point grad, but he'd resigned his commission to avoid a court-martial for drunkenness. He rejoined the army and rose through the ranks to command mainly because, unlike some of his contemporaries, he wasn't afraid to get into a fight with the enemy. "He is the gentlest little man you ever saw," Lincoln remarked. "He makes the least fuss of any man I ever knew." Grant was highly intelligent, determined, compassionate — and a cold-eyed killer, if that's what it took to win.

Hairstyles and hookers

Like most major conflicts, the Civil War gave birth to a number of new terms that are still part of the American language. One of them came from the hairstyle of a Union general who wore his whiskers down the front of his ears along his jaw line, but not as a full beard. His name was Ambrose Burnside, and his whiskers became known as *sideburns*. Another Union general, Joseph "Fighting Joe" Hooker, became known for the large numbers of prostitutes that hung around his army while it was in the Washington area. They were jokingly called "Hooker's Division." Although *hookers* was already a term for ladies of the night, the general helped nationalize it and ensure its lasting place in the language.

The war at sea

The North's first objective was to blockade the Southern coast and cut off the South's ability to trade its cotton in Europe for arms and supplies. The Union Navy already had ships and guns, but the South somehow managed to scrounge up a navy of its own from refitted private ships or ships built for the South in England, as well as scores of captured Union merchant ships.

One of the Confederacy's ships was a Union vessel called the *Merrimac*, which had been sunk. Southern ship fitters raised it, covered it with iron plates, and renamed it the *Virginia*. For a few days, it terrorized the Union fleet off Hampton Roads, Virginia, sinking two Union ships and threatening to decimate the entire group. But the North's own hastily constructed ironclad ship, the *Monitor*, showed up in the nick of time. On March 9, 1862, the two met in a four-hour battle that basically ended in a tie. The *Virginia* was eventually burned and the *Monitor* sunk, but their battle was significant in that it was the first battle between two ironclad ships — ultimately spelling the doom of wooden warships. After a slow start, however, the North's sea blockade was ultimately highly effective.

The war on land

When it came to the ground war, part of the North's strategy included capturing the city of New Orleans and gaining control of the mouth of the Mississippi River. Starting in 1862, largely under the leadership of Grant, the Union Army began taking Tennessee and slowly moving up and down the Mississippi River, cutting the South in half just as Gen. Winfield Scott had suggested.

On the Confederate side, Lee twice took the war to the North, but both times he was forced to return to Southern territory when he was opposed by larger armies and faced uncertain supply lines. Starting in late 1863, the North began grinding down Lee's army in Virginia while another Union Army under Gen. William T. Sherman marched diagonally across Georgia and then up into the Carolinas, destroying everything in its path. "We have devoured the land," Sherman wrote to his wife. "All the people retreat before us, and desolation is behind."

Food for fighting?

Its official name was *hard bread,* a 3-inch-by-3-inch piece of flour and water that the soldiers who ate it — or tried to eat it — called "hardtack." The crackers were often infested with weevils and worms (when they could penetrate it).

"Camp gossip says the crackers have been in storage since the Mexican War," one Pennsylvania soldier wrote in his diary. "They are almost as hard as brick, and undoubtedly would keep for years and be as palatable as they are now."

Here are ten of the key battles or campaigns of the war (check out Figure 10-1 to get a visual of the various locations):

- **Fort Sumter:** After the first Southern states seceded, they began seizing federal forts and shipyards inside their borders. Maj. Robert Anderson, commander of the fort in Charleston Harbor, South Carolina, agreed to surrender as soon as the food ran out. But Southern forces wouldn't wait, and at dawn on April 12, 1861, they fired the first shots of the Civil War. Anderson surrendered when he ran out of ammunition, and the only casualties were two Union soldiers killed when a cannon exploded. But the fact that the South fired first helped recruiting efforts in the North.

- **Bull Run:** The first large fight of the war took place near Manassas Junction, Virginia, on July 21, 1861. Despite the fact that it was a brutally hot day, hundreds of residents from nearby Washington, D.C., came out to picnic and watch the fight, thinking it might be the highlight of what many expected to be a 90-day war. Neither army was trained or prepared, and for most of the day utter confusion reigned. Then Confederate forces got the upper hand, and Union forces panicked and ran. The rebel army was too tired to chase them.

- **Shiloh:** Grant's army was caught napping on April 6, 1862, near this Tennessee church, and was on the brink of being routed when Grant launched a counterattack the next day that pushed the Confederate Army back. The battle solidified the Union Army's dominance in the West.

- **Antietam:** Lee's first push into Northern territory took place near Antietam Creek in Maryland on September 17, 1862. The battle was fought in a narrow field between the creek and the Potomac River. It was one of the bloodiest battles of the war, with 22,000 killed or wounded. Lee was forced to return across the Potomac, providing Lincoln the "victory" he'd been waiting for to announce his Emancipation Proclamation.

- **Chancellorsville:** The Union Army, under Gen. Joseph Hooker, tried to surround Lee's forces in Virginia from May 1–3, 1863. But Lee took a brilliant gamble, divided his smaller army, and attacked first. It was a complete Confederate victory, but a costly one. Lee's top general, Thomas Jackson, who was nicknamed *Stonewall* for his courage and tenacity, was mistakenly shot by his own troops during a reconnaissance after dark. He died of pneumonia a week later, creating a leadership hole the South was never quite able to fill.

- **Gettysburg:** Lee again pushed into Northern territory in early June 1863, this time into Pennsylvania. In a massive battle (a total of more than 50,000 casualties) from July 1 to July 3, Lee's army hurled itself at Union forces led by Gen. George Meade. But the South's effort failed, and Lee was once again forced to withdraw. Considered one of the most important battles in world history, Gettysburg is also regarded by many as the most pivotal fight in the Civil War.

- **Vicksburg:** This Mississippi town was a major Confederate stronghold on the Mississippi River. Coordinating with Union naval forces moving up from New Orleans, Grant masterfully moved his outnumbered army around the city and laid siege to it. Vicksburg surrendered on July 4, 1863, giving the North control of the Mississippi River.

- **Chickamauga and Chattanooga:** These confrontations, which ran from August to November 1863, led to Sherman's march across Georgia. At Chickamauga, Union Gen. George H. Thomas withstood a furious attack and saved the Union Army from a rout. After the Union Army was surrounded at Chattanooga, Grant led a rescue effort and drove off the Confederate forces.

- **The Wilderness:** This was a series of battles in Virginia starting in May 1864 in which Grant used his superior numbers to wear down Lee's army. The carnage was terrible, and Grant's critics accused him of being a butcher. But the strategy worked. Lee's army couldn't break off to try to stop Sherman's march through the heart of the South. By March 1865, the Union forces outnumbered the Confederacy's two to one.

- **Appomattox Courthouse:** This wasn't a battle, but it was the site in Virginia where on April 12, 1865, Lee formally surrendered to Grant. The Southern Army was exhausted, outnumbered, and half-starved. Grant generously fed the defeated Southerners and allowed them to go home, taking their horses and mules with them. Although some units fought on for a few more weeks, the Civil War, for all intents and purposes, was finally over.

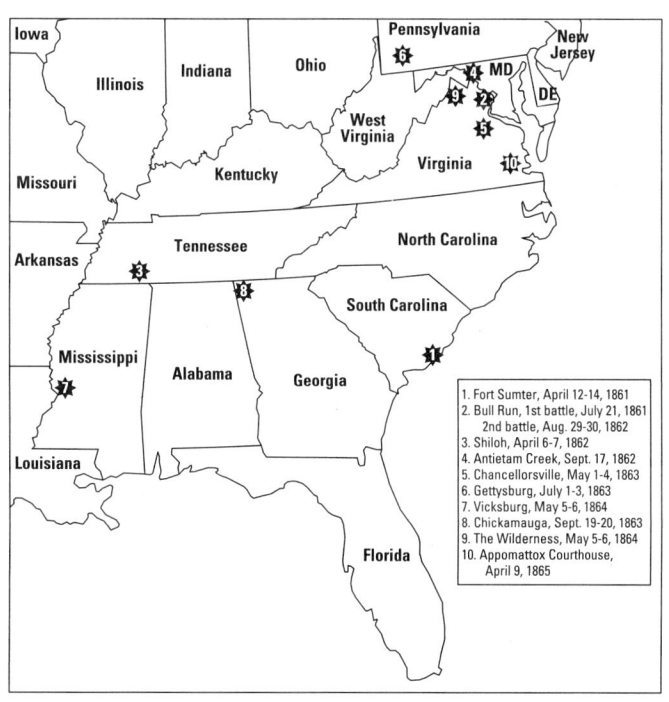

Figure 10-1: Key Civil War battles and campaigns.

1. Fort Sumter, April 12-14, 1861
2. Bull Run, 1st battle, July 21, 1861
   2nd battle, Aug. 29-30, 1862
3. Shiloh, April 6-7, 1862
4. Antietam Creek, Sept. 17, 1862
5. Chancellorsville, May 1-4, 1863
6. Gettysburg, July 1-3, 1863
7. Vicksburg, May 5-6, 1864
8. Chickamauga, Sept. 19-20, 1863
9. The Wilderness, May 5-6, 1864
10. Appomattox Courthouse, April 9, 1865

© John Wiley & Sons, Inc.

Two More Reasons Why the North Won

Winning a war without money or friends is rather difficult, and the South had neither. Its economy, pardon the expression, went south, and it failed to convince any major European powers to join the fight on its side.

The Southern economy was based solely on agriculture. When the Civil War started, there was only one iron foundry in the entire South. Still, the Confederacy's leaders were sure the South's cotton would be enough: "You dare not make war upon our cotton," a Southern politician boasted before the war. "No power on Earth dares make war on it. Cotton is King."

True, European nations, particularly Britain, had depended on Southern cotton to fuel their textile industries. In fact, some 80 percent of Britain's cotton came from America before the war. The South figured that if the Union's blockade cut off Southern cotton to Britain, Britain would intervene on the South's behalf.

But this idea had some holes in it:

- The first hole was that when the war started, Britain had a surplus of cotton, partly because it had stocked up when war clouds loomed on the horizon and partly because it had started getting more cotton from Egypt and India.
- Secondly, British laborers hated slavery and wouldn't support the South even if that meant costing them jobs, which it did. British leaders, even those who favored the South and also favored the idea of two smaller Americas over one big one, didn't want to buck popular sentiment that supported the North.

Actually, Britain and the Union came close to war a couple times, most closely when a Union ship stopped a British ship at sea and arrested two Confederate diplomats on their way to London. This act was clearly against international law and might have given the Brits an excuse to enter the war on the side of the South. But Lincoln wisely released the two diplomats and shrugged the whole thing off as a misunderstanding.

With no European allies and the Union blockade succeeding, the South's economy tanked. In 1861, about $1 million in gold-backed Confederate paper currency was circulating. But by 1863, Confederate printing presses had churned out $900 million in currency, with scarcely any gold supplies to back them. Thus, an 1863 Confederate dollar was worth about two cents in gold.

The North's economy was also buffeted by the war. But because it was stronger going in, it handled the conflict better. Advances in agriculture and manufacturing and supplies of gold and silver from California and Nevada helped fuel the economy despite the war's manpower drain.

Losing a Leader

The worst manpower drain of all came on April 14, 1865, just five days after Lee surrendered to Grant at Appomattox. It was Good Friday, and President Lincoln had decided to go to Ford's Theatre in Washington to see the comedy *Our American Cousin*.

At about 10:30 p.m., during the second act, an actor and Southern sympathizer named John Wilkes Booth snuck into the presidential box and shot Lincoln in the back of the head. Lincoln was taken to a lodging house across the street from the theater, where he lingered until the next morning and then died, surrounded by several members of his cabinet. "Now he belongs to the ages," said Secretary of War Edwin Stanton.

Booth was from a prominent American acting family. He was born in Maryland and was a white supremacist who had plotted to kidnap Lincoln and use him as a bargaining chip to end the war on better terms for the South. But Lee's surrender changed his plot to assassination.

Booth made his escape from the theater after stabbing a Union officer who was in Lincoln's box and jumping to the stage, breaking his leg in the attempt. He was cornered in a Virginia barn a week later and was shot to death or killed himself — it was never clear which. Four of Booth's fellow conspirators were hanged. Four others were convicted of helping the conspirators after the fact and were sentenced to prison.

America's Civil War lasted four awful years. Healing from its wounds would take far longer.

Chapter 11

Putting the Country Back Together: 1865–1876

In This Chapter
- Surveying the damage to the South after the Civil War
- Reconstructing the South — and the Union
- Examining Johnson's road to impeachment and Grant's corrupted administration

The bullet that killed Abraham Lincoln at the end of the Civil War may also have killed any chance of coming up with a practical solution toward putting the country back together — and figuring out what to do with 3.5 million former slaves who had won their freedom but not much else.

In this chapter, a defiant South, a wrathful and power-mad Congress, and a stubborn and nasty-tempered president combine to make a mess of what's known as the Reconstruction period. Additionally, you also see how a very good military leader became a very bad political leader and how one political group managed to steal a presidential election.

A Southern-Fried Mess: Life in the South after the Civil War

The 11 Southern states that had decided to leave the Union in 1860 and 1861 were basket cases by 1865. Only Texas, where there hadn't been that much fighting, was in relatively decent shape. Southern cities such as Atlanta, Charleston, and Richmond were in ruins.

Few businesses of any kind were still operating, little capital was available to start new businesses, and few outsiders were willing to risk investing in the area. For example, 7,000 miles of railroad track were laid in the South between 1865 and 1879. In the rest of the country, 45,000 miles were laid.

Whipped

"A city of ruins, of desolation, of vacant houses, of widowed women, of rotting wharves, of deserted warehouses, of weed-wild gardens, of miles of grass-grown streets, of acres of pitiful and voiceful barrenness — that is Charleston, wherein rebellion loftily reared its head five years ago . . . I fell into some talk with [a local resident] . . . when I asked him what should be done, he said 'you Northern people are making a great mistake in your treatment of the South. We are thoroughly whipped; we give up slavery forever; and now we want you to quit reproaching us. Let us back into the Union, and then come down here and help us build up the country.'" —Massachusetts journalist Sidney Andrews, 1865.

Before the war, the South's economy had been based almost strictly on agriculture, mainly cotton, tobacco, and sugar, and all these industries suffered, especially cotton. Southern cotton production in 1870 was half what it was in 1860. The education system in the South had virtually disappeared, along with the old plantation system. More than 250,000 of the South's young men were gone, too. "Pretty much the whole of life has been merely not dying," wrote the Southern poet Sidney Lanier about the Reconstruction period.

Two postwar changes dominated Southern life. One was the bewildering new world faced by the freed slaves. The other was a new farming practice, known as *sharecropping,* that would ultimately make life more difficult for both ex-slaves and poor whites.

Starting a new life

For more than 3 million African Americans, the whole of life post–Civil War had become pretty darn confusing. They had their freedom but didn't know what they should do with it. Few former slaves had any education or training. Some thought freedom meant freedom from work; others were fearful that to continue working for white people would put them in danger of being enslaved again. And many believed a widespread rumor that the federal government would be giving each slave "40 acres and a mule" to start their own farms.

Such a plan never existed, but in 1865, the federal government did organize the *Freedman's Bureau,* an agency designed to help freed slaves during their transition from slavery to freedom by providing food, education, and other support. From 1865 to 1868, the bureau helped as many as 200,000 former slaves learn to read. About 10,000 black families were settled by the bureau on land that had been confiscated by Union troops, although most of them were eventually forced off the land by whites who swindled them out of it or used dubious legal means.

Chapter 11: Putting the Country Back Together: 1865–1876

Blanche Kelso Bruce

Next time you have a $2 bill that was printed in, say, 1880, take a look at the signatures on it. One of them belongs to a Virginia native who started life as a slave and became a prosperous landowner and United States senator.

Blanche Kelso Bruce was born in 1841 and worked as a field hand. When the Civil War began, Bruce escaped. He eventually settled in Missouri, where he organized the state's first school for African Americans. In 1869, Bruce moved to Mississippi, where he held a series of political offices. In 1874, he became the first African American to be elected to a full term in the U.S. Senate. As a senator, Bruce investigated banking scandals, advocated economic aid for freed slaves, and helped obtain levee system and railroad projects for Mississippi.

In 1880, Bruce was appointed registrar of the U.S. Treasury, where his duties required a facsimile of his signature on U.S. currency. He was also a lecturer, a writer, and an educator. Bruce died in 1898, having left his name in American history — and on a lot of money!

Becoming sharecroppers

Most blacks and many whites couldn't afford to buy land of their own, so a new form of farming became the basis for the Southern agricultural economy: sharecropping. Under *sharecropping,* the farmer farmed land owned by someone else, and the two shared the profits.

That was the ideal, but in most cases, the sharecropper had to borrow money to make ends meet until the next crop was harvested. This borrowing left him with so little when the crop was harvested that he had to borrow on the next crop. Thus, many sharecroppers, both black and white, became virtual slaves to debt.

The sharecropping system dominated many parts of the South, replacing the plantation system. In 1868, perhaps one-third of the area's farms were tended by renters. By 1900, that percentage grew to about 70 percent. The system, coupled with low cotton prices and the ravages of an insect pest called the boll weevil, virtually guaranteed that few farmers could become successful, no matter how hard they worked.

Piecing the Union Back Together

One of the topics American historians like to speculate on is what might have happened if Lincoln hadn't been assassinated. Would he have been able to come up with a widely accepted plan to reunite the states and give the former slaves their rightful place in society? Would that have led to better race relations sooner in America?

Probably not. Lincoln, like most mid-19th century white Americans, felt it was impossible to just free the slaves and make them socially equal. "There is an unwillingness on the part of our [white] people, harsh as it may be, for you free colored people to remain with us," he told a group of African Americans during the war. Lincoln's hope was to resettle the freed slaves somewhere else, either in Africa or the Caribbean. But most black Americans had no firsthand experience with Africa or any other country except the United States — the country in which they were born — and they had no desire to leave.

Lincoln did insist, however, that the former slaves be treated as equals when it came to the law. In 1864 and early 1865, he prodded Congress into passing the 13th Amendment to the Constitution, which barred slavery. He also set out a general plan for reuniting the country when the fighting was done (assuming the North won). Under this plan, most Southerners could become U.S. citizens again simply by taking a loyalty oath. Those who couldn't, mostly high-ranking Confederate officials, could apply for the reinstatement of their citizenship on a case-by-case basis. After Lincoln was killed, his vice president, Andrew Johnson, adopted practically the same plan.

Demanding loyalty, legislating equality

When 10 percent of a state's population had taken an oath of loyalty to the Union, the state could set up a new government and apply for readmission to the Union, as long as it agreed to give up slavery and provide an education system for blacks. By the time Congress convened in December 1865, all the Southern states had organized new governments, ratified the 13th Amendment, and elected new representatives and senators for Congress.

But Congress, dominated by *Radical Republicans* — those who sought harsh reprisals against the South for the war and immediate equal rights for freed slaves — didn't like the deal. For one thing, many of the men elected to represent the Southern states in Washington, D.C., were the same people who'd run the Confederacy — including Alexander Stephens, the ex-Confederate vice president who was in federal prison awaiting trial on treason charges. That kind of in-your-face attitude irritated the Radical Republicans, who felt Southerners weren't sorry enough for causing the war.

Even more infuriating were the *Black Codes.* These codes were established by Southern state legislatures to keep the former slaves "under control." They varied from state to state and did give blacks some rights they hadn't had before, such as the power to sue in court, own certain kinds of property, and legally marry. But the Black Codes also prohibited blacks from bearing arms, working in most occupations other than farming or manual labor, and leaving their jobs without permission. They restricted African Americans' right to travel and fined them if they broke any of the codes. To the Radical Republicans, and even many moderate Northerners, the Black Codes were simply a substitute form of slavery.

Sorry — Not!

"Oh I'm a good old rebel / Now that's just what I am; / For the 'fair land of freedom,' / I do not care a damn. / I'm glad I fought agin it / I only wish we'd won / And I don't want a pardon / For anything I've done." —from a popular Southern song, 1865–1866.

To combat the Black Codes, Congress passed a series of bills designed to strengthen the rights of blacks — and President Johnson vetoed them either as unconstitutional interference in states' rights or as infringing on the powers of the presidency. One thing he couldn't veto, though, was the 14th Amendment, because the Constitution required that proposed amendments go directly to the states for approval. The amendment, ratified in 1868, entitled all people born or naturalized in the United States — including slaves — to U.S. citizenship and equal protection under the law.

Using violence to keep blacks down

Many whites in the South were outraged by the 14th Amendment, particularly poorer whites who already felt they were competing with ex-slaves for jobs. Groups such as the Ku Klux Klan (KKK), Knights of the White Camellia, and Pale Faces sprang up. They used weird costumes and goofy rituals to intimidate blacks from exercising their rights. When intimidation failed, they and other white mobs and paramilitary groups resorted to violence. Hundreds of African Americans were beaten, driven from their homes, or brutally murdered as a result of these groups' actions.

The terrorist activities of the white supremacist groups were very effective in "keeping blacks in their place." And the groups had unwitting allies in the current president of the United States, Andrew Johnson, and Northerners who were losing interest in reforming the South.

Blacks weren't the only targets of the KKK and similar groups; carpetbaggers and scalawags were also terrorized. *Carpetbaggers* were Northerners who came to the South to participate in its reconstruction — and make a lot of money in the process. *Scalawags* were Southerners who worked in concert with the carpetbaggers. Although it's true some of these people were basically just vultures feeding off the defeated Southern corpse, many of both groups actually did a lot of good, reviving the school system, helping rebuild the railroads, and so on.

A lamp, a cow, and a hot, hot town

The year 1871 was a long and dry one in Chicago, Illinois. A drought had made the bustling city tinder-dry and certainly not a place to be careless with fire. But on the morning of October 8, 1871, someone was. Legend has it that someone was a Mrs. O'Leary, on DeKoven Street. Supposedly, she went to her barn to milk the cow, the cow kicked over the kerosene lamp, and one of the most disastrous fires in U.S. history began. (Mrs. O'Leary later denied the story.)

However the fire started, by the time it was out more than 24 hours later, it had killed 250 people, left nearly 100,000 homeless, destroyed more than 17,000 buildings, and done close to $200 million worth of damage.

Contributions poured in from around the world, as did government help. Fortunately, the fire missed the city's vital railroad yards and stockyards, and within a few years Chicago was able to rise from the ashes.

The Tailor-Made President: Andrew Johnson

Andrew Johnson may have been the poorest president ever, at least in terms of his humble beginnings. He was born in North Carolina to impoverished parents, and his father died when Johnson was just 3 years old. He never went to school and instead became a tailor's apprentice at the age of 14.

Johnson taught himself to read and became involved in politics at the age of 17. When the Civil War broke out, he became military governor of Tennessee. In 1864, the Republican Lincoln picked the Democrat Johnson to be his vice presidential running mate. The thought was that a pro-Union Democrat would balance the ticket and attract more votes.

But when Lincoln was killed, the country was left with a stubborn and ill-tempered president who had none of Lincoln's gift of leadership. Johnson didn't like blacks, didn't like rich Southerners, and didn't like the Republican-controlled Congress. In 1866, Johnson took what was called a "Swing around the Circle," traveling around the Northern states to campaign *for* Democrats running for Congress and *against* the 14th Amendment, which would give blacks full citizenship.

Johnson's "Swing around the Circle" was a disaster. The president was booed and jeered by Northern crowds who viewed him as a pro-South bozo. The Republicans dominated the election and had such overwhelming majorities in Congress that they easily passed any bill they wanted — and then just as easily overrode Johnson's vetoes.

Chapter 11: Putting the Country Back Together: 1865–1876

Pushed by Radical Republicans, such as Thaddeus Stevens of Pennsylvania and Charles Sumner of Massachusetts, Congress passed a series of Reconstruction acts designed to force the South into line. One Reconstruction act, passed in 1867, divided the South into five military districts, each governed by a general and policed by the army. To be allowed to reenter the Union and get rid of military rule, Southern states had to agree to ratify the 14th Amendment. They also had to modify their state constitutions to give African Americans the right to vote. This stipulation was particularly galling to Southerners, because many Northern states didn't allow blacks to vote.

Adding salt to the wound, Congress also approved and sent to the states the 15th Amendment, which guaranteed all adult males everywhere the right to vote. This amendment was passed to ensure the Southern states didn't go back on their promise to give blacks the ballot (and also because the Radical Republicans were embarrassed to be from Northern states that didn't let African Americans vote).

Enough Southern state legislatures were dominated by carpetbaggers, former slaves, and other people whose loyalties were to the Radical Republicans to ensure the amendment's ratification. However, Southern states gradually got around the law anyway by requiring blacks to pass difficult "literacy" and "citizenship" tests before they could vote.

The 15th Amendment also greatly angered many American women, who found that they were now second-class citizens to black males as well as white ones when it came to voting.

One result of giving newly freed slaves the right to vote was that they elected some of their own to state legislatures. The resulting black-white governments in some states created sound, fair tax and education systems; built roads and levees; and gave property rights to women. In other states, the government was dominated by leeches and thieves of both races, although white politicians were by far the worst offenders. One carpetbagger governor managed to "save" more than $4 million on an annual salary of $8,000 a year.

Radical Republicans weren't satisfied with being able to overturn Johnson's vetoes. They wanted him out of the White House, which, according to the Constitution, would then fall to the leader of the Senate, Ohio's Benjamin Wade.

To get what they wanted, the Radicals laid a trap. Congress passed a bill that required the president to have Senate approval before he could fire any of his appointees. Johnson, who believed the act was unconstitutional, promptly took the bait and fired his secretary of war, Edwin Stanton, whom he considered a Radical Republican stooge.

Thaddeus Stevens

He had a clubfoot, a razor tongue, and was one of the most sincere white men in America when it came to rights for African Americans. Thaddeus Stevens was born in 1792 in New England. He moved to Pennsylvania, where he practiced law, got into politics, and was first elected to the House of Representatives and later the U.S. Senate.

Stevens was that rarity of rarities — an honest politician. He was unmoved by either flattery or criticism. But he was also fanatical in his hatred for the South, a hatred fueled in part by the destruction of his Pennsylvania factory by Southern troops on their way to Gettysburg. Stevens never married, but for years he had a black housekeeper who was rumored to be his lover. (Stevens never confirmed or denied this gossip.)

As the most radical of the Radical Republicans, Stevens virtually led the country for more than a year because of his power in Congress. He advocated taking the land from the South's wealthiest plantation owners and dividing it among former slaves. But that was too radical even for his colleagues. He did, however, successfully push for other laws designed to protect the basic rights of African Americans.

When Stevens died in 1868, he was buried in a black cemetery. "I have chosen this," read his epitaph, "that I might illustrate in my death the principles which I advocated through a long life: Equality of Man before His Creator."

Following Stanton's dismissal, Congress impeached Johnson in late February 1868 for violating the law, and the Senate put him on trial. The country regarded the whole situation as a great melodrama: Tickets to the Senate gallery were the toughest buy in town. On May 16, 1868, the first of three votes was taken to remove Johnson from office. All three were 35 to 19 — one short of the two-thirds needed. Seven Republican senators voted against removing Johnson from office.

All of these men sacrificed their political careers by voting against Johnson's removal, but they may very well have preserved the U.S. government. Removing Johnson solely on political grounds could've created the basis for a congressional dictatorship, whereby Congress could dominate the presidency by threatening to dump any president who didn't go along with its wishes.

The trial may also have marked the beginning of the end of Northern interest in Reconstruction. Many Northerners were as prejudiced against blacks as many Southerners. They were sick of the issue and wanted to put the war, and its aftermath, behind them. "The whole public are tired out with these autumnal outbreaks in the South," wrote a federal official to a Southern governor, in refusing to provide military aid when the KKK interfered in local elections. "Preserve the peace by the forces of your own state."

> ## "Seward's Folly"
>
> By 1867, Russia was ready to dump Alaska. After all, there didn't seem to be as many fur-bearing animals as there used to be, and the British might take the land anyway. It just so happened that U.S. Secretary of State William Seward was in a buying mood. Seward had heard from Americans in Russia that Alaska had loads of fish, fur, and other natural resources. Plus, buying the area would get the Russians completely out of North America. So in 1867, he offered $7.2 million — about 2 cents an acre — and the Russians said "da."
>
> Most Americans thought buying what they believed amounted to a distant, giant icebox was dumb. The press sneered at the purchase, labeling it "Seward's Folly," "Walrussia," and "Seward's Polar Bear Garden." But Congress went along with the deal, in large part because Russia had been the only European country to support the North during the Civil War. Alaska became the first U.S. possession that wasn't geographically connected to the rest of the country. It also turned out to be a pretty good deal when gold was discovered there in 1897. Then "Seward's Folly" paid off thousands of times over.

Growing Corruption in Politics

When Americans elected Ulysses S. Grant president in 1868, they expected him to be the same kind of chief executive as he was a general — brave, tenacious, and inspiring. But Grant had no political experience and little political philosophy. Neither did many of the people he appointed to be his cabinet advisors and top aides. His one asset was his personal honesty, and, unfortunately, it was an asset not shared by the people around him.

Almost from the time Grant took office, his administration was awash in corruption. Scandal after scandal broke over the White House like waves: Cornering the gold market, attempting to annex the Caribbean island of Santo Domingo, speculating on railroads, ripping off the Native Americans, and stealing liquor tax revenues were all grist for the corruption mill. Grant's administration became known as the "Great Barbecue" because everyone helped themselves.

Political corruption was by no means limited to the federal government or Grant's administration. State and local governments were tainted by scandal as well, and the country was soon caught up in what writer Mark Twain labeled "The Gilded Age." It seemed everyone was in a fever to make money, and the most money-hungry individuals became known, not always with disdain, as *robber barons*.

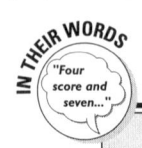

> ### A generous crook
>
> "The Great Fisk died this morning. No loss to the community — quite the reverse — but it's a pity he should have escaped the state prison in this way... By talent and audacity he raised himself to the first rank among business scoundrels... illiterate, vulgar, unprincipled... [but] he was liberal to distressed ballet dancers and munificent to unfortunate females under difficulties." —Lawyer George Templeton Strong, describing the death of "robber baron" James "Jubilee Jim" Fisk in 1872.

In California, Colis P. Huntington and others bribed legislators and congressmen to get concessions for their railroad. In Pennsylvania, John D. Rockefeller bought and bullied lawmakers to aid his Standard Oil Company. The worst situation of all may very well have been in New York City, where a political boss named William M. Tweed created a web of elected officeholders, bureaucrats, and contractors and looted more than $100 million from the city treasury.

Despite the stench of scandal from his first term, Grant was reelected in 1872, easily defeating Democratic candidate Horace Greeley, the longtime editor of the *New York Tribune*. But by 1874, the scandals and the mess of Reconstruction — which ruined Republicans' chances of winning anything in the South — combined to let the Democrats take control of the House of Representatives. The shift added an ingredient of bitter partisan divisiveness to the stinky stew of corruption, but it didn't make it any more palatable. And then an economic panic made things worse.

Riding the railroads to economic ruin

America's post–Civil War economy was driven by a boom in railroad construction. Between 1866 and 1873, 35,000 miles of new track were laid, and railroads trailed only agriculture in their importance to the economic well-being of the country.

For many Americans with a little money to invest, railroads seemed like a can't-miss proposition. Their enthusiasm drove up stock prices far beyond what the stocks were really worth. One such deal involved a major New York–based bank called Jay Cooke & Company.

Cooke, who had become wealthy marketing Union bonds during the war and was known as "the nation's financier," was trying to build a second transcontinental railroad and was seeking investors to pay for it. Sadly for Cooke (and more sadly for his bank's customers), his efforts coincided with a confluence of unfortunate events. One was that banks in Great Britain raised interest rates, which meant fewer Brits were borrowing to invest in U.S. railroad schemes. At the same time, Congress decided to henceforth back U.S. currency with gold only. The U.S. Treasury quit buying silver; silver coins and paper "greenbacks" were devalued; the money supply shrank, and interest rates in America rose.

The economy's tailspin meant Cooke's bank couldn't attract enough cash to keep its vast railroad scheme going. On September 18, 1873, the bank went under. (The bank's collapse was so stunning that a newsboy in Philadelphia was arrested by a disbelieving cop for shouting out the news on a street corner.) The failure triggered a flood of panic selling on the New York Stock Exchange, which actually closed down for ten days.

The stock market collapse, in turn, touched off a deep economic recession that lasted into 1879. Scores of other banks failed, about a quarter of all U.S. railroads went belly up, thousands of auxiliary businesses closed, and unemployment rose to 14 percent by 1876. The country desperately needed strong, honest, and calm political leadership. What it got was the most tainted presidential race in its history.

Fixing a presidency (and not in a good way)

With all the corruption — and the public's growing disgust — it wasn't surprising that in 1876 both political parties nominated presidential candidates known for their integrity. The Republicans put up Rutherford B. Hayes, a former Union general who had been governor of Ohio for three terms. The Democrats countered with New York Governor Samuel B. Tilden, who had gained admiration for helping bring down the Boss Tweed Ring in New York City.

When the returns came in, Tilden had beaten Hayes by more than 250,000 votes, and appeared to have captured 203 of the 369 electoral votes. But Republican Party leaders, who controlled the people who oversaw the elections, arranged to invalidate thousands of Democratic votes in Florida, South Carolina, Oregon, and Louisiana, which changed the electoral vote count to 184–165, with 20 votes in dispute.

Naturally, the Democrats challenged the new results, and a special commission was created to look into the matter. The commission consisted of ten members of Congress, five from each party, as well as five members of the Supreme Court (three Republicans and two Democrats). The commission voted 8–7, not surprisingly along party lines, to give all 20 disputed votes, and the election, to Hayes.

Bounce this idea off the wall

Dr. Benjamin Franklin Goodrich was a Civil War surgeon who became an Ohio businessman after the war. His business was finding things to do with rubber, which a fellow named Charles Goodyear had figured out could be treated with high heat and sulfur — a process called *vulcanization* — so it would stay flexible under hot or cold conditions.

Goodyear died in debt in 1860 before he could find a practical use for the substance. But Goodrich, who had watched a friend's house burn down after a leather fire hose burst, knew exactly what he wanted to produce. In 1870, his company began making the world's first rubber hoses (and one of the first rubber products of any kind).

By the following year, rubber gaskets, bottle stoppers, clothes-wringer rollers, and other items were being produced. Watering can manufacturers may have cursed them, but to gardeners and firefighters, Goodrich's hoses were a godsend.

Northern Democrats were outraged, but Southern Democrats saw an opportunity and offered a deal: They agreed to drop any challenge to the commission's vote if Hayes promised to remove the last of the federal troops from Southern states and let the states run their own affairs. The Republicans eventually agreed, and Hayes became president. As a result, the Reconstruction period came to an ignominious end. African Americans were largely abandoned by the federal government, and white Americans outside the South turned their attentions elsewhere, mostly to the West.

Indigestion on wheels

One day in 1872, a man from Providence, Rhode Island, one Walter Scott, loaded a wagon with sandwiches, boiled eggs, and other food and parked it outside a downtown newspaper office in the evening. Because all the restaurants in town closed at 8 p.m., Scott had plenty of customers. Soon other "lunch wagons" began rolling down streets all over American cities. In 1884, a guy in Worcester, Massachusetts, named Sam Jones got the idea to put stools in his lunch wagon so customers could sit down.

The wagons drew complaints from residents and competing restaurant owners and were banned or restricted in many towns. So the wagon owners simply rolled their wagons onto vacant lots, took off the wheels, and called themselves restaurants. By the 1920s, people were eating as many breakfasts and dinners at the wagons as lunches, and rather than lunch wagons, people started calling them *diners*.

Part III
Coming of Age

Six Main Causes of the Great Depression

- **Bank failures:** Many small banks, particularly in rural areas, had overextended credit to farmers who, for the most part, had not shared in the prosperity of the 1920s and often couldn't repay the loans. Big banks, meanwhile, had foolishly made huge loans to foreign countries. When times got tough, European nations simply defaulted on their outstanding loans. As a result, many banks went bankrupt.

- **Environmental disasters:** The production of vast crops during World War I and the decade that followed resulted in over-plowing of much of America's farmland. The prairie grasses that held topsoil in place were stripped. Coupled with a terrible drought, the unprotected soil turned the Great Plains into the *Dust Bowl*.

- **Farm failures:** Many American farmers were already having a hard time before the Depression, mostly because they were producing too much and farm product prices were too low. The situation was so bad in some areas that farmers burned corn for fuel rather than sell it.

- **Government inaction:** Rather than try to jump-start the economy by pushing the Federal Reserve System to lend money to banks at low interest rates and pumping money into the economy through federal public works projects, the Hoover administration did nothing at first and then took small, tentative actions that weren't enough to head things off.

- **The stock market crash:** The stock market soared throughout most of the 1920s. Many people bought on margin, so when the market crashed in late October 1929, they were forced to pay up on stocks that were worth far less than what they had paid for them. Many had borrowed to buy stock and couldn't repay their loans. The lenders were left holding the empty bag.

- **Too many poor people:** While the overall economy had soared in the 1920s, most of the wealth was enjoyed by relatively few Americans. In 1929, 40 percent of the families in the country were still living at or below the poverty level. That made them too poor to buy goods and services and too poor to pay their debts.

Visit www.dummies.com/extras/ushistory for an article on an interesting American product.

In this part...

- The United States matures as a country after the Civil War.
- America emerges as an economic world power.
- The economy shifts from farms to factories.

Chapter 12

Growing Up: 1876–1898

In This Chapter

▶ Cashing in on animals, minerals, and vegetables
▶ Pushing non-whites out
▶ Watching big business boom while unrest settles in
▶ Remembering some forgettable presidents
▶ Battling with Spain for some islands

*A*mericans have always been restless, and in 1876 they were hungry, too — for success. There seemed to be many ways and places to be successful, and it seemed very important to a whole lot of people.

In this chapter, the country starts its final push toward filling in the gaps between the coasts — and its final pushing aside of the original Americans. Railroads help do both, as well as usher in the birth of truly huge businesses. A string of mediocre presidents don't do much of anything, and a war with Spain launches America on the road to becoming an empire.

Heading West in a Quest for Wealth

When settlers in America first started moving west (about ten minutes after they got here), they generally did so because of the lure of free land and the chance to put down roots. After the Civil War, however, Americans moved west as much to make a buck as to settle into a new life. The West was seen as a bottomless treasure chest of resources to exploit.

Making money from minerals

Some of those resources were mineral. Starting with the California Gold Rush of 1849, the West saw a steady stream of gold, silver, and copper discoveries touch off "rushes," as hordes of miners careened like pinballs from strike to strike. In 1859, thousands descended on Pike's Peak in Colorado, looking for gold. Later that year, it was the Comstock silver lode in Nevada. In 1861, it was Idaho; in 1863, Montana; in 1874, the Black Hills of Dakota; and in 1876, it was back to Colorado.

Towns with 5,000 inhabitants sprang up virtually overnight, composed of miners-who-would-be millionaires, and the gamblers, thieves, swindlers, prostitutes, and liquor sellers that accompanied them. They formed violent societies. Justice was often in the form of vigilance committees or *vigilantes,* who set themselves up as the law and sometimes didn't bother with a trial before stretching a defendant's neck.

Where most of the mining money went reflected what was happening in the rest of the country. Big corporations, financed by stockholders from the East and Europe, had the capital to buy the equipment needed to mine on a large scale, and they reaped most of the profits. Most miners made little, and many of them ended up going to work as laborers for the large companies.

But mining had some positive impact on the West besides the wealth it created. The miners were the first to open much of the West, and they helped encourage the railroads to come. Some of those who came for the booms stayed on after the inevitable busts that followed. Because miners had to set up governments in a hurry to deal with the instant towns, political organization took root. Coupled with the mineral wealth, these organizations gave the mining areas clout in Congress. This helped speed the admission of new states, such as Nevada.

By the dawn of the new century, the big, fever-producing mineral strikes were over in the West. But they were replaced by the rush to extract oil — "Black Gold" — beneath western lands, particularly in Texas and Oklahoma.

Making money from animals

After the Civil War, Texas soldiers returned to find as many as five million cattle roaming around the state. The cattle were descendants of animals brought to the area hundreds of years before by Spanish explorers. There was plenty of grazing land and enough water, and the cattle were a hardy breed.

Now, Texans were as fond of beef as the next state's inhabitants, but they really wanted to find a way to share their wealth on the hoof with the rest of the nation. Cattle worth $3 to $4 a head in Texas could be sold for ten times that much in Eastern states, if you could get them there. Cattle drives to the East and even California had been tried before. But many of the cattle died before the drives were over, and the survivors were worn thin by the effort.

> ## Deadwood
>
> It started as a place full of Americans gambling on their futures, hung tenaciously to life for 113 years, and then re-invented itself as a place full of Americans who were just plain gambling. Along the way, Deadwood, South Dakota, became ensconced in the nation's psyche as the geographical embodiment of the Wild West: The town where "Calamity Jane" Cannary howled and prowled, and "Wild Bill" Hickok was shot in the back while playing poker.
>
> Deadwood (named for an abundance of dead trees) began in 1876 with the gold rush that hit the Black Hills in the southwest corner of what was then the Dakota Territory. By 1880, it had boomed from a few sheds to a city of about 10,000. Telephone lines were there by 1879; electric lights by 1883. Through a series of floods and fires, the town persevered, supported mainly by commercial mining (and, until 1980, an entire block of brothels.) By the 1980s, however, mining operations had waned, and the town was dying.
>
> In an effort to revive what was the first U.S. city to be named a national historic landmark, South Dakota voters approved a measure in 1989 that legalized casino gambling in the town. As of 2013, Deadwood was home to 80 gambling halls, a permanent population of about 1,400 — and tens of thousands of annual visitors seeking a taste of the Old West.

After the war, however, someone got the idea to shorten the distances by driving cattle to the railroads that were moving west, and then shipping them east by rail. Rail met cow at "trailheads" in Abilene and Dodge City in Kansas, Ogalalla in Nebraska, and Cheyenne in Wyoming. By 1871, 750,000 head of cattle were moving through Abilene alone. By 1875, the advent of the refrigerated car allowed cattle to be slaughtered and butchered in Midwest cities like Kansas City and Chicago before being shipped east.

The rise of the cattle industry also gave rise to an American icon: the cowboy. Hollywood turned the cowboy into a romantic figure who was quick on the draw with a six-shooter and spent most of his time drinking whiskey and playing poker in town, with a dance-hall girl hovering at his shoulder.

In truth, the cowboy was more likely an ex-Confederate soldier or former slave who spent most of his life on the back of a short-legged cow pony, hundreds of miles from the nearest bar or woman. He was brave and tough, but he was far less likely to use his pistol on his fellow man than he was on rattlesnakes or as a noisemaker. He was likely in his late teens or early 20s, and about one in five was African American. He worked for $25 a month and ate beans, bacon, and black coffee day after day.

By the early 1890s, the day of the cowboy and the cattle drive was coming to an end. Like other aspects of American life, inventions (such as barbed wire) and investments (by Easterners and Europeans) turned ranching into big business, and cowboys became caretakers on large fenced ranches rather than riders of the range. A far less glamorous, but much more numerous, type of Westerner was now dominant: the sodbuster.

Making money from vegetables

In the wake of the miner and the cowboy came the farmer. The railroads were eager to colonize the areas they controlled with potential customers and offered land near their tracks through giant advertising efforts in the East and Europe. The federal government tried various ways to sell public lands, most of them badly managed.

Regardless, the settlers rushed in. The populations of Minnesota, Kansas, and Nebraska doubled or tripled. The Dakotas went from 14,000 residents after the Civil War to 500,000 in 20 years. In 1889, the "Cherokee Strip" in northern Oklahoma was purchased from Native Americans and thrown open to settlement, and by 1900, the Oklahoma Territory had a population of about 800,000.

Most of the farmers faced a blizzard of hardships: drought, grasshopper invasions, prairie fires, and, well, blizzards. There was even foreign competition. In the 1870s, crop failures in Europe helped drive up prices and open markets for American farmers. But in the 1880s, crop prices fell as new producers in Australia and India came on the scene.

More and more farmers in the West found themselves in the same plight as those in the war-torn South. The number of farms that were either mortgaged or farmed by tenant farmers steadily increased as the last 20 years of the century passed.

Still, between 1870 and 1900, the number of American acres under cultivation more than doubled, from 407 million to 841 million acres. The frontier had been mined, ranched, and farmed into submission.

Happy 100th, America

In 1871, Congress decided to put on a big to-do to celebrate America's 100th birthday. It took awhile to raise the dough, but on May 10, 1876, 13 giant bells chimed, 100 cannons fired a salute, and an 800-voice choir sang the "Hallelujah Chorus" to open the U.S. Centennial Exhibition in Philadelphia.

The fair, spread over a 248-acre park, featured exhibits from all over the world, but the highlights were the proud displays of Yankee know-how. Crowds, which included Pres. Ulysses Grant and Emperor Don Pedro II of Brazil, gasped and gaped at the largest steam engine ever built up to that time; an ice box that used ammonia as its refrigerant; and a printing process that printed, cut, and sorted pages for up to an hour at a time.

The first prize for new inventions went to Alexander Graham Bell for a device he called the telephone. The Brazilian emperor put the thing to his ear and quickly dropped it, exclaiming, "My God, it talks!" But Bell's invention drew smaller crowds than an exotic exhibit from Central America. It featured a strange fruit, called the banana.

Ousting "Undesirables"

Gen. Philip Sheridan never said: "The only good Indian is a dead Indian." What he did say, however, was just as bad: "The only good Indians I ever saw were dead."

There were plenty of dead Native Americans by 1876. When Columbus arrived, there were probably 1 million to 1.5 million Native Americans living in what is now the United States. By the time of the Civil War, that number had dropped to about 300,000, with two-thirds of them living on the Great Plains.

The Plains Indians generally tolerated the white man crossing their territory on the way to California and Oregon. But when the newcomers began to settle in, tensions grew and both sides resorted to violence.

In 1862, a tribe of Sioux went on the offensive in Minnesota against encroaching settlers, killing more than 700 before the militia defeated them and hanged 38 of the tribe's leaders. In 1864, John Chivington, a Colorado militia colonel, attacked a band of Cheyenne at Sand Creek, Colorado, and killed 133 people, most of them women and children. Many white Americans were appalled at Chivington's brutality.

After the Civil War was over, a debate began in earnest on what to do about "the Indian Problem." Ideas ranged from extermination to reservations to ending tribal customs and forcing Native Americans to adopt white culture. All of them were tried to varying degrees. Between 1859 and 1876, soldiers and Native Americans fought at least 200 pitched battles and signed 370 treaties.

"They made us promises more than I can remember," noted one Sioux leader, "but they never kept but one. They promised to take our land, and they did."

They also all but wiped out the American bison, or buffalo, which to the Plains Indians was a walking supermarket. The tribes not only ate the buffalo but also wore clothes and blankets from it and used its bones for tools and its dried dung for fire fuel. In 1840, an estimated 40 million buffalo roamed the Plains.

But buffalo were dumber than rocks when it came to being hunted, placidly grazing while hunters with long-range rifles picked them off one by one for their hides, their meat, or just for the heck of it. By 1875, only a million buffalo were left; by 1893, less than 1,000. The Plains Indians were starved into submission far more than they were outfought.

In 1868, after a series of indecisive battles, both sides agreed to a grand scheme in which two large reservations would be created, one in Oklahoma and one that took in all of western South Dakota. That included the Black Hills, which were sacred to the Sioux (more properly known as Lakota).

Putting up a fight

Six years later, an expedition led by Colonel George Armstrong Custer discovered gold in the Black Hills. White prospectors poured into the area. The government, powerless to stop them, offered to buy the land from the Native Americans but was refused. The last great war against the Native Americans began, and for the first time, the Plains tribes united into a formidable fighting force.

On June 25, 1876, the U.S. 7th Cavalry regiment, led by Custer, rashly attacked a Native American encampment at the Little Bighorn River in Montana. It proved to be populated by 2,500 warriors. Custer and nearly 40 percent of his men were killed.

"Custer's Last Stand" horrified people in the East as well as the West, and greatly diminished sympathy for the Native Americans' situation. The battle proved to be the beginning of the end for the Plains Indians. Over the next decade, tribe after tribe was gradually worn down by hunger and continual pursuit by the army. What happened to the Plains tribes was repeated throughout the West — the Apache in Arizona, the Crow and Blackfoot in Montana, the Ute in Colorado, the Nez Percé in Idaho — all were decimated by hunger, disease, and harassment by the whites.

In 1887, Congress passed a law that divided land into individual allotments for Native Americans, as part of an effort to turn them into small farmers. It also provided for an education system and eventual U.S. citizenship. However well intentioned the law was, it didn't work. Most Native Americans didn't want to be farmers or U.S. citizens, and the education system never amounted to much. Many Native Americans eventually signed away their land for a few cents an acre to speculators, who promptly resold it to settlers for a few dollars an acre.

In 1890, a misunderstanding led to a cavalry attack on a group of Miniconjou and Hunkpapa Lakota who were under military escort, near a creek called Wounded Knee in South Dakota. The soldiers killed more than 200 men, women, and children, and then left their bodies in the snow for three days before burying them in a mass grave. It was the last major violence between the Native Americans and whites, and a tragic and horrifyingly typical response to America's "Indian Problem."

Legalizing discrimination

While white America was pushing the Native Americans to adopt white ways and become part of white culture, it was pushing to keep African Americans out. Reconstruction had failed to give blacks equal rights, and a conservative U.S. Supreme Court ensured the failure would last another 50 or 60 years.

I quit

"I am tired of fighting. The old men are all dead . . . it is cold and we have no blankets. The little children are freezing to death . . . Hear me my chiefs. I am tired; my heart is sick and sad. From where the sun now stands, I will fight no more forever." —Nez Percé Chief Joseph, before surrendering to U.S. Army troops, 1877.

In 1883, the Court ruled the federal government had no right to interfere with discrimination by private enterprises or individuals. In 1896, in a case called *Plessy v. Ferguson,* It decided states had the right to legally segregate public facilities, from schools to trains. And in 1899, the Court ruled that states could erect schools for white kids only, even if there were no schools for blacks.

Encouraged by the decisions, Southern states passed what were called *Jim Crow laws* (named after a popular song that depicted African Americans as shiftless children), which not only tried to completely separate the races, but also take away most of the rights they had been accorded by the 13th, 14th, and 15th Amendments. Blacks couldn't serve on juries, represent themselves in court, or drink from the same public drinking fountains as whites. If they quit a job, they could be arrested for vagrancy. They also established elaborate tests that black would-be voters had to take to get a ballot. The result was that the level of black voting dropped like a boulder off a bridge.

Crazy Horse

Crazy Horse was named after his father, after proving himself in battle, which was probably a good thing, because in his early years he was called "Curly." Born around 1842 near the Belle Fourche River in South Dakota, the Lakota (Sioux) warrior began his fight against the white invaders in 1865. He became known as a daring fighter who used tricks and guerilla tactics well. In 1866, he helped lure 80 soldiers into an ambush in which all of them were killed.

Eleven months after leading the combined tribes against Custer at the Little Big Horn, Crazy Horse surrendered to troops that had been relentlessly harassing his band. He was taken to Fort Robinson, Wyoming, where he was held for several months.

"They say we massacred him [Custer]," he said during his captivity, "but he would have done the same thing to us had we not defended ourselves and fought to the last. Our first impulse was to escape . . . but we were so hemmed in that we had to fight."

In September 1877, while still in custody, he was stabbed to death by a soldier under questionable circumstances. Crazy Horse became a mythic figure among Native Americans of all tribes.

But as if the Jim Crow laws weren't enough, during the 1890s, the South averaged 130 lynchings a year. They were so commonplace that they were sometimes advertised in advance in newspapers. The North generally shrugged at the Jim Crow laws and ignored the lynchings. "The Negro's day is over," observed Yale Professor William Graham Sumner. "He is out of fashion."

Even the best-known African American leader of the day was not ready to challenge the injustices. Born into slavery, Booker T. Washington had become a schoolteacher, the founder of a major vocational school in Alabama called the Tuskegee Institute, and an eloquent advocate of African Americans improving themselves economically.

To improve their economic situations, Washington urged blacks to "accommodate" whites when it came to demands for segregation, in return for white help in obtaining black schools and economic opportunity. "The wisest among my race understand that the agitation of questions of social equality is the extremest of folly," he argued.

White America didn't care much for Chinese immigrants, either. "The Yellow Peril," many of whom were brought to America to work on the railroads at half the wages paid to white workers, were viewed as a competitive labor threat to American-born workers. Anti-Chinese riots broke out in San Francisco in 1877. In 1882, Congress passed a law prohibiting all Chinese immigration for ten years. The ban, called the Chinese Exclusion Act, was later extended to last indefinitely, and wasn't repealed until 1943.

Cramming into Cities

The law that excluded immigration by Chinese also banned criminals, the mentally ill or retarded, and those likely to end up as public charity cases. Otherwise, America's front door was wide open, and people poured in. Between 1866 and 1915, 25 million immigrants came to the United States. Most of them came from Italy and Southeastern Europe, but they also came from Scandinavia, Russia, Poland, Germany, Ireland, England, and France. By 1910, 15 percent of the country's total population was foreign-born. Most of them came to escape hard economic times at home, despotic governments, or both. Many times their expectations were unrealistically high. "America is all puddings and pies!" enthused one young man as he stepped off the ship in New York.

Despite the warning of a popular immigrant guidebook to "forget your past, your customs, and your ideals," many of the new Americans clung to their own languages, customs, and cuisines, and gravitated to communities populated by others from their country. The presence of so many immigrants in so short a time caused alarm in some "natives," who feared the newcomers would weaken their chances in the job market and pollute American culture. But it wasn't until 1921, after World War I had created millions of refugees in Europe, that Congress tightened immigration policies concerning Europeans.

In the meantime, as much as 80 percent of the immigrant wave settled in Northern cities. By the turn of the century, more than a third of Chicago's populace was foreign-born, and there were more Irish in New York City than there were in Ireland. The immigrants weren't the only newcomers in town, because there were plenty of American-born country folks moving to urban areas, as well. By 1900, 30 million Americans lived in cities, about a third of all U.S. residents. The number of cities larger than 100,000 increased from 9 to 50 between 1860 and 1910.

But many parts of the big cities were festering sores. In those areas, fire protection, street cleaning, sewage systems, garbage collection, and water treatment barely existed. The Chicago River was an open sewer. Baltimore's sewers emptied into the tidal basin and in the summer heat, journalist H. L. Mencken wrote, it "smelled like a billion polecats."

Housing was often designed to cram the most people into the least space. It wasn't uncommon for 24 four-room apartments to be built on a 2,500-square-foot lot. Tenement slums took on fitting names, such as "Hell's Kitchen," "Bone Alley," or "Poverty Gap."

Gradually, things improved in the major urban areas. No one, rich or poor, wanted to live in filth, and after the link between disease and poor sanitation was firmly established, city leaders began to develop adequate sewage and water systems. Public transit systems, based on streetcars or trolleys, were put in place. But none of it happened overnight, and more than a few farmers-turned-city-dwellers must have yearned more than once to be home on the range.

Slum life

"All the fresh air that enters these stairs comes from the hall-door that is forever slamming.... The sinks are in the hallway, that all tenants may have access — and all be poisoned alike by the summer stenches.... Here is a door. Listen! That slow, hacking cough, that tiny helpless wail — what do they mean? The child is dying of measles. With half a chance, it might have lived; but it had none." —Reporter Jacob Riis, in "How the Other Half Lives," 1890.

Inventing Big Business

As America reached young adulthood in the last part of the 19th century, it began to shake off its rural roots and become an industrial city slicker. From 1859 to 1899, the value of the country's manufactured products rose 622 percent, from $1.8 billion to $13 billion, and America became the world's leading manufacturer. It rode its way to the top on the train.

Building the railroads

The railroad system was America's first truly big business and its growth and impact were enormous. In the 41 years from 1830 to 1870, about 40,000 miles of track were laid in the country. But in the 20 years from 1871 to 1890, more than 110,000 miles were laid. In 1869, the first transcontinental line linking the East and West coasts was opened, and by 1900, there were four more.

By 1890, annual railroad freight revenues totaled $1 billion — which was more than twice what the federal government gathered yearly in revenue. The railroads not only transported goods and people, they dictated where towns would grow and businesses would locate. They employed more than one million people by 1900. They helped push Congress to create four standard time zones across the country so train schedules could be worked out.

The railroads created or greatly expanded other industries with their demands for materials like steel for rails and passenger and freight cars. And they helped speed development of America's telegraph system, because where the rails went, the wires went. With telegraph stations at most train stations, the Western Union Company was sending 40 million messages a year by 1883, over 400,000 miles of wire.

Despite all those grand and glorious numbers, the railroad boom wasn't exactly a shining example of American free enterprise at its best. The rails were laid mostly on public land given to the railroads by the federal government — more than 240,000 square miles, or an area the size of Germany — along with more than $60 million in taxpayer-financed grants or loans.

Because the federal government didn't want to get directly in the railroad-building business, the land was thought of as an incentive to attract private investment. The idea was that the railroad companies would sell most of the land near their tracks, and that's where they would make their money, because rail operations alone weren't expected to turn a profit for years.

Caveat emptor, chump

"Let the buyer beware; that covers the whole business. You cannot wet-nurse men from the time they are born until the time they die. They have to wade, and get stuck, and that is the way men are educated." —Sugar baron Henry O. Havemeyer, to a congressional committee investigating the sugar industry, 1895.

In May 1886, an AFL strike for an eight-hour day for workers led to a clash at Chicago's Haymarket Square between police and strikers. A bomb killed 7 cops and injured 67 others. The police, who had killed four strikers the day before, fired into the crowd and killed four more. Seven strike leaders were eventually convicted and four were hanged. The incident was condemned by anti-union forces as an example of how the labor movement was controlled by "anarchists" and "radicals."

In 1894, a strike against the Pullman railroad car company spread over 27 states and paralyzed the country's railroads. Federal troops were called out, and a court order ended the strike. The Haymarket Square riot and Pullman strike dealt severe blows to the chances of things getting better for the average working stiff through labor unions. America was progressing, but not all of its citizens were.

Samuel L. Clemens

He was a printer, a prospector, a Confederate army deserter, a riverboat pilot, a world traveler, a lecturer, an inventor, and an investor. Oh yeah, he could write a little too.

Born in 1835 in Missouri, Clemens grew up on the banks of the Mississippi River. After various careers, Clemens settled on journalism, working for newspapers in Nevada and California. His humor-laden dispatches, written under the pen name "Mark Twain" (which in riverboat parlance meant "safe water"), became very popular in the East.

Starting in 1869, Clemens wrote a series of short stories, travel books, autobiographical works, and novels that established him as America's most celebrated man of letters. He was also one of the country's fiercest critics. He termed the post–Civil War period "The Gilded Age" for its venality and corruption. Despite his criticisms, however, Clemens was himself caught up in the chase for wealth, and made and lost several fortunes. At the time of his death in 1910, he was one of the best-known people in the world. His works were translated into more than 70 languages, and he was lionized as "the Lincoln of our literature."

And dribble before you shoot . . .

James Naismith had an unruly class on his hands. The Canadian-born YMCA teacher was training would-be YMCA instructors in Springfield, Massachusetts, in the winter of 1891. His boss had ordered him to come up with a new indoor game that would get the class re-enthused about exercise in the winter.

Naismith tried variations of soccer and lacrosse. They proved too rough. After two weeks, he was still stumped. Then a solution began to fall into place. The first notion was to use a big, round ball that didn't require a stick to hit it. Second, running with the ball was eliminated, so no tackling was required. Third, goals were set up through which to chuck the ball.

"I met Mr. Stebbins, the superintendent of buildings," Naismith later recalled, "and I asked him if he had two boxes about 18 inches square. Stebbins thought a minute, and then said: 'No, but I have two old peach baskets down in the store room.'" By noon, Naismith had nailed up the peach baskets, and two nine-man teams were playing "basket ball" — as opposed to what presumably would have been "box ball."

The system was ripe for corruption, and scandals were plenty. The Union Pacific line, for example, was built by the Credit Mobilier Construction Company, which was owned by the same people who owned the railroad. They took fat federal grants and awarded themselves exorbitant contracts — and bought off inquisitive congressmen with bribes of heavily discounted railroad stock.

The business attracted titans of industry (or robber barons, depending on how you viewed them). There was Cornelius Vanderbilt in the East, Thomas A. Scott in the Midwest, James J. Hill in the Northwest, and Jay Gould in the Southwest. Each had their railroad fiefdoms and battled with the others for government favors. But not all of the country's big wheels concentrated on trains — there were fortunes to be made in other fields, too.

Manufacturing steel more efficiently

Before the Civil War, steel was a rare and expensive building material, mainly because the process to make it from iron ore was a lengthy one. But a method that became widely used in the early 1870s greatly shortened the process while greatly increasing the amount that could be made at one time.

In America, steel-making became synonymous with one man: Andrew Carnegie. Born in Scotland, Carnegie came to America at the age of 13 and got a job working in a Pennsylvania factory for $1.50 a week. He moved on to jobs with Western Union and the Pennsylvania Railroad, made smart investments, and, by the time he was 28, was making $50,000 a year.

Carnegie eventually focused on steel. He hired chemists to perfect the production process, developed markets for steel, reinvested his profits, and expanded. He bought up or leased vast holdings of iron ore and coal in order to corner the supply of raw materials. By 1890, America was producing 4 million tons of steel per year, mostly for the railroads, and 70 percent of it was made by Carnegie's steel plants near Pittsburgh.

In 1901, Carnegie sold out to financier J.P. Morgan for the staggering sum of $447 million. In his later years, he gave away more than $300 million of his fortune through philanthropies that included building 2,811 public libraries and donating 8,000 organs to churches.

Refining (and controlling) oil

In the 1850s, whale oil — the primary fuel for providing light — had become very expensive, and people began to look for an alternative. Gradually, drilling for oil became practical enough that kerosene made from refined petroleum began replacing whale oil.

The most famous — or infamous — of the oil men was John D. Rockefeller, a Cleveland businessman who had made some money during the Civil War selling meat and grain. In 1870, Rockefeller combined five companies he owned into the Standard Oil Company. A ruthless and brilliant businessman, Rockefeller either bought up the competition or drove it out of business by undercutting prices. Political bribery was also a standard tool of Standard Oil: One critic noted that Rockefeller "had done everything to the Pennsylvania legislature except refine it." By 1879, Standard Oil controlled 90 percent of the nation's refining capacity, a huge network of pipelines, and large oil reserves, and by 1892, Rockefeller had amassed a fortune of $800 million.

Getting wired for sound and light

New industries were also springing up around new inventions. In 1876, a teacher of the deaf, Alexander Graham Bell, invented the telephone. By 1880, 85 cities and towns had phone networks, and by 1900, more than 800,000 telephones were in place throughout the country.

In 1879, inventor Thomas A. Edison came up with a practical electric light bulb. Over the next 20 years, America began to wire up. At first, direct current (DC) was used, but DC didn't work over distances of more than a few miles. Then a man named George Westinghouse began using alternating current (AC), which allowed high voltage to be sent long distances through transformers and then reduced to safer levels as it entered buildings. Switching from steam engines to electricity made factories safer and more efficient, too.

The real thing

John Pemberton was an Atlanta pharmacist, but he was also a man with a vision: He wanted to make the perfect drink. So he came up with a syrup that combined the coca leaf and the kola nut. Mixing it in a big kettle, he lugged it down to a local drugstore, where he sold it for five cents a glass — and averaged nine sales a day.

Pemberton died in 1888, and the formula for "Coca-Cola" (a name created by Pemberton's bookkeeper from the two main ingredients) was sold to a clever marketing man named Asa B. Candler. Candler realized that advertis[ing] was the key to making the product a nati[onal] brand, and devoted an unheard-of $50,00[0 a] year to marketing the drink. Other execut[ives] who followed him perfected distribution [and] bottling techniques, and today billions of bot[tles] and cans of "Coke" are sold in more than [200] countries.

PS: Among other things, Pemberton claime[d the] drink could cure headaches and dyspepsia [but] made no rash claims about diet dyspepsia.

Forming trusts and striking against the[m]

In 1882, Standard Oil organized the first of the nation's trusts. A *trust* ov[ersaw] virtually all of an industry's operations, from production to price-settin[g] to distribution and sales. It was supposedly run not by a single compan[y] but by trustees. A trust issued certificates to stockholders in the indust[ry's] companies and paid dividends. Virtual monopolies like Standard Oil cou[ld] then argue that they didn't control an industry; the trust did.

Monopolies weren't all bad. Because of the economies of doing busines[s] on a large scale, costs could be kept down and prices lowered. The pri[ce of] kerosene, for example, dropped a fair amount after Standard Oil domina[ted] the market. Of course with no competition, prices were at the mercy of [the] monopolies and could — and often did — swing up again. In addition, t[he] sheer size and power of the monopolies were worrisome to some Amer[icans].

Carnegie and other giants of capitalism immodestly preached the "Gos[pel] of Wealth," arguing that it was natural for a few people to have most of [the] wealth, a sort of economic "survival of the fittest." As long as they used [their] fortunes to benefit society, they contended there was nothing wrong wi[th it].

But opening libraries and donating church organs didn't put bread on the [table] of the average working guy. Labor unions began to try to do that after the [Civil] War by organizing on a large scale. Most notable were groups called the K[nights] of Labor and the American Federation of Labor (AFL). In 1877, America fa[ced its] first national labor strike when railroad workers walked off the job after w[ages] were cut. State and federal troops were called in, hundreds of strikers we[re] killed or wounded, and service was restored at the point of a gun.

> ### Nickel-and-diming it
>
> The growth of the cities helped spark the development of retail stores designed to do a high volume of business by selling low-cost goods. In February 1879, a self-described "boob from the country" of upstate New York, named Frank W. Woolworth, opened the "Great Five-Cent Store" in Utica, New York. During its first months, it took in a grand total of $2.50 a day.
>
> Undismayed, Woolworth figured his store was just in a bad location and opened another in Lancaster, Pennsylvania. It featured a "5-cent counter" in the front of the store that was supposed to lure customers in the door, where they might buy some higher-priced items.
>
> The idea worked. By 1900, Woolworth had 59 stores, and by 1913, he was wealthy enough to pay $13.5 million in cash to construct what was then the tallest building in the world, the Woolworth Building in Manhattan. By the way, that's 270 million nickels.

Electing a String of Forgettable Presidents

America has had good presidents and bad presidents, but it's doubtful it has ever had as many mediocre presidents in a row as it did between 1876 and 1900. It wasn't a case of boring elections. Party splits and factions, and the fact that winners got to milk the government for jobs, made for intense and nasty campaigns. There were plenty of big issues, too, from tariffs to bank panics to civil service reform. The men elected to deal with them, however, were a forgettable bunch. Here they are, before I forget them:

- **Rutherford B. Hayes** (Republican, 1877–1881): Hayes was a Civil War hero who was very politically cautious. He hated making tough decisions, so he avoided them. The Democrats controlled Congress most of the time he was president, so he accomplished little. He chose not to run for a second term and might not have been nominated anyway.

- **James A. Garfield** (Republican, 1881): Garfield was assassinated by a disgruntled office seeker four months after taking office. He was also the last president to be born in a log cabin.

- **Chester A. Arthur** (Republican, 1881–1885): Arthur was a lifelong politician who never won an election, except as Garfield's running mate. He was a fairly dignified and businesslike president, but he accomplished little.

- **Grover Cleveland** (Democrat, 1885–1889 and 1893–1897): Cleveland was the only president to serve two non-consecutive terms and the only one to have personally hanged a man. He accomplished the latter feat as sheriff in Buffalo, New York. He managed the former by losing his reelection bid in 1888 to Benjamin Harrison, and then defeating Harrison in 1892. Cleveland was elected the first time despite the revelation that he fathered a son by a woman he never married. His second term was marked by an economic depression. He didn't win nomination for a chance at a third term.

- **Benjamin Harrison** (Republican, 1889–1893): Harrison was the grandson of Pres. William Henry Harrison. Six new states — Washington, Idaho, Montana, Wyoming, North Dakota, and South Dakota — were admitted during his administration. That was pretty much it.

- **William McKinley** (Republican, 1897–1901): By most accounts, McKinley was a nice guy. He was an Ohio congressman and governor and very devoted to his invalid wife. He also had friends in high places, especially political boss Mark Hanna. Hanna and others helped elect McKinley president. He defeated Democrat-Populist William Jennings Bryan in 1896, and again in 1900. He was assassinated by a crazy anarchist named Leon Czolgosz in 1901. As he lay wounded, McKinley urged that his killer not be harmed. But they executed him in the electric chair anyway.

The Rise of Populism

Times were tough on the farm in the 1890s. Crop prices fell as production rose. Credit was hard to get and interest rates were high. Many of the rural areas' best and brightest had taken off to seek their fortunes in the cities.

These hard times triggered a political movement called *Populism*. Populists sought higher crop prices and lower interest rates. They wanted a system where farmers could deposit crops in storage facilities and use them as collateral for low-interest government loans.

They also wanted more money put into circulation and more silver coins made. The idea was that more money in circulation would raise prices, while their mortgage payments would stay the same. But it was also risky. Money based on the amount of gold reserves the country had was more stable than money based on silver, because the amount of silver reserves was increasing and therefore could "cheapen" the value of money as the price of silver dropped.

Republicans generally opposed the Populist ideas, while Democrats generally lined up with the Populists. The Democrats nominated 36-year-old Nebraska Congressman William Jennings Bryan as their 1896 presidential candidate. Bryan, an outstanding orator, gave a rousing speech at the Democratic convention in favor of "free silver," by exclaiming "you shall not crucify mankind upon a cross of gold." But Bryan lost to Republican William McKinley anyway, in large part because McKinley's supporters raised and spent $3 million on his campaign.

And dribble before you shoot...

James Naismith had an unruly class on his hands. The Canadian-born YMCA teacher was training would-be YMCA instructors in Springfield, Massachusetts, in the winter of 1891. His boss had ordered him to come up with a new indoor game that would get the class re-enthused about exercise in the winter.

Naismith tried variations of soccer and lacrosse. They proved too rough. After two weeks, he was still stumped. Then a solution began to fall into place. The first notion was to use a big, round ball that didn't require a stick to hit it. Second, running with the ball was eliminated, so no tackling was required. Third, goals were set up through which to chuck the ball.

"I met Mr. Stebbins, the superintendent of buildings," Naismith later recalled, "and I asked him if he had two boxes about 18 inches square. Stebbins thought a minute, and then said: 'No, but I have two old peach baskets down in the store room.'" By noon, Naismith had nailed up the peach baskets, and two nine-man teams were playing "basket ball" — as opposed to what presumably would have been "box ball."

The system was ripe for corruption, and scandals were plenty. The Union Pacific line, for example, was built by the Credit Mobilier Construction Company, which was owned by the same people who owned the railroad. They took fat federal grants and awarded themselves exorbitant contracts — and bought off inquisitive congressmen with bribes of heavily discounted railroad stock.

The business attracted titans of industry (or robber barons, depending on how you viewed them). There was Cornelius Vanderbilt in the East, Thomas A. Scott in the Midwest, James J. Hill in the Northwest, and Jay Gould in the Southwest. Each had their railroad fiefdoms and battled with the others for government favors. But not all of the country's big wheels concentrated on trains — there were fortunes to be made in other fields, too.

Manufacturing steel more efficiently

Before the Civil War, steel was a rare and expensive building material, mainly because the process to make it from iron ore was a lengthy one. But a method that became widely used in the early 1870s greatly shortened the process while greatly increasing the amount that could be made at one time.

In America, steel-making became synonymous with one man: Andrew Carnegie. Born in Scotland, Carnegie came to America at the age of 13 and got a job working in a Pennsylvania factory for $1.50 a week. He moved on to jobs with Western Union and the Pennsylvania Railroad, made smart investments, and, by the time he was 28, was making $50,000 a year.

Carnegie eventually focused on steel. He hired chemists to perfect the production process, developed markets for steel, reinvested his profits, and expanded. He bought up or leased vast holdings of iron ore and coal in order to corner the supply of raw materials. By 1890, America was producing 4 million tons of steel per year, mostly for the railroads, and 70 percent of it was made by Carnegie's steel plants near Pittsburgh.

In 1901, Carnegie sold out to financier J.P. Morgan for the staggering sum of $447 million. In his later years, he gave away more than $300 million of his fortune through philanthropies that included building 2,811 public libraries and donating 8,000 organs to churches.

Refining (and controlling) oil

In the 1850s, whale oil — the primary fuel for providing light — had become very expensive, and people began to look for an alternative. Gradually, drilling for oil became practical enough that kerosene made from refined petroleum began replacing whale oil.

The most famous — or infamous — of the oil men was John D. Rockefeller, a Cleveland businessman who had made some money during the Civil War selling meat and grain. In 1870, Rockefeller combined five companies he owned into the Standard Oil Company. A ruthless and brilliant businessman, Rockefeller either bought up the competition or drove it out of business by undercutting prices. Political bribery was also a standard tool of Standard Oil: One critic noted that Rockefeller "had done everything to the Pennsylvania legislature except refine it." By 1879, Standard Oil controlled 90 percent of the nation's refining capacity, a huge network of pipelines, and large oil reserves, and by 1892, Rockefeller had amassed a fortune of $800 million.

Getting wired for sound and light

New industries were also springing up around new inventions. In 1876, a teacher of the deaf, Alexander Graham Bell, invented the telephone. By 1880, 85 cities and towns had phone networks, and by 1900, more than 800,000 telephones were in place throughout the country.

In 1879, inventor Thomas A. Edison came up with a practical electric light bulb. Over the next 20 years, America began to wire up. At first, direct current (DC) was used, but DC didn't work over distances of more than a few miles. Then a man named George Westinghouse began using alternating current (AC), which allowed high voltage to be sent long distances through transformers and then reduced to safer levels as it entered buildings. Switching from steam engines to electricity made factories safer and more efficient, too.

The real thing

John Pemberton was an Atlanta pharmacist, but he was also a man with a vision: He wanted to make the perfect drink. So he came up with a syrup that combined the coca leaf and the kola nut. Mixing it in a big kettle, he lugged it down to a local drugstore, where he sold it for five cents a glass — and averaged nine sales a day.

Pemberton died in 1888, and the formula for "Coca-Cola" (a name created by Pemberton's bookkeeper from the two main ingredients) was sold to a clever marketing man named Asa B. Candler. Candler realized that advertising was the key to making the product a national brand, and devoted an unheard-of $50,000 a year to marketing the drink. Other executives who followed him perfected distribution and bottling techniques, and today billions of bottles and cans of "Coke" are sold in more than 150 countries.

PS: Among other things, Pemberton claimed his drink could cure headaches and dyspepsia. He made no rash claims about diet dyspepsia.

Forming trusts and striking against them

In 1882, Standard Oil organized the first of the nation's trusts. A *trust* oversaw virtually all of an industry's operations, from production to price-setting to distribution and sales. It was supposedly run not by a single company, but by trustees. A trust issued certificates to stockholders in the industry's companies and paid dividends. Virtual monopolies like Standard Oil could then argue that they didn't control an industry; the trust did.

Monopolies weren't all bad. Because of the economies of doing business on a large scale, costs could be kept down and prices lowered. The price of kerosene, for example, dropped a fair amount after Standard Oil dominated the market. Of course with no competition, prices were at the mercy of the monopolies and could — and often did — swing up again. In addition, the sheer size and power of the monopolies were worrisome to some Americans.

Carnegie and other giants of capitalism immodestly preached the "Gospel of Wealth," arguing that it was natural for a few people to have most of the wealth, a sort of economic "survival of the fittest." As long as they used their fortunes to benefit society, they contended there was nothing wrong with it.

But opening libraries and donating church organs didn't put bread on the table of the average working guy. Labor unions began to try to do that after the Civil War by organizing on a large scale. Most notable were groups called the Knights of Labor and the American Federation of Labor (AFL). In 1877, America faced its first national labor strike when railroad workers walked off the job after wages were cut. State and federal troops were called in, hundreds of strikers were killed or wounded, and service was restored at the point of a gun.

Caveat emptor, chump

"Let the buyer beware; that covers the whole business. You cannot wet-nurse men from the time they are born until the time they die. They have to wade, and get stuck, and that is the way men are educated." —Sugar baron Henry O. Havemeyer, to a congressional committee investigating the sugar industry, 1895.

In May 1886, an AFL strike for an eight-hour day for workers led to a clash at Chicago's Haymarket Square between police and strikers. A bomb killed 7 cops and injured 67 others. The police, who had killed four strikers the day before, fired into the crowd and killed four more. Seven strike leaders were eventually convicted and four were hanged. The incident was condemned by anti-union forces as an example of how the labor movement was controlled by "anarchists" and "radicals."

In 1894, a strike against the Pullman railroad car company spread over 27 states and paralyzed the country's railroads. Federal troops were called out, and a court order ended the strike. The Haymarket Square riot and Pullman strike dealt severe blows to the chances of things getting better for the average working stiff through labor unions. America was progressing, but not all of its citizens were.

Samuel L. Clemens

He was a printer, a prospector, a Confederate army deserter, a riverboat pilot, a world traveler, a lecturer, an inventor, and an investor. Oh yeah, he could write a little too.

Born in 1835 in Missouri, Clemens grew up on the banks of the Mississippi River. After various careers, Clemens settled on journalism, working for newspapers in Nevada and California. His humor-laden dispatches, written under the pen name "Mark Twain" (which in riverboat parlance meant "safe water"), became very popular in the East.

Starting in 1869, Clemens wrote a series of short stories, travel books, autobiographical works, and novels that established him as America's most celebrated man of letters. He was also one of the country's fiercest critics. He termed the post–Civil War period "The Gilded Age" for its venality and corruption. Despite his criticisms, however, Clemens was himself caught up in the chase for wealth, and made and lost several fortunes. At the time of his death in 1910, he was one of the best-known people in the world. His works were translated into more than 70 languages, and he was lionized as "the Lincoln of our literature."

populated by others from their country. The presence of so many immigrants in so short a time caused alarm in some "natives," who feared the newcomers would weaken their chances in the job market and pollute American culture. But it wasn't until 1921, after World War I had created millions of refugees in Europe, that Congress tightened immigration policies concerning Europeans.

In the meantime, as much as 80 percent of the immigrant wave settled in Northern cities. By the turn of the century, more than a third of Chicago's populace was foreign-born, and there were more Irish in New York City than there were in Ireland. The immigrants weren't the only newcomers in town, because there were plenty of American-born country folks moving to urban areas, as well. By 1900, 30 million Americans lived in cities, about a third of all U.S. residents. The number of cities larger than 100,000 increased from 9 to 50 between 1860 and 1910.

But many parts of the big cities were festering sores. In those areas, fire protection, street cleaning, sewage systems, garbage collection, and water treatment barely existed. The Chicago River was an open sewer. Baltimore's sewers emptied into the tidal basin and in the summer heat, journalist H. L. Mencken wrote, it "smelled like a billion polecats."

Housing was often designed to cram the most people into the least space. It wasn't uncommon for 24 four-room apartments to be built on a 2,500-square-foot lot. Tenement slums took on fitting names, such as "Hell's Kitchen," "Bone Alley," or "Poverty Gap."

Gradually, things improved in the major urban areas. No one, rich or poor, wanted to live in filth, and after the link between disease and poor sanitation was firmly established, city leaders began to develop adequate sewage and water systems. Public transit systems, based on streetcars or trolleys, were put in place. But none of it happened overnight, and more than a few farmers-turned-city-dwellers must have yearned more than once to be home on the range.

Slum life

"All the fresh air that enters these stairs comes from the hall-door that is forever slamming.... The sinks are in the hallway, that all tenants may have access — and all be poisoned alike by the summer stenches.... Here is a door. Listen! That slow, hacking cough, that tiny helpless wail — what do they mean? The child is dying of measles. With half a chance, it might have lived; but it had none." —Reporter Jacob Riis, in "How the Other Half Lives," 1890.

Inventing Big Business

As America reached young adulthood in the last part of the 19th century, it began to shake off its rural roots and become an industrial city slicker. From 1859 to 1899, the value of the country's manufactured products rose 622 percent, from $1.8 billion to $13 billion, and America became the world's leading manufacturer. It rode its way to the top on the train.

Building the railroads

The railroad system was America's first truly big business and its growth and impact were enormous. In the 41 years from 1830 to 1870, about 40,000 miles of track were laid in the country. But in the 20 years from 1871 to 1890, more than 110,000 miles were laid. In 1869, the first transcontinental line linking the East and West coasts was opened, and by 1900, there were four more.

By 1890, annual railroad freight revenues totaled $1 billion — which was more than twice what the federal government gathered yearly in revenue. The railroads not only transported goods and people, they dictated where towns would grow and businesses would locate. They employed more than one million people by 1900. They helped push Congress to create four standard time zones across the country so train schedules could be worked out.

The railroads created or greatly expanded other industries with their demands for materials like steel for rails and passenger and freight cars. And they helped speed development of America's telegraph system, because where the rails went, the wires went. With telegraph stations at most train stations, the Western Union Company was sending 40 million messages a year by 1883, over 400,000 miles of wire.

Despite all those grand and glorious numbers, the railroad boom wasn't exactly a shining example of American free enterprise at its best. The rails were laid mostly on public land given to the railroads by the federal government — more than 240,000 square miles, or an area the size of Germany — along with more than $60 million in taxpayer-financed grants or loans.

Because the federal government didn't want to get directly in the railroad-building business, the land was thought of as an incentive to attract private investment. The idea was that the railroad companies would sell most of the land near their tracks, and that's where they would make their money, because rail operations alone weren't expected to turn a profit for years.

"A Splendid Little War"

When Cuba revolted against Spain in 1868, most Americans weren't very interested. But in 1898, when the Caribbean island rebelled again, America took notice. The difference was that by 1898, the United States was Cuba's best customer for its sugar and tobacco crops, and its biggest investor. So when the fighting destroyed American property in Cuba, the country's interest was aroused.

Some Americans wanted to free Cuba from Spanish oppression. Some wanted to protect U.S. economic interests, and others saw it as a chance to pick off some of Spain's colonies for America.

The anti-Spain flames were fanned by New York newspapers that tried to outdo each other in reporting about Spain's "atrocities." "You furnish the pictures," New York publisher William Randolph Hearst told an illustrator for his *New York Journal,* "and I'll furnish the war."

In January 1898, the U.S. battleship *Maine* was sent to Havana when it was reported that American lives were in danger. On February 15, the *Maine* mysteriously exploded, killing 260 U.S. sailors and officers. By April, America and Spain were at war.

It was, in the words of one American official, "a splendid little war." In the Philippines, a U.S. fleet commanded by Commodore George Dewey blasted a Spanish fleet and U.S. soldiers easily took the islands. Cuba took a little longer to conquer, but the Spanish forces there also fell. The four-month war cost 5,642 American lives, all but 379 to disease. And a grown-up America now had the makings of an empire on its hands.

How are ya, Hawaii?

The islands of Hawaii have always been a great place to visit for Americans. Yankee traders visited there in the 1790s. In the 1840s, the islands were home to American whaling ships. And by 1860, many U.S. citizens owned land there.

In 1875, America dropped a ban on Hawaiian sugar that had been urged by U.S. sugar growers and became the islands' best customer; and in 1887, Hawaii granted America exclusive rights to use Pearl Harbor as a coaling station and repair base for U.S. ships.

But making Hawaii a U.S. territory took some doing. In 1893, white businessmen led a successful rebellion against Queen Liliuokalani. The rebels promptly petitioned to be annexed to the United States. But Pres. Grover Cleveland rejected the offer. The new Hawaiian government asked again in 1897, but this time the Senate rejected it. Finally, in 1898, Hawaii became a U.S. territory. In 1959, it became the 50th state.

> ### Nickel-and-diming it
>
> The growth of the cities helped spark the development of retail stores designed to do a high volume of business by selling low-cost goods. In February 1879, a self-described "boob from the country" of upstate New York, named Frank W. Woolworth, opened the "Great Five-Cent Store" in Utica, New York. During its first months, it took in a grand total of $2.50 a day.
>
> Undismayed, Woolworth figured his store was just in a bad location and opened another in Lancaster, Pennsylvania. It featured a "5-cent counter" in the front of the store that was supposed to lure customers in the door, where they might buy some higher-priced items.
>
> The idea worked. By 1900, Woolworth had 59 stores, and by 1913, he was wealthy enough to pay $13.5 million in cash to construct what was then the tallest building in the world, the Woolworth Building in Manhattan. By the way, that's 270 million nickels.

Electing a String of Forgettable Presidents

America has had good presidents and bad presidents, but it's doubtful it has ever had as many mediocre presidents in a row as it did between 1876 and 1900. It wasn't a case of boring elections. Party splits and factions, and the fact that winners got to milk the government for jobs, made for intense and nasty campaigns. There were plenty of big issues, too, from tariffs to bank panics to civil service reform. The men elected to deal with them, however, were a forgettable bunch. Here they are, before I forget them:

- **Rutherford B. Hayes** (Republican, 1877–1881): Hayes was a Civil War hero who was very politically cautious. He hated making tough decisions, so he avoided them. The Democrats controlled Congress most of the time he was president, so he accomplished little. He chose not to run for a second term and might not have been nominated anyway.

- **James A. Garfield** (Republican, 1881): Garfield was assassinated by a disgruntled office seeker four months after taking office. He was also the last president to be born in a log cabin.

- **Chester A. Arthur** (Republican, 1881–1885): Arthur was a lifelong politician who never won an election, except as Garfield's running mate. He was a fairly dignified and businesslike president, but he accomplished little.

- **Grover Cleveland** (Democrat, 1885–1889 and 1893–1897): Cleveland was the only president to serve two non-consecutive terms and the only one to have personally hanged a man. He accomplished the latter feat as sheriff in Buffalo, New York. He managed the former by losing his reelection bid in 1888 to Benjamin Harrison, and then defeating Harrison in 1892. Cleveland was elected the first time despite the revelation that he fathered a son by a woman he never married. His second term was marked by an economic depression. He didn't win nomination for a chance at a third term.

- **Benjamin Harrison** (Republican, 1889–1893): Harrison was the grandson of Pres. William Henry Harrison. Six new states — Washington, Idaho, Montana, Wyoming, North Dakota, and South Dakota — were admitted during his administration. That was pretty much it.

- **William McKinley** (Republican, 1897–1901): By most accounts, McKinley was a nice guy. He was an Ohio congressman and governor and very devoted to his invalid wife. He also had friends in high places, especially political boss Mark Hanna. Hanna and others helped elect McKinley president. He defeated Democrat-Populist William Jennings Bryan in 1896, and again in 1900. He was assassinated by a crazy anarchist named Leon Czolgosz in 1901. As he lay wounded, McKinley urged that his killer not be harmed. But they executed him in the electric chair anyway.

The Rise of Populism

Times were tough on the farm in the 1890s. Crop prices fell as production rose. Credit was hard to get and interest rates were high. Many of the rural areas' best and brightest had taken off to seek their fortunes in the cities.

These hard times triggered a political movement called *Populism*. Populists sought higher crop prices and lower interest rates. They wanted a system where farmers could deposit crops in storage facilities and use them as collateral for low-interest government loans.

They also wanted more money put into circulation and more silver coins made. The idea was that more money in circulation would raise prices, while their mortgage payments would stay the same. But it was also risky. Money based on the amount of gold reserves the country had was more stable than money based on silver, because the amount of silver reserves was increasing and therefore could "cheapen" the value of money as the price of silver dropped.

Republicans generally opposed the Populist ideas, while Democrats generally lined up with the Populists. The Democrats nominated 36-year-old Nebraska Congressman William Jennings Bryan as their 1896 presidential candidate. Bryan, an outstanding orator, gave a rousing speech at the Democratic convention in favor of "free silver," by exclaiming "you shall not crucify mankind upon a cross of gold." But Bryan lost to Republican William McKinley anyway, in large part because McKinley's supporters raised and spent $3 million on his campaign.

Chapter 13

Growing into the 20th Century: 1899–1918

In This Chapter

- Winning colonies from Spain
- Bringing in Teddy Roosevelt
- Improving conditions across America
- Getting America in the air and on the road
- Fighting for women's right to vote
- Hunting for jobs in the North, African-American style
- Joining World War I with Woodrow Wilson

As the 1800s turned into the 1900s, America had just won a short and sloppily fought, but easily won, war with Spain. As a result, the country found itself, for the first time in its history, with an overseas empire formed by the colonies it won from Spain.

This chapter covers how America reacted to its new role as a force to be reckoned with in the world, and how Americans handled changes in how they worked, how they got around, and how they governed themselves.

Here Today, Guam Tomorrow: Colonizing Spain's Lands

At the end of the 19th century, the American government suddenly had a lot more territory to take care of. There was Hawaii, which was formally annexed in 1898, and also Guam, Puerto Rico, and the Philippines, which were all won from Spain. Cuba was technically free, but because of restrictive treaties, it was in reality an American fiefdom.

On February 6, 1899, the U.S. Senate ratified the treaty with Spain that gave the U.S. Guam and Puerto Rico. The Spanish threw in the Philippines, too, after American negotiators offered $20 million for the islands. The Senate vote on the treaty was 57 to 27 — only two more than the two-thirds needed. The close vote mirrored a sharp division of opinion about whether it was a good idea for America to have colonies.

Arguing about American imperialism

Imperialism is a political idea that sounds something like this: "We can run your country better than you can because we have a better system of government." In practical terms, imperialists also view occupied territory as a sort of automatic teller machine for withdrawals of natural resources, or as a great place for strategically located military bases.

In June 1898, opponents to the idea of American colonies formed the Anti-Imperialist League, a group of strange bedfellows that included author Mark Twain, steel tycoon Andrew Carnegie, and labor leader Samuel Gompers. The folks who opposed imperialism all had different reasons for their opposition. Some believed it was un-American to impose American culture or government on other people. Others were afraid of "mingling" with "inferior" races. Laborers feared competition from poorly paid workers in other countries, and conservative business leaders feared foreign entanglements would divert capital.

Proponents, led by Theodore Roosevelt, who was then the governor of New York, argued that annexation would open the Orient for U.S. business. He said it would also prevent other nations from seizing the former Spanish colonies, and better position the United States as a world military power. Pres. William

---

Fighting with the Filipinos

After suffering under Spanish rule for 350 years, Filipinos weren't keen on a continuance of domination by a foreign country. Theirs was an antipathy that led to what is perhaps America's least-known war.

In 1899, led by Emilio Aguinaldo, Filipino *insurrectos* who had fought alongside U.S. troops against the Spanish now took up arms against their former allies. Aguinaldo commanded an army of about 80,000. Many of the insurrectos lacked weapons other than spears or machetes, so the Filipinos resorted to guerilla warfare and terrorism. American soldiers responded with a vengeance, torturing and executing prisoners and burning entire villages.

After four years of fighting, 4,230 Americans and more than 25,000 Filipinos had been killed. After Aguinaldo was captured and took an oath of allegiance to the United States, the fighting ended. A U.S. judge named William Howard Taft (who would later become the 27th president of the United States) took over as civilian governor of the islands. Taft gave the Filipinos wide latitude in governing themselves. But formal U.S. control didn't end until July 4, 1946.

McKinley opined it was America's duty to "educate the Filipinos and uplift and civilize and Christianize them," conveniently ignoring the fact that most Filipinos were already Roman Catholic. Such attitudes sparked a war with the newly liberated Filipinos. The war took several years and thousands of casualties on both sides before the United States prevailed.

Keeping a high profile in international affairs

To a large extent, the nasty fight in the Philippines soured the American appetite for imperialism. But protecting U.S. business interests overseas remained a priority, and a strong feeling still existed that the country needed to maintain a high profile in international affairs. No one felt that way more strongly than McKinley's new vice president, Theodore Roosevelt. McKinley's original vice president, Garret Hobart, had died in late 1899, and Republican Party leaders added the headstrong Roosevelt to McKinley's ticket in 1900 mainly as a way to shut him up in the obscurity of the vice presidency.

But on September 6, 1901, while visiting the Pan-American Exposition in Buffalo, New York, McKinley was shot by a self-proclaimed anarchist. The president died a week later, and Roosevelt moved into the spotlight.

"Now look!" cried GOP political boss Mark Hanna of McKinley's death and Roosevelt's succession to the presidency. "That damned cowboy is President of the United States!"

Making a Lot of Noise and Carrying a Big Stick: Roosevelt Takes Office

Depending on whether you liked him or not, Theodore Roosevelt was either the energetic embodiment of the nation he led, or a macho blowhard who really should have taken more cold showers.

A puny, asthmatic child, Roosevelt literally built himself into a human dynamo with strenuous exercise and a nonstop personal regimen. His walrus mustache, thick round spectacles, and outsized teeth made him a political cartoonist's dream (see Figure 13-1). However, his relative youth — at 43, he was the youngest president the country had ever had — his energy, and his unpredictability made him the bane of GOP political bosses.

Figure 13-1: Political cartoonists had fun with Theodore Roosevelt's appearance and personality.

THE MAN WHO CAN MAKE THE DIRT FLY.

© Bettmann/CORBIS

Roosevelt was fond of repeating an old African proverb that suggested "Speak softly, and carry a big stick; you will go far." In practice, however, he was much fonder of the stick than of speaking softly. A leading imperialist under McKinley, Roosevelt relished America's role as policeman to the world — and he took great advantage of his position as the top cop. In 1903, for example, Roosevelt encouraged Panama to revolt against Colombia so the United States could secure rights from the Panamanians to build the Panama Canal. In 1905, he brokered the treaty that settled a war between Russia and Japan, for which he won a Nobel Peace Prize. (In 2001, Roosevelt was posthumously awarded the Congressional Medal of Honor for his service in the war with Spain — the only man to win the top prize for peace and war.)

Roosevelt set the tone for presidents who followed him. Both William Howard Taft and Woodrow Wilson had their own versions of *gunboat diplomacy* (using the force, or threat of force, to help negotiations along), particularly in Latin America.

For example, in 1912, Taft sent U.S. Marines to Nicaragua after a revolution there threatened American financial interests. In 1915, when Wilson was commander in chief, U.S. troops went to Haiti when revolution began to

The Panama Canal

Roosevelt considered the construction of the Panama Canal his greatest accomplishment as president. And so did a lot of sea-goers. After all, it cut 7,800 miles off the voyage from New York to San Francisco by eliminating the necessity to sail around the tip of South America. The canal took about 10 years to build and cost $380 million. That cost broke down to about $7.5 million for each of its 50.72 miles. At the height of construction in 1913, more than 43,400 people were working on the canal; approximately 75 percent of these laborers were from the British West Indies. Hundreds of workers died from disease or accidents. About 240 million cubic yards of earth were moved during construction.

bubble; the troops stayed until 1934. Also in 1915, Wilson sent U.S. Army troops into Mexico under Gen. John J. "Black Jack" Pershing. The troops were to chase Mexican revolutionary Francisco "Pancho" Villa, who had raided American territory. The "punitive expedition" (as it was referred to by the War Department) almost triggered a war with Mexico and added to a widely held notion in the rest of the hemisphere that Uncle Sam was something of a bully. The expedition was also an example of a U.S. tendency to get involved in other countries' affairs. The tendency, which sprang sometimes from idealism and sometimes from pure self-interest, would last the rest of the 20th century.

The World Series

For 25 years, the National Baseball League had squashed all challenges to it as *the* only major organization when it came to the national pastime. In 1901, however, a tough and savvy longtime minor-league executive named Byron Bancroft "Ban" Johnson started an eight-team league of his own, with franchises in major cities. Johnson's new American League lured many of the National League's top stars away with higher salaries. Forced to match salaries to keep its best players, the National League sued for peace and signed a National Baseball Agreement in January 1903, recognizing the American League as an equal.

As part of the deal, the leagues agreed to stage a postseason "world" championship between the pennant winners in each league. The first of these, a best-of-nine-games affair, was played in October 1903 between the National League's Pittsburgh Pirates and the American League's Boston Red Sox. To the shock of most baseball fans, the upstart league's Red Sox won, 5 games to 3.

Progressing toward Political and Social Reform

While America was busy reforming other countries, a burgeoning movement for reforms was in full swing at home, in virtually every business and social institution. At the core of the effort was a loose and diverse coalition of journalists, politicians, and single-cause crusaders who, because they sought progress, were called *Progressives*. These Progressives helped turn the first two decades of the century into what's known as the *Progressive Era*.

The "muckrakers" expose evil and initiate change

The first step in many of the causes undertaken by the Progressives was in exposing particular evils. This was often done by reporters and writers who looked into everything from machine politics to child labor to the preparation of food. Roosevelt dubbed them "muckrakers," after a character in the 17th century allegorical novel *Pilgrim's Progress*, who constantly cleaned up the moral filth around him.

While journalists had written exposés for years, the muckrakers' impact was magnified by the fact that they were often published in a fairly new medium: the popular (and cheap) magazine. The magazines included *McClure's, The Saturday Evening Post,* and the *Ladies' Home Journal.* The muckrakers included Ida Tarbell, who exposed the inner workings of the Standard Oil monopoly; Lincoln Steffens, who wrote about the corruption of many big-city governments; and Upton Sinclair, whose novel on meatpacking practices in Chicago, called *The Jungle,* made the entire country queasy.

The muckrakers were joined in their quest for reforms by political figures at the local, state, and national levels, such as California Governor and then-U.S. Senator Hiram Johnson, Mayor Tom Johnson of Cleveland, and Governor Robert LaFollette of Wisconsin.

When the Progressives couldn't prevail over entrenched corrupt political machines, they sought to change the rules, pushing for reforms such as

- **Direct primary elections:** Voters — not bosses — picked party nominees
- **The initiative:** Allowed voters to circumvent balky legislatures and propose laws directly
- **The recall:** A means of removing officials before their terms expired
- **The referendum:** Voters could repeal unpopular laws

Anyone for vegetables?

"There would be meat that had tumbled out on the floor, in the dirt and sawdust where workers had tramped and spit uncounted billions of consumption germs. There would be meat stored in great piles in rooms; and the water from leaky roofs would drip over it, and thousands of rats would race about on it . . . a man could run his hand over these piles of meat and sweep off handfuls of the dried dung of rats. These rats were nuisances, and the packers would put out poisoned bread for them, they would die, and then rats, bread and meat would go into the hoppers together." —Upton Sinclair, writing in *The Jungle* about meatpacking practices in Chicago.

Improving working conditions — and other people's drinking habits

Other groups, meanwhile, fought to improve working conditions for women and children, secure welfare assistance for widows, and get insurance for workers who were hurt in industrial accidents. Spurred mainly by fundamentalist religious groups in the South and Midwest and women's temperance groups, a decade-long effort to abolish the production and sale of alcoholic beverages gained momentum, culminating in the 18th Amendment — also referred to as "Prohibition" — which went into effect on January 16, 1920. The amendment was repealed in 1933. (See Chapter 14 to find out why.)

One of the Progressives' ideas was that people who made more money could afford to pay more taxes. A federal income tax had been tried before — once during the Civil War and once during the hard economic times of 1894 — but neither attempt was successful. In fact, the U.S. Supreme Court, on a 5 to 4 vote, struck down the 1894 effort as unconstitutional. The 16th Amendment, which was pushed by Progressives, was proposed in 1909 and ratified in 1913. This amendment gave Congress the power to slap a federal tax on income, which it promptly did. Congress required a 1 percent tax on annual income above $4,000, and a 2 percent tax on income above $20,000. Of course, the rates have gone up since.

The result of all this progress was impressive, and included

- **The Meat Inspection Act and Pure Food and Drug Act in 1906:** This act created new rules and regulations for the preparation and handling of food and medicine.
- **The breakup of monopolies:** The bank and beef monopolies ended in 1907 and the Standard Oil trust came to a halt in 1911.

- **The Federal Reserve Act of 1913:** This act divided the country into 12 districts, each with its own bank and board of directors. This division helped to better oversee banking practices and policies and prevent panics and bank failures.
- **The 17th Amendment in 1913:** This amendment provided for the direct election of U.S. Senators instead of having them selected by state legislatures.

Contracting Labor Pains

While the nation generally prospered in the early 20th century, it was by no means a uniform prosperity. For every oil millionaire or steel tycoon in 1900, there were hundreds of thousands of people making the average annual wage of $400 to $500 — about $100 less than was needed to maintain what was deemed a "decent" standard of living. To make matters worse, the working conditions for these people were often miserable.

Struggling in a changing workforce

A change was occurring in the U.S. workforce. As manufacturing expanded, jobs moved from the farm to the factory. In 1900, for example, there were about 10 million farm-related jobs as opposed to about 18 million nonfarm jobs. By 1920, there were still about 10 million farm-related jobs, but there were more than 30 million jobs not related to agriculture. Women held 20 percent of all manufacturing jobs, and 1.7 million children under the age of 16 had full-time jobs.

"Full-time" meant just that. In the Pittsburgh steel mills, for example, 10-year-old boys were paid 14 cents an hour to work 12 hours a day, six days a week. Factory conditions were often horrendous. Between July 1906 and June 1907, 195 people died in the steel mills of Pittsburgh — about one person every other day. In 1911, 146 workers, most of them women, were killed when a fire roared through the Triangle Shirtwaist Factory in New York. Casualties were high because fire exits had been locked to keep workers from sneaking out for breaks.

Bosses know best

"I beg of you not to be discouraged. The rights and interests of the laboring man will be protected and cared for — not by the labor agitators, but by the Christian men to whom God in His infinite wisdom has given control of the property interests of this country." —George F. Baer, president of the Philadelphia and Reading Coal & Iron Co., in response to a letter from a stockholder worried about a coal strike in 1902.

Initiating improvements to working conditions

Anxious to improve conditions, American workers increasingly tried to follow the example of the industrialists and combine into large groups — labor unions — to have strength through numbers. In 1904, the American Federation of Labor, which focused mainly on skilled workers, had 1.7 million members. The number grew to more than 4 million by 1920. But the unions often faced brutal reprisals from companies and law enforcement. In Ludlow, Colorado, a 1914 strike against the Colorado Fuel & Iron Company resulted in state militia and private police firing on strikers. Fourteen people were killed, eleven of which were children.

Sometimes the government intervened. In 1902, a strike of more than 800,000 coal miners dragged on for months when mine operators refused to negotiate. Fed up, President Roosevelt summoned both sides to Washington and threatened to send federal troops into the mines and appropriate the coal for the national good. Finally, a presidential commission granted the miners a raise and a shorter workday.

A more typical strike was the 1912 textile mill strike in Lawrence, Massachusetts. After a state law required mill owners to limit the weekly hours of women and children to 54, the owners responded by speeding up production paces and cutting wages by 32 cents a week — the price of eight loaves of bread. The International Workers of the World organized a strike of more than 10,000 men and women. After 63 days that included beatings by police, the killing of a

---

"The Wobblies"

Formed in 1905 by socialists and militant unionists, the Industrial Workers of the World (IWW) was a radical labor force that favored action rather than negotiations, and it often resorted to violence. For reasons somewhat unclear, the IWW was disparaged as "The Wobblies." Foes of the union also said IWW stood for "I Won't Work."

The group favored one all-encompassing union rather than many unions divided by craft or industry, and it targeted unskilled laborers, minorities, and women. Although it probably never had more than 150,000 members in any one year, the IWW had great influence on labor relations because of its zeal and the threat it posed to business owners. By the end of World War I, however, the union had become hugely unpopular because of its association with socialism, and it was all but defunct by 1920.

woman, the sending of strikers' children to other cities because strikers couldn't feed them, and a failed attempt to bomb one of the mills and frame the strike leaders, the owners gave in and granted the strikers all of their demands. Within a year, however, most of the concessions had been rescinded, and the pre-strike conditions returned. It would be at least another generation before unions became a national force.

Transporting America

Unions weren't alone in their aspirations for improving the lives of working-class Americans. In Detroit, a generally unlikable, self-taught engineer named Henry Ford decided that everyone should have an automobile, and, thus, the right to go where they wanted, when they wanted. So Ford's company began making one model in 1908 — the Model T. Contrary to popular belief that it only came painted black, it actually came in a choice of several colors (none of them black). And because of his assembly-line approach to putting them together, you could have it relatively cheaply.

Ford's plan was a good one. The price of a Model T dropped from $850 in 1908 to $290 by 1924. As prices dropped, sales went up. Sales went from 10,000 in 1909 to just under a million in 1921. Within two decades, Ford and other carmakers had indelibly changed American life. The average family could now literally get away from it all, which created a new sense of independence and self-esteem. Because of the availability of the automobile, new industries, from tire production to roadside cafes, sprang up. And by the end of the 1920s, it could be persuasively argued that the automobile had become the single most dominant element in the U.S. economy.

When it came to getting from here to there, others were looking up to the skies. In December 1903, two brothers who owned a bicycle shop in Dayton, Ohio, went to Kitty Hawk, North Carolina. There they pulled off the world's first powered, sustained, and controlled flights with a machine they had built. Fearful of losing their patent rights, Orville and Wilbur Wright didn't go public with their airplane until 1908, by which time other inventors and innovators were also making planes. Unlike the automobile, however, the airplane's popularity didn't really take off until after its usefulness was proved in World War I.

Suffering for Suffrage

By the time the 20th century arrived, American feminists had been seeking the right to vote for more than 50 years. Their desire was fanned even hotter in 1869, when African American males were given the right to vote through the 16th Amendment, while women of all races were still excluded.

One place where women were increasingly included was in the workplace. As the country shifted away from a rural, agrarian society to an industrial, urban one, more and more women had jobs — eight million by 1910. Moreover, they were getting better jobs. In 1870, 60 percent of working women were in domestic service. By 1920, it was only 20 percent, and women made up 13 percent of the professional ranks. Women were getting out of the house for more than just jobs, too. In 1892, membership in women's clubs was about 100,000. By 1917, it was more than one million. And women's increasing independence was reflected in the fact that the divorce rate rose from 1 in every 21 marriages in 1880 to 1 in 9 by 1916.

Because women had always had nontraditional roles in the West, it wasn't surprising that Western states and territories were the first to give females the right to vote: Wyoming in 1869, Utah in 1870, Washington in 1883, Colorado in 1893, and Idaho in 1896. By 1914, all the Western states except New Mexico had extended the voting franchise to women.

By 1917, the suffrage movement was building momentum (see Figure 13-2). In July of that year, a score of suffragists tried to storm the White House. They were arrested and taken to the county workhouse. Pres. Woodrow Wilson was unamused, but sympathetic, and pardoned them. The next year, a constitutional amendment — the 19th — was submitted to the states. When ratified in 1920, it gave women the right to vote in every state.

Jeannette Pickering Rankin

Jeanette Pickering Rankin was the first woman to serve in Congress and the only member who voted against both world wars. Born on a ranch near Missoula, Montana, in 1880, Rankin graduated from the University of Montana in 1902 and was a social worker before becoming a field secretary for the National American Woman Suffrage Association. After Montana approved the vote for women in 1914, Rankin decided in 1916 to run for one of the state's two seats in the House of Representatives as a Republican, and won. As a congresswoman, she was one of 56 members of Congress who voted against President Wilson's call for a war resolution in 1917.

As a result, she lost the race for a U.S. Senate seat in 1918, moved to Georgia, and devoted her energies to pacifist organizations. In 1940, Rankin returned to Montana, where she ran again for Congress and won — in time to be the lone member of either house to vote against war with Japan in 1941. She didn't run for reelection and died in California in 1973 at the age of 92.

Of Rankin's vote against two world wars, John F. Kennedy said: "Few members of Congress have ever stood more alone while being true to a higher honor and loyalty."

Hands off!

"A woman's body belongs to herself alone. It does not belong to the United States of America or any other government on the face of the earth." —Margaret Sanger, who first coined the term "birth control" and founded the first birth control clinic in the United States in 1916. In 1921, she organized the American Birth Control League, the forerunner of Planned Parenthood.

Figure 13-2: Women marching for the right to vote.

© CORBIS

Despite the significance of the 19th Amendment, many leaders of the women's movement recognized that the vote alone wouldn't give women equal standing with men when it came to educational, economic, or legal rights.

"Men are saying, perhaps, 'thank God this everlasting women's fight is over,'" said feminist leader Crystal Eastman after the 19th Amendment was ratified. "But women, if I know them, are saying, 'now at last we can begin.'"

Leaving the South: African Americans Migrate to Northern Cities

Women weren't the only Americans on the move. Between 1914 and 1918, more than 500,000 African Americans left the farms of the South for jobs in Northern cities. The movement was part of the "Great Migration," which stretched from the 1890s to the 1960s, and eventually resulted in more than 6 million black people leaving the South.

This migration was spurred first by the Jim Crow laws, the lynchings, and the poverty of the post–Civil War South. Then, as the war in Europe simultaneously sparked U.S. industrial expansion and cut off the flow of immigrant workers, Northern jobs opened up by the thousands. Henry Ford, for example, offered to pay the astronomical sum of $5 a day in his plants, and despite his racist views, he hired blacks. The black populations of Northern cities swelled. In Chicago, for example, the African American community grew from 44,000 in 1910 to 110,000 by 1920.

But moving North didn't mean that African Americans left racism behind. Many Northern whites resented their new neighbors. The resentment was fueled in 1915 when the wildly popular new movie, *The Birth of a Nation,* portrayed blacks as deranged and dangerous creatures who lorded their emancipation over white Southerners. Nor was there much interest in black issues among Progressive leaders. When a delegation of black leaders met with Pres. Woodrow Wilson in 1914 to protest segregation in federal offices, he all but pushed them out the door.

Racial unrest led to race riots. In 1917 in East St. Louis, Illinois, white rioters went on a rampage in the black community. When it was over, 39 blacks and 9 whites were dead. In the summer of 1919, more than 25 race riots broke out in cities across the country. The worst was in Chicago, where an incident at a segregated swimming beach sparked a six-day riot that resulted in 38 people dead and more than a thousand left homeless by riot-sparked fires. The beachfront riots didn't stop until federal troops were called in.

Still, when President Wilson called on Americans to "help make the world safe for democracy" in 1917, more than 375,000 African Americans entered the military. "If this is our country," explained black leader W.E.B. DuBois, "then this is our war." (For more information, check out *African American History For Dummies* by Ronda Racha Penrice, published by Wiley.)

W. E. B. DuBois

William Edward Burghart DuBois was decidedly not what most white Americans thought of when they thought about black Americans. He was born in 1868 to a poor but respected family in a Massachusetts town with a population that was less than 1 percent black; he had degrees from Harvard and the University of Berlin; he became one of the country's leading sociologists; and he was an eloquent orator and stylish writer.

DuBois was best known for his forceful disagreements with another African-American leader, Booker T. Washington. These disagreements were most famously expressed in DuBois's 1903 book, *The Souls of Black Folk*. Washington stressed self-help and material gain over seeking equal legal and social rights with whites, but DuBois believed Washington's approach would only continue black oppression. In 1905, DuBois took a leading role in the Niagara Movement, the forerunner of the National Association for the Advancement of Colored People (NAACP), which he helped found in 1909. Disillusioned with the direction of the NAACP, he resigned in 1934. From 1934 to 1944, he was head of the Department of Sociology at Atlanta University and has been called the Father of American Sociology. He died in Ghana in 1963, at the age of 95.

The War to End All Chapters

Theodore Roosevelt had been president nearly eight years by the time of the 1908 election, having filled most of the assassinated McKinley's second term and winning his own term in 1904. Even though there were no term limits to stop him, Roosevelt decided not to run in 1908. Instead, he gave his blessing to William Howard Taft, a fellow Republican. But in 1912, Roosevelt became restless and decided to run against Taft, as the candidate of the Progressive, or "Bull Moose," Party. Americans ended up choosing the Democrat in the race, a scholarly former president of Princeton University and son of the South named Thomas Woodrow Wilson.

Progressive in his domestic policies, Wilson was something of a cautious imperialist abroad. He subscribed to the idea that America had a leading role to play in world affairs; he just didn't want to fight about it. The country did get embroiled in a few Latin American fights, and Wilson did send troops into Mexico in 1916 after Mexican revolutionaries led by Pancho Villa raided into American soil. But as the European powers squared off in 1914 in what was to be four years of mind-numbingly horrific war, America managed to somewhat nervously mind its own business. Wilson, in fact, won reelection in 1916 using the phrase "he kept us out of war."

As time passed, however, the country began to side more often with Britain, France, and other countries that were fighting Germany. The sinking of the British passenger ship, *Lusitania,* by a German submarine in 1915, which resulted in the deaths of 128 Americans, inflamed U.S. passions against "the Huns." Propagandistic portrayals of German atrocities in the relatively new medium of motion pictures added to the heat. And finally, when it was revealed that German diplomats had approached Mexico about an alliance against the United States, Wilson felt compelled to ask Congress for a resolution of war against Germany. He got it on April 6, 1917.

The U.S. military was ill-prepared for war on a massive scale. Only about 370,000 men were in the Army and National Guard combined. Through a draft and enlistments, however, that number swelled to 4.8 million in all the military branches by the end of World War I.

At home, about half of the war's eventual $33 billion price tag was met through taxes; the rest was funded through the issuance of war bonds. Organized labor, in return for concessions such as the right to collective bargaining, agreed to reduce the number of strikes. Labor shortages drove wages up, which in turn drove prices up. But demand for goods and services because of the war soared, and the economy hummed along, despite government efforts to "organize" it.

In Europe, however, no one was humming. American troops, like their European counterparts before them, found that modern warfare was anything but inspiring. The first U.S. troops were fed into the lines as much to shore up the morale of the Allies as anything else. But by the time the Germans launched their last desperate offensive, in the spring of 1918, more than 300,000 American troops had landed in France. By the war's end in November, the number of Yanks had swelled to 1.4 million.

Led by Maj. Gen. John "Black Jack" Pershing, a celebrated veteran of the Spanish-American and Philippines wars, the U.S. forces, known as the American Expeditionary Force (AEF) fought off efforts by Allied commanders to push the AEF into a subordinate role as replacement troops.

The great "Spanish" flu of 1918

Despite conflict and war, civilians and soldiers around the world had at least one thing in common in 1918 — a killer flu. Erroneously dubbed "Spanish influenza" because it was believed to have started in Spain, it more likely started at U.S. Army camps in Kansas and may not have been a flu virus at all. A 2008 study by the National Institute of Allergy and Infectious Diseases suggested that bacteria might have caused the pandemic.

Whatever caused it, it was devastating. Unlike normal influenza outbreaks, whose victims are generally the elderly and the young, the Spanish flu often targeted healthy young adults. By early summer, the disease had spread around the world. In New York City alone, 20,000 people died. Western Samoa lost 20 percent of its population, and entire Inuit villages in Alaska were wiped out. By the time it had run its course in 1921, the flu had killed from 25 million to 50 million people around the world. More than 500,000 Americans died, which was a greater total than all the Americans killed in all the wars of the 20th century.

Starting with the battles of Cantigny, Chateau-Thierry, and Belleau Wood in France, the AEF proved itself an able force. In September 1918, the Americans launched an attack on a German bulge in the lines near Verdun, France. U.S. and French troops captured more than 25,000 prisoners, and the German military's back was all but broken. At the 11th hour of the 11th day of the 11th month of 1918, Germany called it quits, and the fighting stopped.

American losses — 48,000 killed in battle, 56,000 lost to disease — seemed trifling compared to the staggering costs paid by other countries. Germany lost 1.8 million people; Russia, 1.7 million; France, 1.4 million; Austria-Hungary, 1.2 million; and Britain, 950,000. "The War to End All Wars," as it was called, turned out to be just another test of humans' aptitude for killing other humans in large quantities.

Chapter 14

Gin, Jazz, and Lucky Lindy: 1919–1929

In This Chapter

- Pushing for the League of Nations
- Terrorizing minorities and turning immigrants away
- Electing Harding, Coolidge, and Hoover
- Making the rich richer and the poor poorer
- Creating a thriving popular culture
- Experimenting with Prohibition
- Looking to the stars and heroes of the 1920s

*W*ith World War I over, America turned its attention back toward itself — and it was kind of uneasy about what it saw. Things seemed to be happening at too fast a pace. Young people were challenging old ways. An attempt to make the country more moral with a prohibition on liquor had the opposite effect, and the economy was making some Americans rich (and causing a lot more to spend like they were rich).

In this chapter, I visit the heroes and villains of the 1920s, along with the rise of mass media and its impact on the country. It was only a decade-long trip, but it was a helluva ride.

Wilson Goes Out of His League for Peace

Nearly a year before World War I was over, President Woodrow Wilson had already come up with a plan of *14 Points,* in which he outlined his version of a peace treaty. Leaders of America's allies viewed it as both simplistic and overly optimistic. The French prime minister even sneered that because humankind couldn't keep God's Ten Commandments, it was unlikely that folks could keep Wilson's 14 Points.

But so eager was Wilson to play a major role in the making of peace that he did something no other American president had ever done: He left the country while in office. In December 1918, a month after the fighting ended, Wilson went to Paris to meet with the leaders of France, England, and Italy. The Big Four (which soon became the Big Three after the minister from Italy left in a snit) soon drafted a peace treaty that included *almost* nothing that Wilson wanted.

Instead, the Treaty of Versailles required Germany to accept the blame for the war, pay $15 billion to the winning countries, give up most of its colonies, and limit the future size of its military forces. But the treaty did include something Wilson *really* wanted: the formation of a League of Nations, whose members would promise to respect one another's rights and settle their differences through the league.

Wilson brought the treaty and the idea of the league back to America and presented them to the U.S. Senate for its constitutionally required approval. But the Democratic president was facing a Senate dominated by Republicans and led by Massachusetts Sen. Henry Cabot Lodge, chairman of the Foreign Relations Committee.

Lodge, California Sen. Hiram Johnson, and some other "isolationist" senators were adamantly against the idea of "foreign entanglements" like the league. Lodge used his position to both stall consideration of the treaty and offer amendments to it that would have watered it down somewhat.

If Wilson had agreed to go along with a few changes, he may have gained the two-thirds approval he needed. But Wilson stubbornly refused to negotiate. Each side dug in and launched thunderous attacks on the other. Wilson made more than 40 speeches in three weeks on an 8,000-mile journey around the country.

In the end, Wilson's valiant effort proved politically futile and personally tragic. In early October, he had a stroke. The next month, the Senate resoundingly rejected the league and the peace treaty. The Senate rejected it again in March 1920 when Democratic senators brought it back for reconsideration. America would go it alone for another generation, or until the next world war.

Peace plan now or war later

"I can predict with absolute certainty that within another generation there will be another world war if the nations of the world do not concert the method by which to prevent it." —Woodrow Wilson, during his tour to drum up support for the League of Nations, September 1917.

Restricting Immigration and Challenging the Natives

One of the reasons many Americans opposed joining a League of Nations was because they connected foreigners with domestic economic problems, even when there was little or no real connection. A 1919 economic mini boom created high inflation, which meant higher prices, which meant labor strife as millions of workers struck for higher wages. In 1919 alone, more than 3,500 strikes involving more than 4 million workers took place. Then the economy dropped sharply, unemployment soared, and Americans looked for someone to blame.

They found plenty of targets. One group was the communists. The Russian Revolution scared many Americans by demonstrating how an uprising by a small group of radicals could overthrow the government of a mighty nation. Actually, there were relatively few communists in America, and they wielded relatively little clout. But nearly every labor strike was denounced as communist-inspired. A series of bombs mailed to leading American capitalists like J. P. Morgan and John Rockefeller, as well as some elected officials and judges, also alarmed the country, even though few of the explosives reached their targets. It all added to what became known as the *Red Scare*.

The chief Red-hunter was U.S. Attorney General A. Mitchell Palmer, who had hopes of becoming president. In August 1919, Palmer created the General Intelligence Division within the Justice Department and put an ardent young anti-communist named J. Edgar Hoover in charge of it. On January 2, 1920, Palmer's agents arrested about 6,000 people — many of whom were U.S. citizens — in 33 cities. Some were held for weeks without bail. Many were beaten, and some were forced to sign confessions. But only 556 were eventually deported. When a gigantic communist uprising predicted by Palmer failed to materialize, the Red Scare, and his presidential hopes, deflated.

Closing the gate

The bad taste left by World War I also showed itself in anti-immigration feelings. Immigration increased from 110,000 in 1919 to 430,000 in 1920 and 805,000 in 1921. Fear that war-torn Europe would flood America led to the Emergency Quota Act of 1921. The act limited immigration from any one country to 3 percent of the number from that country already in the United States.

Later, in 1924, the quotas were cut to 2 percent, and all Japanese immigration was banned, an action that deeply humiliated and angered Japan. In 1929, Congress limited total immigration to no more than 150,000 per year. The fire under America's melting pot had cooled off considerably.

And we look stupid, too

"We are a movement of plain people, very weak in the matter of culture, intellectual support, and trained leadership.... It lays us open to the charge of being 'hicks' and 'rubes' and 'drivers of secondhand Fords.' We admit it." —Hiram Evans, Imperial Wizard of the Ku Klux Klan, 1926.

Return of the Klan

Xenophobia — the fear or hatred of strangers or foreigners — also showed itself in the resurgence of the Ku Klux Klan in the early 1920s. The Klan had all but died out by 1880, but it was revived in 1915 in Georgia and spread around the country. By 1924, it probably had 4.5 million members, many of them in the Midwest. Approximately 40,000 Klansmen marched in Washington, D.C., in August 1925. Both major political parties felt the organization's influence in local, state, and even national elections.

The new Klan targeted not only African Americans but also Latinos, Jews, Roman Catholics, socialists, and anyone else who didn't embrace the Klan's views of what was moral and patriotic.

But in 1925, an Indiana Klan leader was convicted of abducting and assaulting a young girl, who subsequently killed herself. The widely publicized scandal, coupled with exposés about how some Klan leaders had siphoned off funds from the group, led to a demise in its popularity. The klowns of the KKK never again approached their earlier influence.

Darwin versus God

The Klan's greatest influence developed in smaller cities and in rural areas. The repressive attitudes it catered to were also quick to embrace *fundamentalism,* or the idea that everything in the Bible was literally true. In 1925, fundamentalists pushed through the Tennessee legislature a law prohibiting the teaching of Darwin's theory of evolution in public schools.

When a young high school teacher named John Scopes decided to challenge the law, America had the show trial of the decade (and the basis for the play *Inherit the Wind*). Scopes was defended by Clarence Darrow, a great trial lawyer and a leader of the American Civil Liberties Union. William Jennings Bryan, the aging, thrice-defeated Democratic presidential candidate and famous orator, joined the prosecution.

American Faces: Aimee Semple McPherson

Aimee Semple McPherson preached glory and salvation instead of fire and brimstone; thought heaven would look like a cross between Washington, D.C., and Pasadena, California; and was adored by millions as *Sister*.

McPherson was born in 1890 in Canada. With her first husband, she became a missionary and toured the world, but when her husband died in China, she returned to America and married an accountant. That marriage fell apart, however, when McPherson refused to give up her evangelical career.

In 1921, she showed up in Los Angeles and started the Foursquare Gospel Mission. She opened the Angelus Temple in Los Angeles's Echo Park in 1923 and used brass bands, massive choirs, and fancy sets to draw nightly crowds in the thousands. She became a national figure, and people came from all over the country to hear her preach and to be "healed" by her touch.

While swimming at a local beach in 1926, McPherson disappeared. Thirty-seven days later, she reappeared with a story about being kidnapped and held in the Arizona desert before escaping. The story was a sensation, at first for its own sake and then when skeptical reporters suggested she had really been on a month-long tryst with a married man.

McPherson's popularity waned in the 1930s, but she continued to preach until 1944, when she died at the age of 53 from a possible accidental overdose of sleeping pills. The church she founded still uses Angelus Temple as its headquarters and claims a worldwide membership of nearly 8 million.

Bryan repeatedly ridiculed the idea that humans could be descended from apes. But he made a big mistake when he took the stand himself to defend the Bible. Under shrewd questioning by Darrow, Bryan admitted that parts of the Bible couldn't logically be interpreted literally. Scopes was found guilty anyway and fined $100, but the conviction was later overturned on a technicality. The trial took the wind out of the fundamentalist sails for a while, but debate over evolution and education has never fully left the American scene.

Warren, Cal, and Herbert: Republicans in the White House

Three Republicans succeeded Wilson as president in the 1920s — Warren G. Harding, Calvin Coolidge, and Herbert Hoover — and all three were firmly in favor of the status quo, or at least what the status quo was before the war.

Harding was a handsome, affable newspaper publisher and politician from Ohio. His record as a state legislator and U.S. senator was almost entirely without distinction, but he was a popular guy anyway — especially with newly enfranchised women voters — and was easily elected in 1920.

Harding's administration was ripe with scandal, much of it involving buddies he appointed to various offices. The worst scandal was called *Teapot Dome* and involved the secret leasing of public oil reserves to private companies by Harding's Secretary of Interior Albert B. Fall, in return for $400,000 in interest-free "loans."

Harding himself was never implicated in any of the scandals, but he suffered nevertheless. "I have no trouble with my enemies," he told a reporter, "but my damned friends . . . they're the ones that keep me walking the floor nights."

Harding died suddenly while visiting San Francisco in August 1923, probably of a stroke. (His wife inexplicably refused to allow an autopsy, so the exact cause was never established.) He was succeeded by Coolidge, his vice president.

Silent Cal, as he was called, was from Vermont and was quite possibly less interested in being president than any man who ever held the office. (But he did enjoy playing mean practical jokes on the White House staff and having his photo taken while wearing silly headgear.) After finishing out Harding's term, Coolidge was easily elected to his own term in 1924. His winning platform was that government should do what it could to promote private enterprise and then get out of the way.

"The man who builds a factory builds a temple," Coolidge pronounced. "The man who works there worships there." Coolidge fit the times perfectly. His philosophy was that not doing anything was the best course nine times out of ten. Most of the voting public didn't want or need anything from the federal government other than a military in time of war and someone to deliver the mail. Even though he wasn't exactly overworked in the job, Coolidge decided he had had enough in 1928 and chose not to run again.

In 1928, the country elected Hoover as president. He was an Iowa farm boy turned civil engineer who had won international kudos for organizing massive food programs for Europe after World War I. Hoover easily defeated New York Gov. Al Smith, extending Republican control of the White House. Like Harding and Coolidge, Hoover was a firm believer that America was on the right track economically.

"We in America are nearer to the final triumph over poverty than ever before in the history of the land," Hoover said. "We shall with the help of God be in sight of the day when poverty will be banished from the nation." As it turned out, he was wrong.

Marcus Garvey

Marcus Garvey was born in Jamaica, lived in New York and England, and wanted to go to Africa and take all of black America with him. The youngest of 11 children, Garvey moved to New York in 1916, started a newspaper, and organized a back-to-Africa movement he had begun in Jamaica, called the *Universal Negro Improvement Association*.

Garvey believed African Americans would never get a fair chance in America and should therefore go to Africa — a philosophy that, ironically, was enthusiastically supported by the Ku Klux Klan. He was openly contemptuous of whites, opposed interracial marriages, and denounced efforts by some African Americans to "look white" by using skin lighteners and hair straighteners.

Some black leaders thought Garvey — who liked to wear outlandish military-style uniforms in public — was a demagogue, but his appeal to black pride earned his efforts a large following. By the early 1920s, Garvey had more than 2 million followers. He used their financial support to start more than 30 black-owned businesses, including a steamship company that he hoped would help take African Americans to Liberia. But those plans fell apart when Liberia's government, fearful of a possible Garvey-led revolution, refused to deal with him.

In 1925, Garvey was convicted on what quite possibly were trumped up federal mail fraud charges. He served two years of his prison sentence, and then he was deported to Jamaica on orders of President Coolidge. When Garvey died in 1940 in England, he was largely forgotten. But his efforts helped form the roots of black pride and black nationalism that flourished later in the 20th century.

Good Times (Or Were They?)

One of the overriding themes sung by Harding and chorused by Coolidge and Hoover was "a return to normalcy," and nothing was more normal, as far as they were concerned, than the pursuit of financial wealth. So their administrations established policies that were designed to help that pursuit.

Helping the rich

Harding, Coolidge, and Hoover all reduced the national debt by cutting spending on government programs. They increased tariffs to protect U.S. manufacturing from foreign competition. They also cut taxes for the wealthy, arguing it would help create incentives for the rich to invest more, which would create more jobs, more products, and more wealth for everyone. And the Federal Reserve Board kept interest rates low so that those who weren't wealthy could borrow money to invest.

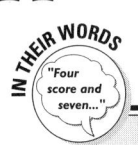

> ### Rich, or feeling like it
>
> "You can't lick this prosperity thing. Even the fellow that hasn't got any is all excited over the idea." —Will Rogers, American humorist, 1928.

These tactics seemed to work. Businesses became more productive by using new techniques that made workers and machinery more efficient. Chemical processes, for example, tripled the amount of gasoline that could be extracted from crude oil. Advances in electricity transmission sped development of larger manufacturing plants. U.S. manufacturing output rose 60 percent in the 1920s. And greater efficiency and productivity naturally translated to more profit for business owners.

Increasing American spending habits

The 1920s saw the rise of two elements that are still both banes and blessings to the American consumer: advertising and installment buying. Advertising was spurred by the development of national media, such as radio and popular magazines, which made it possible to reach audiences from coast to coast. It became a $1.25 billion-a-year industry by 1925.

In addition, the idea of buying *on time* — paying a little each week or month, plus interest — became more and more popular. Between 1920 and 1929, installment buying increased 500 percent. By 1929, more than 60 percent of American cars, large appliances, and pianos were being purchased on time.

The drive to sell government bonds during World War I made the average American more confident in buying securities like stocks and more willing to invest money rather than save it. The increased availability of capital enabled industries and retailers to expand, which in some cases meant lower prices. The Piggly Wiggly grocery store chain grew from 515 stores in 1920 to 2,500 in 1929; A&P grew from 4,621 stores to more than 15,000.

Making it difficult on the poor

Below the veneer of prosperity, there were indications of trouble. More and more wealth was being concentrated in fewer and fewer hands, and government did far more for the rich than the poor. It was estimated, for example, that federal tax cuts saved the hugely wealthy financier Andrew Mellon (who also happened to be Hoover's treasury secretary) almost as much money as was saved by all the taxpayers in the entire state of Nebraska.

Bruce Barton

Bruce Barton invented Betty Crocker, wrote one of the best-selling books of the 1920s, and proclaimed that "advertising is the very essence of democracy," even though he privately had doubts about its worth.

Born in Tennessee in 1886, Barton graduated from Amherst College in 1907 and had trouble finding a job. After a mediocre career as a writer and editor, Barton started a New York City advertising firm that eventually became Batten, Barton, Durstine & Osborn, one of the largest such companies in the world. It was a perfect 1920s fit: Barton had a genius for catchy phrases, and America had a big thirst for buying stuff. In addition to creating the ultimate housewife character in Betty Crocker, Barton ran campaigns for U.S. Steel, General Electric, and Lever Brothers, among others.

A deeply religious man, Barton also wrote books designed to renew the public's enthusiasm for religion. In 1925, he published *The Man Nobody Knows,* which portrayed Jesus Christ as a super salesman and a role model for businessmen. The book sold a stunning 700,000 copies in two years.

Even though he spent most of his life in advertising, Barton privately expressed misgivings as to whether much of it was wasteful and dishonest. Perhaps fittingly for a consummate pitchman, he spent two terms as a congressman from New York City. Barton died in 1967 at the age of 80.

Supreme Court decisions struck down minimum wage laws for women and children and made it easier for big businesses to swallow up smaller ones and become de facto monopolies. And union membership declined as organized labor was unable to compete with the aura of good times.

Probably worst off were American farmers. They had expanded production during World War I to feed the troops, and when demand and prices faded after the war, they were hit hard. Farm income dropped by 50 percent during the 1920s, and more than 3 million farmers left their farms for towns and cities.

For farmers in ten states along the Mississippi River and its tributaries, things were made tragically worse in 1927, when rains of biblical proportions triggered the most devastating river flood in U.S. history. More than 27,000 square miles of mostly agricultural land were inundated. At least 250 people were killed, and hundreds of millions of dollars in damage was done before the waters finally receded.

Most of those hit the hardest were poor farmers, and unfortunately for them, the affection the Harding, Coolidge, and Hoover administrations felt for business didn't extend to agriculture. Flood relief was scant and sporadic, and much of it was siphoned off to benefit white landowners in the region at the expense of African-American tenant farmers.

> ### Let's eat
>
> "Bell's Sunday Dinner, 12 noon to 9 p.m.: Radishes, olives, green onions, sliced tomatoes and mayonnaise, vegetable salad, rice and cocoanut fritters with vanilla sauce, roast young turkey with dressing and jelly, chicken fricassee with egg dumplings, fried Belgian hare and country gravy, prime ribs of beef, mashed potatoes, fresh string beans, fresh peach pudding, layer cake, assorted pies, coffee, tea, milk or buttermilk: 75 cents." —from a newspaper ad for a Sacramento, California, restaurant in 1925.

Coolidge also twice vetoed bills that would have created government-guaranteed minimum prices for some farm goods, an idea called *parity*. "Farmers have never made money," he explained. "I don't believe we can do much about it."

Ain't We Got Fun?

A lot of people think the Roaring Twenties was a decade in which everyone spent a huge amount of time dancing the Charleston and drinking. That, of course, isn't true. People also went to the movies, listened to the radio, read, and played games. The decade, in fact, was marked by an explosion of popular culture, pushed by the development of mass media, which was pushed by postwar advances in technology.

Going to the movies

By the mid-1920s, moviemaking was one of the top five industries in the country in terms of capital investment. A former farm community in California called Hollywood recently had become the film capital of the world. In 1928, America had 20,000 movie theaters, and movie houses that looked like ornate palaces and seated thousands of patrons were built in every major city. Millions of Americans flocked each week to see stars like Charlie Chaplin and Rudolph Valentino on the silent screen.

In 1927, with the release of *The Jazz Singer*, the screen was no longer silent, and "talkies" made the movies even more popular. Perhaps fittingly, the first words spoken in the first talkie were "Wait a minute! Wait a minute! You ain't heard nothin' yet!"

Movies and their stars had a huge impact on the culture of the '20s. They influenced fashion, hairstyles, speech patterns, and sexual mores — and reinforced cultural and racial stereotypes and prejudices.

Clara Bow

One producer said Clara Bow "danced even while she was standing still," and the writer F. Scott Fitzgerald called her "someone to stir every pulse in the nation." She was the movies' first true female sex symbol.

Bow was born in 1905 in Brooklyn to an alcoholic father and a mother so unbalanced she tried to cut Bow's throat when she learned her daughter was going into movies. By the time she was 25, Bow had already starred in almost 50 films and was making as much as $7,500 a week. Moreover, she was the ultimate 1920s flapper: the "It Girl" ("it" referring to sex appeal) who did what she wanted when she wanted with whom she wanted.

Personal scandals and the coming of sound to movies (she had a thick Brooklyn accent) marked the end of Bow's career by 1933. She married a cowboy star named Rex Bell (who later became lieutenant governor of Nevada) and was in and out of mental institutions until her death in 1965. Like many of her successors, it's questionable how much Bow really liked the role of femme fatale. "The more I see of men," she once observed, "the more I like dogs."

Listening to the radio

At the beginning of the 1920s, radio was entirely for amateurs. "Ham" operators listened mostly to messages from ships at sea over homemade sets. But in 1920, the Westinghouse Company in Pittsburgh established the first commercial radio station, KDKA. Almost overnight, stations sprang up all over the country. By 1924, there were more than 500 stations, and by 1927 the Radio Corporation of America (RCA) had organized a 19-station National Broadcasting Company (NBC).

Radio brought major sporting events and election returns "live" into American homes. It also encouraged the makers of soap, the sellers of life insurance, and the purveyors of cornflakes to reach out to consumers over the airwaves. U.S. business had its first true national medium for advertising, and Americans accepted that the price of "free" radio was commercials. By 1929, more than 12 million American families had radio sets.

Listening to music and writing literature

Radio, along with the increasing popularity of the phonograph, made popular music even more popular. The hottest sound was called *jazz,* which stressed improvisation and rhythm as well as melody. This sound had its roots deep in the musical traditions of African Americans. Its stars included Bessie Smith, Ferdinand "Jelly Roll" Morton, and Louis Armstrong, and it was a key part

> **IN THEIR WORDS**
>
> ### Radio? It stinks!
>
> "What have you done with my child? You have sent him out on the street in rags of ragtime to collect money... you have made him a laughingstock of intelligence, surely a stench in the nostrils of the gods of the ionosphere." —Dr. Lee De Forest, inventor and guiding force behind long-distance radio transmissions, objecting in 1928 to the commercialization of the medium.

of what became known as the *Harlem Renaissance,* a confluence of African-American genius in the arts that flourished in the 1920s in New York City. Jazz became wildly popular in other parts of the world as well and was recognized as the first truly unique form of American music.

Literature, on the other hand, was most heavily influenced by writers who were disillusioned with postwar America or who chose to satirize Americans' seeming penchant for conformity. These writers included novelists F. Scott Fitzgerald (*The Great Gatsby,* 1925), Sinclair Lewis (*Babbitt,* 1922), and Ernest Hemingway (*A Farewell to Arms,* 1929); playwright Eugene O'Neill (*Strange Interlude,* 1928); and poets E. E. Cummings, Carl Sandburg, and Langston Hughes.

Playing games

When it wasn't being entertained, America was seemingly entertaining itself in the 1920s, so much so that one contemporary observer called it "the age of play." Shorter workdays and weeks and more disposable income (or at least what seemed like more disposable income) gave Americans more time and money to enjoy themselves. Sports like golf and tennis boomed. Public playgrounds for kids became popular. Crossword puzzles and a game called Mah Jong were all the rage.

Drying Out America: Prohibition Begins

Even before the country's formal inception, Americans had been a hard-drinking bunch, and the social and private costs they paid for it had been high. But on January 16, 1920, the nation undertook a "noble experiment" to rid itself of the effects of "demon rum." It was called *Prohibition,* and it was a spectacular failure.

> ### Tiled out
>
> Parlor games have come and gone in American culture, but the Mah Jong craze of the 1920s may have been the only one to require costumes. An ancient Chinese game played with a set of 144 colored tiles, Mah Jong hit the West Coast in 1922 and soon became immensely fashionable across the nation. Many women refused to play, however, unless they were suitably attired in elaborate Oriental robes.
>
> So many Mah Jong sets were being produced at the height of the craze that Chinese manufacturers ran out of the traditional calf shins they made the tiles from. As a result, they were forced to ask Chicago slaughterhouses for cow bones. The fad faded after about five years of wild popularity. One possible reason was ennui created by confusion: By mid-decade, more than 20 different sets of rules for the game had been published.

There is some statistical evidence that Americans drank less after Prohibition started than they did before it began. But overall, the ban on booze was a bad idea. For one thing, it encouraged otherwise law-abiding citizens to visit *speakeasies* where alcohol was sold illegally. The number of "speaks" in New York City at the end of the decade, for example, was probably double the number of legal saloons at the beginning.

Gangsters like "Scarface" Al Capone and George "Bugs" Moran made fortunes selling bootleg booze, and they became celebrities doing it, despite the violence that was their normal business tool. Capone's Chicago mob took in $60 million a year at its peak — and murdered more than 300 people while doing it. But bullets weren't the gangsters' only tools. They also bought off or bullied scores of federal, state, and local officials to look the other way, which only added to public disrespect for law and government.

Part of the disrespect for government was well deserved. Even though Congress and a string of presidents paid lip service to the idea of Prohibition to make the anti-liquor lobby happy, many of the politicians were regular customers for the bootleggers. Congress provided only 1,550 federal agents to enforce the ban throughout the entire country, and criminal penalties for bootlegging were relatively light.

Changing Morals

At the time, many observers saw Americans' unenthusiastic support of Prohibition as an example of the country's slipping morals. So was the behavior of young people. Perhaps more than any generation before them, the youth of the 1920s embraced their own music, fashion, and speech. The automobile gave them a way to get away from home, at least temporarily, and also a place to be sexually intimate.

Other things contributed to the shifting moral patterns of the times: the sexy images from Hollywood, the growing availability of birth control devices, the use of sex by advertisers to sell everything from cars to toothpaste, and the growing emancipation of women.

There was no question, however, that the inequities between the sexes continued. Women made less than men in the same jobs and were still subject to a double standard that their place was in the home with the kids. But women now had the right to vote, and more and more of them were entering the workplace — from 8.4 million in 1920 to 10.6 million in 1930.

Short-haired, short-skirted young women — referred to as *flappers*— flaunted their freedom to smoke and drink and go out with men alone without the certainty of being morally condemned as "loose." And perhaps most important, fewer of them cared if they were.

George Remus

He was known as *King of the Bootleggers,* an attorney whose most famous client turned out to be himself. Remus was born in Germany in 1876 and came to America when he was 5 years old. He trained as a pharmacist but became a lawyer in 1900 and specialized in criminal defense. When Prohibition began, his clients were often bootleggers, and Remus observed that the occupation paid a lot more than practicing law.

Moving to Cincinnati, which was near most of the major distilleries that could still legally make alcohol for medicinal purposes, Remus used his pharmacist's license to buy huge amounts of legal alcohol. Then he had an army of employees "steal" it on the way to his warehouses and turn it into illegal hooch. Despite five arrests, Remus lived a lavish life, complete with a $125,000 swimming pool at his mansion. He once threw a party where each of the 200 guests received diamond jewelry or cars.

During one of his jail stints, Remus's wife took up with a federal Prohibition agent. On his release from prison, Remus promptly shot and killed his errant spouse. Acting as his own attorney, he pleaded temporary insanity and was acquitted after the jury deliberated all of 19 minutes. Remus eventually retired from bootlegging when the business got too violent for him. He died in 1952 at the age of 75. One more thing: The King of the Bootleggers never touched the stuff himself.

Girls just wanna have more...

"The outstanding characteristic of the flapper is not her uniform, but her independence and will to be prosperous... they will no longer marry men who merely support them... they have awakened to the fact that the 'Superior Sex' stuff is all bunk." —journalist Samuel Crowther, 1926.

An Age of Heroes

If there was one thing the 1920s had a lot of, it was heroes. The advent of radio and the increasing popularity of national magazines and tabloid newspapers provided an arena for stars to shine. And armies of public relations agents pushed and shoved their clients into the spotlight.

There were movie stars. Clara Bow reportedly got 45,000 fan letters a week. When screen heartthrob Rudolph Valentino died of a perforated ulcer in 1926, several women reportedly committed suicide. More than 30,000 mourners filed past his $10,000 casket, which had a glass plate above his face so they could have one last look. There were also vaudeville stars like magician Harry Houdini and humorist Will Rogers.

Every sport had its own gods or goddesses: In swimming, there were Gertrude Ederle and Johnny Weissmuller; in football, Red Grange and Knute Rockne; in boxing, Jack Dempsey and Gene Tunney; in golf, Bobby Jones; and in tennis, Bill Tilden.

And in baseball, there was the moon-faced son of a Baltimore saloonkeeper. His name was George Herman Ruth, but everyone called him *Babe*. For most of the decade, Ruth was perhaps the most photographed man in the world. A fine pitcher, he became the greatest slugger in history and almost single-handedly restored baseball as the national pastime after a fixed World Series in 1919 had threatened to ruin it. Ruth was so popular that when his team, the Yankees, moved into a new stadium in New York, it was dubbed "the house that Ruth built."

But as big as Babe Ruth was, he was only second to a tall, thin, and modest airmail pilot from Michigan named Charles A. Lindbergh. On May 20, 1927, Lindbergh lifted off alone from a New York airfield in a $6,000 plane laden with gasoline and sandwiches. When reporters asked him if sandwiches were all he was taking to eat, Lindy replied, "If I get to Paris, I won't need any more, and if I don't, I won't need any more either." Lindbergh headed over the Atlantic, and 33½ hours later, he landed in Paris. He was proclaimed the first man to fly nonstop between the two continents.

The world went nuts. Lindbergh was mobbed everywhere he went. In New York City alone, an estimated 4 million people turned out for a parade and celebration in his honor. In later years, Lindbergh's luster was badly tarnished by his pre–World War II enthusiasm for Hitler's Germany.

But his flight proved a giant shot in the arm for aviation. Suddenly, flying wasn't so scary. By the end of the decade, more than 40 U.S. airline companies were carrying close to 200,000 passengers per year.

Lindbergh's *Spirit of St. Louis* wasn't the only thing in the air as the 1920s came to a close. The economy continued to hum along at a frenetic pace, as well. "Stock prices have reached what looks like a permanently high plateau," said Yale economics professor Irving Fisher on October 16, 1929. Eight days later, the plateau collapsed. An overinflated stock market crashed, costing investors $15 billion in a week. America was plunged into an economic mess the likes of which it had never seen before.

Chapter 15

Uncle Sam's Depressed: 1930–1940

In This Chapter
- Enduring the Great Depression
- Failing minorities
- Fashioning a New Deal
- Naysayers, crusaders, nuts, and desperadoes

During one of his last speeches as president, in December 1928, Calvin Coolidge noted that America could "regard the present with satisfaction and anticipate the future with optimism." And much of the country did both. But as the 1930s dawned, it became painfully apparent that Americans had been prematurely satisfied and overly optimistic.

This chapter takes a look at what triggered the Great Depression and what it meant. You also meet Franklin Roosevelt, another of those great men who seem to come along every now and then in American history just when the country needs them. (For a more detailed look at this era, see *Lessons from the Great Depression For Dummies,* written by Steve Wiegand — that's me! — and published by Wiley.)

The Great Depression: Causes and Consequences

America had gone through economic hard times before. There had been bank panics, recessions, and boom-and-bust cycles of varying degrees of severity and length triggered by political battles, the collapse of particular industries, or world events. But never did it suffer an economic illness so deep and so long as the Great Depression of the 1930s. Economists have argued ever since as to just what caused it. But it's safe to say that a bunch of intertwined factors contributed. Among them were

- **Bank failures:** Many small banks, particularly in rural areas, had overextended credit to farmers who, for the most part, had not shared in the prosperity of the 1920s and often couldn't repay the loans. Big banks, meanwhile, had foolishly made huge loans to foreign countries. Why? So the foreign countries could repay their earlier debts from World War I. When times got tough and U.S. banks stopped lending, European nations simply defaulted on their outstanding loans. As a result, many banks went bankrupt. Others were forced out of business when depositors panicked and withdrew their money. The closings and panics almost completely shut down the country's banking system.

- **Environmental disasters:** The production of vast crops during World War I and the decade that followed resulted in over-plowing of much of America's farmland. The prairie grasses that held topsoil in place were stripped. Coupled with one of the worst droughts in recorded history, the unprotected soil turned the Great Plains into what would become known as the *Dust Bowl*. Dry winds picked up tons of topsoil and blew it across the prairies, creating huge, suffocating clouds of dirt that buried towns and turned farms into deserts.

- **Farm failures:** Many American farmers were already having a hard time before the Depression, mostly because they were producing too much and farm product prices were too low. The situation was so bad in some areas that farmers burned corn for fuel rather than sell it.

- **Government inaction:** Rather than try to jump-start the economy by pushing the Federal Reserve System to lend money to banks at low interest rates and pumping money into the economy through federal public works projects, the Hoover administration did nothing at first and then took small, tentative actions that weren't enough to head things off.

- **The stock market crash:** The stock market soared throughout most of the 1920s, and the more it grew, the more people were eager to pour money into it. Many people bought *on margin,* which meant they paid only part of a stock's worth when they bought it and the rest when they sold it. That worked fine as long as stock prices kept going up. But when the market crashed in late October 1929, they were forced to pay up on stocks that were worth far less than what they had paid for them. Many had borrowed to buy stock, and when the stock market went belly up, they couldn't repay their loans, and the lenders were left holding the empty bag.

- **Too many poor people:** That may sound sort of goofy, but it's a real reason. Though the overall economy had soared in the 1920s, most of the wealth was enjoyed by relatively few Americans. In 1929, 40 percent of the families in the country were still living at or below the poverty level. That made them too poor to buy goods and services and too poor to pay their debts. With no markets for their goods, manufacturers had to lay off tens of thousands of workers, which, of course, just created more poor people.

Whatever the causes, the consequences of the Great Depression were staggering. In the cities, thousands of jobless men roamed the streets looking for work. It wasn't unusual for 2,000 or 3,000 applicants to show up for one or two job openings. If they weren't looking for work, they were looking for food. Bread lines were established to prevent people from starving (see Figure 15-1). And more than a million families lost their houses and took up residence in shantytowns made up of tents, packing crates, and the hulks of old cars. They were called *Hoovervilles,* a mocking reference to President Hoover, whom many blamed for the mess the country was in.

Figure 15-1: Many wait hours in line for bread.

© Bettmann/CORBIS

Plus to minus

If you doubt that the Great Depression deserves that "Great" adjective, look at these numbers:

- More than 5,000 banks closed between 1930 and 1933, 9 million savings accounts were wiped out, and depositors lost $2.5 billion.

- Unemployment rose from less than 1 million in 1929 to more than 12 million by 1933 — equal to about 25 percent of the total U.S. workforce.

- Capital investment dropped from $10 billion in 1929 to $1 billion in 1932, and the stock market's industrial index dropped from 452 in September 1929 to 58 in July 1932.

- The gross national product went from $104 billion in 1929 to $59 billion in 1932.

- Farm income dropped 60 percent in the three years after 1929. In 1932, per capita income from farming was only $80 a year for farmers.

> ### The Lindbergh kidnapping
>
> Almost everybody loved Charles Lindbergh. The lanky aviator had remained a true American hero after his historic solo flight across the Atlantic in 1927. So it made national headlines when someone climbed in a second-story window of Lindbergh's Hopewell, New Jersey, home and snatched his 20-month-old son, Charles Jr.
>
> The nation held its breath for six weeks, during which time Lindbergh responded to a ransom demand by paying $50,000. But on May 12, the body of the missing baby was found in the woods about 5 miles from the Lindbergh home. An illegal immigrant and escaped convict from Germany named Bruno Richard Hauptmann was arrested for the crime after most of the ransom money was found in his garage. Hauptmann was convicted and executed in the electric chair in 1936, still declaring his innocence.
>
> As a result of the crime, Congress passed what became known as the *Lindbergh Law*, which made kidnapping a federal crime and thus allowed the FBI to enter the hunt for kidnappers.

Americans weren't sure what to do. In the summer of 1932, about 20,000 desperate World War I veterans marched on Washington, D.C., to claim $1,000 bonuses they had been promised they would get, starting in 1946. When Congress refused to move up the payment schedules, several thousand members of the *Bonus Army* built a camp of tents and shacks on the banks of the Potomac River and refused to leave. Under orders of President Hoover, federal troops commanded by Gen. Douglas MacArthur used bayonets and gas bombs to rout the squatters. The camp was burned. No one was killed, but the episode left a bad taste in the mouths of many Americans.

Thousands of farmers left their homes in states like Oklahoma and Arkansas and headed for the promise of better days in the West, especially California. What they found there, however, was often a backbreaking existence as migrant laborers, living in squalid camps and picking fruit for starvation wages.

Shoving Aside Racial Minorities

The majority of America's minorities had never had it good, so it's not surprising that the Depression made their lot even more miserable.

More than half of African Americans still lived in the South, most as tenant farmers or *sharecroppers,* meaning they farmed someone else's land. Almost all of those who worked and weren't farmers held menial jobs that whites hadn't wanted — until the Depression came along. When it did, the African Americans were shoved out of their jobs. As many as 400,000 left the South for cities in the North, which didn't help much. By 1932, it's estimated that half of the black U.S. population was on some form of relief.

There also wasn't much of a "we're all in this together" mentality. Segregation continued in nearly every walk of life, more than 60 blacks were murdered by lynching and other mob violence during the decade, and federal anti-lynching laws were defeated in Congress. Even many of the bold federal programs that came into being in the 1930s blatantly discriminated against African Americans. Wage-setting programs allowed employers to pay black workers less than whites, farm aid programs often ignored African-American farmers, and job creation programs provided disproportionately fewer jobs to African Americans.

Some of the programs, however, helped everyone. Segregation in federal jobs did begin to slowly crumble, and some labor unions opened their membership to minorities. Such crumbs were enough to make many black voters leave the party of Lincoln behind, which they felt had done nothing for them, and vote Democratic for decades to come.

Other minority groups suffered similarly. Mexico had been exempted from the immigration restrictions of the 1920s, and as a result, hundreds of thousands of Mexicans came to the United States, mostly to the Southwest. Prior to the Depression, they were at least tolerated as a ready source of cheap labor. In the 1930s, however, they were pushed out of jobs by desperate whites. Many thousands were deported, even some who were legal U.S. citizens, and as many as 500,000 returned to Mexico. Those of Asian descent, mostly on the West Coast, were likewise pushed out of jobs or relegated to jobs only within their own communities.

Native Americans had been largely ignored by the U.S. government since the 1880s. The general idea had been to gradually have Native Americans disappear into the American mainstream. In 1924, Congress made U.S. citizens of all Native Americans who weren't already citizens, whether they wanted to be or not.

Justice, Southern-style

In March 1931, nine young black males were taken from a freight train near Scottsboro, Alabama, and arrested for vagrancy. Then two white women who were traveling in the same freight car accused the boys of gang-raping them.

Despite mountains of evidence that the women were lying, an all-white jury quickly convicted the youths, and eight of them were sentenced to death. A communist-backed group called the *International Labor Defense* took up their cause, and the U.S. Supreme Court ordered a new trial. Five of them were retried and found guilty again, and again the verdict was thrown out by the Supreme Court as unconstitutional because blacks had been excluded from the jury.

None of the defendants were ever executed. One escaped, and the other four were paroled after serving years in prison for the crime of being black in the wrong place at the wrong time. In November 2013, the state of Alabama posthumously pardoned the three men who had not yet been formally exonerated. "The Scottsboro boys have finally received justice," said Alabama Gov. Robert J. Bentley.

But preliminary studies done in the 1920s found that assimilation had failed. In 1934, Congress changed direction and passed laws that allowed Native Americans to retain their cultural identity. That did little for their economic well-being, and they remained perhaps the worst off of America's minority groups.

Keeping Women at Home — or Work

With jobs scarce, a strong feeling prevailed that women should stay home and let men have the jobs. There was even a federal rule that two people in the same family couldn't both be on the government payroll. But two things occurred that actually increased the number of women in the workforce during the decade. The first was that many families simply couldn't survive without an extra income. The second was that many men abandoned their families to look for work or because they were ashamed that they couldn't find work. Marriage rates dropped for the first time since the early 1800s.

Inventing an antidepressant

Charles B. Darrow had known better times. Broke and unemployed in 1933, the Germantown, Pennsylvania, heating engineer combined memories of a past family vacation to Atlantic City, New Jersey, with an existing board game called "The Landlord's Game." Darrow's version used Atlantic City addresses like Marvin Gardens and Park Place. He called his get-rich-quick, real-estate board game "Monopoly." Darrow took his idea to the folks at the Parker Brothers game company in 1934. They promptly kicked him out the door, calling the game too long, too dull, and burdened with at least 52 "fundamental play errors." Undaunted, Darrow produced the game on his own and sold 5,000 sets to a Philadelphia department store. The sale changed the mind of Parker Brothers. It bought the game from Darrow in early 1936; bought the rights to "The Landlord's Game" from its inventor, Elizabeth Magie; and soon was churning out 20,000 sets of Monopoly a week. People forgot their hard times for a few hours while rolling dice, buying railroads, and going directly to jail without passing "Go."

Monopoly is now produced in 26 languages and in more than 100 variations and is sold in more than 40 countries. Darrow retired at 46 on his royalties. He lived to 76, the first American millionaire to make his fortune by designing a game — and in the midst of the Great Depression yet!

Developing Organized Labor

If the sun peeked through the Depression's clouds on anyone, it may have been organized labor. The 1930s saw captains of industry and business lose much of their political clout to unions, and new laws made organizing easier.

The decade also saw a telling split in labor. The traditionalists who ran the American Federation of Labor (AFL) wanted to concentrate on organizing workers according to their specific skills or craft. But that left out thousands of workers who had no specific skills and also sometimes pitted workers for the same company against one another.

In 1936, John L. Lewis, the bombastic leader of the United Mine Workers, led a split from the AFL and formed the Congress of Industrial Organizations (CIO). The CIO was more receptive to not only unskilled workers but also women and minorities. By 1938, it had 4 million members.

The United Auto Workers (UAW) also flexed its muscles in the decade. The UAW used sit-down strikes, where workers would simply stop and sit down at their posts, making it much more difficult to use strikebreakers. In 1937, General Motors, the third-largest company in the country, recognized the UAW after a 44-day strike.

That same year, steelworkers won recognition of their union by U.S. Steel, the giant of the industry. Other steel companies, however, refused to go along, and confrontations were often violent. On Memorial Day, 1937, police opened fire on marching strikers and their families in South Chicago, killing 10 and wounding 90. The tragedy became known as the *Memorial Day Massacre* and served as a rallying cry for labor.

All told, there were more than 4,500 strikes in 1937, and labor won more than three-quarters of them. By 1940, more than 8 million Americans were members of organized labor.

Every bit helps

How bad were things in the Great Depression? Consider this Associated Press report that appeared in U.S. newspapers in mid-June 1931: "The Presbyterian Missions Board had $3.77 to use for the hungry and unemployed today, a contribution from the Batanga Church in Cameroon, West Africa, which raised the money at a cocanut (sic) bazaar.

"The Bulu tribe's newspaper 'Efou' had published an article saying: 'There are actually people in America who do not have enough to eat.' Pastor Eduma Musambi and his son, a church elder, concluded aid must be forthcoming to the United States and arranged the church festival."

FDR: Making Alphabet Soup

In 1932, Herbert Hoover was the U.S. president. In 1933, he was toast. Much of the country blamed Hoover for the Depression, although the groundwork for it had been laid long before he was elected in 1928. Hoover's big mistake was that he kept saying things would get better if everyone was just a little patient — and things just got worse.

Electing a reformer

By the time the 1932 presidential election came along, it was pretty clear that the Democrats could nominate a dead dog and still beat Hoover. Fortunately for the country, they passed up deceased canines and chose the governor of New York. His name was Franklin Delano Roosevelt, an appellation reduced in newspaper headlines and the popular parlance to *FDR*.

A distant cousin of Theodore Roosevelt and the only son of a wealthy railroad executive, FDR attended the best private schools and graduated from Harvard. Trained as a lawyer, Roosevelt served in the state legislature, became assistant secretary of the Navy, and had a boundless future. Then, in 1921, he was struck by polio and crippled.

But Roosevelt had an indomitable spirit. He was elected New York's governor in 1928, earning a reputation as a reformer. The Democrats nominated him for the presidency in 1932 after some behind-the-scenes maneuvering by newspaper publisher William Randolph Hearst and business tycoon Joseph Kennedy. He campaigned on a "New Deal" platform and easily defeated Hoover.

Despite his aristocratic background, Roosevelt was wildly popular with the average guy, many of whom didn't know he could walk only with leg braces and crutches. (News photographers and newsreel cameramen took care not to take shots of him in "awkward" poses.) But many conservatives and business leaders, who considered him a traitor to his class, hated him.

FDR may have been the perfect president for the time. He was friendly and approachable and exuded sympathy and self-confidence. He knew how to compromise, and like Lincoln and Washington, he knew how to get the best out of people. He was lucky — before taking office he narrowly escaped an assassin's bullets while riding in a car with Chicago Mayor Anton Cermak in Miami (Cermak was killed). He wasn't afraid to do something, even if it proved to be wrong: "Take a method," he said, "and try it. If it fails, try another. But above all, do something."

AMERICAN FACES

Eleanor Roosevelt

She began her marriage to her distant cousin in his shadow — and became his "legs." She also became one of the most beloved — and hated — First Ladies in U.S. history.

Eleanor was born into a wealthy New York family in 1884. After an unhappy childhood marked by the death of her parents, she married Franklin in 1905. Over the next decade, Eleanor had six children, found out her husband was playing around, and seemed destined to be either divorced or in the background as a politician's wife.

But Eleanor rose to the occasion. As First Lady, she broke tradition and held more than 350 press conferences of her own — but for female journalists only. She was a tireless champion for civil rights and women's issues and often represented her husband, whose polio prevented him from traveling easily, around the country. But her activism also earned her vitriolic hatred from people who didn't like her husband, her politics, or the fact that she was an independent woman.

After FDR's death, Eleanor served as a U.S. delegate to the United Nations and as a roving ambassador-at-large. She died in 1962 at the age of 78.

Creating hope through a New Deal

Roosevelt heeded his own advice and did something. Supported by healthy Democratic majorities in Congress, FDR pushed through a dazzling array of programs (many of them best known by their initials) in his first 100 days in office. The products of the first 100 days (and in some cases a bit longer) included the

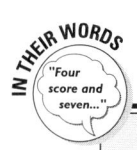

IN THEIR WORDS

Who's afraid of a little depression?

"First of all, let me assert my firm belief that the only thing we have to fear is fear itself — nameless, unreasoning, unjustified terror that paralyzes needed effort to convert retreat into advance." —Franklin Roosevelt, inaugural address, March 4, 1933.

"We ain't gonna die out. People is goin' on — changin' a little, maybe, but goin' right on." —Ma Joad in John Steinbeck's *The Grapes of Wrath*, 1939.

- **Agricultural Adjustment Act (AAA):** Basically, it paid farmers not to produce so much food. That bailed farmers out, at least a little, and increased farm prices to more profitable levels.
- **Civil Works Administration (CWA):** The CWA provided about 4 million jobs in building roads, airports, schools, sewer systems, and other civic projects.
- **Civilian Conservation Corps (CCC):** This created 1,300 camps around the country to give young men new jobs (at $30 a month, with $22 sent home to their families) in conserving natural resources. By 1941, the CCC employed 2.5 million men, who planted more than 17 million trees and made improvements in scores of state and national parks.
- **Emergency Banking Act:** Three days after he took office, FDR closed all banks. Then, on March 9, he pushed through Congress a bill that reopened the banks under close supervision. The bill, which took all of eight hours to go through, also authorized the treasury to issue more currency.
- **Federal Emergency Relief Act (FERA):** The FERA eventually provided a total of $500 million in aid to state and local governments.
- **Glass-Stegall Banking Act:** This act mandated that banks get out of the investment business and restricted use of bank money on stock speculation. It also created federal guarantees for personal bank accounts.
- **Homeowners Loan Act:** This provided funds to help keep homeowners from losing their homes to mortgage foreclosures.
- **National Industrial Recovery Act (NIRA):** This ambitious program was designed to get industries to cooperate in setting maximum hours, minimum wages, and price controls through an organization called the National Recovery Administration (NRA). The NIRA was declared unconstitutional by the Supreme Court in 1935 for giving too much power to the program's nongovernment administrators.
- **Tennessee Valley Authority Act (TVA):** One of the most innovative of the New Deal programs, the TVA created an independent public agency that oversaw the development of dams and other projects in the Tennessee River Valley. The TVA covered 40,000 square miles in seven states. It built 16 dams, took over 5 more, and provided electric power to 40,000 families that previously had none. The TVA also supplied fertilizer, provided flood control and better river navigation, and reforested vast areas.
- **Truth in Securities Act:** This act required new stocks and bonds offered for sale to be registered with the new Securities Exchange Commission (SEC) and required brokers to fully disclose all background information.
- **Work Projects Administration (WPA):** This organization created a host of federal projects that ranged from cleaning slums and providing electricity to rural areas to painting murals on the walls of public buildings and putting on plays for audiences that paid only what they could afford.

Harry Hopkins

He was the big dealer in the New Deal, a super social worker who was Franklin Roosevelt's most trusted aide and whose no-b.s. approach to things earned him the nickname *Lord Root of the Matter* from Winston Churchill.

Hopkins was born the son of a harness maker in Iowa in 1890. After graduating from college, he became a social worker and eventually ran relief programs in New York for FDR when Roosevelt was governor. In the White House, Hopkins ran several New Deal programs and agencies and was made secretary of commerce in 1938.

He wasn't shy about spending government money, either: One Hopkins-run program spent $1 billion in less than six months, making even FDR wince. When a New Deal congressional critic suggested there were better ways to deal with the Depression in the long run, Hopkins snapped: "People don't eat in the long run, senator; they eat every day."

When World War II broke out, Hopkins served as FDR's alter ego and go-between with other world leaders. After FDR's death, Hopkins helped plan the United Nations. Never in good health, he died in 1946 at the age of 55.

In 1935 Roosevelt added to his alphabet soup of programs by getting Congress to pass the Social Security Act, which began a sweeping federal system of unemployment insurance and retirement pensions paid for by both employers and employees through payroll taxes. In 1938, he signed the Fair Labor Standards Act, which created a national minimum wage of 25 cents per hour and a maximum workweek of 44 hours.

By the time the 1936 elections rolled around, things were looking up. Unemployment had dropped from 12 million to about 9 million. Average weekly earnings had increased from $17 to $22. So despite Republican predictions that the Democrats were creating a socialist state, FDR was easily reelected.

Packing the Supreme Court

One of the things that stuck in FDR's craw during his first term was the nine-member U.S. Supreme Court, which was dominated by conservatives and had thwarted some of Roosevelt's plans. So in February 1937, he proposed that he be allowed to appoint a new federal judge for every judge that refused to retire within six months of reaching the age of 70. This "court-packing" tactic would have raised the number of Supreme Court justices to 15.

Roosevelt's ploy worked — sort of. Although Congress ultimately rejected it, the high court began making decisions that were more favorable to the New Deal. Within a few years, six justices retired, enabling Roosevelt to appoint liberals to the court. But the fight also weakened FDR politically.

Assessing the New Deal

How well the New Deal actually worked is debatable. Many of the programs had big price tags. The national debt, which was about $22.5 billion when FDR took office, was nearly double that by 1940, and so was the size of the federal bureaucracy. After winning reelection in 1936, FDR began scaling back federal spending to help keep inflation in check. As soon as he did, unemployment began to climb again, and industrial production slowed.

What is undebatable, however, is the fact that the New Deal greatly increased the role of the federal government in people's lives. It laid the foundation for a government "safety net" of services for Americans most in need, it fostered the development of the modern labor movement, and it made the federal government a key player in regulating the U.S. economy.

And whether all that was a good or bad idea, most people felt a lot better in 1940 than they did in 1932. Americans were pleased enough, in fact, with FDR's performance by 1940 to give him what they had given no other president — a third term.

The birth of a hero

You may have read that Superman was born on the planet Krypton, but it was really Cleveland, Ohio, on a hot summer night in 1934. And his parents were a couple of teenagers looking for careers in Depression-ravaged America.

Jerry Siegel was a 19-year-old would-be writer who dallied in science fiction. His pal, 19-year-old Joe Shuster, was an artist. So when Siegel came up with an idea for a comic character with superpowers during a sleepless night, the two decided to put together a comic strip. They dressed their hero in a red, blue, and yellow costume and took him around to every comic strip syndicate in America — and were rejected faster than a speeding bullet.

In 1938, however, DC Comics decided to take a chance, and Superman appeared for the first time in Action Comics #1 (a mint copy of which sold in 2011 for slightly more than $2 million.) Siegel and Shuster got relatively little for their creation, despite decades of legal battles over who owned the rights to the Kryptonian crusader.

Created as an antidote for Depression blues, the Man of Steel has become an icon perhaps second only to Mickey Mouse as a larger-than-life pen-and-ink character. And who knows? Without him, we might not have Super Bowls, superstars, or super-sized fast-food meals.

Critics, Crooks, and Crime Fighters

Of course, not everyone was in love with FDR. Many Republicans refused to even say his name, referring to him as "that man in the White House." The 1930s also spawned a gaggle of colorful critics and crusaders who made themselves heard above the hard times.

Huey Long

He was a traveling salesman, a lawyer, and a world-class demagogue. Huey Long was elected governor of Louisiana in 1928 on a populist platform, and he actually did some good things for the state, such as making school textbooks free and improving roads and highways. But he also ran a corrupt administration that was not above roughing up, blackmailing, or slandering those who opposed him. By 1930, the "Kingfish" was as close to an absolute dictator as there was in the country. He controlled the legislature and, after winning a U.S. Senate seat, refused to promptly vacate the governor's office, thus holding both jobs for a while.

Originally an FDR supporter, Long broke with the White House mostly for egotistical reasons. He proposed a "Share Our Wealth" program that called for confiscating family fortunes of more than $5 million and annual incomes over $1 million and guaranteeing every family $2,500 a year, a homestead, and a car. Long had a national following and announced he would run against FDR at the head of a third party in 1936. Private polls showed he might garner 4 million votes, enough to tip the election to the Republicans. But he never got the chance. In September 1935, Long was shot to death on the steps of the Louisiana capitol by a man whose family he had ruined.

Francis E. Townsend

Francis Townsend was an elderly California doctor who was selling real estate in Long Beach in 1935 when he had an idea that he just couldn't help sharing: providing $200 a month for life to everyone 60 or older. It would be financed by sales taxes, and every pensioner would have to spend his entire pension every month, which Townsend said would stimulate the economy. Actually, more experienced economists pointed out the scheme would take half the national income to provide for 8 percent of the population.

> ### IN THEIR WORDS
>
> ## A "democratic" kingmaker
>
> "I'm for the poor man — all poor men. Black and white, they all gotta have a chance. 'Every man a king,' that's my motto." —Huey Long to a journalist, 1932.

Despite the crackpot smell of the idea, "Townsend Clubs" sprang up all over the country, with as many as 5 million members. The idea gradually died out after Roosevelt proposed the Social Security system.

Charles E. Coughlin

A Roman Catholic priest, Charles Coughlin was, after Roosevelt himself, the best radio orator in America. Broadcasting from the Shrine of the Little Flower in Royal Oak, Michigan, Coughlin was a super-patriot who ripped into Wall Street, big business, and oppressive bosses. Originally, he supported FDR, but soon he became an ardent foe, advocating the nationalization of banks and ripping into Roosevelt as a communist tool of Jewish bankers.

Coughlin created the National Union for Social Justice, which drew more than 5 million members in less than two months. But his increasingly shrill attacks on Jews and Roosevelt created a backlash, and by mid-1940, the bombastic cleric had quieted down considerably.

Despite the fact that their schemes were pretty looney-tunes, FDR's more vocal and visible critics did put some pressure on him to continue to press for reform, especially during his first term. "I am fighting communism, Huey Longism, Coughlinism, Townsendism," FDR said with some exasperation. "I want to save our system, the capitalist system [but] I want to equalize the distribution of wealth."

Meanwhile, a guy named Hoover was fighting "outlawism."

Bad guys and G-men

While some were coming up with political proposals to redistribute wealth, others had a more pragmatic approach: They stole it. The 1930s saw the rise of the modern outlaw. Instead of six-guns and horses, they used Tommy guns and Fords. Some of them became folk heroes, robbing banks that many people felt had robbed their customers.

Shirley Temple

She was less than 4 feet tall, and she was the biggest thing in Hollywood: dancing, singing, and mugging her way into the hearts of a country that really needed someone to hug.

Born in 1928 in Santa Monica, California, Shirley Temple made her first movie at the age of 3. She went on to make 24 more during the 1930s and was the number-one box-office attraction every year from 1935 to 1938. Movies like *Little Miss Marker* and *Captain January* earned the curly-headed charmer $300,000 a year. And thousands more were added by royalties from the sales of Shirley dolls, dresses, dishes, soap, and books. Little girls all over the country wanted to look like, sound like, and be adored as much as Shirley.

Temple retired from films in the late 1940s and had a brief career on TV. She married oil executive Charles A. Black in 1950 and gradually became active in politics. She served as a U.S. representative to the United Nations, ambassador to Ghana, and chief of protocol for the State Department in the 1970s. She died in February 2014 at the age of 85.

There was Charles "Pretty Boy" Floyd, who reportedly robbed more than 30 banks and killed ten men before he was gunned down in 1934. There was Arizona "Ma" Barker, whose gang consisted mainly of her four sons and who died in a shootout with the law. There were Bonnie Parker and Clyde Barrow, a pair of Texas lovers-robbers-murderers who became folk heroes despite the fact that many of their fellow desperadoes regarded them as trigger-happy bunglers. And there was John Dillinger.

An Indiana native, Dillinger robbed a grocery store in 1924 and was caught. He did nine years in prison, and when he got out he started a 14-month crime spree that made him one of the most famous, or infamous, men in America. Dillinger killed ten men, engineered three daring jailbreaks, escaped from two gun battles with the law, and stole as much as $265,000.

He also became something of a Robin Hood. "Dillinger does not rob poor people," a fan wrote to the newspapers. "He robs those who became rich robbing poor people. I am for Johnnie." In the end, such popularity did Dillinger little good. Federal agents killed him in 1934 as he left a movie theater in Chicago.

Fighting the bad guys were the *G-men,* a nickname given to Federal Bureau of Investigation (FBI) agents by George "Machine Gun" Kelly. The *G* stood for government, and the head G-man was an owlish-looking, fiercely intense man named J. Edgar Hoover. As head of the FBI, Hoover combined a fanatical sense of duty and a flair for public relations to make his agency a beacon of heroism and integrity.

The panic of a Martian invasion

Mercury Theater players had a dull story on their hands and a deadline looming for their live Halloween-eve performance on CBS radio in 1938. But writer Howard Koch did his best with H. G. Wells's novel *The War of the Worlds*, bringing the Martian invasion into the 1930s and relocating it from England to New Jersey. And Mercury leader Orson Welles used all his considerable acting talent to make it as realistic as possible.

In fact, he and the rest of the cast did too good a job. Despite several announcements that it was just a radio show, many in the show's audience of several million thought there was a real Martian invasion going on. Panic spread (although just how much is a subject of debate among historians). People called police to ask what to do. In New Jersey, families hastily packed and took to the roads. There were several reports of attempted suicides.

It took two days to calm things down, and criminal charges were even considered against Welles. In the end, however, the show got a big new sponsor, Campbell Soup, and Welles was invited to the White House.

"You know, Orson," President Roosevelt told him, "You and I are the two best actors in America."

Serving as director from 1924 until his death in 1972, Hoover was one of the most powerful figures in 20th-century America. His almost pathological hatred of communism, his dictatorial manner, and his unethical and, quite probably, illegal use of the bureau against political and personal enemies eventually stained his name. But in the 1930s, millions of American boys wanted to be him.

Chapter 16

The World at War: 1941–1945

In This Chapter

- Heading toward war
- Contributing to the war effort
- Fighting overseas and at sea
- Using the first atomic bomb

*V*ery few Americans had any use for the dictators of Europe and Asia, but even fewer had a burning desire to fight them. World War I had left a bad taste in the mouths of many, and the lingering effects of the Depression were still being felt. The United States didn't need a foreign headache.

But as this chapter shows, sometimes a fight just can't be avoided, particularly when it seems half the world is being run by monsters. Faced with the most widespread and horrific war in human history, Americans respond magnificently. They also develop and unleash a weapon that will forever change the future of mankind.

Trying to Avoid War — Again

Despite the hangover from World War I and America's refusal to join the League of Nations, the country didn't exactly become a hermit in the 1920s and 1930s. In 1922, U.S. government and private interests helped feed more than 10 million starving Russians. The country also provided more than $100 million in aid to Turkey, Greece, and other Mediterranean countries in the 1920s and forgave or reduced World War I debts.

On the diplomatic front, the United States, Great Britain, Japan, France, and Italy agreed in 1922 to limit their warship building. And in 1928, French foreign minister Aristide Briand and U.S. Secretary of State Frank Kellogg convinced themselves and 15 other countries to formally agree not to go to war with each other. As completely unrealistic as the agreement may have been, so eager for peace was the U.S. Senate that it ratified the Kellogg-Briand Pact on an 85-to-1 vote.

Playing the role of a good neighbor

Closer to home, the administrations of presidents Harding and Coolidge were not at all shy about interfering in Latin American countries' internal affairs if it suited the interests of U.S. businesses. Starting with President Hoover, however, and continuing under Roosevelt, America began a "good neighbor" policy toward Central and South America. The policy basically pledged that we would maintain pleasant relations and generally mind our own business.

America tried to keep to that policy elsewhere in the world as well. In Asia, Japan was becoming more and more hostile toward its neighbors, and U.S. diplomats made periodic attempts to convince the Japanese to slow down. But Japan had been insulted in 1924 when the United States closed its doors to Japanese immigration and wasn't in much of a mood to listen. And Americans weren't interested in a fight, even after Japan invaded China, nor even after Japanese planes "accidentally" sank a U.S. gunboat in a Chinese river in 1937.

In Europe, Italy, run by a buffoonish thug named Benito Mussolini, invaded Ethiopia in 1936 with not much more than a whimper from the United States. When Germany, under an evil madman named Adolf Hitler, took Austria and Czechoslovakia in 1938, President Roosevelt did send letters to both Hitler and Mussolini, asking them not to conquer any more countries. They laughed at him.

Roosevelt was not being timid as much as he was being a practical politician. America was still reeling from the effects of the Great Depression, and most Americans were more interested in figuring out how to pay next month's rent than in who ran Austria. A 1937 survey found that 94 percent thought U.S. policy should be directed at keeping out of foreign wars rather than trying to stop them.

An "isolationist" movement, whose most popular leader was aviator hero Charles Lindbergh, gained strength and held rallies around the country, exhorting Roosevelt and Congress to keep the United States sheltered from the growing storm clouds in Asia and Europe. Congress and FDR agreed, approving laws in 1935 and again in 1937 that prohibited the sale of American weapons to any warring nation.

But much of the rest of the world continued to rush toward conflict. On September 1, 1939, Germany invaded Poland. Great Britain and France had signed a pact pledging to come to Poland's defense and declared war on Germany. World War II had begun. France was badly prepared for war and collapsed quickly under the German "Blitzkrieg," or "lightning war." By mid-1940, England stood alone against Hitler and his allies, which for the time being included the Soviet Union, led by its own evil madman, Josef Stalin.

Sensing impending doom

Roosevelt, like most Americans, was still not eager for war. But unlike the ardent isolationists, he also figured it was inevitable and began to take steps to get ready for it in 1940 and 1941. They included

- Authorizing the doubling of the size of the U.S. Navy.

- Pledging to come to the aid of any North, Central, or South American country that was attacked.

- Pushing Congress to approve the first peacetime military draft in U.S. history. The draft required the registration of all men between the ages of 21 and 35 (about 16 million men). About 1.2 million were drafted for a year's service, and 800,000 reservists were called to active duty. (In October 1941, just before the 18-month period expired, Congress fortuitously voted to extend the draft. But it was a very close vote: 203 to 202.)

- Trading 50 old U.S. Navy destroyers to England in return for leases on military bases on English possessions in the Caribbean.

- Pushing the Lend-Lease Act through Congress, which authorized FDR to sell, trade, lease, or just plain give military hardware to any country he thought would use it to further the security of the United States.

- Ordering the Navy to attack on sight German submarines that had been preying on ships off the East Coast.

The great stone faces

John Robinson had this idea for a sculpture. A *big* sculpture. Robinson was the state historian of South Dakota in the 1920s, and he thought it would be cool to turn a cliff in the state's Black Hills into a tribute to figures from the Old West, such as Buffalo Bill Cody. So he and other supporters of the idea hunted up an Idaho sculptor named John Gutzon de la Mothe Borglum. Borglum liked the concept, but not the subject.

In 1927, with the blessing of South Dakota — and eventually about $1 million from Congress — Borglum began using dynamite to blast away granite from the side of a mountain named after a New York lawyer named Charles Rushmore. Instead of Old West figures, however, Borglum carved the heads of four American presidents: George Washington, Abraham Lincoln, Thomas Jefferson, and Theodore Roosevelt. The job wasn't finished until October 1941, when Mt. Rushmore National Memorial opened to the public. Borglum didn't live to see it. He died in March 1941. But his son (somewhat appropriately named Lincoln) carried on his work, and more than 2.7 million visitors view the mammoth effort every year. Very few ask, "Where's Buffalo Bill?"

No bloodshed, I promise

"And while I am talking to you mothers and fathers, I give you one more assurance. I have said this before, but I shall say it again and again and again: Your boys are not going to be sent into any foreign wars." —Franklin Roosevelt, a few days before being elected to a third term as president, November 1940.

Despite all the preparations, many Americans still refused to believe war was inevitable. Then, on a sleepy Sunday morning less than three weeks before Christmas, 1941, a Japanese naval and air force launched a surprise attack on the U.S. naval base at Pearl Harbor, Hawaii. More than 2,400 U.S. military men were killed, 150 planes were destroyed, and eight battleships were sunk or badly damaged.

December 7, in Roosevelt's words, had become "a day that shall live in infamy."

The Andrews Sisters

They didn't have great voices and they weren't especially beautiful, but they sure struck a chord with Americans in the 1940s. LaVerne (1911–1967), Maxene (1916–1995) and Patty (1918–2013) Andrews were born in Minneapolis, and were performing three-part harmonies in vaudeville by the time they were in their teens.

Their first big hit, a Yiddish tune called "Bei Mir Bist Du Schon," came out in 1937 and sold 350,000 copies in a month. Other hit records included "Beat Me Daddy, Eight to the Bar," "Boogie Woogie Bugle Boy," "Don't Sit Under the Apple Tree," "Rum and Coca Cola," and "Don't Fence Me In." They sold more than 70 million records, sang with virtually every big star of the day — from Glenn Miller to Bing Crosby — and appeared in 17 films where they usually played themselves.

But the sisters (who often quarreled and sometimes didn't speak to each other except on stage) were best known as "America's Wartime Sweethearts" because of their tireless travels to entertain U.S. troops, both in the United States and overseas. "We never got tired of trying to bring a little smile and a little music to the boys," Maxene later recalled. "They didn't have much else to smile about."

Gearing Up for War

Despite all the warnings, the United States wasn't completely prepared when war broke out. The Depression had rubbed out many of the country's machine and tool industries, the military was woefully under-supplied, and many soldiers found themselves drilling with toy guns and wooden tanks. In a way, however, the Depression was a good preparation for what was to come: Americans had learned to scrimp and persevere. And having been pushed into a fight, they were eager to oblige.

Getting industry and the economy in shape for World War II

Gearing up of the industry needed to wage a global war on two fronts was handicapped by a lack of manpower. More than 15 million Americans eventually served in the military. Training and supplying them was a staggering challenge. It took more than 6,000 people to provide food, equipment, medical services, and transportation to 8,000 soldiers. In addition, many raw materials, such as rubber, manila fiber, and oil, were in short supply. And to top it off, President Roosevelt was a great leader, but not a great administrator.

Nevertheless, Americans rose to the occasion. When FDR called for the production of 50,000 planes in a year, it was thought to be ridiculous. By 1944, the country was producing 96,000 a year. Technology blossomed. When metals became scarce, plastics were developed to take their place. Copper was taken out of pennies and replaced with steel; nickel was removed from nickels. War-inspired pragmatism even affected fashions: To save material, men's suits lost their pant cuffs and vests, and women painted their legs to take the place of nylons.

Other sacrifices were made as well. Gasoline and tires were rationed, as were coffee, sugar, canned goods, butter, and shoes. But the war proved to be more of an economic inconvenience than a real trial for most people.

The statistics of war supplies

Production boomed during the war, to the tune of the following figures:

- **Aircraft:** 296,429
- **Artillery:** 372,431
- **Bullets:** 41.59 million
- **Naval ships:** 87,620
- **Tanks and self-propelled guns:** 102,351
- **Trucks:** 2.46 million

> ### "Da" for the working Yank
>
> "To American production, without which this war would have been lost." —toast by Soviet dictator Josef Stalin, October 1943.

Of course, all that military hardware had a hefty price tag. The federal government spent about $350 billion during World War II — or twice as much as it had spent *in total* for the entire history of the U.S. government up to that point. About 40 percent of that came from taxes; the rest came through government borrowing, much of that through the sale of bonds.

All that money had to go someplace. A lot of it went to the West, especially California, where 10 percent of all the federal war spending took place. But the American economy rose just about everywhere else too. The civilian workforce grew 20 percent. The *Gross National Product* (the total of goods and services produced) more than doubled between 1939 and 1945. Wages and corporate profits went up, as did prices.

In October 1942, Congress gave the president the power to freeze agricultural prices, wages, salaries, and rents. The Roosevelt administration created the Office of Price Administration (OPA) to oversee prices and wages. But the OPA proved generally ineffective, and the economy mostly ran itself.

Working with labor unions during war times

The serious labor shortage created by the war was a big boost to union membership. Early on, FDR got labor to agree to a "no strike" pledge and a 15 percent limit on wage increases.

Even so, there were thousands of work stoppages, especially as the war wore on. The government actually seized the nation's coal mines in 1943 after a major strike and also seized the railroads in late 1943 to avert a strike. Congress eventually passed a law requiring unions to wait 30 days before striking.

AMERICAN FACES

Henry J. Kaiser

Henry Kaiser had never built a ship before, so he didn't know he was doing it "wrong." All he knew was that he was doing it fast — and helping to win the war. Kaiser was born in New York in 1882. He left school at the age of 13 to go to work and eventually ended up on the West Coast as an engineer. During the Depression, he helped to build major dams in the West, such as Boulder and Grand Coulee, and when the war started, he was asked to help provide ships.

He did it by using assembly line methods, building sections and then welding them together. Traditional shipbuilders were skeptical that it would work. But Kaiser's method streamlined the process of building a cargo vessel, called a *liberty ship*, from 245 days to 17. By 1943, Kaiser's shipyards were producing an average of two ships a day, helping to keep England fed, providing supplies for overseas troops, lowering enemy morale, and earning Kaiser the nickname "Sir Launch-a-lot."

Kaiser's interests were by no means limited to ships. He also built magnesium and aluminum plants to provide parts for planes and built the first steel-producing plant in the West. After the war, he made Jeeps and got into healthcare. He died in 1967, having proved that you can't stop a Kaiser when he's on a roll.

Many perceived the strikes as slightly treasonous, and "there are no strikes in foxholes" became a popular response to labor stoppages. Still, as labor leaders pointed out, things were a lot better for a lot of working Americans: Average weekly wages went from $24 in 1939 to $46 in 1944.

Employing women for the war effort

Millions of women entered the workforce to take the place of the men who were off to the military. By 1943, 17 million women filled a third of civilian jobs, 5 million of them in war factories (see Figure 16-1). "If you've followed recipes exactly in making cakes, you can learn to load shells," proclaimed billboards recruiting women to the workplace.

Some companies offered childcare or provided meals to take home as incentives to lure women into the workplace. But women were still given the short end of the stick when it came to wages: In 1944, women got an average of $31.21 a week for working in war-related factories, while men doing the same jobs were paid $54.65.

Figure 16-1: Woman working in a war plant.

© Bettmann/CORBIS

Rose Monroe

It was a classic case of life imitates art imitates life. Early on in World War II, the government started propaganda campaigns to help get women involved in the war effort. One such campaign was built around a poster of an attractive (and well-muscled), bandana-wearing woman named "Rosie the Riveter." There was even a popular song to go along with it.

But Rosie was a fictional character — until actor Walter Pidgeon visited an aircraft plant in Ypsilanti, Michigan, to make a short film promoting war bonds. There he met a young widow named Rose Monroe, who was riveting planes to support her family. Pidgeon signed her up to be in the film, and she became an inspiration for millions of women entering the workforce for the first time.

Born in 1920 in Kentucky, Monroe went to work after her husband died in a car accident. After the war, Monroe drove a cab, owned a beauty shop, started a construction company, and earned a pilot's license. She died in 1997, still an inspiration to new generations of working women.

Making strides — African Americans achieve greater equality

Many African Americans had hoped their service in World War I would help bring them equality in postwar America. But they were wrong. So when World War II started, some black leaders were wary. "Our war is not against the Hitler in Europe," editorialized one black newspaper, "but against the Hitlers in America." Some black leaders demanded assurances that loyalty this time around would be rewarded with more decent treatment.

In response, Roosevelt established the Fair Employment Practices Commission and charged it with investigating cases where African Americans were discriminated against in war industries. The commission enjoyed some success. But the real economic boost for blacks came from the labor shortage, which fueled the movement of many from the South to industrial cities in the North and West.

About 700,000 African Americans also served in the military and some strides in equality were made. Blacks were admitted into the Air Force and Marines for the first time. The Air Force enlisted some 600 black pilots and the first African-American general was appointed in the Army. Some military units were even integrated toward the end of the war, although it was more for practical reasons than to further civil rights.

The "Battle of Los Angeles"

On February 2, 1942, less than two months after Pearl Harbor was attacked, U.S. Naval intelligence in Southern California issued a warning that a Japanese attack might occur that night.

Sure enough, in the wee hours of February 25, radar picked up unidentified blips about 120 miles off the coast of Los Angeles. Then planes were reported near Long Beach, and then four anti-aircraft batteries began firing at something over Santa Monica. Within minutes, other military guns opened fire. Confusion reigned over the next three hours as contradictory reports poured in.

By the dawn's early light, Los Angeles residents saw the results of the attack: no downed enemy planes, no bomb damage, a few traffic accidents, and one man dead from a heart attack.

Eventually it was decided that it had been a false alarm and the fuss had probably been caused by weather balloons (or UFOs, as some folks now insist). Whatever the cause, for a few hours the fighting had come uncomfortably close to the home front.

Even so, race relations remained mired in racism and distrust. Several cities had race riots, the worst of which was in Detroit in 1943, when 34 people died. Angry that the racism of Hitler was being fought against while the racism at home was largely ignored, many African Americans began taking a more active role in asserting their legal rights. The ranks of the National Association for the Advancement of Colored People (NAACP) swelled from 50,000 before the war to more than 400,000 at war's end.

Returning for work after being kicked out — Latinos

In 1942, the U.S. and Mexican governments reached an agreement to allow Mexican workers — *braceros* — to enter the United States to help make up the manpower shortage. Thousands of Mexicans, some of whom had been thrown out of America during the Depression, entered the country, mostly to take agricultural jobs in the West.

The sudden influx sometimes caused friction, particularly in California. In Los Angeles, tensions between outlandishly garbed Latino youths and sailors led to the "zoot suit" riots of 1943. City officials actually passed a law prohibiting the wearing of zoot suits in public as a way to avoid further confrontations.

Treating the Japanese Americans poorly

By far the most shameful aspect of World War II on the home front was the treatment of Japanese residents. About 125,000 people of Japanese descent lived in the United States, 110,000 of them on the West Coast. Seventy thousand, called *Nisei,* were born here. The rest, called *Issei,* were born in Japan and emigrated.

In the wake of Pearl Harbor, many of both groups' neighbors began to view them with suspicion and even hatred. "A Jap's a Jap," said Lt. Gen. John DeWitt, who was in command of the West's defense. "It makes no difference whether he is an American or not."

In February 1942, Roosevelt ordered the forced evacuation of all Japanese residents from the West Coast, supposedly to lessen the potential for them to engage in seditious or traitorous acts. They were moved to bleak concentration camps in remote areas. Many lost virtually everything they owned: homes, farms, businesses, and even personal possessions.

Despite their treatment, about 8,000 Nisei volunteered to serve in the military. One group, the "Fightin' 442nd," was one of the most decorated combat units of the war.

> ### Winning cuisine
>
> If an army travels on its stomach, the United States rode to victory in World War II on Spam. Yes, Spam, the ubiquitous canned meat product made from pork shoulder and ham.
>
> Invented in 1937 by the Hormel Foods Corporation, Spam hit its culinary stride when the war began, as a substitute for rationed beef. Because it didn't need refrigeration, it was ideal for feeding troops — and they ate more than 100 million pounds of it.
>
> Spam was also fodder for G.I. humor: "meatloaf without basic training," "the ham that didn't pass its physical," "the reason war is hell." But Spam was a lifesaver for countries whose food supplies had been pinched by the war. Soviet leader Nikita Khrushchev once stated that without Spam, the Russian army would have starved. And it fries up so much better than caviar.

It wasn't until the 1980s and 1990s that the Nisei were compensated for some of what they lost. In the meantime, Roosevelt's action was upheld by the U.S. Supreme Court as a justifiable hardship. "Hardships are a part of war," said Justice Hugo Black, "and war is an aggregation of hardships."

Dealing with the War in Europe

Shortly after Pearl Harbor, FDR met with English Prime Minister Winston Churchill to decide what the forces of the Allies should do against the *Axis* powers — Germany, Italy, and Japan. The most pressing threat, they decided, was Hitler's Germany. The German army seemed to be on the brink of defeating the Soviet army, its one-time ally. If the Russians fell, Germany could turn its full attention to Britain.

Soviet dictator Josef Stalin wanted the Allies to launch an invasion of German-held Europe as soon as possible, because Russia was being mauled by the Germans. But Churchill wanted to nibble at the edges of the German empire while bombing Germany from the air, and FDR went along with the Brits.

Roosevelt, Churchill, and Stalin managed to put their sharp differences aside and generally cooperate. That proved to be a key ingredient in the Allies' ultimate success. The trio met several times during the war to plot strategy and negotiate about what the world would be like after the war.

Meeting at Yalta

The most important of the meetings of FDR, Churchill, and Stalin actually came toward the end of the war at Yalta, a former palace on the Black Sea in the Soviet Union.

Roosevelt came to Yalta hoping to establish the groundwork for a practical and powerful United Nations, to be formed after the war, and also to convince the Russians to enter the war against Japan and help speed up the end of the war.

Stalin eventually agreed, but at a price. In return, the Soviet dictator got the other two to agree to give the Soviets control over broad areas of Europe and a promise that each of the major nations on the UN Security Council would have veto power over council decisions. As it turned out, the price Roosevelt paid was far too high for what he got in return.

Winning one step at a time

One of the most immediate problems was dealing with the menace posed by German submarines, or *U-boats,* in the Atlantic. Traveling in packs, the subs sank three million tons of Allied shipping in the first half of 1942 alone. But the Allies worked out a system of convoys and developed better anti-sub tactics. Most importantly, they built far more cargo ships than the Germans could possibly sink.

In the summer of 1942, Allied planes began bombing targets inside Germany. Eventually, the bombing would take a terrible toll. In 1943, 60,000 people were killed in the city of Hamburg, and the city of Dresden was all but destroyed.

In February 1943, U.S. forces in North Africa had their first significant confrontation with the German army. It did not go well. The green American troops were driven back from the strategic Kasserine Pass in Tunisia. But under a new commander, Major Gen. George S. Patton, the U.S. forces rallied and counterattacked. Combined with victories by the British and other Allies, the effort drove German forces out of North Africa.

From Africa, the Allies invaded Sicily, and then advanced into the Italian mainland. Mussolini was overthrown and eventually executed by his own people. But the German army poured troops into the country and it took until the end of 1944 for Italy to be completely controlled.

On the Eastern Front, meanwhile, the Russian army gradually had turned the tables on the invading Germans and begun pushing them back, despite staggering civilian and military losses. And in England, the Allies, under the leadership of Eisenhower, were preparing the greatest invasion force the world had ever seen.

Making the final push

On June 6, 1944 — *D-Day* — the Allied forces swept ashore on the beaches of Normandy in France. It was a staggering logistical feat. Some 175,000 men were landed on the first day, a number that swelled to 325,000 in the first week and eventually to 2.5 million. They were delivered by 5,300 ships and supported by 50,000 vehicles and 11,000 planes.

By August, the U.S. 3rd Army, under the brash and aggressive Patton, pushed deep into France and to the edge of Germany itself. A little more than a week before Christmas, 1944, however, the Germans launched a desperate counterattack. Known as the Battle of the Bulge, the surprise attack succeeded at first, costing the United States 77,000 casualties. But the Germans were low on men and supplies and could not sustain the attack. By late January 1945, the Allies were again on the offensive.

Discovering the war's greatest crime

As Allied troops moved deeper into the heart of German-held territory, they began to make stomach-churning, heart-wrenching discoveries: concentration camps holding what was left of millions of Jews and other "undesirables" that German leaders had ordered to be murdered as a "final solution" to "cleansing" Germany of all but the "Aryan Race."

Hitler's "final solution" became known to the civilized world as the Holocaust, and resulted in the murders of 6 million Jews and 4 million non-Jews, including gays, Gypsies, and the mentally and physically handicapped. The Holocaust had not been a complete secret to the Allies, but finding a way to stop it had not been as big a priority as winning the war.

In addition, anti-Semitic feelings were not unknown in Congress, the U.S. State Department, or among the American public — although certainly not to the point that Americans would have approved of Nazi atrocities. But the enormity of the crimes was not fully understood until the camps were discovered and their stories told by survivors.

Late in the war, the Roosevelt administration established the War Refugee Board, which helped organize the rescue of some European Jews. And the United States was the first country to formally recognize the Jewish state of Israel in 1948. But stopping the Holocaust, as it was happening, was simply not at the forefront of the war effort.

> ### Nazi nitwits
>
> Adolf Hitler had an itch to bring the war to America. So in mid-June, 1942, German subs landed four men on Long Island, New York, and four more on a Florida beach. They also landed cases of explosives. All the men had lived in America before and spoke fluent English. Their mission was to sabotage U.S. factories, incite terror, and disrupt the economy.
>
> But they turned out to be an octet of oafs. Several of them went on shopping sprees. Several blabbed about their mission to relatives — and two of them blabbed to federal agents.
>
> Within two weeks of their arrival, all of them had been arrested by the FBI. After a military trial, all eight were convicted of espionage. Six of the Germans were executed, while the two who confessed were imprisoned for the rest of the war and then deported.
>
> Hitler's itch was never scratched. Not a single case of enemy-directed sabotage was ever verified during the war.

Ending the war in Europe, and the end of FDR

In April, the U.S. and Russian armies joined up at the Elbe River and advanced on Berlin. Hitler committed suicide, and on May 7 — *V-E* or *Victory in Europe* Day — Germany surrendered.

Roosevelt did not live to see the victory. The president had won a fourth term in 1944, despite rumors about his failing health. But on April 12, 1945, while vacationing at Warm Springs, Georgia, FDR died suddenly of a cerebral hemorrhage. The nation was staggered at the loss of the man who had led them through the Depression and the war. One New York housewife was asked if she heard the radio bulletins of FDR's death and replied "For what do I need a radio? It's on everybody's face."

The new president, a former hat salesman from Missouri named Harry S. Truman, was as stunned as anyone. "Being president is like riding a tiger," Truman later wrote. "I never felt that I could let go for a single moment."

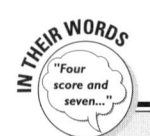

> ### That's a negative
>
> "Nuts." — Reply of U.S. Gen. Anthony McAuliffe to a German demand for surrender at Bastogne, France, during the Battle of the Bulge. McAuliffe's troops held on until relieved.

Dealing with the War in the Pacific

Less than 12 hours after the bombing of Pearl Harbor, the Japanese attacked U.S. air bases in the Philippines, destroying scores of U.S. planes. Within a few months, they conquered Guam, Wake Island, Hong Kong, Singapore, the Dutch East Indies, Burma, and the Philippines. Drunk with victories, Japanese forces continued to expand their dominance in the Pacific during the first few months of the war.

About the only good news for the Allies came on April 18, 1942, when a squadron of B-25 bombers launched from an aircraft carrier and led by Col. James Doolittle managed to bomb Tokyo. The planes did little damage and none of the planes made it back, with most of the crews having to ditch them in China. Still, Doolittle's raid was a huge shot in the arm for sagging American morale.

Fighting back

U.S. strategists decided to strike back on two fronts. The first, under Gen. Douglas MacArthur, would move north from Australia, through New Guinea, and then back to the Philippines. The second, under Adm. Chester Nimitz, would move west from Hawaii and then hopscotch from island to island toward Japan itself.

But first the Japanese offense had to be stopped. The initial halt came in early May 1942, at the Battle of the Coral Sea, northwest of Australia. It was the first naval fight in history where the fighting ships never actually saw each other: All the combat was done by planes from each side's aircraft carriers. The battle was pretty much a draw, but the Japanese fleet carrying invasion troops to New Guinea had to turn back, marking the first time the Japanese had not won outright.

Turning the tide

The real turning point, however, came between June 3 and June 6, in a fierce naval battle near the U.S.-held Midway Island. Tipped to Japanese plans by intercepting their messages and breaking their codes, U.S. forces managed to sink four Japanese aircraft carriers, losing only one. The victory returned control of the central Pacific to the Allies.

A few months after the Battle of Midway, the United States took the offensive in the Solomon Islands, winning battles at Gavutu, Tulagi, and Guadalcanal. It took six grueling months to take Guadalcanal, but by mid-1943, the Japanese forces were either retreating or on defense nearly everywhere.

Now it was America's turn. In February 1944, forces under Nimitz won victories in the Marshall Islands, and in the fall, Allied forces reopened supply lines in Southeast Asia into China. In mid-1944, a U.S. armada struck the Marianas Islands of Tinian, Guam, and Saipan, and on October 20, 1944, MacArthur made good on an earlier promise and returned to the Philippines.

As the Germans did at the Battle of the Bulge, the Japanese threw everything they had into a counteroffensive. And, like the Germans, they lost. The Battle of Leyte Gulf cost Japan four more carriers and all but ended its ability to mount an offensive. Next came the battle for the island of Okinawa, just 370 miles south of Japan itself. The Japanese sent suicide planes called *kamikazes* ("divine wind") on one-way trips into U.S. ships, and while they were horrifyingly effective, they weren't enough. After 50,000 Allied and 100,000 Japanese were killed or wounded, Okinawa fell in late June 1945.

U.S. submarines were taking a huge toll on Japanese supply lines, sinking more than half of all the enemy's cargo ships by the end of the war. American planes, meanwhile, had been softening up the Japanese mainland. In May 1945, they dropped napalm on Tokyo, killing 80,000 people. The bombings were designed to make the eventual invasion of Japan easier. Even so, U.S. strategists figured it would take more than a year of fighting and more than 1 million American soldiers would be killed or wounded before the Japanese homeland would fall.

What the strategists did not count on was a terrible new weapon that had been conceived in New York and Tennessee and spawned on the deserts of New Mexico.

Another "useless" war product

The Japanese conquests in Southeast Asia cut off many of America's rubber supplies. So the United States turned to synthetic rubber and went looking for an alternative that would be even cheaper.

In 1943, a General Electric (GE) scientist named James Wright mixed boric acid and silicone oil and formed a gooey substance that bounced, stretched, and even picked up impressions from newsprint and comic books.

Trouble was, no one could find a practical use for it. In 1949, however, a Connecticut man named Paul Hodgson borrowed $147, bought the rights to the stuff from GE, and began marketing it in little plastic eggs in time for Easter.

"Silly Putty" was a smash hit with kids, and Hodgson left a tidy $140 million estate when he died in 1976, proving that it is possible to make gold from goo.

Audie Murphy

He was a pint-sized Texas orphan who joined the Army as a buck private at the age of 16. When he came home, he weighed a lot more — mostly because of the medals on his chest.

Murphy was born in 1926 to poor sharecropper parents. After joining the Army, Murphy saw action in nine major campaigns in North Africa, Italy, and France, single-handedly killing more than 200 enemy soldiers while rising to the rank of second lieutenant. On Jan. 26, 1945, in France, Murphy took on an attack by six German tanks and supporting infantry. Despite being wounded, he fought until he ran out of ammunition, which was long enough to direct artillery fire and beat back the German attack.

His heroism won Murphy more than 30 citations, including the Congressional Medal of Honor and the French Croix de Guerre. After the war, America's most decorated soldier became a movie actor, making 44 films. One of them, *To Hell and Back,* was based on his own best-selling autobiography. Murphy died in a plane crash in 1971, at the age of 45.

Dropping the Bomb

Even before the war began, scientists fleeing from Nazi Germany had warned U.S. officials the Germans were working on developing a huge new bomb that would be triggered through an atomic reaction. The U.S. government then began pouring what would amount to more than $2 billion into what would be called the "Manhattan Project," because it started in New York.

Work continued at top-secret bases in Oak Ridge, Tennessee, and Los Alamos, New Mexico, under the direction of physicist J. Robert Oppenheimer. The project was so hush-hush that Vice President Harry Truman wasn't told of it until he assumed the presidency after FDR's death. On July 16, 1945, the world's first atomic bomb was detonated at a testing ground in New Mexico.

On July 26, 1945, Allied leaders delivered a surrender ultimatum to Japan, but it was rejected by that country's military leaders. Then on August 6, 1945, a single B-29 bomber nicknamed *Enola Gay* dropped an atomic bomb on the city of Hiroshima. The bomb killed 75,000 people and injured another 100,000 in the city of 340,000. Thousands more eventually died from the radiation.

Debate has raged ever since as to whether Japan would have surrendered if the bomb had not been dropped. But at the time, there was little hesitation about its use on the part of the man who made the decision, President Truman. "I regarded the bomb as a military weapon," he said later, "and never had any doubt that it should be used."

IN THEIR WORDS

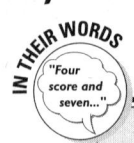

A witness to doom

"It worked." —J. Robert Oppenheimer, after witnessing the first atomic bomb explosion. Oppenheimer later said he was thinking of an ancient Indian poem: "I am become Death, the Shatterer of Worlds."

Japan was stunned by the destruction of the Hiroshima bomb, but its leaders hesitated in surrendering. Three days later, another A-bomb was dropped on Nagasaki. The next day, Japan surrendered. The final ceremony took place on September 2, aboard the USS *Missouri* in Tokyo Bay.

World War II, the bloodiest and most devastating war in human history, was over.

About 30 million civilians and military personnel around the world had been killed. American losses, compared to the other major combatant countries, had been light: About 300,000 were killed and another 750,000 were injured or wounded.

But while the war was over, a new age that included the threat of even more horrible wars was just beginning.

Part IV
America in Adulthood

Five Terrible Facts about the Vietnam War

- Number of Americans killed: 58,174
- Number wounded: 304,000
- Cost, 1950–1974: $150 billion
- Average age of U.S. soldier killed: 23
- Average number of days in combat by U.S. infantry soldier in one year in Vietnam: 240

Visit www.dummies.com/extras/ushistory for an article about an extremist group in the 1960s and 1970s.

In this part...

- America emerges as a world power after World War II.
- Tensions build with the USSR and plunge the United States into a Cold War.
- Fast-moving technology and mass media shape American life in the last few decades of the 20th century.

Chapter 17

TV, Elvis, and Reds under the Bed: 1946–1960

In This Chapter

▶ Cooling down relations with Russia and heating things up in Korea

▶ Testing Americans' loyalty

▶ Letting the good times roll (and rock)

▶ Working against segregation

*I*f you had asked most Americans in 1945 how they felt about the Union of Soviet Socialist Republics (USSR), they probably would've responded with warm and fuzzy statements about our brave ally against Hitler. Had you asked them in 1950, however, you would have received a very different answer.

In this chapter, Americans combat communism at home and abroad, real and imagined. They move to the suburbs, eat in their cars, and discover a new medium/religion called television. They also embrace a form of music with its roots in African-American culture — but are much less willing to embrace African Americans themselves.

A Cold War and a Hot "Police Action"

The foundations of the Cold War were broader than just the ideological struggle between capitalism and communism. The Soviet Union had suffered terribly during World War II and was hungry to recover. Soviet leaders feared and distrusted the United States, which was the only country with the atomic bomb — and which had used it. They were also determined to surround the Soviet Union with countries that would not be a threat to it in future wars.

But America saw its former ally as a nation led by men who were as duplicitous and dangerous as those the Allies had just defeated. The Soviets desire to forcibly impose itself on other counties was unacceptable.

Heavy drapes

"From Stettin in the Baltic to Trieste in the Adriatic, an 'iron curtain' has descended across the continent." —Winston Churchill, referring to the spread of Soviet influence across Europe in a March 5, 1946, speech in Fulton, Missouri.

Gauging the United Nations

After World War I, the U.S. Senate voted against joining the League of Nations. The second time around, however, it jumped at the chance to join the League's successor. On July 28, 1945, senators voted 89 to 2 in favor of joining the United Nations (UN), which had its first meeting in 1946 in London and then moved to its permanent home in New York City.

The UN's two main bodies were the General Assembly, where every member nation had a seat, and the Security Council, which had five permanent members — the United States, the Soviet Union, Great Britain, France, and China — and six seats that rotated among other countries. Each of the permanent members could veto council actions, which meant it was impossible for the UN to do anything that any one of the top powers didn't like.

While the United Nations did have some success in international cooperation when it came to subjects like health and education, it could do little to slow down the nuclear arms race or prevent the Super Powers from interfering in other countries.

The world as a chessboard

The first big test of wills between the United States and the Soviet Union came in the Mediterranean. Communist-backed rebels in Greece and Turkey were trying to overthrow the governments in those two countries. Britain had been assisting the Greek and Turkish governments, but was in deep economic trouble at home and couldn't continue.

So Harry Truman went to Congress. Truman was a former U.S. senator from Missouri who had been made vice president in 1944 and succeeded Franklin Roosevelt as president when Roosevelt died in 1945. Truman was blunt, honest, and outspoken. He often complained about what a tough job it was to be president. But most of the time he wasn't shy about doing it — and to hell with anyone who didn't like the way he did it.

In March 1947, Truman asked Congress for $400 million to help the Greek and Turkish governments. He also asked to send U.S. military advisors to both countries, at their request. In what became known as the "Truman Doctrine," Truman drew a sharp distinction between the communist way of life and the Free World. Congress went along, sending more than $600 million to the two countries by 1950.

Truman's doctrine was part of an overall strategy to "contain" communism. The idea was to make other countries prosperous enough that they wouldn't be tempted to go red. Other elements of the containment strategy included

- **The Four Point Program:** This was sort of a junior Marshall Plan. Proposed by Truman in 1949, it provided about $400 million to under-developed countries in Asia, Latin America, and Africa for developing industry, communications, and technological systems.

- **The Marshall Plan:** Named after General George C. Marshall, who became Truman's secretary of state, the plan provided about $12 billion in U.S. aid to 16 countries in Western Europe to help them recover from the ravages of the war. The plan was a rousing success, and by 1952, much of Western Europe was well on its way to economic recovery.

- **NATO:** In 1949, the United States and 11 Western nations formed the North Atlantic Treaty Organization (NATO). The countries agreed to come to the aid of any member nation that was attacked, and to develop an international security force that would help discourage aggression by non-NATO countries.

The Berlin airlift

The Soviet Union didn't watch all this U.S. activity while lazing in a hammock. After the war, temporary governance of Germany had been divided among France, Britain, the United States, and Russia. The city of Berlin was deep in the Russian sector but run by all four nations. So when the Soviets became irritated at all the containment in 1948, they blockaded Berlin, hoping to force the Western countries out of the city completely.

Instead, the Western countries mounted a huge airlift, shipping food and other supplies over the blockade and into the city. In May 1949, the Soviets lifted the blockade. But the tensions made both sides realize that there would be no easy solution to reestablishing a new Germany. So the Western powers agreed to create one country out of their half and the Soviets created another country out of the other half. East Germany and West Germany would not be united again for more than 40 years.

> ## Big Red in the corn
>
> One reason behind the distrust between the United States and the Soviet Union was that the countries didn't really know each other very well. So it was big news in 1959 when leaders of the two countries exchanged visits.
>
> In July, Vice President Richard Nixon went to Moscow to attend an exhibit of American products, including a six-room, ranch-style model home. Nixon and Soviet Chairman Nikita Khrushchev got into a heated — and televised — quarrel over the relative merits of each country's economic system.
>
> In September, Khrushchev came to America. Among his stops were Hollywood, San Francisco, Franklin Roosevelt's grave — and Coon Rapids, Iowa. It seems the chairman had been invited to visit the farm of a fellow named Roswell Garst, who had been selling corn seed to the Soviet Union since 1955, and fancied himself a bit of a diplomat as well as a farmer.
>
> After a tour of Garst's farm, Khrushchev offered what could have been a summary of his whole trip. Garst, the chairman said, was a "class enemy," but was generously willing "to trade secrets with others — even us."

The "miracle of '48"

Despite some success overseas, Truman was considered a political dead duck as the 1948 elections drew near. The Republicans had gained seats in Congress in 1946. Truman's former secretary of commerce, Henry Wallace, had decided to run as a liberal third-party candidate, sure to take votes from Truman. Segregationist Strom Thurmond, governor of South Carolina, also decided to run as an independent candidate. The Republicans were running Governor Thomas Dewey of New York, a man who was considered solid, if a bit dull (someone suggested he looked like the little plastic guy on wedding cakes).

But true to form, Truman decided to "give 'em hell." He stumped around the country, ragging on the Republican-controlled Congress as a bunch of do-nothings and pledging to change things at home and abroad if given another term. When the votes were counted, Truman had pulled off the biggest upset in presidential political history, and the Democrats had taken back Congress. Their reward was another war.

The Korean War

The Cold War was at its hottest in Korea. After World War II ended, the Russians controlled the northern part of the country and the United States the south. In 1949, the Soviets left a communist government in charge in the north and the United States left a pro-Western government in the south. China, meanwhile, finished its civil war and was now firmly in the control of communists.

On June 24, 1950, the North Koreans invaded South Korea. A few days later, Truman ordered U.S. troops to the aid of South Korea and convinced the UN to send military aid as well, in what was referred to in diplomatic circles as a "police action."

The UN troops, which were mostly American, were under the command of General Douglas MacArthur. Because the North Korean attack was such a surprise, the U.S. and South Korean forces were pushed into the far southern corner of the Korean peninsula by September. But MacArthur pulled off a risky but brilliant amphibious landing behind the North Koreans. By November, he had driven the enemy deep into North Korea and was poised to push them into China.

Then the Chinese army poured troops into the fight and forced the UN troops back into South Korea. But the UN forces reorganized and counterattacked, forcing the Chinese back behind the 38th parallel of latitude, where the war had started in the first place.

For the next 18 months, an uneasy truce, sporadically interrupted by skirmishing, was in place. Finally, in July 1953, an agreement to call the whole mess a draw was reached.

The Korean War cost more than $50 billion and 33,000 U.S. lives, plus another 110,000 or so were wounded. It also cost Truman politically. When MacArthur publicly disagreed with Truman over Truman's decision not to invade China, the general was fired. MacArthur returned to a hero's welcome in America, and Truman was unfairly pilloried as being soft on communism.

Truman didn't run for reelection in 1952. Instead, the country turned to its most popular military figure in decades, Dwight David Eisenhower. "Ike" was so apolitical he didn't even decide which political party to join until shortly before accepting the Republican nomination.

Eisenhower had been a bold and decisive military leader in World War II. But as president his approach, at least on domestic issues, was to move cautiously, if at all. He does deserve credit for investing in and jump-starting America's interstate highway system, but only reluctantly involved the federal government in the struggle for civil rights.

Uncle Sam's big stick

One thing Eisenhower's administration wasn't shy about was injecting itself into other countries' internal affairs. In 1953, Central Intelligence Agency (CIA) operatives helped topple a communist-influenced government in Iran and reinstate the dictatorial Shah. The following year, the CIA aided a coup in Guatemala, ousting a communist-backed but constitutionally elected leader and replacing him with a U.S.-friendly president.

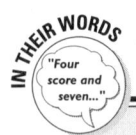

"Doominoes"

"You have a row of dominoes set up, and you knock over the first one, and what will happen to the last one is the certainty that it will go over very quickly." —President Eisenhower, explaining why the United States needed to stop the communists in Vietnam, April 7, 1954.

It wasn't only ideology that motivated America. In Iran, the United States made sure Iranian oil was kept flowing toward America and not the Soviet Union. In Guatemala, the interests of American fruit companies were being protected.

In Asia, the United States was busy providing aid to France to help it fight a communist rebellion in its colony of Vietnam. By 1954, the French had lost the northern half of the country, and by 1956, the United States was steadily increasing the amount of aid it was sending to South Vietnam.

Finding Commies under the Bed

Not all the world's communists were in other countries. Since the 1920s, there had been a communist party in the United States that had taken orders from party leaders in the Soviet Union. But the average American didn't pay much attention. After World War II, however, "communist" became a much dirtier word. U.S. government officials helped fuel the fire by talking almost daily about spies and the dangers of communists and communist sympathizers.

Part of the reason for the anti-communist fears was that communists ran America's biggest post-war rivals, the Soviet Union and China. Part was bewilderment over the success the communists were having in Asia and Eastern Europe. And part was there really were some spies, and the U.S. government failed to keep the atomic bomb the exclusive property of America.

Whatever the reason, commie hunting became a national pastime. In 1947, the House Un-American Activities Committee (HUAC) — dominated by Republicans who included a freshman member from California named Richard M. Nixon — began searching for communists within and without government. One place they looked was Hollywood. Actors, directors, and writers were called before the committee, and 10 who refused to testify were jailed. Others were "blacklisted" and couldn't get jobs in the industry for years afterward. But no great plot to undermine America through the movies was ever uncovered.

Casting suspicion on Hiss

The committee caught a bigger fish in 1948. Whittaker Chambers, a *Time* magazine editor who said he had been a communist until 1937, told the committee that a former member of Roosevelt's State Department, Alger Hiss, had passed information to Russian spies.

Hiss denied the charges, even after Chambers produced from a hollowed-out pumpkin what he said was microfilm passed between the men. Neither could be prosecuted for espionage because too much time had passed. But Hiss was found guilty of perjury and sentenced to five years in prison. The Hiss conviction helped Nixon get elected to the Senate in 1950 and win a place as Eisenhower's running mate in 1952.

Leaking scientific secrets: The Rosenbergs

Hiss wasn't the only trophy for the commie hunters. In February 1950, it was revealed that a British scientist had given atomic secrets to the Soviets. Among his allies, it was announced, were a New York couple named Julius and Ethel Rosenberg. The Rosenbergs were charged with getting information from Ethel's brother, who worked on the U.S. bomb project in New Mexico. They were convicted of treason and executed in 1953.

Helen Gahagan Douglas

Helen Gahagan Douglas was the "pink lady" of American politics. Douglas was born in New Jersey in 1900. She left college in 1922 to become an opera singer and a leading Broadway actress. With her husband, actor Melvyn Douglas, Helen moved to California and became active in Democratic politics. After working to better the plight of migrant farm workers, she won a seat in Congress in 1944, representing a heavily African-American district in Los Angeles.

In 1950, Helen ran for the U.S. Senate against another member of Congress, Richard Nixon.

Nixon had won a national reputation as a communist hunter and wasted little time implying that Helen was, if not an outright commie, "pink right down to her underwear."

Helen's liberalism did not play well with voters, especially after the Korean War broke out, and Nixon easily defeated her. She left politics, became an author, and died in 1980. As part of her legacy, she left behind a nickname she gave Nixon that stuck with him all the way to the White House: "Tricky Dick."

> ### A shot at polio
>
> Every summer it showed up: a crippling disease that most often struck children and left them paralyzed or dead. In 1952 alone, more than 21,000 U.S. children were infected.
>
> Jonas Salk wanted to do something about the poliomyelitis virus. Salk, a University of Pittsburgh Medical School researcher, worked for almost eight years to develop a vaccine. Finally, after exhaustive trials, the government licensed the vaccine on April 12, 1955. Salk refused to become rich by patenting the vaccine and hoped the federal government would take over its distribution. The Eisenhower administration greeted the idea icily. Secretary of Health, Education, and Welfare Oveta Culp Hobby called it "socialized medicine by the back door."
>
> But Salk's vaccine, delivered via injections, eventually was distributed free by the government and saved thousands of children from the disease. In 1961, an oral vaccine developed by Dr. Albert Sabin was licensed and administered around the world. Polio is now virtually unknown in the United States. By 2013, there were only 328 cases of polio reported in the entire world.

Checking the loyalty of federal workers

Despite some reservations that things were getting out of hand, President Truman didn't leave all the ferreting out of communists to Congress. In 1947, Truman ordered a government-wide "loyalty" review. By the time it was done, more than 3 million federal workers had been reviewed. More than 2,000 workers resigned and about 200 were fired.

Not to be outdone, Congress passed bills in 1950 and 1952 — over Truman's vetoes — that made it illegal to do anything "that would substantially contribute to the establishment . . . of a totalitarian dictatorship." The bills also required "communist front organizations" to register with the Justice Department and denied admission to the country to aliens who had been members of "totalitarian" groups, even as children.

Telling tall tales: "Tail-Gunner Joe"

He was a liar and a drunk — and for a few years he was one of the most powerful men in America. In February 1950, Senator Joseph McCarthy of Wisconsin gave a speech in West Virginia. In the speech, McCarthy said he had a list of 205 known communists working in the State Department. It was nonsense, but it made national headlines, and McCarthy repeated it and similar charges over the next four years.

> ### Shut up, Senator
>
> "Let us not assassinate this lad further, Senator. You have done enough. Have you no sense of decency, sir? At long last, have you no sense of decency?" —Army counsel Joseph Welch to Senator Joseph McCarthy during hearings on suspected communists in the U.S. Army, June 9, 1954.

McCarthy, who claimed to have been a tail gunner who saw lots of action during World War II, actually had never seen any combat. But he was a formidable opponent in the commie-hunting field. He ripped even General George Marshall and President Eisenhower. Every time he made a charge that proved to be untrue, McCarthy simply made a new charge. The tactic became known as "McCarthyism."

By the summer of 1954, however, McCarthy's antics were wearing thin. When he began a series of attacks on the Army for "coddling" communists during congressional hearings, they were televised. Many Americans got their first look at McCarthy in action and were repulsed. In December 1954, the Senate censured him. He died in obscurity three years later of problems related to alcoholism.

Having It All

After World War II, the American economy hummed along. There were plenty of jobs for returning servicemen. There was also the G.I. Bill of Rights, which passed Congress in 1944 and provided veterans more than $13 billion in the decade after the war for college tuition, vocational training programs, or money to start a business. Perhaps most important, the bill offered vets no-money-down, low-interest loans to buy homes.

A booming economy

Thanks to a $6 billion tax cut and all the savings from buying bonds during the war, Americans had plenty to spend. The high consumer demand for goods triggered high inflation — 14 to 15 percent the first two years after the war for goods in general, and a painful 25 percent for food. Such high costs in turn triggered a lot of labor unrest, with 5,000 strikes in 1946 alone, and major troubles in the coal and rail industries. President Truman reinstated wartime price controls to deal with inflation, and the Republican Congress passed a bill called the Taft-Hartley Act in 1947 that restricted labor union power.

By 1949, the economy had adjusted to the ending of the war, and the country entered an almost unprecedented economic boom. From 1945 to 1960, the Gross National Product (the amount of goods and services produced) increased from $200 billion to $500 billion per year. Thousands of smaller companies merged or were gobbled up by large corporations. So were many family farms, by large "company" farms.

The economy wasn't the only thing growing. The birthrate boomed as men and women pushed apart by the war made up for lost time. The population grew 20 percent in the 1950s, from 150 million to 180 million, and the generation born between 1946 and 1964 became known as the baby boomers. Along with the economy and the population, Americans' appetite for the good life (the number of private cars purchased doubled in the 1950s) and the perceived need to "keep up with the Joneses" also grew.

Moving to the burbs

Having your own car meant you could live farther away from where you worked. The suburbs grew 47 percent in the 1950s as more and more Americans staked out their own little territory. New housing starts, which had dropped to 100,000 a year during the war, climbed to 1.5 million annually. To fill the need, homebuilders turned to assembly-line techniques.

The leading pioneer was a New York developer named William J. Levitt. A former member of the Navy construction battalion known as the Seabees, Levitt knew how to build things in a hurry. He bought 1,500 acres on Long Island, and on March 7, 1949, opened a sales office — with more than 1,000 customers already waiting. A basic Levitt four-room house on a 6,000-square-foot lot sold for $6,900, about 2½ years' wages. The cookie-cutter approach in Island Trees (later changed to Levittown) was criticized as stifling individuality. But to the 82,000 people living in 17,000 new houses, it was home. Other builders followed suit all over the country, and 13 million new homes were sold during the decade.

"No man who owns his own house and a lot can be a communist," Levitt said. "He has too much to do." Of course, his sentiments didn't extend to African Americans: They were excluded from buying homes at his developments for fear they would scare away white buyers.

Chapter 17: TV, Elvis, and Reds under the Bed: 1946–1960 277

The golden age of grease

Brothers Richard and Maurice McDonald were bored with the drive-in barbeque joint they had opened in 1940 in San Bernardino, California, and they were tired of all the teens that hung around the place after they ate, as if it were a clubhouse.

So in 1948, the McDonalds fired their carhops, cut their menu to nine items, dropped the price of a hamburger from 30 cents to 15 cents, replaced tableware with paper bags and cups, and pre-assembled much of the food. The "fast food" was perfect for the speeded-up postwar society.

A Chicago milkshake machine salesman named Ray Kroc loved the idea. Kroc convinced the McDonalds to make him their franchising agent and then bought the brothers out in 1961. By the time he died in 1984, there were 7,500 McDonald's outlets. Today, there are more than 31,000, serving 47 million people a day in 119 countries.

And why did Kroc stick with the brothers' name even after he bought them out? Because, he once explained, no one was going to buy a "Kroc burger." Or a "Big Kroc," for that matter.

Tuning in to the tube

There was less discrimination when it came to selling consumer products, and one of the most popular products in the 1950s was the TV (see Figure 17-1). At the start of the decade, there were about 3 million TV owners; by the end of it, there were 55 million, watching shows from 530 stations. The average price of TV sets dropped from about $500 in 1949 to $200 in 1953.

Figure 17-1: A family gathers around a TV to watch their favorite program.

© Frank Martin/ Getty Images

Like radio before it, the spread of TV had a huge cultural impact. Beginning with the 1948 campaign, it made itself felt in U.S. politics. One wonderful effect was that it made speeches shorter. Politicians and commentators alike began to think and speak in "sound bites" that fit the medium. By 1960, the televised debates between candidates Richard Nixon and John F. Kennedy were considered a crucial element in Kennedy's narrow victory. TV also helped make professional and college sports big businesses, and sometimes provided excellent comedy and dramatic shows to vast audiences that might not otherwise have had access to them.

But even to its mildest critics, much of what was on the often-aptly nicknamed "boob tube" was mindless junk. It was designed to sell products, it homogenized cultural tastes to the point of blandness, and it created feelings of inadequacy in some, who felt their real lives should compare with the insipidly happy characters they saw on shows like *Leave It to Beaver*.

Federal Communications Commission (FCC) chairman Newton Minnow called it "a vast wasteland." Nonetheless, it was a popular wasteland. Comedian Milton Berle's show was so loved, for example, that movie theaters in some towns closed down Tuesday nights because everyone was home watching "Uncle Miltie." And in 1954, the Toledo, Ohio water commissioner reported that water consumption surged at certain times because so many people were simultaneously using their toilets during commercial breaks on the most popular shows.

What A doll!

Ruth Handler went shopping in Switzerland in the 1950s — and found retail gold. Handler, with her husband Elliot and his business partner, Harold Mattson, had started a toy company in 1945 that they named by combining Mattson's name and Elliot's to form "Mattel." Anyway, Ruth Handler bought a German-made doll named Lilli while on her Swiss shopping spree. Unlike most American dolls, which were modeled after babies, Lilli was modeled after babes — as in buxom, long-legged young women. Handler had seen her own daughter playing with similar-looking paper dolls, and figured a U.S. version of Lilli might catch on.

So in 1959, Mattel introduced a very grown-up-looking doll with an impressive wardrobe (which of course was sold separately). It was a hit, and the company sold $500 million worth of dolls and related products in the first decade after its introduction.

The line has added heaps of supporting characters ever since, but the original mainstays have remained "Barbie" and "Ken," named after the Handlers' own son and daughter. And doll collectors the world over are glad the Handlers didn't name their kids "Attila" and "Hortense."

Rockin' 'n' rollin'

America had 13 million teenagers by the mid-1950s, and they had a lot of money to spend — an average of about $10 a week. One of the things they spent it on was their own music. It was a mix of blues and country that was as much about youthful rebellion as it was the sound, and it was called *rock 'n' roll,* a term coined in 1952 by a Cleveland radio personality named Alan Freed, who became the new sound's Pied Piper.

Adult backlash was fierce. Ministers decried it as satanic, racists called it "jungle music," and law enforcement officials deemed it riot-inciting. Most troubling to some older Americans was that the music tended to blur racial divides among young people: You couldn't easily segregate the radio dial.

And of course the more adults squawked about it — surprise! — the more their kids wanted it. In 1954, "Shake, Rattle and Roll" by Bill Haley and the Comets sold more than 1 million records. Scores of rock stars came and went almost overnight. Others, such as Jerry Lee Lewis and Little Richard, were stars with more staying power.

An American king

And then there was Elvis. Born in Mississippi in 1935 and raised in Tennessee by poor, working-class parents, Elvis Presley became perhaps the most recognized personality in the world during the decade. In 1956 alone, he was selling $75,000 worth of records *per day* and had signed a three-picture movie deal. A staggering 54 million people tuned in to see him on the Ed Sullivan TV show. By the time he died in 1977, Presley was the undisputed "King of Rock 'n Roll," and composer Leonard Bernstein had referred to him as "the greatest cultural force in the 20th century."

One effect of the new music was to open up new audiences for African-American performers. Chuck Berry became the first black rock star to have a hit on the mainstream charts. More than 90 years after the end of slavery, music was one of the few fields that were open to African Americans.

Moving, Slowly, to the Front of the Bus

By the 1950s, after fighting through two world wars and struggling through the Depression, many African Americans had had enough of running in place. The result was a series of events that added up to the beginning of the civil rights movement.

Buddy Holly

His career lasted only 18 months, but his influence on American music has lasted more than half a century. Charles Hardin Holley was born in Lubbock, Texas, in 1936. After high school, Holley played in a trio, focusing on country music. But his heart was in the new sounds of rock 'n' roll. In May 1957, "Holly" (his name had been spelled wrong on a record label, and he just went along with it) and his group, the Crickets, released their first hit, "That'll Be the Day." By the end of the year, Holly had three million-sellers, and by the end of 1958, he had sold 10 million records.

Unlike other teen stars, Holly not only played guitar and sang, but also wrote, arranged, and produced most of his music, and experimented with techniques such as double-tracking. He was also one of the first U.S. rock stars to tour abroad. But on Feb. 3, 1959, his career came to a sudden end. After a concert in Clear Lake, Iowa, the 22-year-old Holly and three others were killed when their small plane crashed. The tragedy was immortalized in the 1972 song "American Pie" as "the day the music died."

Holly's musical influence lived on not only in America, but overseas as well. A fledgling rock group in Liverpool, England, for instance, named itself a variation of Holly's group, the Crickets. They called themselves "The Beatles."

Brown against the board

On May 17, 1954, the U.S. Supreme Court issued one of its most important decisions. In a case called *Brown v. the Board of Education of Topeka, Kansas*, the court ruled that the segregation of public schools was unconstitutional. It overturned an 1896 Supreme Court decision that had said schools could be segregated if the facilities that were offered different groups were equal (which of course they seldom, if ever, were). "We conclude that in the field of public education, the doctrine of 'separate but equal' has no place," wrote Chief Justice Earl Warren.

The court followed its decision a year later with broad rules for desegregating America's schools, but they included no timetable. Some communities moved quickly. But others, mostly in the South, made it clear they were in no hurry to comply with the court's ruling. By 1957, only about 20 percent of Southern school districts had even begun the process.

In September 1957, a federal court ordered Central High School in Little Rock, Arkansas, desegregated. A white mob decided to block the admission of nine black students, and Arkansas Governor Orval Faubus refused to do anything about it. So a reluctant President Eisenhower sent in 1,000 federal troops and activated 10,000 members of the National Guard to protect the students and escort them to class.

Fair ball

Branch Rickey needed an African American who was smart, had the ability to play baseball at the major league level — and could keep his mouth shut under trying circumstances.

Rickey, the general manager of the Brooklyn Dodgers, thought he had found him in John Roosevelt Robinson. Known to his friends as "Jackie," Robinson was a 28-year-old UCLA graduate and former Army officer whom Rickey had signed to play for Montreal in the minor leagues in 1945. Robinson was irritated when Rickey kept telling him about all the virulent hatred he would face as the first African-American player in the major leagues.

"Mr. Rickey, do you want a ballplayer who's afraid to fight back?" Robinson asked.

Rickey replied, "I want a player with guts enough *not* to fight back."

On April 15, 1947, Robinson stepped to the plate for the first time in a major league game. By the end of the year, he was the National League's best rookie, and two years later, its most valuable player. Robinson opened the gates for thousands of African Americans in professional sports and inspired millions of Americans of all races with his dignity, courage, and refusal to lose.

In the same month, Congress passed a bill that

- Authorized the attorney general to stop Southern elected officials from interfering with African Americans registering to vote
- Established a federal Civil Rights Commission
- Created a civil rights enforcement division within the U.S. Justice Department.

The sad fact, however, was that in many places in the South, the laws went largely unenforced.

Boycotting the bus

Like a rock dropped in a still pond, the Supreme Court decision on school desegregation started ripples of change throughout the country. One of them hit Montgomery, Alabama, on December 1, 1955. A 42-year-old African-American woman named Rosa Parks was tired after a long day working, and she was tired of being treated as a second-class human being. So Parks refused to get up from her seat on the bus when the driver demanded she give it to a white man. That was against the law, and Parks was arrested.

> ## Sput-what?
>
> Frankly, it didn't look like much: a little blip of a light in the evening sky that appeared to be moving much slower than its 18,000 miles per hour.
>
> But to Americans watching on October 5, 1957, the blip represented a terrible thought: The commies might someday rule the world from outer space. That's because the little blip was a Soviet satellite called *Sputnik* (Russian for "fellow traveler"). It was the first such object, and within a few weeks it was followed by Sputnik II.
>
> Americans were shocked. Fears of super weapons orbiting above the United States competed with the feeling that a new day was dawning for humanity. During the next year, the United States launched four satellites of its own, and within two years, U.S. efforts to catch up with the Soviet Union in space were in full gear. The Space Race had joined the Arms Race in the political Olympics between the Super Powers.

Her arrest sparked a boycott of the bus system by the black community. Facing the highly damaging boycott and a 1956 Supreme Court decision that declared segregation on public transportation unconstitutional, the Montgomery bus company dropped its race-based seating plan in 1957.

More important than getting to ride in the front of the bus was the example the boycott set as to how effective organized demonstrations against segregation could be. Equally important was the emergence on the national scene of the boycott's leader, an eloquent, charismatic son of a well-known Atlanta minister, who admired the non-violent protest philosophies of India's Mohandas Gandhi. His name was Martin Luther King Jr., and he was to become one of the most important men in America in the coming decade.

Chapter 18
Camelot to Watergate: 1961–1974

In This Chapter
- Electing and losing JFK
- Entering the war in Vietnam
- Trying to put an end to discrimination
- Forming a counterculture in protest
- Impeaching Nixon

The decade of the 1960s began with a defeat for Richard Nixon and ended in victory for him. In between, America became mired in a war it never understood and saw its citizens take to the streets in the name of peace, justice, and racial rage.

By the mid-1970s, U.S. streets were clearing, Nixon had suffered the last — and worst — defeat of his career, and America was trying to figure out just what the heck had happened in the preceding 14 years.

Electing an Icon

He was rich, handsome, witty, and married to a beautiful woman, and he looked good on the increasingly important medium of television. His opponent was middle class, jowly, whiny, and married to a less beautiful woman, and on TV he looked like 50 miles of bad road.

Even so, Massachusetts Senator John F. Kennedy won the presidency in 1960 over Vice President Richard Nixon by a very narrow margin — and only, some said, because his father, bootlegger-turned-tycoon Joseph Kennedy, had rigged the results in Illinois and Texas.

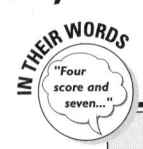

Call for volunteers

"Let the word go forth from this time and place, to friend and foe alike, that the torch has been passed to a new generation of Americans. . . . Ask not what your country can do for you, but what you can do for your country." —John F. Kennedy, inaugural address, January 20, 1961.

After eight years of the colorless, fatherly Eisenhower, "Jack" and Jacqueline Kennedy excited the interest of the country. The administration was dubbed "Camelot," after the mythical realm of King Arthur. Kennedy — known to headline writers as "JFK" — gave off an aura of youth, vigor, and shiny virtue. In truth, however, he was plagued with health problems from a bad back to venereal disease, popped pain pills and took amphetamine injections, was an insatiable womanizer, and didn't mind bending the truth when it suited his purposes.

Kennedy called on Americans to push toward a "new frontier" of challenges, and the first big challenge came very soon after he took office.

The Bay of Pigs

Cuba had been a thorn in the United States' side since 1959, when dictator Fulgencio Batista was overthrown by a young communist named Fidel Castro. Castro soon became an ardent anti-American, ordering the takeover of U.S.-owned businesses in Cuba and establishing close ties with the Soviet Union.

Kennedy gave his approval to a scheme that centered on anti-Castro Cuban exiles being trained by the Central Intelligence Agency (CIA) for an invasion of the island. The idea was that the Cuban people would rally to the invaders' side and oust Castro. The invasion took place April 17, 1961, at the Bay of Pigs on Cuba's southern coast. It was a disaster. No one rushed to their side, and many of the invaders were captured and held for two years before being ransomed by the U.S. government.

The resulting embarrassment to America encouraged the Soviet Union to increase pressure in Europe by erecting a wall dividing East and West Berlin and resuming the testing of nuclear weapons. Kennedy, meanwhile, tried to counter the Soviet moves by renewing U.S. weapons testing, increasing foreign aid to Third World nations, and establishing the Peace Corps to export U.S. ideals, as well as technical aid. The Soviets weren't impressed, and tensions between the two super-powers escalated.

Advocating for birds: Rachel Carson

Because a friend of hers noticed some birds dying, Rachel Carson saved millions more.

Carson was born in Pennsylvania in 1907. She earned a zoology degree from Johns Hopkins University, and after teaching awhile, went to work for the U.S. Bureau of Fisheries. In 1951, her second book, *The Sea Around Us,* became a bestseller, allowing Carson to devote herself to writing full-time.

One day, Carson got a letter from a friend in Massachusetts who had a small bird sanctuary. The friend had noticed that a lot of birds had died after the area was sprayed with the insecticide DDT to kill mosquitoes. Carson decided to investigate.

The result, in 1962, was *Silent Spring,* a carefully researched and eloquently written indictment of the pesticide's impact on the reproductive functions of fish and birds. The book started an avalanche of controversy around DDT. Finally, in 1972, the Nixon administration ordered a ban on the substance.

Carson didn't live to see the ban. She died of cancer in 1964, at the age of 57. But her landmark work is considered by many to be the start of the modern environmental movement in America.

Facing the possibility of nuclear war

During the summer of 1962, the Soviets began developing nuclear missile sites in Cuba. That meant they could easily strike targets over much of North and South America. When air reconnaissance photos confirmed the sites' presence on October 14, JFK had to make a tough choice: Destroy the sites and quite possibly trigger World War III, or do nothing, and not only expose the country to nuclear destruction but, in effect, concede first place in the world domination race to the USSR.

Kennedy decided to get tough. On October 22, 1962, he went on national television and announced the U.S. Navy would throw a blockade around Cuba and turn away any ships carrying materials that could be used at the missile sites. He also demanded the sites be dismantled. Then the world waited for the Russian reaction.

On October 26, Soviet leader Nikita Khrushchev sent a message suggesting the missiles would be removed if the United States promised not to invade Cuba and eventually removed some U.S. missiles from Turkey. The crisis — perhaps the closest the world came to nuclear conflict during the Cold War — was over, and the payoffs were ample.

A hotline was installed between the leaders of the United States and the Soviet Union to help defuse future confrontations, and in July 1963, all the major countries except China and France agreed to stop aboveground testing of nuclear weapons.

A dark day in Dallas

Even with his success in the Cuban missile crisis, Kennedy admitted he was generally frustrated by his first thousand days in office. Despite considerable public popularity, many of JFK's social and civil rights programs had made little progress in a Democrat-controlled-but-conservative Congress. Still, Kennedy was looking forward to running for a second term in 1964, and on November 22, 1963, he went to Texas to improve his political standing in that state.

While riding in an open car in a motorcade in Dallas, Kennedy was shot and killed by a sniper. A former Marine and one-time Soviet Union resident named Lee Harvey Oswald was arrested for the crime. Two days later, a national television audience watched in disbelief as Oswald himself was shot and killed by a Dallas nightclub owner named Jack Ruby, while Oswald was being moved to a different jail. Whether Oswald and Ruby acted alone, or were part of conspiracies, has been debated for decades.

America was stunned. The age of Camelot was over. And a veteran politician from Texas named Lyndon B. Johnson was president of the United States.

Sending Troops to Vietnam

If John F. Kennedy represented a fresh new face in the White House, his successor, Lyndon Baines Johnson, was a classic example of the old school of U.S. politics. A Texan, LBJ had served in both houses of Congress for more than 20 years before being elected as JFK's vice president in 1960, and was considered one of the most effective Senate leaders in history.

As president, Johnson inherited a host of problems, not the least of which was a growing mess in Southeast Asia, particularly Vietnam. Before World War II, Vietnam had been a French colony, and after the Japanese were defeated and driven out, it reverted to French control. But despite U.S. monetary aid, France was driven out of the country in 1954 by communist forces led by a man named Ho Chi Minh. The country was divided in two, with the communists controlling the northern half. Elections were scheduled for 1956 to reunite the two halves.

But they never took place, mostly because South Vietnam dictator Ngo Dinh Diem was afraid he would lose. The U.S. supported Diem (at least until 1963, when he became so unpopular he was assassinated with the U.S. government's unofficial blessing). At first, the support amounted to financial aid. Then U.S. military "advisors," who were not directly engaged in combat, were sent. But the pressure to do more mounted as the fighting dragged on, and by the time of Kennedy's assassination, 16,000 "advisors" had been sent to Vietnam.

Sinking deeper into a confusing war

Shortly after taking office, Johnson ordered 5,000 more U.S. troops to Vietnam and made plans to send another 5,000. In August 1964, he announced that U.S. Navy ships had been attacked in international waters near the Gulf of Tonkin. Congress reacted by overwhelmingly approving a resolution that gave Johnson the power to "take all necessary measures" to protect U.S. forces. A few months later, LBJ ordered U.S. bombings of targets in North Vietnam. By March 1965, more than 100,000 U.S. troops were in the country. Within three years, that number had swelled to more than 500,000.

It was a lot of people to fight a war no one seemed to understand how to win. The United States had overwhelming military superiority. But it was mostly designed for fighting a conventional war, with big battles and conquered territories.

Vietnam was different. It was essentially a civil war, which meant it was sometimes tough to figure out who was on whose side. The communists in the south were called the Vietcong. They were aided by North Vietnamese Army troops, referred to as the NVA. The dense jungle terrain made it difficult to locate and fight large concentrations of the enemy. There were conflicts between U.S. political leaders who wanted to contain the war and military leaders who wanted to expand it. Finally, the lack of clear objectives and declining public support demoralized many American soldiers.

Taking a look at the Tet Offensive

On January 31, 1968 — the Vietnamese New Year, called *Tet* — communist forces unleashed massive attacks on U.S. positions throughout Vietnam. The Tet Offensive, televised nightly in the United States, shocked many Americans who had the idea that the United States was rather easily handling the enemy. In fact, U.S. forces eventually pushed the North Vietnamese forces back and inflicted huge casualties on them. But the impact the fighting had on U.S. public opinion was equally huge. Opposition to the war grew more heated and contributed mightily to LBJ's decision not to run for reelection in 1968.

Muhammad Ali

He was the most famous sports figure in the world, perhaps the most famous person, period, and if you didn't believe it, all you had to do was ask him. "I am," he would reply, "the Greatest."

Ali was born Cassius Clay in Louisville, Kentucky, in 1942. After a successful amateur boxing career, which included winning a gold medal at the 1960 Olympics, he turned pro. In 1964, Clay won the heavyweight championship and successfully defended it nine times over the next three years. Flamboyant, witty, charming, and arrogant, he was resented and disliked by many white Americans for not being humble enough.

He became even more controversial when he became a Black Muslim and changed his name. Then in 1967, he was stripped of his title and sentenced to five years in prison for refusing to be drafted into the military, on grounds of his religious beliefs. The Supreme Court eventually reversed the conviction and Ali won the title back in 1974 from George Foreman, defending it 10 more times before losing it in 1978 to Leon Spinks and then winning it for a third time in a rematch with Spinks later that year.

Ali announced his retirement from the ring in 1979 (although he returned for two losing matches in 1980). The onset of Parkinson's disease made it difficult for him to speak in subsequent years, but he managed an electrifying appearance as a torchbearer at the 1996 Olympics.

Increasing Pressure in 'Nam and Escalating Fears at Home

With Johnson out of the 1968 race, Republican Richard Nixon narrowly defeated Johnson's vice president, Hubert Humphrey, and Alabama Gov. George Wallace, an ardent segregationist who ran as an independent.

Nixon and his top foreign affairs advisor, Henry Kissinger, tried several tactics to extricate the United States from the war without just turning over South Vietnam to the communists. One tactic was to coerce the South Vietnamese government into taking more responsibility for the war. To force the issue, the United States began withdrawing some troops in 1969. At the same time, however, Nixon tried another tactic by ordering an increase in the bombing of North Vietnam, as well as in the neighboring countries of Laos and Cambodia. In essence, he was trying to put pressure on both sides to stop the fighting.

> ## Vietnam by the numbers
>
> The following numbers tell a story of their own:
>
> - Number of Americans killed: 58,174
> - Number wounded: 304,000
> - Cost, 1950–1974: $150 billion
> - Peak number of U.S. troops stationed in Vietnam: 535,000
> - Average age of U.S. soldier killed: 23
> - Age of youngest U.S. soldier killed: 16
> - Age of oldest U.S. soldier killed: 62
> - Average number of days in combat by U.S. infantry soldier in one year in Vietnam: 240

In 1970, Nixon approved the invasion of Cambodia by U.S. troops who were pursuing North Vietnamese soldiers based there. The decision intensified opposition to the war, and massive anti-war demonstrations spread across the country. At Kent State University in Ohio, National Guard troops shot and killed four student demonstrators.

Anti-war fever grew even stronger in 1971, when *The New York Times* published what became known as the Pentagon Papers. The documents, leaked by a former defense department worker named Daniel Ellsberg, proved the government had lied about the war's conduct. Later that year, an Army lieutenant named William Calley was convicted of supervising the massacre of more than 100 unarmed civilians at a village called My Lai.

Despite the mounting opposition, Nixon easily won reelection in 1972, in part because of a politically inept opponent (U.S. Sen. George McGovern of South Dakota), and in part because Kissinger announced a few weeks before the election that a peace settlement was not too far off.

After the election, however, Nixon ordered heavy bombing of North Vietnam's capital of Hanoi. The bombing failed to break North Vietnamese resolve, and 15 U.S. bombers were shot down. On January 27, 1973, the United States and North Vietnam announced they had reached an agreement to end the fighting and would work to negotiate a settlement.

The peace treaty proved to be a face-saving sham, allowing U.S. troops to be withdrawn before the communists closed in. In April 1975, North Vietnamese troops overran South Vietnam and took over the entire country. America had suffered its first decisive defeat in a war, touching off a reassessment of its role in the world — and on how it would approach involvement in conflicts in the future.

Continuing the Fight for Civil Rights

Although the civil rights movement began in the 1950s, it reached full steam in the 1960s, marked by several new tactics that proved effective in breaking down discrimination.

Enforcing their rights: African Americans

In February 1960, four African-American students sat down at a segregated lunch counter in Greensboro, North Carolina, and refused to leave after they were denied service. The "sit-in" became a strategy used across the country, and by the end of 1961, some 70,000 people had taken part in sit-ins. In May 1961, black and white activists began "freedom rides," traveling in small groups to the South to test local segregation laws (see Figure 18-1).

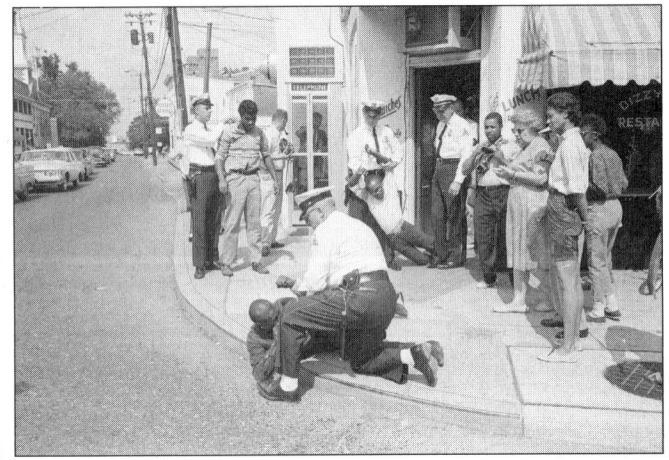

Figure 18-1: Police removing demonstrators from a restaurant.

© Bettmann/CORBIS

The inspirational leader of the movement was the Rev. Martin Luther King Jr., a courageous and eloquent orator who founded the Southern Christian Leadership Conference and won the 1964 Nobel Peace Prize for his civil rights work.

But not all African Americans were enamored of King's non-violent-demonstration approach. They also didn't believe equality could be attained through cooperation among the races. Leaders such as the Black Muslims' Elijah Muhammad and Malcolm X warned African Americans to neither expect nor seek help from whites. "If someone puts a hand on you," said Malcolm X, "send him to the cemetery."

Looking for legal remedies to discrimination

Both approaches eventually put pressure on the federal government to act. President Kennedy and his brother Robert (who was also his attorney general) used federal troops and marshals to force the admission of black students to the state universities in Alabama and Mississippi. In June 1963, JFK proposed a bill that would ban racial discrimination in hotels, restaurants, and other public places and give the federal government more authority to clamp down on state and local agencies that dragged their feet in enforcing civil rights laws. Black organizers gathered 200,000 demonstrators for a march in Washington, D.C., to support the Kennedy proposal.

After Kennedy's assassination, JFK's efforts were taken up by Johnson. Despite his Southern roots, LBJ was a committed liberal whose "Great Society" programs mirrored the New Deal of Franklin Roosevelt in the 1930s. In addition to providing more federal aid to America's down-and-outs, LBJ pushed the 1964 Civil Rights Act through Congress. It featured many of the same elements Kennedy had proposed. Johnson followed it with another bill in 1965 that strengthened federal safeguards for black voters' rights.

But events and emotions moved faster than politics. In early 1965, Malcolm X, who had softened his earlier opposition to interracial cooperation, was murdered by Black Muslim extremists who considered such talk traitorous. A few months later, a march led by Martin Luther King Jr. from Selma to Montgomery in Alabama was viciously attacked by state and local police, while a horrified national television audience watched.

Tired of waiting for an equal chance at the U.S. economic pie, many African Americans began demanding affirmative action programs in which employers would actively recruit minorities for jobs. "Black Power" became a rallying cry for thousands of young African Americans.

Taking it to the streets

The anger manifested itself in a rash of race riots in the mid- and late 1960s. The first was in August 1965, in the Los Angeles community of Watts. Before it was over, six days of rioting had led to 34 deaths, 850 injuries, 3,000 arrests, and more than $200 million in damages. Riots followed in the next two years in dozens of cities, including New York, Chicago, Newark, and Detroit, where 43 people were killed in July 1967.

Then things got worse. On April 4, 1968, Martin Luther King Jr. was assassinated in Memphis, Tennessee. A white man named James Earl Ray was eventually arrested and convicted of the crime. More riots followed across the country, most notably in Washington, D.C.

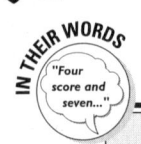

> ### Big dreams
>
> "I have a dream that one day this nation will rise up, live out the true meaning of its creed. . . . I have a dream that my four little children will one day live in a nation where they will not be judged by the color of their skin but by the content of their character." —Martin Luther King Jr., August 28, 1963, before the Lincoln Memorial, Washington, D.C.

The riots, in turn, triggered a backlash by many whites. George Wallace, a racist and ardent segregationist, got 13.5 percent of the vote in the 1968 presidential election, and much of the steam of the civil rights movement had dissipated by the time Richard Nixon moved into the White House.

Challenging the system: Latin Americans

African Americans weren't the only minority group on the move in the 1960s. Americans of Latin American descent had been treated as second-class citizens since the 1840s. While their numbers increased during and after World War II, mainly because thousands of Mexicans came to the country as a source of cheap labor, Latinos were largely ghettoized in inner-city *barrios* and rural areas of the Southwest. They were generally invisible in terms of the political process.

Between 1960 and 1970, however, the number of Latinos in the United States tripled, from three million to nine million, with perhaps another five million living in the country illegally. Cubans came to Florida, Puerto Ricans to New York, and Mexicans to California. With the increase in numbers came an increased interest in better political, social, and economic treatment for *La Raza* (the race). Leaders, particularly among Mexican Americans or *Chicanos,* sprang up: Reies Lopez Tijerina in New Mexico, Rodolfo "Corky" Gonzales in Colorado, and Cesar Chavez in California.

Latinos began to pursue organized efforts to gain access to the educational and economic systems and fight racial stereotypes. Latin Americans were elected to municipal and state offices and gradually began to organize themselves into a formidable political force in some parts of the country.

Cesar Chavez

His opponents accused him of "sour grapes," but to Cesar Chavez, it was merely a question of tactics. Chavez was born in 1927 on a small family farm near Yuma, Arizona. During the Depression, his family lost the farm and was forced to move, becoming laborers on other people's farms in California and the Southwest. Chavez only occasionally attended school because the family moved so much, following the crops. After serving in the Navy during World War II, Chavez settled in San Jose, California, and became an official in a Latino community service organization.

In 1962, using his life savings, he founded the United Farm Workers (UFW), a union for a group that no other union was interested in. Chavez was an advocate of nonviolence, and he believed the interests of the union should extend beyond labor contracts to other areas of social justice for farm workers.

By the mid-1960s, Chavez and the UFW had begun to organize farm workers in earnest. When strikes failed to work, he began boycotting products, particularly grapes. The aim of the boycotts was to get consumers not to buy the product until a fair labor agreement was in place. By the end of the 1970s, the UFW's membership was more than 70,000, the state of California had created a state board to mediate disputes between growers and workers, and for the first time, the nation's most downtrodden workers had union contracts.

Chavez died in 1993. The following year, his work not only as a union leader but also as a civil rights leader and humanitarian was recognized when he was posthumously awarded the Presidential Medal of Freedom, the nation's highest civilian honor.

Maintaining their culture: Native Americans

No minority group had been treated worse than Native Americans, nor had any group been less able to do anything about it. They had lower average incomes, higher rates of alcoholism, and shorter life expectancies than any other ethnic group. And because their numbers were few, the federal government since the turn of the century had largely ignored them.

In the 1950s, federal laws and policies had tried to push Native Americans into white society and into abandoning traditional ways. But in the 1960s, some Native Americans began to push back. In 1961, the National Indian Youth Council was established, followed by the American Indian Movement in 1968. The efforts of these and other groups helped lead to the Indian Civil Rights Act in 1968, which granted U.S. rights to Native Americans living on reservations while allowing them to set their own laws according to tribal customs.

It would be nice to say that all the racial wrongs in America were made right by the tumultuous events of the 1960s. It would also be absurd. But it isn't absurd to say the period was an overall success in terms of civil rights. It established key new laws, instilled a sense of self-pride in minority groups, and served notice that the issue would not be swept under the rug.

"Lord, we ain't what we ought to be," observed Martin Luther King Jr. "We ain't what we wanna be. We ain't what we gonna be. But, thank God, we ain't what we were."

Entering a Generation in Revolt

Not all the groups fighting the status quo were tied to each other by race or national origin. The war in Vietnam and the blooming civil rights movement triggered political activism among many young Americans, particularly on college campuses. Groups like Students for a Democratic Society appeared, and activities like draft card burnings became as common as pep rallies.

Draft dodging, drugs, and demonstrations

Because of opposition to the war, thousands of draft-age males fled to Canada and other countries rather than serve in the military. Their actions baffled many of their parents, whose generations had served in World War II and Korea, and widened the gap of misunderstanding between the age groups.

The gap was also evident in the younger generation's freer attitudes toward sex, public profanity, and hairstyles. More troubling, and longer lasting in terms of its impact, was the use of drugs by the counterculture. The use of marijuana and hallucinogenics like LSD became commonplace. Most of it could be attributed to the excesses of youth. But it was also a disturbing preview of the plagues of drug use that would sweep over the country during the rest of the century.

Perhaps nowhere was the generation gap more visible than at the 1968 Democratic National Convention in Chicago. While mostly middle-aged and middle-class delegates debated an anti-war plank for the party platform, hundreds of mostly young and poor demonstrators battled with club-swinging police in the streets outside the convention center. "The whole world is watching!" the demonstrators taunted. Ironically, many of those watching were so troubled by the sight of young people defying authority that they voted for Richard Nixon in 1968, and again in 1972. Nixon appealed to these voters, whom he called the "silent majority," because he spoke out strongly against the demonstrations.

The rise of feminism

Draft cards weren't the only things being burned during the period. Women who resented their secondary roles in the workplace, the home, and the halls of government periodically protested, too — and they had plenty to protest. Women faced barriers in getting jobs, and when they did find jobs, they were paid far less than men doing the same work: In 1970, women earned 60 cents for every dollar paid a man. Married women were denied credit in their own names, even when they had jobs of their own.

The women's liberation movement gave birth to the National Organization of Women (NOW) in 1966, and by 1970 NOW was organizing women's rights demonstrations and winning court battles over equal pay for equal work. In 1972, Congress approved a constitutional provision called the Equal Rights Amendment and sent it to the states for ratification. But a coalition of conservative and religious groups combined to fight the ERA, and in 1982 it was dead, 3 states short of the 38 needed for ratification.

As it turned out, the amendment hardly mattered, because many of the rights it would have provided were awarded in court decisions. One key decision came in 1973, when in *Roe v. Wade,* the Supreme Court essentially legalized abortion in the first three months of pregnancy. The ruling meant women now had a wider range of legal choices when faced with pregnancy. It also meant the beginning of an intense political, legal, social, and religious battle over abortion that continues today.

Coming out of the closet

The subject of homosexuality was so unspoken in America for most of its history that many Americans at the beginning of the 20th century had never heard of it or didn't believe it was real. Even into the 1960s, many psychiatrists believed homosexuality was a mental illness, and same-gender sex between consenting adults was still a crime in many states.

That began to change in the late 1960s, however, as gay men and women began to assert themselves. In June 1969, New York City police busted a gay nightclub called the Stonewall and began arresting patrons. The bust sparked a riot in the predominantly gay and lesbian community of Greenwich Village. Gay activist organizations like the Gay Liberation Front were started. But changing anti-gay laws and homophobic attitudes was still a work in progress in the first decade of the 21st century.

> ### Harvey Milk
>
> When the first openly gay elected official of any big U.S. city stepped in it, he *really* stepped in it. As a San Francisco supervisor, Milk once pushed for a city ordinance to force dog owners to clean up after their pets in public places. Accompanied by reporters, he staged a stroll through a city park that ended with his foot in a pile of dog droppings, for the benefit of the cameras. The measure was approved.
>
> Milk was born in 1930 in New York. He served in the Navy during the Korean War as a deep-sea diver, but was dishonorably discharged after his homosexuality was revealed. After a career as a Wall Street stockbroker, Milk moved to San Francisco's predominantly gay Castro Street district, opened a camera store, and began running for office as an openly gay candidate. He was finally elected, on his fourth try, in 1977.
>
> In 1978, Milk and San Francisco Mayor George Moscone were shot to death at City Hall by a disgruntled former city official named Dan White. White received only a five-year sentence for the killings, triggering gay riots. But Milk's death also inspired many gay professionals to "come out of the closet," and encouraged other gays to run for office. "If a bullet should enter my brain," Milk had said in a tape-recorded will, "let that bullet destroy every closet door."

Weirdness in the White House

Vietnam and a whole bunch of unhappy people in the streets of America weren't the only problems Richard Nixon faced when he took over as president in early 1969. Inflation was running wild. Much of the problem was a result of President Johnson's economic policy of "guns *and* butter": paying for the war and expanding social programs at the same time.

Making strides: The Nixon administration

Nixon responded to the situation by cutting government spending and balancing the federal budget for 1969. He also rather reluctantly imposed wage and price freezes on the country. But he wasn't reluctant at all about dropping federal efforts to enforce school integration laws: He had been elected with Southern support and was mindful that polls showed most Americans opposed forcing kids to take buses to schools in other neighborhoods to achieve racial balance.

Outside of Vietnam, Nixon enjoyed success in foreign policy. He went to China in early 1972, ending 20 years of diplomatic silence between the two countries, and he pursued a policy of *détente* (a French term for relaxing of tensions) with the Soviet Union.

Chapter 18: Camelot to Watergate: 1961–1974

These accomplishments, coupled with vague hints of looming peace in Vietnam and a backlash among voters Nixon called the "silent majority" against all the protesting, helped Nixon easily win reelection in 1972. In early 1973, the peace settlement with North Vietnam was announced. And despite Democratic majorities in Congress, Nixon was able to veto bills that challenged his authority in a number of areas. He took advantage of it to greatly expand the White House's power and cloak its actions from public scrutiny. And then an ex-FBI agent named James McCord wrote a letter to a judge, and the wheels of the Nixon White House began to come off.

Watching it all fall apart: Watergate

In a nutshell, here's what happened in the greatest presidential scandal in U.S. history (or second-greatest — see Chapter 20):

- On June 17, 1972, McCord and four other men working for the Committee to Re-Elect the President, or CREEP (really), broke into the Democratic Party's headquarters in the Watergate, a hotel-office building in Washington, D.C. They got caught going through files and trying to plant listening devices. Five days later, Nixon denied any knowledge of it or that his administration played any role in it.

- The burglars went to trial in 1973 and either pleaded guilty or were convicted. Before sentencing, McCord wrote a letter to Judge John Sirica, contending that high Republican and White House officials knew about the break-in and had paid the defendants to keep quiet or lie during the trial.

- Investigation of McCord's charges spread to a special Senate committee. John Dean, a White House lawyer, told the committee McCord was telling the truth and that Nixon had known of the effort to cover up White House involvement.

- Eventually, all sorts of damaging stuff began to surface, including evidence that key documents linking Nixon to the coverup of the break-in had been destroyed, that the Nixon reelection committee had run a "dirty tricks" campaign against the Democrats, and that the administration had illegally wiretapped the phones of "enemies," such as journalists who had been critical of Nixon.

- In March 1974, former Atty. Gen. John Mitchell and six top Nixon aides were indicted by a federal grand jury for trying to block the investigation. They were eventually convicted.

- While Nixon continued to deny any involvement, it was revealed he routinely made secret tapes of conversations in his office. Nixon refused to turn over the tapes at first, and when he did agree (after firing a special prosecutor he had appointed to look into the mess and seeing his new

> attorney general resign in protest), it turned out some of them were missing or had been destroyed. (They were also full of profanity, which greatly surprised people who had an entirely different perception of Nixon.)
>
> ✔ In the summer of 1974, the House Judiciary Committee approved articles of impeachment against the president for obstructing justice.

The tapes clearly showed Nixon had been part of the coverup. On August 8, 1974, he submitted a one-sentence letter of resignation, and then went on television and said, "I have always tried to do what is best for the nation." He was the first and, so far, only U.S. president to quit the job.

The Watergate scandal rocked the nation, which was already reeling from the Vietnam disaster, economic troubles, assassinations, and all the social unrest of the preceding 15 years. It fell to Nixon's successor, Vice President Gerald R. Ford, to try to bring back a sense of order and stability to the nation. And no one had voted for him to do it.

Small steps and great leaps

It started with a challenge from John F. Kennedy and ended with perhaps the greatest technological feat in human history: Man on the moon.

On May 25, 1961, Kennedy asked Congress for money to put a U.S. astronaut on the moon before the end of the decade. Congress agreed, and more than $1 billion was spent to get to the afternoon of July 20, 1969. At 1:17 p.m. (PDT), a craft carrying two men landed on the lunar surface. A few hours later, astronaut Neil A. Armstrong stepped out. "That's one small step for a man," he said, "one giant leap for mankind."

Armstrong was joined on the surface by Buzz Aldrin, while a third astronaut, Michael Collins, circled above in the mother ship, *Columbia*.

A worldwide television audience estimated at 1 billion people watched from a quarter-million miles away.

Some lunar visit facts: Armstrong and Aldrin spent 21 hours on the surface, but only 2 hours, 15 minutes actually walking around and never ventured farther than 275 yards from their craft. They collected 46 pounds of rocks. And they left behind a plaque attached to the base of the landing craft (they got back to the *Columbia* in the top half of the two-stage lander).

The plaque reads: "Here men from the planet Earth first set foot upon the moon, July 1969 A.D. We came in peace for all mankind."

Chapter 19

Hold the Malaise, or, Ayatollah So: 1975–1992

In This Chapter
- Wading through Watergate
- Fueling a failing economy
- Smiling for the camera — and the country
- Thawing after the Cold War

Nothing puts a damper on a country's attitude like an unscrupulous president followed by a couple of well-meaning but relatively inept ones, and that's just what occurred in the 1970s. Throw in an oil crisis, a very unsettled economy, and a hostage situation in Iran, and we're not exactly talking about the Golden Age of America here.

In this era, a charismatic figure from, of all places, Hollywood, rides to the rescue, smiles a lot, and generally makes America feel better about itself by the end of the 1980s.

Wearing Nixon's Shoes

No one voted for Vice President Gerald R. Ford when he became president of the United States on August 8, 1974. Come to think of it, no one had voted for him when he became vice president, either.

Ford was elected to Congress from Michigan in 1948 and reelected every two years through 1972. In December 1973, President Nixon appointed Ford vice president after the incumbent vice president, Spiro T. Agnew, resigned. Agnew was a blustering eccentric who proved to be an even bigger crook than Nixon.

Finding himself under investigation for extorting bribes from contractors while he was governor of Maryland, Agnew pleaded no contest to a charge of tax fraud, quit the vice presidency, and faded into richly deserved obscurity.

A month after becoming president when Nixon resigned in the wake of the Watergate scandal, Ford determined the country needed to put Watergate behind it. The best way to do that, Ford decided, was to pardon Nixon for any crimes he may have committed while in office. About 40 of Nixon's assistants weren't so lucky and were indicted for various offenses. Some of them — including Nixon's attorney general, John Mitchell, and Nixon's top aides, John Ehrlichman and Bob Haldeman — went to prison.

Doing the best he could

As an honest, hardworking, and amiable man, Ford did his best as president. Unfortunately, his best wasn't great. Although he had been a college football star and a leader in Congress, he developed an undeserved reputation as a not-too-coordinated, not-too-bright guy. Falling down a flight of airplane stairs, hitting a spectator with a ball during a golf tournament, and occasionally misspeaking didn't help. Lyndon Johnson joked that Ford had "played one too many games without his helmet."

Ford's pardon of Nixon angered many Americans who felt the former president shouldn't have escaped facing the justice system. But even without the Watergate hangover, 1975 wasn't a great time to be president, for Ford or anyone.

In late April 1975, the communists completed their takeover in Vietnam. American diplomats scrambled onto escape helicopters from the roofs of buildings near the U.S. embassy in Saigon, with the whole world watching from living room TVs. Most of the rest of Indochina had already fallen under communist control or fell soon after.

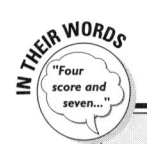

Not on my shift

"I did not take the sacred oath of office to preside over the decline and fall of the United States of America." —Gerald R. Ford, after assuming the presidency, August 1974.

Whipping inflation

Even worse for Ford than the humiliation of the fall of Saigon, the U.S. economy was a mess. Inflation was soaring, and the unemployment rate reached 9 percent, the highest level since 1941. Ford's response included asking Americans to wear buttons that bore the acronym *WIN,* for *whip inflation now.* The buttons didn't have much of an impact, however.

Despite the buttons' ineffectiveness, Ford refused to take stronger measures. He neglected to address such issues as wage and price controls and did little to lessen the country's growing dependence on foreign oil. So when oil-producing nations, mainly in the Middle East, dramatically jacked up oil prices — 400 percent in 1974 alone — the United States suffered a price increase on just about every other product as well.

The Nixon pardon, the humiliating end to Vietnam, and the staggering economy proved to be three strikes against Ford. After barely winning the Republican nomination over former California Gov. Ronald Reagan, Ford lost the 1976 presidential election to Jimmy Carter, the former governor of Georgia. The way things turned out, Ford may have been the lucky one.

Good Intentions, Bad Results

America turned 200 in 1976, and for its bicentennial birthday, it gave itself a new president. His name was James Earl Carter, but everyone called him Jimmy. He was a Naval Academy graduate, a nuclear engineer, a peanut farmer, and the former governor of Georgia. He ran for the presidency as a Washington outsider. Because U.S. voters were pretty sick of Washington insiders, they elected him in a close race over the incumbent, Jerry Ford. Carter was the first candidate since 1932 to defeat an incumbent president. He was also the first president from the Deep South since the Civil War.

Ford had started his administration with the controversial pardoning of Richard Nixon, and Carter started his with the controversial pardoning of Vietnam War draft evaders. The two men had other similarities. Both seemed to have a tough time being consistent in their policy- and decision-making. And both had real troubles with the economy because of runaway inflation and oil shortages.

Measuring misery

During the 1976 campaign, Carter added up the nation's unemployment rate and inflation level, called it a "misery index," and used it as an effective rhetorical weapon against Ford. Unfortunately for Carter, by the time he left office, the level of misery was higher than when he took over. The annual *inflation rate* — the change in the price of various consumer goods — went from 5 percent in 1970 to 14.5 percent in 1980. The price of gasoline went from about 40 cents a gallon to more than 70 cents ($1.98 in 2013 dollars). Part of the reason for both higher inflation and high oil prices was America's increasing dependence on foreign oil. Simply put, the country was using more oil — for everything from running cars to making textiles — than it was producing.

In the early 1970s, Arab oil-producing countries cut off supplies to the United States and other Western nations as a way of pressuring Israel to give back Arab territory it had taken during a 1967 war. When the embargo was lifted in 1974, the Western countries' oil reserves had dried up, and the oil-producing countries could charge pretty much whatever they wanted for their product.

Higher oil prices helped fuel inflation, and inflation helped trigger higher interest rates. Companies couldn't afford to borrow money to expand, so unemployment rose. Carter tried various ways to combat the problems, including voluntary wage and price controls, but they didn't help much. Things got so bad that Carter went on national TV to acknowledge that a "crisis of confidence" had struck the nation. The address became known as "the malaise speech," and to many people it made Carter appear to be a self-pitying crybaby.

A nuclear "oops"

One of the great hopes of weaning America from its dependence on foreign oil was nuclear power from plants like the one on the banks of the Susquehanna River in a bucolic area of Pennsylvania called Three Mile Island.

On March 28, 1979, one of the plant's thousands of valves went on the fritz. The malfunction caused temperatures in the plant's reactor chamber to climb to 5,000 degrees, melting the lining of the reactor chamber before being stopped by the thick concrete floor.

Pregnant women and children were evacuated, and as many as 60,000 other people voluntarily fled the area. As it turned out, only relatively low levels of radiation escaped, and no claims of personal or property damage were ever proven.

But the accident effectively exploded the hopes of expanding nuclear power as an energy source in America. Although 104 nuclear plants were still operating in the United States in 2008, supplying 20 percent of the country's energy, no new plants had been built since the Three Mile Island accident.

Befriending the enemy

On the foreign front, Carter had mixed results. He negotiated treaties to gradually transfer the Panama Canal territory to Panama. He reached an agreement with the Soviet Union to restrict the development of nuclear arms, and he furthered the restoration of relations with Communist China that Richard Nixon had started.

Carter's biggest triumph was in engineering a historic peace agreement between Israel and Egypt, which had been at each other's throats for decades. At Camp David, the presidential retreat in Maryland, Carter brokered a deal in 1978 with Israeli Prime Minister Menachim Begin and Egyptian President Anwar Sadat. Sadat and Begin got the Nobel Peace Prize for their efforts; Carter got nothing but trouble in the form of multiple disasters involving Iran.

The United States had backed the shah of Iran since 1953, when the Central Intelligence Agency (CIA) helped him regain power in that country. When the shah was thrown out again in 1979 and replaced with a Muslim religious leader named the Ayatollah Ruhollah Khomeini, the United States allowed the shah to receive medical treatment in America.

Jesse Jackson

He could've been a professional athlete but became a preacher instead — and as a result became known as "the president of black America."

Jesse Jackson was born in 1941, the illegitimate son of a South Carolina cotton buyer who ignored Jackson for much of his early life. After a career as an all-state football player in high school, Jackson passed up a pro baseball contract and went to college instead. He also became active in the civil rights movement and was with Martin Luther King Jr. when King was assassinated in Memphis in 1968. In that same year, Jackson was ordained a Baptist minister.

Basing his work in Chicago, Jackson founded a program in 1971 called Operation PUSH (People United to Save Humanity). The program was designed to address problems facing inner-city youth. In 1984, he formed the National Rainbow Coalition, the aim of which was to bring together members of all races to address common goals. Jackson also ran for president in 1984 and 1988, generating enough support to become a major player in national Democratic Party politics. He has also been something of a diplomat-without-a-portfolio, negotiating the release of hostages in Syria, Cuba, and Iraq.

In 2001, it was revealed that Jackson had had an affair with a staff member and fathered a daughter with her in 1999. The revelation resulted in Jackson temporarily withdrawing from public life, but he returned to his role as an inspirational — if sometimes divisive — advocate for human rights.

That angered Iranian mobs, which invaded the U.S. embassy in the Iranian capital of Teheran on November 4, 1979. The mobs held the occupants of the embassy hostage. Some hostages were allowed to leave, but 52 were kept as prisoners. In April 1980, Carter ordered a team of Marine commandos to Iran on a rescue mission. Because of a series of screw-ups and accidents involving the rescue aircraft, eight commandos were killed before the actual rescue even began, and the mission was called off.

Finally, after the shah died in July, negotiations for the hostages' release began. They ended with the hostages being freed on January 20, 1981, after 444 days in captivity. The day the hostages were freed was, coincidently, the last day of Carter's presidency.

There's a First Time for Everything

If you told someone in 1951 that Ronald Reagan would someday be president of the United States, he would've suggested you check into a rest home for the politically delusional. After all, the veteran actor had just starred in *Bedtime for Bonzo,* in which his costar was a chimpanzee. That qualified him for Congress, certainly, but hardly the White House.

In addition to being the first president to have starred in a movie with an ape, Reagan was also the first president to have been divorced, and at the age of 69, the oldest president when he took office. Reagan was born in Illinois in 1911 and after college became a sportscaster in Iowa. In 1937, a screen test led to Hollywood, and Reagan became a second-tier star, first in movies and then on TV. His taste for politics grew from serving two terms as president of the Screen Actors Guild, and as his politics became increasingly conservative, he found himself a favorite of the Republican Party's right wing. He ran for governor of California in 1966, defeating incumbent Pat Brown, and served two terms.

In 1976, he came in a strong second for the GOP presidential nomination, and then in 1980, he swept both the nomination and the presidency over the unpopular Carter. His two greatest campaign tactics turned out to be a single question — "Ask yourself, are you better off than you were four years ago?" — and not being Jimmy Carter.

As president, Reagan was essentially a cheerleader for a vision of America that counted on everyone trying not to be too different from one another and not relying on the federal government to do much. He seemed to have an inexhaustible supply of both good and bad luck. He bounced back from being shot and seriously wounded after giving a speech at a Washington hotel in 1981, and in 1985 he won a bout with cancer. Despite his health problems, he managed an easy reelection victory in 1984 over Democrat Walter Mondale, who had been vice president under Jimmy Carter.

> ## Death in the jungle
>
> He was handsome, charismatic, and a mesmerizing speaker. He was also crazier than an outhouse rat. But to his followers, the Rev. Jim Jones was a messiah, the man who would show them the path to interracial happiness and a utopia on earth.
>
> Jones, an Indiana native who once sold monkeys door to door (seriously), became a preacher and eventually settled his "Peoples Temple" in San Francisco. By the mid-1970s, he had as many as 5,000 followers and wielded considerable political clout. But negative news stories about some of the temple's shady dealings triggered interest by various government agencies. In 1977, Jones left the Bay Area for a settlement in the jungles of Guyana, in South America, that some of his followers had started several years before. It was called Jonestown.
>
> In November 1978, a California congressman named Leo Ryan, some aides, and a few reporters visited Jonestown to investigate allegations of mistreatment of some of the residents, who were mostly African American (Jones wasn't). After a tense meeting with Jones, Ryan's party was attacked at a nearby airfield. Ryan and four others were killed. After the attack, Jones ordered his followers to commit suicide by drinking or injecting poison. Those who refused were slain. In the end, 913 men, women, and children, including Jones, died.

Reagan greeted political setbacks with boundless good cheer and a joke or two. And no matter what else happened, Reagan's personal popularity stayed high — so much so that he became known as the "Teflon president": Like the nonstick coating used on pots and pans, nothing seemed to stick to him. But his nice-guy persona didn't mean he was wishy-washy. When the country's air traffic controllers ignored federal law and went on strike in 1981, Reagan promptly fired all 11,400 of them and refused to rehire them after the strike ended.

Buying into the "Reagan Revolution"

One of the fastest-growing portions of America's population during the 1980s didn't have a clue what Reagan was talking about when he laid out his vision of the country and probably wouldn't have liked it had they understood. They were immigrants from countries like Mexico, Cuba, Haiti, and Vietnam who came to the United States by the tens of thousands during the 1980s. Many of them were counting on some form of government assistance to get started in their new lives in a new land.

But the people who had voted for Reagan knew exactly what he was talking about. Many of them were part of the *Sunbelt,* the fast-growing states of the Southeast, Southwest, and West. As the region's population grew, so did its representation in Congress — and its political clout. (The area became so powerful that every president elected between 1964 and 2008 was from a

Jim Bakker

He once spent $100 on cinnamon rolls so his hotel room would smell nice, which was okay because he was doing God's work — and had plenty of cash to spare.

Jim Bakker was born in 1940 and grew up in a small town in Michigan. After high school, he attended a Bible college and became a minister. In the early 1970s, Bakker began a Christian puppet show on a local TV station in Virginia. He developed a TV ministry that became known as the PTL Club, which to followers stood for "praise the Lord" and to critics stood for "pass the loot."

There was plenty of that. With contributions from hundreds of thousands of his followers, Bakker and his wife Tammy Faye (who wore what seemed to be pounds of makeup and wept at the drop of a psalm) built Heritage USA, a 2,300-acre Christian-themed resort, water park, and entertainment complex in South Carolina. In 1988, however, it was revealed that PTL had paid $265,000 to a former secretary named Jessica Hahn to keep her quiet about a sexual encounter she had had with Bakker eight years before.

The revelation was only one of many that followed over the next year. In 1989, Bakker was convicted of bilking more than 100,000 people of $158 million. He served five years in federal prison, and the scandal helped put the brakes on the momentum of the Christian right.

Southern or Western state.) In the West, in particular, Reagan's call for less government was in perfect harmony with the *Sagebrush Rebellion.* The rebellion, which was mostly rhetorical, was a reaction to land use and environmental regulations made in faraway Washington that were considered a threat to development of urban areas and resource-based industries, such as timber and mining. Reagan was the beneficiary of the growth in the Sunbelt's clout.

Reagan also benefited from a revival in Christian evangelicalism that married itself to conservative politics in the late 1970s and 1980s. Conservative evangelicals — those who said they had been "born again" through a direct personal experience with Jesus Christ and who were often referred to in a political sense as the *Christian right* — were alarmed at what they saw as the country's moral laxity in the 1960s and early 1970s. America's real problems, they argued, could be traced to feminism, abortion, rising divorce rates, and homosexuality.

Groups like the Moral Majority, led by a Virginia-based TV evangelist named Jerry Falwell, became powerful political forces in terms of raising money and mobilizing mass support — or opposition — for legislation and political candidates. Another "religious right" leader, Marion G. "Pat" Robertson, founded the Christian Coalition and twice ran for president himself.

Finally, Reagan was supported by followers of a more secular cause — tax-cutting. The high inflation of the 1970s caused many people's income and property values to rise — and also pushed them into higher tax brackets that ate up much of the increases. That naturally fueled taxpayers' anger. In California, a cranky political gadfly named Howard Jarvis successfully pushed through an initiative that dramatically cut property tax rates and required state and local governments to drastically shift their way of financing government operations. The success of Proposition 13 led to similar efforts in other states. It also helped Reagan push through his own brand of tax-cutting.

Paying for "Reaganomics"

Reagan figured that if you cut taxes on companies and the very wealthy and reduced regulations on business, they would invest more, the economy would expand, and everyone would benefit. Of course, this approach, based heavily on the views of economist Milton Friedman, a Reagan advisor, would require cutting government services, which would most affect Americans on the bottom of the economic ladder. But the benefits would eventually "trickle down" from those on the top of the ladder to those on the bottom. At least, in theory. So, early in his administration, Reagan pushed through a package of massive tax cuts, and the economy got better. Unemployment dropped from 11 percent in 1982 to about 8 percent in 1983. Inflation dropped below 5 percent, and the gross national product rose.

While Reaganistas were quick to point to the president's policies as a great deal, critics pointed in a different direction. Although Reagan had cut taxes, he and Congress had failed to cut government spending. In fact, he greatly increased spending on military programs. Because the government was spending far more than it was taking in, the national debt rose from about $900 billion in 1980 to a staggering $3 *trillion* in 1990. Moreover, most of the benefits of Reagan's trickle-down approach failed to trickle, priming the pump for another economic downturn after he left office.

Dealing with foreign affairs

As a true conservative, Reagan didn't much care for the Soviet Union or communists in general. He heated up the Cold War by, among other things, referring to the Soviets as amoral and irreligious. (Toward the end of his second term, however, Reagan's anti-Soviet feelings began to soften, particularly after a moderate named Mikhail Gorbachev became Soviet leader.)

Reagan also irritated the Soviets by proposing a giant military program called the Strategic Defense Initiative (SDI, more popularly known as "Star Wars" after the popular science-fiction film). Reagan's plan included

> ## The Challenger tragedy
>
> It was cold and windy at Cape Canaveral the morning of January 28, 1986, but U.S. space program officials were determined to go ahead with the launch of the space shuttle *Challenger*. After all, the *Challenger* had already made 9 successful trips into space, and the National Aeronautics and Space Administration (NASA) had run 24 space shuttle missions without a major problem.
>
> At 11:38 a.m. (EDT), NASA launched its 25th mission. At 11:40, as thousands of spectators watched in horror at the launch site and millions more watched on TV, the shuttle exploded shortly after lifting off. All seven of the crew members were killed, including a Concord, New Hampshire, schoolteacher named Christa McAuliffe, who was along for the ride as a way of increasing children's interest in the space program.
>
> The cause of the explosion was later traced to a flaw in the rocket's booster system and led to a complete reevaluation of the shuttle and an examination of more than 1,000 of its parts. More than 2 years passed before the shuttle program was allowed to resume — and 17 years passed before the next space shuttle disaster: The *Columbia* fell apart over Texas on its reentry on February 1, 2003, killing all seven crew members.

missile-destroying lasers based on satellites in space. His vision never went anywhere, however, because Congress refused to go along with the program's enormous costs.

Reagan also supported virtually any government that was anti-communist, including repressive regimes in Latin America, and he was quick to respond to provocations by terrorist acts supported by Libya. But he did withdraw American peacekeeping troops from war-torn Lebanon after a 1983 terrorist attack killed 241 U.S. marines stationed there. One of the anti-communist groups Reagan's administration supported was called the *contras* in Nicaragua, and it resulted in the biggest embarrassment of Reagan's presidency. In 1986, it was revealed that the White House had approved the sale of weapons to Iran as part of a mostly unsuccessful effort to win the release of some U.S. hostages in the Middle East.

It turned out that some of the money from the arms deal had been illegally siphoned off to the contras. Most of the blame for the scandal was pinned on an obscure Marine lieutenant colonel named Oliver North. But like other calamities, the Iran-contra mess did little to harm Reagan's popularity or inflict any lasting damage on his administration. In fact, it didn't even hurt the election of his successor in the White House, a one-time Reagan political foe who had become Reagan's dutiful vice president. His name was George Bush.

Warming Up after the Cold War

For more than four decades, the ideological conflict between the free world and the communist world had influenced just about every aspect of U.S. life. The federal budget was built around the idea of defending the country against communism. Advances in science and medicine were often driven by the fervor to stay ahead of the communists. Schoolchildren were indoctrinated as to the evils of the communist menace and chided to do better than commie kids. Even international sporting events became intense political struggles.

But the boogeyman began to deflate in 1979, when the Soviet Union intervened in a civil war in Afghanistan. Over the following decade, the Soviets poured thousands of troops and millions of rubles into what became the equivalent of America's Vietnam. The difference was that the U.S. economy was strong enough and flexible enough to survive Vietnam, whereas the ponderous Soviet economy all but creaked to a halt.

In 1985, Mikhail Gorbachev became the Soviet leader. Gorbachev realized that the old Soviet system couldn't continue to dominate Eastern Europe. In fact, the Soviet Union couldn't even continue to function as a country without some dramatic changes. He initiated two major concepts: *perestroika,* or changes in the Soviet economic structure, and *glasnost,* or opening the system to create more individual freedoms.

On November 9, 1989, the wall that divided East and West Berlin was opened. By the end of the year, Soviet-dominated regimes in a half-dozen European countries, including East Germany, had collapsed and been replaced by more democratic governments. By the end of 1991, the Soviet Union itself had dissolved into a set of mostly autonomous republics. The Cold War was over.

The collapse of the Soviet Union left the United States as the world's only true superpower. But it took no time at all for one of the planet's seemingly inexhaustible supply of thugs and bullies to test the United States' will to live up to its role as the world's leader.

Engaging in the Gulf War

If impressive résumés translated into leadership, they'd be carving George Bush's bust on Mt. Rushmore right now. After all, he was a Yale graduate, a World War II hero, an ambassador to China, a CIA director, and vice president under Reagan.

Bush was easily elected president in 1988 after waging a rather sleazy campaign against Democratic nominee Michael Dukakis. Voters were so turned off by the campaign and politics in general that the turnout was the lowest for a

> ### Oil all over the place
>
> On March 24, 1989, Alaska's Prince William Sound was one of the most scenic and beautiful inlets in the world, teeming with birds, fish, and marine mammals. On March 25, 1989, it was a heartbreaking, stomach-turning mess: the site of the biggest oil spill in U.S. history.
>
> It began when a giant tanker, the *Exxon Valdez*, hit a well-marked reef after picking up a load of crude oil in the town of Valdez. More than 11 million gallons of oil oozed into the sound and spread over hundreds of square miles. More than 250,000 birds were killed, along with thousands of other animals.
>
> It was quickly determined that the 984-foot ship's captain, Joseph Hazelwood, had been drinking before the accident. He was convicted the following year of negligence and sentenced to 1,000 hours of community service. He began the service in 1999, after nine years of appeals. Exxon spent $2.2 billion on cleanup efforts and paid another $900 million in a settlement to the state and federal government. As the 21st century began, there was still oil to be found on the shores of Prince William Sound.

presidential election since 1924. As president, several things hampered Bush. Democrats controlled both houses of Congress. Reagan's personal popularity was a hard act to follow. And Bush was simply not much of a leader, especially when it came to solving domestic problems.

Bush's leadership was put to a stern test in 1990. On August 2, the army of Iraq invaded the small neighboring country of Kuwait and quickly took over. Iraq was led by a brutal bozo named Saddam Hussein, who proclaimed he was annexing Kuwait to Iraq, and anyone who didn't like it could stuff it.

Bush chose not to stuff it. To Bush supporters, his decision to intervene was based on his desire to defend the defenseless. To his critics, it was to protect U.S. interests in Kuwait's oil production. Whatever the reason, in the weeks following the Iraqi invasion, Bush convinced other world leaders to establish a trade embargo on Iraq. Almost simultaneously, the United States, Britain, France, Egypt, Saudi Arabia, and other countries began assembling a massive armed force in case the economic pressure didn't work.

When that proved to be the case, the United States and its allies launched a gigantic aerial assault on Iraq on January 16, 1991. After six weeks of massive bombardment, the Allied forces sent in ground troops. The vaunted Iraqi military turned out to be made of papier-mâché. U.S. casualties were light, and about 100 hours after the ground war started, Iraq threw in the towel.

The victory, however, wasn't all that victorious. Kuwait was free, but the Iraqi dictator Hussein remained in power. Nine years after the war, the United States was still spending $2 billion a year to enforce a no-fly zone over Northern Iraq, kept an armada of Navy ships in the area, and maintained a force of 25,000 troops in the region.

Byting off the apple

Steve Jobs was a college dropout with marketing talents, and Steve Wozniak was an electronics nerd with an inventive mind. When the two got together, interesting things occurred.

First it was a device that allowed them to make free, if illegal, long-distance calls. Then it was an early video game called "Breakout." But the two Steves yearned to do something really radical: create an affordable computer that the average American could use at home.

So Jobs sold his Volkswagen van and Wozniak his favorite calculator. With the $1,300 they raised, they began work on their "personal" computer, laboring in a garage, an attic, and a spare room in the home of Jobs' parents in Palo Alto, California. They called it "Apple," partly in tribute to the Beatles' recording company of the same name and partly because Jobs just liked apples.

In 1976, the duo sold their first 50 computers for $500 each, but they sold only 125 more through the rest of the year. In 1977, however, they developed Apple II. It was the first true PC, with color graphics, a keyboard, a power supply, memory, a carrying case, and a floppy disk drive. It sold for $1,195 (around $4,600 in 2014 dollars). By 1981, sales had reached $335 million — and by 2012, $156 billion worldwide. That's a lot of Apples, no matter how you slice them.

Back on the home front

If the Gulf War left a sour taste in the mouths of Americans who questioned its purpose, necessity, and results, things at home weren't much sweeter. For one thing, the economy was in the dumpster. Like the federal government, many individuals and corporations had borrowed heavily in the 1980s, causing the number of bankruptcies in the country to soar. That, in turn, triggered a mess in the savings and loan (S&L) industry.

The Reagan administration, in its quest to lessen the role of government, had pushed to loosen up regulations on savings and loan companies. The result was that many S&Ls overextended credit and made stupid investments. Many of them collapsed. Tens of thousands of investors lost their savings, and the federal government had to spend billions of dollars to bail many of the S&Ls out.

Not all the disharmony was economic. On March 3, 1992, a 25-year-old black man named Rodney King was pulled over for reckless driving by Los Angeles police. A witness happened to videotape several of the police officers beating King. Despite the videotaped evidence, an all-white jury acquitted the police. Los Angeles erupted in the worst U.S. domestic violence in more than a century. Before it was over, 53 people died, 4,000 were injured, 500 fires had been set, and more than $1 billion was lost in property damage (see Figure 19-1).

Figure 19-1: Aftermath of the Los Angeles riots.

Peter Turnley/CORBIS

All this didn't bode well for the incumbent president. Not only were Americans generally dissatisfied with the way things were, but an eccentric Texan named Ross Perot also compounded Bush's troubles. Perot was a billionaire who decided to run for president as a third-party candidate. Despite his immense wealth (he financed his own campaign), Perot ran as a populist, railing against the influence of special interests in the political process.

When the votes were counted, Perot had gathered an impressive 19 percent, the best showing by a third-party candidate since Theodore Roosevelt in 1912. Bush finished second. The winner was a 46-year-old Democrat who had been elected governor of Arkansas five times.

His name was William Jefferson Clinton, and the name of his hometown said a lot about the feelings of the country as it headed down the homestretch of the 20th century. The name of the town was Hope.

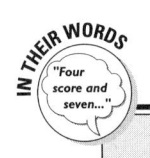

Good question

"People, I just want to say, you know, can we all get along? Can we just get along?" —Rodney King, to reporters during the Los Angeles riots, May 2, 1992.

Chapter 20

No Sex, Please, I'm the President: 1993–1999

In This Chapter
- Taking a look at President Clinton
- Handling homegrown terrorism
- Dealing with the outbreak of AIDS and the use of drugs
- Introducing e-mail, the Internet, and a global economy

*I*n the last decade of the 20th century, America was on top of the world. Communism had crumbled. The economy, after a slow start, spent much of the decade in overdrive, sparked by revolutions in how people communicate and do business with one another and the rest of the world.

But the 1990s weren't all fun and games. Terrorism and violent confrontations between the government and domestic fringe groups came home to this country after having been regarded as events that were confined to foreign shores. Oh, and the president of the United States got caught with his zipper down.

Bill, Newt, and Monica

Fewer than half the people who voted for a presidential candidate in 1992 voted for Bill Clinton, which shows there was a pretty fair number of people who either disliked him or didn't trust him. At 46, he was the youngest president since John F. Kennedy. Like JFK, Clinton could be charming and affable, was a convincing public speaker, and had a weakness for women. A Democrat, Clinton was the first of the baby-boomer generation — those born between 1946 and 1964 — to be president. He had avoided the draft during Vietnam and admitted that he smoked marijuana at least once. In short, he was a new kind of chief executive.

Treading lightly abroad

REMEMBER

On the foreign front, Clinton was cautious. He did push through the North American Free Trade Agreement (NAFTA), which greatly reduced barriers among the United States, Canada, and Mexico. But his biggest challenge came in what was the former country of Yugoslavia. It had split into smaller states after the collapse of Soviet dominance in Europe in the late 1980s. In Bosnia, which was one of those states, Serbian, Croatian, and Bosnian groups were fighting a civil war that threatened to spread. When diplomatic efforts failed, the United States and other nations sent in peacekeeping troops to enforce a fragile truce. Later in the decade, U.S. military forces and other countries also intervened (and eventually restored order) when the former Yugoslavian state of Serbia invaded and terrorized neighboring Kosovo.

Clinton was much less successful — and apparently less interested — in solving problems in Africa. He inherited a mess in Somalia, where U.S. troops had been sent in as part of a United Nations peacekeeping force. They failed to quiet things down. In October 1993, Americans were repulsed by video of the bodies of U.S. soldiers being dragged through the streets of Somalia's capital. U.S. troops were removed in 1994. Clinton also failed to intercede in the genocidal conflict in Rwanda, where millions were killed or forced to become refugees. A decade later, and presumably wiser, Clinton apologized for his "personal failure" to do more.

In 1998, a radical Islamic terrorist group called al-Qaida bombed U.S. embassies in Kenya and Tanzania. Clinton ordered retaliatory missile attacks against suspected al-Qaida havens in Sudan and Afghanistan, to little effect. Frustrated with Iraqi dictator Saddam Hussein's refusal to cooperate with UN weapons inspections, the United States and Great Britain launched air strikes against Iraq in late 1998, also to little effect. Both the terrorist group and the dictator would prove to be even bigger headaches for Clinton's successor.

Pushing harder on the home front

Clinton was much more interested and engaged when it came to domestic policies. His first big battle as president was over his ambitious plan to reform the country's healthcare system. It was a system plagued by soaring costs, confusing programs, and increasing unavailability to the unemployed and the uninsured. As the baby boomers aged and needed more medical care, the strain on the system would only get worse.

Clinton put his wife, Hillary, in charge of getting his reforms through Congress. But her efforts were hampered when she became embroiled in a probe into the financial dealings of an Arkansas company called the

Whitewater Development Corporation. The Whitewater probe led to Hillary Clinton becoming the first First Lady to be subpoenaed in a criminal investigation. The scandal, Hillary's stubbornness in refusing to compromise with legislators, and a massive and well-financed campaign by the health and pharmaceutical industries combined to sink the president's healthcare reforms.

In turn, the failure of Clinton's healthcare reforms, a series of mini-scandals at the White House, and the clever political strategy of a Georgia congressman named Newt Gingrich gave the Republicans control of both houses of Congress in 1995 for the first time since 1946. Gingrich was elected House speaker.

Pushing the "Contract with America"

During the 1994 congressional campaign, Republicans had come up with a conservative litany of policies they said they would pursue if they came to power. They called it the *Contract with America*. After the election, they began pushing an array of programs that were aimed at reducing federal spending on social programs, softening environmental rules, cutting taxes, and easing government regulations on business and industry.

Clinton, sensing that the political mood of the country was shifting to the center, went along for the ride. In August 1996, he signed into law the Welfare Reform Act, which tightened up federal aid to those who wouldn't or couldn't work and shifted more responsibility to the states. By the end of the decade, welfare rolls in much of the country had shrunk considerably. Well before the welfare bill, however, Clinton had shown his willingness to hug the middle. Shortly after taking office in 1993, he tried to end the ban on gays in the military. When a firestorm of opposition arose, he retreated to a "don't ask, don't tell" policy that said gays could serve in the military as long as they didn't tell anyone they were gay.

But most Americans were far more interested in pocketbook issues than gays in the military, and when it came to the economy, Clinton shone. The federal budget deficit of $290 billion in 1993 was transformed to a surplus of about $70 billion by 1997. Clinton had backed a tax increase in 1993 to balance the budget; when it was balanced in 1997, he signed a bill cutting U.S. income taxes for the first time since 1981.

He was also more stubborn on economic issues than on some other issues. When the president and Congress couldn't agree on a federal budget, the government all but shut down in November 1995 and January 1996. The public largely blamed the Republicans in Congress, in part because Gingrich was viewed as something of a political weasel outside of Washington. By 1998, the "Republican resurgence" was over, although Republicans continued to hold majorities in both houses of Congress. In November 1998, Democrats picked up a total of 5 congressional seats when they had expected to lose 20. Gingrich stepped down as speaker and soon left Congress altogether.

The public's apathy toward the Republicans' "contract," combined with the fact that the economy was doing well, allowed Clinton to easily win reelection over Kansas Senator Bob Dole in 1996. One of Clinton's most ardent supporters in his reelection effort was a young White House intern named Monica Lewinsky.

Judging a president

Bill Clinton had troubles with women before Miss Lewinsky. During the 1992 presidential campaign, a nightclub singer named Gennifer Flowers claimed she and Clinton had a long affair while he was governor of Arkansas. Clinton first denied it and then acknowledged that during his marriage he had committed adultery. As president, he was also unsuccessfully sued for allegedly sexually harassing a former Arkansas state employee named Paula Jones while he was governor.

Then in January 1998, it was revealed that an independent investigator named Kenneth Starr — appointed by Congress to look into the Whitewater real estate mess around Hillary Clinton — was looking into a possible sexual relationship between Clinton and Lewinsky. Lewinsky had come to the White House in 1995 as a 21-year-old, unpaid intern. She went on the White House payroll a few months later but was transferred to the Pentagon after some Clinton aides thought she was getting too cozy with the president.

At first, Clinton and Lewinsky denied any hanky-panky. Clinton also adamantly denied he ever asked Lewinsky to lie about their relationship. As the months passed, however, the truth began to emerge. In a national TV address in August 1998, Clinton admitted to "a relationship with Miss Lewinsky that was not appropriate."

On October 8, the GOP-controlled House of Representatives brought impeachment charges against Clinton, basically for fooling around with Lewinsky and then lying about it (although the formal charges were obstructing justice, tampering with witnesses, and lying under oath). He was impeached a few weeks later, the second president in U.S. history (Andrew Johnson was the first) to be tried in the Senate.

But public polls showed that while most Americans were pretty disgusted with Clinton's morals, they didn't want to see him thrown out of office for them. The Senate agreed, and on February 12, 1999, it voted to acquit him.

> ## Bettor days
>
> Americans have always been gamblers. Many American ancestors gambled big-time just to get here in the first place. But chances are that very few of them envisioned just how much legal U.S. gambling would eventually grow.
>
> Fueled by relaxed moral views, more leisure time, and governments looking to raise money without raising taxes, legal gambling boomed in the last quarter of the 20th century and into the 21st. By 2013, 44 states ran lotteries and 42 had casinos of some kind. Only 2 states — Utah and Hawaii — had no forms of legal wagering.
>
> Some of the biggest beneficiaries of all this betting were Native Americans — although by no means all. Thanks to their status as sovereign nations and a 1988 congressional act, 240 tribes (out of a total of 562) in 28 states had gambling operations in 2012, with revenues of $29.2 billion.
>
> And don't bet on Americans giving up their betting ways anytime soon. In 2013, Nevada, New Jersey, and Delaware began allowing their residents to legally gamble online within the state. And other states were watching to see whether it paid off.

Homegrown Terrorism

For most of the 20th century, *terrorism* — using acts of violence to make a political point — was something most Americans regarded as a foreign problem. But in the 1990s, a series of events brought terrorism closer to home.

Some domestic terrorism stemmed from small-but-fervent groups or individuals who believed the U.S. government was part of various international conspiracies bent on world domination. By 1997, right-wing paramilitary or survivalist groups had developed in every state. Some were led by Vietnam-era vets who felt betrayed by the government, others by religious fanatics, and still others by white supremacists.

Rallying around Ruby Ridge

One such group formed in Idaho, about 40 miles from the Canadian border, at a place called Ruby Ridge. On August 21, 1992, U.S. marshals were watching a white supremacist named Randy Weaver when shots were fired. A marshal and Weaver's 14-year-old son were killed. The next day, an FBI sniper killed Weaver's wife and wounded another man. At a subsequent trial, Weaver and another defendant were acquitted of all but one minor charge, and the government agreed to pay $3.1 million to the Weaver family for the incident. "Ruby Ridge" became a rallying cry for militia groups of all types.

Taking down a cult: Waco

By his own admission, Vernon Wayne Howell had an unhappy childhood, and by the time he was 22, he was still seeking somewhere to belong. In 1981, he chose the Branch Davidians, a religious sect that in 1935 had settled about 10 miles outside of Waco, Texas. By 1990, Howell had changed his name to David Koresh and was head of the cult. Koresh called himself "the Messiah" and took multiple wives from among his followers.

On February 28, 1993, federal agents looking for illegal weapons and explosives tried a surprise raid on the Branch Davidian compound. But Koresh had apparently been tipped off that they were coming, and a gunfight erupted. Four agents and two cult members were killed, and a 51-day siege of the compound began.

On April 19, after negotiations with Koresh to surrender had stalled, federal agents attacked the compound and fired tear gas inside. A fire broke out and spread rapidly. When it was over, at least 82 people were dead, including 17 children. The government contended it had acted responsibly. Critics contended it was at best a reckless mistake, and at worst, murder. One of the critics was a skinny, 29-year-old, former soldier named Timothy McVeigh.

The People versus "The Juice"

It may have been unique in U.S. history: a national icon who was an accused double murderer.

Orenthal James Simpson — better known to his fans as "O.J." or "The Juice" — was a Hall-of-Fame football player who had been a successful movie actor and TV commercial spokesman. On June 12, 1994, Simpson's former wife, Nicole Brown Simpson, and her friend, Ronald Goldman, were brutally knifed to death in front of Nicole's Los Angeles condominium.

Simpson was a suspect and agreed to surrender to police. Instead, he led them on an incredible, slow-motion, nationally televised chase along L.A. freeways before surrendering in the driveway of his mansion. The evidence against Simpson seemed overwhelming. But after a trial that became an international media circus, Simpson was acquitted.

The verdict was characterized as an example of a rich man being able to buy justice by hiring defense attorneys who were smarter than the jury. Simpson lost a 1997 civil suit to the families of Nicole and Goldman and was ordered to pay $33.5 million for being responsible for their deaths. But he vowed never to pay a dime of the award because he insisted he was innocent of the murders.

In December 2008, Simpson was convicted in Las Vegas of robbery, assault with a deadly weapon, and several other charges. He was sentenced to a minimum of nine years in prison.

Bombings rock the nation

Not all the mayhem of the 1990s involved the U.S. government. On February 26, 1993, a 1,210-pound bomb that had been packed in a van rocked the World Trade Center building in New York City. The bomb killed six people. Members of a radical Islamic group, some of whom were also accused of plotting to bomb the UN building and two New York City tunnels, were arrested and convicted.

But it was Waco that stuck in the mind of Timothy McVeigh. A Gulf War veteran, McVeigh believed the U.S. government had become part of an international totalitarian conspiracy. With a friend, Terry Nichols, McVeigh decided to do something about it.

On the morning of April 19, 1995, the nine story Alfred P. Murrah Building, a federal office complex in Oklahoma City, was blasted by a powerful bomb. The blast rained down concrete and glass for blocks around. A total of 168 people were killed, including 19 children who had been at the building's day-care center. At the time, it was America's worst act of terrorism, and it stunned the nation. "This is why we live in Oklahoma," exclaimed a disbelieving woman. "Things like this don't happen here."

McVeigh and Nichols were arrested shortly after the bombing. At their trials, prosecutors charged that the bomb — a mixture of fertilizer and fuel oil in a truck parked outside the building — had been set to mark the second anniversary of the Waco tragedy. McVeigh was sentenced to death in 1997 and executed in 2001. Nichols received a life sentence.

In between the bombing and the sentencings of McVeigh and Nichols, America was shook by yet another bombing, this one in a park in Atlanta during the 1996 summer Olympics. Two people died and 111 were injured. An antiabortion homophobe named Eric Rudolph was arrested in 2003 for the bombing and sentenced in 2005 to life in prison.

Don't open that mail: The Unabomber

Theodore Kaczynski was a university math professor who retreated to life in a tiny plywood shack in Montana. From there he mailed bombs to people he deemed were part of society's "evil" homage to technology. Over 18 years, Kaczynski mailed 16 bombs, killing 3 people, injuring 23, and triggering a massive manhunt. He became known as the "Unabomber" because his initial targets were universities and airlines.

He was caught after he successfully demanded that *The Washington Post* publish a long and rambling "manifesto" he had written. Kaczynski's brother recognized the thoughts as his brother's and contacted federal agents. Kaczynski was arrested. He pleaded guilty in 1997 to avoid the death penalty and was sentenced to life without parole.

The tragedies served notice on America that it was no longer a safe oasis in a dangerous world. Mindful of potential terrorist attacks, Pennsylvania Avenue, the street in front of the White House, was closed to traffic.

Making Ourselves Sick

While the bombs and terrorism of the 1990s were scary, many more Americans were affected by different kinds of horrors: the twin plagues of AIDS and drugs.

Suffering from AIDS

First documented in 1981, AIDS (acquired immune deficiency syndrome) was found to come from the HIV virus, which in turn was spread by the exchange of bodily fluids, such as blood and semen. People could have the virus — be *HIV-positive* — and not have AIDS. After the virus transmuted, however, death was a near certainty. Most of the early cases were among gay men, and "only" 21,517 total cases were reported in 1986.

Still, AIDS was sobering on two levels besides the most important, which was the loss of life. Medical science had conquered many diseases by the end of the 20th century and lessened the impact of many others. AIDS was a chilling reminder that man was still not master of his own medical fate.

The other impact was political. Gays and lesbians had made important strides in gaining the status of other minority groups. Openly gay candidates had won elective office, and some states and cities had begun banning discrimination on the basis of sexual orientation. But the spread of AIDS was seen by many homophobes as God's revenge against gays, and many people who previously considered themselves open-minded on the issue began to worry about contracting the disease from even casual contact with homosexuals.

As the disease spread from the gay community to intravenous drug users and heterosexuals, the numbers became epidemic. By the early 1990s, as many as 1.5 million Americans were believed to have the HIV virus, and 280,000 had died. But as the number of victims grew, so did public tolerance of the afflicted. Public sympathy was fueled in part by the revelations of public figures with the disease, such as basketball star Magic Johnson and Olympic diver Greg Louganis.

In 1997, the U.S. Supreme Court ruled that federal disability laws covered people with the HIV virus. Though no cure had been found by the end of 2013, drug treatments had some success in blocking the HIV virus from developing into full-blown AIDs. In 2013, the Centers for Disease Control and Prevention reported that the number of new HIV infections, about 50,000 per year, had remained "relatively stable" for a decade.

Dealing with drugs

A much longer-lived American malady than AIDS was its drug habit. It was a habit that could be traced back to the addictions of Civil War veterans to laudanum and other painkillers used in the war.

But drug use really became epidemic in the 1980s and 1990s, especially in the country's inner cities, with the spread of *crack,* a cheap, potent, and smokable form of cocaine. The production and distribution of crack and other drugs became a multibillion-dollar business, and America became the most lucrative market in the world for drug cartels in Asia and Central and South America.

The blossoming drug trade triggered deadly turf wars in U.S. cities, as rival gangs battled for control of the local drug markets. Not since the gang wars of Prohibition had American streets seen so much gunfire — and this time it was with automatic weapons that sprayed bullets all over the place and killed many innocent bystanders.

By 1990, more people were being sent to U.S. jails and prisons for drug-related offenses than for any other crime. The war on drugs ground on through the 1990s, and when the use of crack declined, the use of methamphetamine, or *crank,* grew.

By the end of the decade and into the new century, it became apparent that the weight of the U.S. justice system had made little lasting impact on America's addictions. A 2010 national survey found that 22 million Americans said they used illegal drugs. A World Health Organization report concluded that America had the highest level of illegal drug use in the world.

And despite federal laws that made marijuana use illegal in all cases, 19 states had legalized its use for medical reasons by 2013. In that same year, voters in Washington and Colorado approved proposals to legalize "recreational" marijuana use. The U.S. Justice Department announced it would not actively enforce the federal laws prohibiting it.

AMERICAN FACES

Toni Morrison

She turned to writing because of an unhappy marriage, and her husband's loss turned out to be the literary world's gain.

Chloe Anthony Wofford was born in Ohio in 1931 to an African-American family who had left the South to escape racism. After graduating from college (where she took the name "Toni" because some people had trouble pronouncing her name), she became a university teacher. She married a young architect named Harold Morrison in 1958. But the marriage was an unhappy one, and she joined an amateur writing group to escape.

After getting a divorce, Morrison moved to New York and became a book editor. She also continued to write, and published her first novel, *The Bluest Eye*, in 1970. Her fifth novel, *Beloved*, won the 1988 Pulitzer Prize, and in 1993 she was given the Nobel Prize for Literature, the first African-American woman to win the award.

"Tell us," she challenged black writers in her acceptance speech, "what it is to live at the edge of towns that cannot bear your company."

A World of Change

The last decade of the 20th century saw America — and the rest of the world — undergo some pretty revolutionary changes. One of the biggest was in the development of technology, particularly in computers. The speed of their development was staggering.

As the chips got more complex, their uses grew, and as their uses grew, their prices dropped. In 1994, a computer sophisticated enough to do high-speed, three-dimensional graphics for things like military flight simulators cost $300,000. In 2000, better computers than that were available in kids' video game systems for $400. (And if you think that's something, take a look at Chapter 24 to see how quickly technology was changing.)

Many of the advances were in communications, and sharing information became as big a business as manufacturing a product. The number of cell-phones in the country, for example, jumped from fewer than 10 million in 1990 to more than 100 million in 2000. (For where all this tech stuff took America in the 21st century, see Chapter 24.)

You've got mail!

In the early 1960s, some American scientists began kicking around the idea of a computer system, using research computers called *nodes*, which could continue to function even in the event of a nuclear war. That possibility was of keen interest to the Pentagon, which financed much of the work.

Chapter 20: No Sex, Please, I'm the President: 1993–1999

The result, in late 1969, was the birth of the Internet, which led to e-mail, which led to a communications revolution. By the late 1990s, virtually every part of the world was linked to every other part. Americans alone sent an estimated 2.2 billion e-mail messages *per day,* or about 7 times the number of pieces of first-class mail. By the end of 2000, it was estimated that e-mail messages had replaced 25 percent of what was now referred to as "snail mail."

But the Internet, which gave birth to a network of information sources called the World Wide Web, did far more than make it easier to check in on Grandma or chat with Uncle Louie in the old country. It allowed businesses to reduce their costs and be more efficient by instantly knowing how much inventory they needed to keep on hand, how much of a product they needed to make, and who could supply them with the raw materials and needed parts.

Retail customers could comparison-shop in businesses across the country and around the world — and they did. Online shopping for the Christmas holidays in 1999 was estimated at $7.3 billion. In 2000, it had jumped to more than $12 billion.

The computer revolution had impacts far beyond shopping and business. It led to amazing advances in medicine and biological research. It led to a very real reduction in the time and space between America and the rest of the world, creating a true global economy.

A pawn for Deep Blue

Garry Kasparov didn't offer to shake hands after winning a chess match in February 1996. It wasn't just Kasparov's well-known arrogance: His opponent had no arms. Kasparov, the world chess champion since 1985, had beaten IBMRS/6000SP, a computer christened *Deep Blue* by its IBM Corporation designers.

The win was called a victory for man over machine, and Kasparov readily agreed to a rematch the following year. It was a bad move for the grandmaster. On May 11, 1997, Kasparov stormed out of a small room in New York City after being soundly thrashed by the computer, which had been considerably tweaked since the first match and could analyze 200 million possible moves in a second.

Kasparov was a sore loser. Much more gracious was Ken Jennings, a champion of the TV quiz show *Jeopardy,* after Jennings and another human contestant lost a 2011 match to a room-sized IBM computer named "Watson."

"I, for one, welcome our new computer overlords," Jennings jokingly wrote on his video screen at the end of the game.

Trading under a global economy

The global economy — an economy that closely tied together the production and consumer patterns of many nations — was created not only by the development of information-sharing technologies but also by many countries dropping trade barriers and opening their markets to the rest of the world.

One of the effects of the global economy was the creation of a wave of megamergers among big corporations from different countries: Daimler Benz of Germany with Chrysler in automobiles, British Petroleum of England with Amoco in oil. The bigger companies promised, and often delivered, more efficiencies, better products, and lower prices.

But there were drawbacks. The intertwining of economies meant America was more affected by downturns in other parts of the world than it had been before. International products were often more attractive to American consumers than their U.S.-made counterparts, and the country's trade deficit steadily rose — from $155 billion in 1997 to $299 billion in 1999.

And many U.S. companies exported jobs as well as products by transferring their manufacturing operations to countries where the cost of labor was much lower. In Thailand, for example, a worker might be paid $2 for a nine-hour day making footwear, or a worker in Haiti might be paid $2.50 a day to make shirts. But though critics complained that such outsourcing was exploiting foreign workers, the companies responded that the wages were fair by third-world standards and helped the countries build their own manufacturing bases.

Most Americans weren't complaining. In 1997, the average U.S. family's annual income passed $40,000 for the first time. The number of people below the poverty level set by the federal government fell to 11.8 percent, the lowest since 1979, and the poverty rates among African Americans and Asian Americans fell to their lowest levels ever. Even Congress couldn't spend fast enough to keep up. The federal budget went from having an annual deficit of $300 billion at the beginning of the decade to a surplus of $123 billion at the end.

And because it was so easy to spend money, Americans did it with enthusiasm. Savings rates dropped to almost nothing by the end of the decade, leaving many Americans in a precarious position if the economy went into a tailspin.

Which, as you see in Chapter 22, it did.

Part V
Facing the New Millennium

Three Stats That Show How American Families Are Changing

- In 1970, 81 percent of U.S. households contained families of some kind. In 2012, it was down to 66 percent.
- In 1970, 40 percent of U.S. households were comprised of a married couple with children. In 2012, it was 20 percent.
- In 1980, about 18 percent of all births in America were to unmarried women. In 2010, it was 41 percent. A quarter of all American children lived in one-parent households.

Visit www.dummies.com/extras/ushistory for an article about the invention of microchips.

In this part...

- A controversial election marks the start of the 21st century.
- The United States goes to war after the attacks of September 11, 2001.
- The U.S. economy plunges into the Great Recession in 2008.

Chapter 21

Terror Comes Home; America Goes to War(s)

In This Chapter
- Winning ugly: The 2000 presidential election
- Going to war with terrorism
- Dealing with Saddam
- Watching a city drown

As the 21st century began, the United States found itself the Big Kahuna on an increasingly shrinking planet. Technological innovations occurred at a geometric pace and jumped national boundary lines. That helped create an even more tightly knit international economy. Environmental and political problems also crossed borders, all of which added up to the fact that the world's troubles were inescapably America's, and vice versa.

This chapter covers one of the closest presidential elections ever, two wars, the most horrific terrorist attack in modern history, and a pretty nasty natural disaster or two. It was a bumpy start for the new century.

Whew! A Squeaker: Bush and Gore, 2000

One was the son of a former president; the other was the son of a former U.S. senator. By the time the 2000 presidential election campaign was over, George W. Bush and Al Gore had staged a race that was a son of a gun.

Gore, the offspring of former Tennessee Sen. Al Gore Sr. and a former senator himself, had served dutifully, if a bit distantly, for eight years as vice president to Bill Clinton and was the obvious choice to succeed Clinton as the Democratic Party's standard-bearer.

Bush, the governor of Texas and the son of the 41st president, George H. W. Bush, was a former oil man and major league baseball executive. The younger Bush parlayed his familiar name and financial backing from much of the Republican establishment to win the GOP nomination, after beating back a challenge from Arizona Sen. John McCain.

The campaign was a roller-coaster affair. Gore tried to run on the positive aspects of the Clinton administration while taking pains not to be too closely associated with Clinton himself, who was viewed as damaged political goods because of the Lewinsky scandal and his subsequent impeachment.

Bush dubbed himself a "compassionate conservative" and focused on the need for a "new morality" in the White House. He also criticized the Clinton administration's military intervention in the Balkans and Somalia, contending that the U.S. military shouldn't be used for "nation building" elsewhere. By the time Election Day arrived, polls showed the two were neck and neck.

Hanging chads and butterfly ballots

It all came down to Florida. Outside the Sunshine State, Gore had captured (or would capture) 266 of the 270 electoral votes needed to win the White House. Bush had 246. It appeared at first that Gore had won Florida's 25 electoral votes, giving him the presidency. But as the night of November 7 turned into the morning of November 8, it looked like Bush had won. TV networks that had originally projected Gore as the winner reversed themselves and declared Bush the winner. Around 2 a.m., Gore called Bush to concede. Around 4 a.m., he called back to withdraw his concession.

And the confusion was just getting warmed up. Over the next 35 days, both sides engaged in a titanic legal struggle over whether recounts should occur and, if so, which votes should be recounted. Ballots where voters had failed to completely punch out the little cardboard squares — and therefore left *hanging chads* — were challenged.

So were *butterfly ballots* that had candidates' names on one page and the punch holes on another, leading to voter confusion. A post-election study of ballots in Palm Beach County found that more than 8,000 voters had punched holes for Gore *and* for one of two minor party candidates.

The whole mess eventually went to the U.S. Supreme Court. On December 12, the court voted 5–4 to reverse a decision by the Florida Supreme Court that would have continued the recounts. The next day, Gore conceded.

Count 'em all — and be a good loser

"An election is not over until all the votes are counted. If the U.S. Supreme Court does not come down on the side of this most revered principle of democracy, then this presidential election will be forever tainted." —U.S. Sen. Barbara Boxer, D-CA, two days before the court's decision.

"There's an important responsibility for the loser to lose with grace." —U.S. Sen. Mitch McConnell, R-KY, on the same day.

Post-election scrutinizing

Gore's concession ended an election filled with ironies and what-ifs. Gore had won the popular vote by about 500,000 votes out of about 100 million cast. It was only the fourth time in U.S. history that the popular vote winner didn't win the White House (1824, 1876, and 1888 were the others). If Gore had only won his home state of Tennessee or Clinton's home state of Arkansas, he would have won. If Green Party candidate Ralph Nader hadn't been on the Florida ballot, most of his 97,000 votes may have gone to Gore.

Post-election studies by several major newspapers found that if the recount had been limited to only the counties in which Gore had sought recounts, Bush still would have won. But if all the disputed ballots throughout the state had been recounted, Gore would have won.

As something of a consolation prize, Gore won the 2007 Nobel Peace Prize for his work in bringing attention to the role of humans in global warming. A film that he narrated on the same topic also won an Academy Award for best documentary. Bush, meanwhile, got the job his dad had held eight years before — and some of the same headaches.

Bush came into office with slightly more than half of the voters preferring someone else and with polls showing that more than half the country thought the Supreme Court's decision was politically motivated. That's hardly anyone's idea of a good way to start an administration.

But Americans don't hold a grudge for long. By April 2001, polls were showing that though only 50 percent thought Bush had won fair and square, 59 percent said they supported him, and 62 percent approved of the way he was handling the job. (Of course, it didn't hurt that Bush had started his tenure by proposing a $1.6 trillion tax-cut package.) The new president also unveiled an ambitious energy program that called for relaxing environmental protections in favor of aggressively expanding fossil-fuel development.

> ### Lifting the curse
>
> Dave Roberts stole second, David Ortiz homered, Curt Schilling bled through his sock, and the "Curse of the Bambino" was forever lifted. That's one way of summing up the Boston Red Sox' improbable 2004 season, in which the 103-year-old baseball team won its first world championship since 1918. The Sox hadn't won since then-owner Harry Frazee sold the legendary Babe Ruth to the New York Yankees in 1920. The Yankees went on to win 27 World Series and become one of the most successful sports franchises in U.S. history.
>
> As for the Red Sox, they managed to get into the World Series in 1946, 1967, 1975, and 1986, but won none of them. Year after year, Boston fans dutifully filled the ancient architectural curiosity called Fenway Park (which opened in 1912, just six years before the team won its last World Series, with Ruth as its star pitcher), and waited.
>
> Then came 2004. After beating the Anaheim Angels in the first round of the American League playoffs, Boston lost the first three games of the best-of-seven second round to the Yankees and was trailing 4-3 in the 9th inning of Game 4. Then Roberts stole second base and eventually scored the tying run. In the 12th inning, Ortiz homered to win the game. The Red Sox went on to whip the Yankees three more times, then swept the St. Louis Cardinals four games to none to win the World Series. Schilling, pitching on an injured ankle, won Game 2 of the series with blood seeping through his sock. "I know one thing," Boston pitcher Tim Wakefield said after the last series game. "We won't hear that '1918' chant again."

But less than nine months into his administration, Bush faced a crisis that would put most domestic programs on the back burner, define his presidency, and change the way many Americans thought about their own security.

A Nation Stunned

At 8:46 (EDT) on the morning of September 11, 2001, a hijacked commercial jet crashed into the North Tower of the World Trade Center in New York City. Seventeen minutes later, a second hijacked passenger jet flew into the center's South Tower (see Figure 21-1). Both towers soon collapsed, pulling down or heavily damaging surrounding buildings.

At 9:37, a third jet plowed into the Pentagon in Washington, D.C., followed 26 minutes later by the crash of a fourth flight into a field about 70 miles southeast of Pittsburgh, Pennsylvania. It appeared passengers aboard the fourth plane, having learned of the fate of the other three through cellphone calls, confronted the hijackers before the plane could reach its intended target, which was believed to have been the Capitol in Washington, D.C.

Figure 21-1: Devastation at the World Trade Center.

AFP/Getty Images

The United States had suffered the worst attack on its soil in its history, and the country plunged into a war against terrorism.

al-Qaida and Osama bin Laden

The attacks, carried out by 19 members of a fundamentalist Islamist group called *al-Qaida* ("the base"), killed a total of about 3,000 people, including some 400 New York City police and firefighters who responded to the disaster at the World Trade Center.

Americans — and much of the rest of the world — were shocked. Millions had watched horrified as TV cameras that had been focusing on the North Tower after the first attack captured the second plane hitting the South Tower. The subsequent collapse of the towers was also carried live. National, state, and local officials scrambled to prepare for more attacks. Air travel was shut down. Stock markets in the United States and around the world were badly shaken and posted severe losses.

On September 17, President Bush formally identified al-Qaida leader Osama bin Laden as the mastermind behind the attacks. A wealthy member of a prominent Saudi Arabian family, bin Laden had operated out of Afghanistan since the mid-1990s, under the protection of a group called the Taliban. The *Taliban* (which means "student") followed an extreme version of Islamic law and had seized control in Afghanistan in 1998.

Taking on the Taliban

Speaking to a joint session of Congress on September 20, Bush demanded the Taliban hand over bin Laden and other al-Qaida leaders and dismantle terrorist training camps within Afghanistan. "They will hand over the terrorists or share their fate," Bush warned.

On October 7, after Taliban leaders had rejected Bush's demands, U.S. and British aircraft unleashed a massive bombing attack on major Afghan cities. By mid-November, the Afghan capital of Kabul had fallen. By mid-December, air attacks coupled with allied nations' ground forces that included about 30,000 troops from the United States and anti-Taliban Afghan militia had toppled the Taliban regime.

While out of power, the Taliban was not out of business. After a year of licking their wounds, Taliban forces began an insurgency. Their efforts were fueled by funds from control of much of Afghanistan's vast opium production, which grew to record levels in 2013. The enemy also took advantage of safe havens in mountainous areas along the Afghanistan-Pakistan border by scampering into Pakistan, where it was logistically and politically difficult for U.S. troops to follow.

President Barack Obama, Bush's successor, countered in 2009 by gradually building U.S. forces to more than 100,000 while warning that "our troop commitment in Afghanistan cannot be open-ended." By mid-2013, U.S. forces had been drawn down to about 65,000, with plans to withdraw all combat troops by the end of 2014. Left unsettled, however, was whether as many as 10,000 U.S. military advisors and other "support personnel" would remain — and for how long.

And while bin Laden was killed by Navy SEALs in his Pakistan hiding place in May 2011, Taliban leader Mullah Mohammad Omar remained at large. After suffering more than 2,000 military deaths, spending more than $800 billion, and fighting for three times longer than it had in World War II, America was still far from certain about the ultimate outcome in Afghanistan.

Terror with a stamp on it

If the events of September 11 weren't enough to stamp the word *terrorism* firmly in the minds of Americans, some letters postmarked September 18 from Trenton, New Jersey, finished the job.

The letters, to NBC News and the *New York Post*, contained a note bearing the date "9-11-01" and a short note. They also contained spores of anthrax, a nasty bacterial disease. Similar letters were apparently received at ABC News and CBS News in New York and the *National Enquirer* in Boca Raton, Florida, because people at those organizations were also exposed to anthrax. A few weeks later, anthrax-bearing letters addressed to U.S. senators Tom Daschle of South Dakota and Patrick Leahy of Vermont were found.

By the end of November, 22 people who either worked at the targeted sites or worked for the postal service had contracted the disease. Five of them died. Americans became nervous about something as mundane as opening the mail. Government officials issued dozens of warnings while emergency personnel practiced responding to any bioterrorism and chemical attacks.

In late July 2008, Bruce E. Ivins, a longtime researcher at the federal biodefense lab at Ft. Detrick, Maryland, committed suicide. Within a week, federal prosecutors announced Ivins was the man behind the attacks and had acted alone. Some of Ivins' colleagues, however, doubted he had done it, and no convincing motive was established. The attacks remain ample fodder for conspiracy theorists everywhere.

Fighting terrorism on the home front

The Bush administration never formally declared war on Afghanistan (which allowed it to claim it didn't have to treat those captured as prisoners of war). But it did declare war on terrorism, and Bush proclaimed the war would continue and be fought on every front "until every terrorist group of global reach has been found, stopped, and defeated."

A month after the September 11 attacks, Bush pushed for a proposal called the "Uniting and Strengthening America by Providing Appropriate Tools Required to Intercept and Obstruct Terrorism Act" — or the USA Patriot Act.

The far-reaching "temporary" act (most of which was made permanent by Congress in 2006) greatly expanded the authority of the FBI and other law enforcement agencies to conduct searches, look at medical and other personal records (such as what materials an individual took out from public libraries), and spy on those suspected of potential terrorist acts without court approval. It allowed foreigners to be held for up to seven days without charges or deportation proceedings.

The act was approved 357–66 in the House of Representatives. In the Senate, the vote was 98–1, with only Sen. Russell Feingold, D-WI, opposed.

In July 2002, Bush secretly authorized the National Security Agency (NSA) to listen in on phone calls American citizens made to other countries and to monitor e-mails. (See Chapter 24 for more on the NSA and electronic surveillance.) The order wasn't made public until 2005, and Congress didn't sanction the actions until 2008. In November, Bush signed a bill creating the Department of Homeland Security, consolidating dozens of government agencies, from the Secret Service to the Coast Guard, into one super-agency.

Imprisoning "non-POWs" at Guantanamo Bay

Because America had not actually declared war against Afghanistan, it didn't treat captured al-Qaida and Taliban fighters as prisoners of war (POWs). Instead, they were taken to a prison erected on the U.S. Naval base at Guantanamo Bay on the island of Cuba. Administration officials contended that because the prison wasn't on U.S. soil, the prisoners had no rights and could be held indefinitely without trial or even formal charges being filed.

In 2004, international observers reported some of the detainees at Guantanamo had been subjected to what the U.S. Central Intelligence Agency (CIA) referred to as "enhanced interrogation techniques," which the observers characterized as "tantamount to torture." One such technique, called *waterboarding*, consisted of covering a person's face with a towel and then pouring water over it, creating a sensation like drowning.

It was also revealed that the CIA had abducted suspected terrorists and held them in secret prisons in Europe.

Defending controversial tactics

Civil libertarians complained that such actions were counter to American ideals and violated basic human rights. But administration officials, notably Vice President Dick Cheney, defended the practices as justifiable and necessary to fight terrorism. They also pointed out that no terrorist attacks had occurred on U.S. soil since September 11, while several terrorist plots had been sniffed out and stopped. In 2008, Congress approved a bill to ban some of the interrogation methods used, but Bush vetoed it. When Bush left office, an estimated 245 prisoners were still at Guantanamo.

His successor, Barack Obama, had promised during his campaign to close the base and repeated variations of that pledge in subsequent years. Shortly after taking office in January 2009, he signed an executive order closing down the CIA's secret prisons. But Congress repeatedly blocked efforts to transfer Guantanamo detainees to U.S. prisons or other countries, and at the end of 2013, 164 prisoners remained.

That Damn Saddam

With his approval ratings as high as 90 percent in some polls after the 9/11 attacks and U.S. retaliation in Afghanistan, Bush made the war on terror the centerpiece of his administration's efforts. And with the overthrow of the Taliban at least temporarily accomplished, the administration turned its attention to an old nemesis: Iraqi dictator Saddam Hussein.

The United States, under the first President Bush, had decided in 1991 not to prolong the Gulf War by seeking Saddam's ouster. But it did persuade the United Nations to impose economic sanctions against Iraq, as well as to monitor the country's clandestine development of nuclear, biological, and chemical weapons, known collectively as *weapons of mass destruction* (WMD).

In 1998, after Iraqi officials had consistently interfered with UN inspectors, President Clinton ordered the bombing of several Iraqi military installations. Iraq countered by banning the UN inspectors. Moreover, the impact of economic sanctions had waned as some countries quietly resumed trading goods for Iraqi oil.

Toughening the stance against Iraq

In 2002, the second President Bush began demanding that the UN toughen its dealings with Iraq. Bush argued the Iraqis had, or were close to having, weapons of mass destruction. Further, he said, they were harboring members of the al-Qaida terrorist group that had engineered the 9/11 attacks. On October 10 and 11, Congress approved a resolution authorizing the use of military force against Iraq. The vote was 297–133 in the House and 77–23 in the Senate.

On February 5, 2003, U.S. Secretary of State Colin Powell went before the UN Security Council to restate American claims about WMDs, displaying aerial photographs of purported chemical weapons sites and mobile nerve gas labs. "Ladies and gentlemen, these are sophisticated facilities," Powell said. "For example, they can produce anthrax and botulinum toxin — in fact, they can produce enough dry biological agent to kill thousands upon thousands of people." Powell was countered by UN inspectors who said they were again making progress with Iraq and had found no evidence of WMDs.

On March 17, 2003 — despite the objections of U.S. allies such as France and Germany, but with the backing of most of Congress — an undeterred Bush issued an ultimatum that gave Saddam 48 hours to resign and get out of Iraq. When he didn't, U.S. and British forces on March 20 launched air attacks on Iraqi targets, including a bunker in which Saddam was thought to be meeting with aides.

The U.S. invasion

Within days, U.S. forces invaded from neighboring Kuwait. By April 9, the Iraqi capital of Baghdad had fallen. Saddam's sons were killed, and Saddam went into hiding. He was captured in December and turned over to Iraqi authorities. On December 30, 2006, he was executed.

The ongoing war

On May 1, Bush landed on a U.S. aircraft carrier off the coast of San Diego and declared an end to major combat. Standing in front of a large banner proclaiming "Mission Accomplished," Bush told the crew that "because of you, the target has fallen, and Iraq is free. The war on terror is not over, yet it is not endless. We do not know the day of final victory, but we have seen the turning of the tide."

But if the tide had turned, it seemed to have turned the wrong way. The United States lacked a comprehensive postwar plan for rebuilding the country. Looting and riots dismantled much of Iraq's infrastructure and damaged public buildings. U.S. occupation leaders barred members of Saddam's Baath Party from serving in the provisional government and largely disbanded the Iraqi army. That resulted in a dearth of experienced political leaders and military officers to help with the country's reconstruction.

In the aftermath, guerrilla warfare caused far more casualties than the brief war had, and fighting between militias of the rival Islamic Sunni and Shiite sects threatened to plunge the country into civil war. Worse for Bush, an intensive search failed to turn up any weapons of mass destruction, and it became clear that Saddam had almost no connection with al-Qaida.

Losing popularity at home

At home, the war had quickly lost popularity after its initial successes had given way to a protracted fight. In 2004, Bush won reelection over U.S. Sen. John Kerry of Massachusetts by the narrowest margin of any incumbent president since Woodrow Wilson in 1916. In 2006, public dissatisfaction with the progress of the wars in Afghanistan and Iraq helped Democrats wrest control of both houses of Congress for the first time since 1994.

In January 2007, with no light visible at the end of the dark Iraqi tunnel, Bush announced he was sending in 21,500 more U.S. troops, for a total of 170,000, in an effort to quell the almost ceaseless violence in the country. In what was called "the Surge" strategy, he also announced renewed U.S. efforts to rebuild Iraq's infrastructure and economy.

Although U.S. military deaths reached 907 in 2007, the highest of any year, they dropped to 284 in the first 10 months of 2008. While administration officials claimed the decline was proof the Surge was working, critics contended it was due to the Shiite militia having largely defeated the Sunni and to insurgent forces adopting a strategy of waiting until U.S. forces began withdrawing.

In February 2009, new President Barack Obama announced U.S. combat troops would pull out of Iraq by the end of August 2010, which they did. Thousands of American military "advisers," however, remained for another year. On December 15, 2011, Secretary of Defense Leon Panetta officially declared the war over.

The eight-year war had cost the United States about 4,500 military personnel killed, more than 32,000 wounded, and at least $1 trillion. Estimates for Iraqi civilian deaths ranged from 115,000 to more than 500,000. And the sectarian fighting continued almost unabated since the U.S. withdrawal: More than 400 civilians were killed in November 2013 alone.

Meanwhile, in the Rest of the World...

As the wars in Afghanistan and Iraq dragged on, America was waging wars of words with other countries. In 2002, Bush had labeled Iran and North Korea, along with Iraq, as parts of an "Axis of Evil."

The primary beef with North Korea was the country's defiant insistence in developing its nuclear weapons program. After several years of public posturing and private negotiating, North Korea formally agreed in June 2008 to halt its program in return for the easing of economic sanctions against it.

But the agreement didn't last. In April 2009, North Korea launched a rocket that was believed to be part of a test of the country's nuclear missile capabilities. Later that year, and again in 2013, North Korean leaders announced they had conducted successful nuclear tests. The announcements were surrounded by a flurry of bellicose threats of war against the United States and South Korea. At the center of the country's bellicosity was its dictator, 30-year-old Kim Jong-un, who assumed power after his father, Kim Jong-il, died in December 2011.

Iran was another thorny problem. Bush administration officials insisted Iran was aiding the insurgency in neighboring Iraq by arming the insurgents and was developing a nuclear weapons program that further threatened the already unstable region. Although evidence as to the exact status of the Iranian nuclear program was conflicting, the administration viewed Iran as a real threat to the region's stability.

So did much of the rest of the world. As 2013 wound down, representatives of the United States, France, Britain, Russia, China, and Germany negotiated with Iranian leaders to seek a trade: If Iran would give up its nuclear aspirations, the UN would ease its economic sanctions against the country.

Oprah Winfrey

In nearly every field of human endeavor, there are individuals who are so dominant that they're instantly recognized by just their first name. In rock 'n' roll, it's *Elvis*. In soccer, it's *Pele*. For nearly everything else, it's *Oprah*. Born in 1954 to an unwed teenage mother, Winfrey was raised in poverty by various relatives. Following college, Winfrey became host of a daytime TV talk show in Maryland and then moved to Chicago in 1984. From 1986 to 2011, she hosted a nationally syndicated program that launched her into a highly varied — and highly lucrative — career. Winfrey became an Academy Award-nominated actress, a movie and TV producer, a magazine publisher, an author, and an arbiter of America's popular tastes.

All that made Winfrey a billionaire several times over and one of the world's most generous philanthropists. It's estimated that through 2013, she had given more than $400 million to various educational programs and raised or donated tens of millions more for other causes.

She also became extremely influential. For example, she was once sued by Texas cattlemen for saying on her show that she wouldn't eat another hamburger because of mad cow disease. The cattlemen claimed her remarks drove down the price of beef. (A Texas jury sided with Winfrey.) In 2013, *Forbes* magazine named Winfrey the world's most powerful celebrity, and *Vanity Fair* magazine suggested she had more cultural influence than any politician or religious leader "except perhaps the Pope." Of course, he's known by his first name only, too.

Winds and Losses

While the war on terrorism dominated Bush's presidency, he did attempt to make changes on domestic issues as well. In 2001, Bush proposed an ambitious education reform program called the *No Child Left Behind Act*. Approved by Congress, the plan boosted federal education funding; increased standards expected of schools, including annual reading and math skills testing; and gave parents more flexibility in choosing schools. The program was variously praised for making schools more accountable and criticized for forcing educators to take cookie-cutter approaches to teaching.

In late 2003, Bush pushed a plan through Congress to reform Medicare, the federal health insurance program for the elderly. The plan gave senior citizens more choices when picking a private insurance plan through which they received medical services, as well as in obtaining prescription drugs.

Bush had far less success in trying to reform Social Security and U.S. immigration policies. He proposed replacing the government-run pension program with a system of private savings accounts. But the plan died in the face of criticism that it would put too much of a burden on individuals and be too expensive in the transition.

Bush also supported a bipartisan plan that would allow an estimated 12 million illegal immigrants to remain in the country on a temporary basis and to apply for citizenship after returning to their own countries and paying a fine. The plan was crushed by the weight of opposition from those who thought it was too draconian and those who thought it was too soft.

But all the blustery rhetoric in Washington was like a gentle summer breeze when compared to a natural disaster that blew into the South.

Big blow in the Big Easy

On August 23, 2005, a hurricane formed over the Bahamas and headed toward the southeastern United States. Called *Katrina,* it crossed Florida, picked up strength over the Gulf of Mexico, and made landfall in southeast Louisiana on August 29.

While Katrina's 125-mile-per-hour winds — sending beds flying out of hotel windows — and 10 inches of rain were bad enough, a storm surge of more than 28 feet devastated the Mississippi coastal cities of Gulfport and Biloxi. But the greatest damage was reserved for the region's largest city — New Orleans.

Nicknamed the *Big Easy,* most of New Orleans is below sea level. Under Katrina's onslaught, levees that were supposed to protect the city gave way in more than 50 places, and 80 percent of the city was flooded. While most of New Orleans' 1.2 million residents were evacuated (many to the city of Houston, Texas), thousands either refused to leave or could not (see Figure 21-2).

Figure 21-2: The aftermath of Hurricane Katrina.

AFP/Getty Images

The disaster claimed more than 1,800 lives and destroyed 200,000 homes. Damage estimates ranged as high as $125 billion, making it the most expensive hurricane in U.S. history. It wasn't until October 11 that the last of the floodwaters were pumped out.

By then, a hurricane of criticism had whipped up over the federal government's response to the disaster. The criticism ranged from condemning the government's slow response in some areas with regard to the evacuation process to providing adequate temporary housing after the storm. There were also charges that the slow response was due in part to the fact that many of New Orleans's residents were poor African Americans. Bush's approval ratings sank to the lowest of his presidency. But they would go even lower.

Ike hits Texas

In September 2008, New Orleans was again evacuated when threatened by Hurricane Gustav. This time, the preparations and responses were better and the levees held. But on the heels of Gustav came Ike.

The hurricane hit the Gulf Coast of Texas on September 13, dragging up a massive storm surge that drowned much of the city of Galveston. The storm killed 82 in the United States, with as many as 200 people missing, and did an estimated $27 billion worth of property damage.

Once again, the federal government was criticized for its post-storm performance. Texas officials complained that the Federal Emergency Management Agency (FEMA) had been slow to provide housing for those left homeless by the hurricane and to provide funds for cleaning up the mess. "The response from Washington has been pretty underwhelming," Texas Gov. Rick Perry said in mid-November, two months after the storm. "This is really irritating."

But hurricanes, and even irritated governors, paled in the face of another kind of storm, an economic tempest that enveloped the nation and most of the rest of the world.

Chapter 22

Recessions Can Be Really Depressing

In This Chapter
▶ Popping economic bubbles filled with "dot-coms" and houses
▶ Concocting cures for an ailing economy
▶ Losing jobs — and not finding them again
▶ Carving a larger piece of the economic pie for a smaller percentage of Americans

An old economists' joke (told mainly by old economists) says that a *recession* is when your neighbor loses his job, and a *depression* is when you lose yours. Whatever you call it, the country's unsettled financial situation as the new century unfolded permeated nearly every aspect of Americans' lives, from politics to lifestyles to how Americans got along with the rest of the world — and one another.

In this chapter, I look at the web of elements that ensnared the economy; the government's efforts to fix things; the impacts that technology, global competition, and corporate profits had on employment; and the growing gap between the very richest Americans and everyone else.

Ouch! The Economy Stubs Its Toe

Here's what happened to the U.S. economy in the first years of the 21st century: A lot of people got rich (and then poor) creating and/or investing in high-tech companies. Then people in California bought homes they couldn't afford. And then Iceland went broke. And thus America had what has been called the *Great Recession*.

Of course, that interpretation is way too simple; there really isn't a linear, cause-effect explanation. The recession was actually a lot of causes and effects linked together. Think of it as sort of a spider's web of events and results.

Dot-com dreams and investor nightmares

As the 20th century ended and the 21st century began, there was an explosion of technological innovation, much of it centering on the Internet. This innovation was heralded as the gateway to a new economy, based on information-sharing as much as producing goods and services. And it triggered what was labeled the *dot-com boom*. Investors poured millions of dollars into hundreds of companies that were founded on great ideas but that often lacked sound business plans, large potential markets, and in some cases, even a product or service to sell.

This situation was a classic example of what Alan Greenspan, the chairman of the Federal Reserve Board, had labeled in 1996 as *irrational exuberance:* when investors' enthusiasm to make dollars overwhelms their common sense.

By March 2001, the dot-com bubble had burst. Scores of companies went belly up, their stocks became worthless, and America had its first economic recession in a decade. The terrorist attacks on September 11 of that year also dealt a sharp blow to the economy.

The dot-com bubble-bursting was fairly mild as recessions go. But some economists were troubled that, though the overall economy began improving by the end of 2001, unemployment rates that had risen when the recession began stubbornly refused to go down again to anything near their previous levels.

The houses that went upside down

A much nastier recession — in fact, the worst the country had suffered since the Great Depression of the 1930s — began with another bubble bursting in late 2007. This one was centered on the American dream of owning your own home and came about partly because of credit default swaps.

Under federal law, banks and other lending institutions have to keep lots of capital in reserve to protect investors if any of the big loans the lenders make go bad. To free up those reserves so they can be used to turn a profit elsewhere, the lending industry came up with a sort of insurance policy in the 1990s, called a *credit default swap*. It involved having a third party — individual investors, insurance companies, hedge funds, and so on — assume the risk of a loan going bad in return for regular payments from the firm that had actually made the loan.

The federal government didn't regulate the deals, so no one had a good handle on how widespread they were or which companies and economic sectors were most at risk. By the middle of the decade, the arrangements had morphed into more than $60 trillion — that's *trillion*, with a *t* — of swaps, and banks and other lenders had trillions of dollars to lend to people who, say, wanted to buy a house.

Buying up houses

In the late 1990s, interest rates were low, and real estate was an attractive investment. Americans began buying homes like crazy. Annual U.S. home sales set records for five straight years, peaking at 7.5 million in 2005. The greater the demand, the higher real estate prices went. Average home prices soared from less than $200,000 in 2000 to more than $300,000 in 2007.

But the higher prices went, the fewer people there were who could qualify for mortgage loans, at least under traditional methods of measuring qualifications — such as whether the borrower had enough income to make the payments.

So lenders and mortgage brokers got creative. They pushed loans with no down payments, loans that started out with low interest rates and then ballooned after a few years, and loans on which the borrower paid only interest for the first few years. By 2005, more than 200 kinds of mortgage products were available. And if there came a time when the borrowers couldn't meet the mortgage payments, heck, they could just refinance or sell the house for more than they paid for it and walk away with a profit. The risky mortgages boomed from about $160 billion in 2001 to more than $600 billion four years later.

There was even a bonus for people who could afford their mortgage payments: Their homes became giant piggy banks! They could borrow on the equity in their homes and buy a new car or pay for Junior's college. And *flipping* — buying a house, fixing it up, and reselling it for hefty profits — became a hip way to get rich quick — as long as prices kept rising.

Meanwhile, all those new mortgages were being pooled and sold by the lenders, in the form of investment bonds, to commercial banks, mutual funds, pension funds, and investors all over the world. And the bonds were "insured" by credit default swaps issued by many of Wall Street's largest financial institutions.

Defaults and foreclosures

The housing market was fine for a while, but then it cooled off — big time. Sales of all homes sagged from a record 7.5 million in 2005 to an estimated 4.9 million in 2008, a 35 percent drop. Sales of brand-new homes dropped even more precipitously, from more than 1.2 million in 2005 to slightly more than 300,000 by 2011.

> ### Depression? Recession? Broke?
>
> Never mind the old economists' joke at the beginning of this chapter; here's a more technical explanation of the difference between a recession and a depression: An economic recession occurs when a country's *gross domestic product* (GDP) — that's the value of all the country's reported goods and services — goes down for two consecutive quarters (six consecutive months) or more. A depression happens when the GDP drops by 10 percent or more.
>
> During America's Great Depression, which stretched over a decade, the GDP dropped a whopping 27 percent between 1929 and 1933 and another 18 percent between 1937 and 1938.
>
> In contrast, in the new century's worst year, 2008, the GDP decreased "only" 2.8 percent. In fact, the Great Recession officially only lasted from December 2007 to June 2009, according to the National Bureau of Economic Research, which is the private, nonprofit organization of economists that has kept official track of such things since 1920.
>
> Still, the Great Recession of 2007 is considered by most economists to be the worst of the ten recessions America has suffered since World War II because of its duration, worldwide scope, and stubborn refusal to go away and take all its effects and impacts with it.

Millions found their gimmicky mortgages had caught up with them. They couldn't make their payments, and they owed more than they could sell their houses for — hence the term *upside down* mortgages. So they defaulted — big time. Between July and September 2008 alone, foreclosure notices were sent to 766,000 U.S. homes. A quarter of those were in California, where housing prices had climbed the fastest and came down the same way. Median housing prices across the nation dropped about 10 percent in 2008 compared to 2007 — and more than 30 percent in much of California.

Mortgage-based bonds went in the tank, and big lenders faced making good on hundreds of billions of dollars in credit default swaps. Some couldn't, and they declared bankruptcy or were bought up by other firms.

Credit dries up, spending shrinks, Iceland sinks

As the financial institutions foundered, lending dried up in other parts of the economy, from car loans to credit card limits. People who had relied on equity in their homes to pay for their boats or vacations or college tuition suddenly had no equity. So consumer spending shrunk, which caused businesses to cut back, often resulting in massive layoffs. The nation's unemployment rate doubled, from 5 percent in January 2008 to 10 percent by October 2009. At one point an average of 750,000 people per month were losing their jobs.

And because the U.S. market was the dominant force in the world economy, other countries felt the pain. In Iceland, for example, the government was forced to nationalize the country's three major banks. The banks relied heavily on foreign investment. When the world's credit markets became tight, the Icelandic banks ran short on funds to meet their obligations. And it wasn't just Iceland. The recession spread around the world, which in turn meant less foreign investment and business for the United States.

"We're from the Government; We're Here to Help..."

Perhaps because of lessons learned from the Great Depression of the 1930s, the federal government reacted quickly, if somewhat reluctantly, to the financial calamity. The U.S. Treasury Department seized the government-backed mortgage finance firms known as *Freddie Mac* and *Fannie Mae*. The government also bailed out American International Group (AIG), the nation's largest insurance company, but allowed Lehman Brothers, one of the country's largest savings and loan firms, to crash into bankruptcy.

On September 24, 2008, with his approval ratings wallowing below 30 percent, President Bush warned a national television audience that "the entire economy is in danger." The speech was part of an effort to sell Congress on a plan to bail out the teetering financial industry.

Known as the *Troubled Asset Relief Program* (TARP), the plan was to use $700 billion in taxpayer money to buy up the mortgage-backed securities of floundering financial institutions. "Without immediate action by Congress, America could slip into a financial panic," Bush said, "and a distressing scenario could unfold."

The scenario did unfold five days later, when a defiant House of Representatives rejected the Bush proposal. The U.S. stock market reacted with the biggest one-day point drop in its history. Two days later, the House reversed itself and approved a version of the bailout plan that the Senate had revised. The plan gave Treasury Secretary Henry Paulson wide latitude to use the money to shore up financial and mortgage institutions.

But to work, it would take time, and the bad economic news just kept coming. Toward the end of November, the stock market had sunk to its lowest level in more than a decade, dragging down pension plans and individual retirement accounts with it.

The crash dashed the dreams of millions of baby boomers (those born from 1946–1964), many of whom had counted on cashing in on healthy stock prices and soaring home values to finance an early retirement. Now they were desperately hoping to hold on to their jobs.

Brand new president, same old problems

In January 2009, President Bush handed off the crisis to his successor, Barack Obama. (For the lowdown on Obama and the 2008 presidential campaign, see Chapter 23.) Less than a month later, the new Democratic president and a Democrat-controlled Congress agreed to a sweeping — and expensive — plan to revive the economy and get as much of the country back to work as possible.

The plan, known formally as the *American Recovery and Reinvestment Act of 2009* and informally as the *stimulus package,* called for spending $787 billion (estimated to eventually climb to $831 billion) on a combination of tax incentives; direct aid to states and local governments; public works projects; extensions of unemployment benefits and funding for job training; and infusions of cash for education, healthcare, housing, energy, and other programs.

The immediate goals of the act were to save jobs and create new ones; help prop up state and local government programs and services, such as those for public safety and education; and inject capital directly into the economy for public works projects that would encourage private investment.

The act's economic philosophy was rooted in the theories of John Maynard Keynes, a British economist who had been greatly influential in guiding the New Deal policies of President Franklin D. Roosevelt during the Great Depression. Keynes had argued that when recessions cause private spending to shrink, governments should spend more to make up the difference, combat unemployment, and prevent the economy from further decline.

"Today does not mark the end of our economic troubles," Obama said while signing the act in Denver on February 17, 2009. "Nor does it constitute all of what we must do to turn our economy around. But it does mark the beginning of the end."

Buying time by buying bonds

While the president and Congress were busy with bailouts and job-saving, another branch of the federal government was also looking for ways to keep U.S. finances afloat. First, some explanation.

Congress created the Federal Reserve System in 1913 in essence to function as the federal government's bank and oversee U.S. monetary policy. Among other things, "the Fed" sets the *federal funds rate,* which is the interest rate banks charge one another for short-term loans and which influences the rates of almost all other kinds of loans. That comes in handy during recessions because lower interest rates help keep the economy moving.

The Fed can also influence the nation's money supply by buying or selling securities such as government bonds. If it wants to increase the amount of available money in recessionary times, for example, it buys bonds by crediting the reserves various banks must have on hand. That lets the banks lower their reserves and use the money to make money through loans and investments.

When the Great Recession hit, the Fed wielded its financial tools with frequency. Starting in late 2007, it cut the federal funds rate nine times in 15 months, dropping the rate from 4.75 percent to near zero, the lowest in its history. Moreover, it went on a bond-buying spree, averaging $85 billion a month by late 2013. Overall, the Fed's balance sheet rose from about $900 billion in mid-2008 to more than $3.7 trillion by the beginning of 2014.

"These purchases have made a meaningful contribution to economic growth and improving the outlook," Federal Reserve Board Vice Chair Janet Yellen told a congressional committee in November 2013. "A strong recovery will ultimately enable the Fed to reduce its monetary accommodation and reliance on unconventional policy tools such as asset purchases. I believe that supporting the recovery today is the surest path to returning to a more normal approach to monetary policy."

Did government intervention work?

The answer to the above question is clear: It depends on whom you ask.

Even before much of the Bush/Obama plans were put in place or the Federal Reserve System's actions had taken hold, there was deeply divided debate on what kind of lifeline could rescue America's economy. A few weeks before the stimulus plan was approved, for example, a group of about 200 economists took out ads in national newspapers opposing it. A week after that, a similar-sized group of economists sent a letter to Congress endorsing the plan. (All of which brings to mind the famous quote by President Harry Truman: "Give me a one-handed economist! All my economists say 'on the one hand, on the other.'")

Some studies have suggested that the efforts saved or created more than 3 million jobs while keeping inflation in check. Other studies concluded they were only temporary fixes that would do more harm than good in the long run or had little effect. Some liberal economists contended that the efforts didn't go far enough and even more government spending was needed. Conservatives argued that the recession would have waned without the stimulus plan, and the biggest result of the plan was to increase the size of the federal budget debt. Moreover, they warned, the "free money" policies of the Fed had pumped up stock prices to unsustainable levels and would trigger high inflation down the road.

Whatever the true impact of the federal government's efforts, the aftershocks of the Great Recession were decidedly mixed, as a look at some facts and figures can attest:

- Four years after the official end of the Great Recession, the median income of U.S. households had actually decreased 4.4 percent, from $54,500 in June 2009 to $52,100 in June 2013.
- The nation's October 2013 unemployment rate of 7.3 percent was nearly 60 percent higher than it had been at the end of 2007, when the Great Recession began.
- On the other hand, total household debt in America had declined $1.2 trillion, or almost 10 percent, between the end of the Great Recession in June 2009 and June 2013. The percentage of U.S. housing units that received some form of foreclosure notice also declined, from 2.2 percent in 2009 to 1.4 percent in 2012.

So, several years after the official end of the worst economic collapse since the 1930s, Americans were making less money and had a higher chance of being out of work, but they had less debt and were less likely to lose their homes. Which overall is good or bad news, depending on whether your neighbor was unemployed or you were.

Brother, Can You Spare a Job?

The most vexing effect of the Great Recession was its swollen jobless numbers. Prior to December 2008, America's monthly unemployment rate had not been *above* 7 percent since June 1993. From December 2008 through November 2013, however, it never went *below* 7.3 percent. And that figure didn't include Americans who were *underemployed* and could only find part-time work or who gave up looking altogether. People were out of work longer, new jobs were being created at a frustratingly slow pace, and many companies were making more money with fewer employees than before the recession.

Looking for work. And looking...

In November 2013, *The New York Times* ran a story about a 53-year-old Massachusetts woman who had been unemployed most of the time since 2008. A college graduate, she had been turned down for dozens of low-paying, low-skill positions for reasons that included "too pretty," "too articulate," and because "we don't hire the unemployed."

She was far from alone in her lengthy quest for work. By November 2013, more than 4 million people, defined as the *long-term unemployed,* had been out of work for longer than 26 weeks. That was triple the number of long-term jobless before the recession began and 50 percent more than the highest figure in any of America's other recessions since World War II.

In July 2008, Congress approved extending unemployment benefits from 26 weeks to as long as 99 weeks and subsequently approved further extensions. But the extensions came with a $250 billion price tag, and there was growing congressional opposition to continuing the program indefinitely. Some economists suggested extending benefits had exacerbated the problem by serving as an incentive for jobless people not to actively seek work and a disincentive for employers to create new jobs.

As 2013 ended, about 2.5 million Americans had exhausted their benefits. That number was predicted to double in 2014, absent another extension.

Detroit

It began as a small fur-trading post and rose to become the nation's fourth-largest city and center of the automobile universe — and eventually the poster child for urban blight. Founded in 1701, Detroit exploded in size and prominence at the beginning of the 20th century, when Henry Ford and other car manufacturers located there. The city attracted tens of thousands of unskilled workers, many of them immigrants or African Americans from the South, who were seeking stable jobs with decent wages and benefits.

By 1950, the population reached 1.9 million, and Detroit was synonymous with automaking. But increasing competition from foreign car companies, overreliance on a single industry, and years of incompetent and sometimes corrupt leadership took their toll. By 2010, the city had shrunk to 714,000. Entire blocks consisted of abandoned buildings. City services had deteriorated to the point that police response to emergency calls could take 45 minutes.

And no U.S. city was hit harder by the Great Recession. Billions of dollars in debt, Detroit sought bankruptcy protection in federal court in July 2013, the largest American city ever to do so.

Where the work went

Economists reckon it takes about 130,000 new jobs each month to provide for Americans who are entering the workforce for the first time. So it was good news when the federal government reported in October 2013 that the economy was adding new jobs at a rate of about 204,000 per month.

The bad news, however, was that an estimated 9.1 million jobs had either been lost or not created as expected during the Great Recession and its aftermath. That meant it could take until 2020 to make up the shortfall. To do it would require plugging some of the holes through which U.S. jobs had leaked.

One of them was *outsourcing,* or the transfer of jobs by American companies to other countries with lower costs of doing business. The Department of Commerce reported that from 2000 to 2012, the largest U.S. multinational corporations cut their domestic workforces by 2.9 million while increasing their foreign payrolls by 2.4 million. The outsourcing issue was hotly debated during the 2012 presidential race, with each candidate accusing the other of supporting the practice.

Many of the outsourced jobs were in manufacturing. Between 2000 and 2009, about 6 million U.S. factory jobs were lost, and only 520,000 had been recovered. Technological changes and automation also contributed to the loss.

The costs of providing worker benefits, such as meeting new federal mandates for healthcare, also played a factor in reduced payrolls. (For more on this subject, see Chapter 23.) Employers with more than 49 workers faced fines if they didn't provide healthcare to full-time employees. Some companies responded by cutting workers to part-time status — or just cutting workers.

Another key factor was cutbacks by state and local governments. In previous recessions, public agencies had been quicker than the private sector to restore jobs. But by the end of 2013, state and local governments and schools still employed about 600,000 fewer people than they had four years earlier.

And as the recession waned, many companies found they could make more money by sharing less of it with employees. As workers scrambled to hold on to their jobs — forget about asking for a raise — productivity increased. That enabled employers to get by with fewer employees. A 2010 Northeastern University study found that while pretax corporate profits *increased* 57 percent from the end of 2008 to the beginning of 2010, wages *decreased* 2 percent. By the end of 2012, U.S. corporations had amassed a record $1.45 trillion in cash reserves, more than half of it stashed overseas to avoid U.S. taxes.

Unspreading the Wealth

The first part of the 21st century wasn't painful for all Americans. Those with a substantial part of their money in assets other than real estate — and a substantial enough pile of dough to ride out the rough times — were for the most part sitting pretty by the end of 2013.

The stock market, for example, emerged relatively unscathed from the Great Recession. In October 2007, the Dow Jones Industrial Average (an index of 30 large-company stocks) reached a high of 14,198. By March 2009, it had plunged 55 percent. But by November 2013, it had passed the 16,000 mark. Trouble was, most Americans had no stocks. Quickly recovering from the recession's ills was a boon enjoyed mostly by those at the very top of the wealth scale.

The rich get richer

On March 2, 2009, the giant insurance company AIG announced it had lost a staggering $62 billion during the last quarter of 2008. The government responded by hastily funneling $30 billion to the firm. Federal officials deemed the company "too big to fail," meaning its collapse would do irreparable harm to the nation's economy. Two weeks later, AIG announced it was paying $450 million in bonuses to the firm's top executives, in part so they wouldn't quit.

The outrage was quick — and loud. "The first thing that would make me feel a little bit better towards them [is] if they would follow the Japanese example," said Sen. Chuck Grassley of Iowa, "and come before the American people and take that deep bow and say I'm sorry and then either do one of two things: resign or go commit suicide."

As it turned out, taxpayers "invested" a total of $182 billion in AIG. The firm eventually restructured, and by 2012, the federal government had recouped the bailout and made a $22.7 billion profit. But the flap became a symbol of a deepening divide between America's haves and have-nots.

The divide was intensified by the fact that whatever wealth most middle-class families had was in the value of their homes or in retirement savings. When the housing market flopped and the stock market plunged, so did their nest eggs. Median household wealth plunged a whopping 39 percent between 2007 and 2011.

"Overall it is estimated that the bottom 80 percent of households lost two decades' worth of wealth," a congressional research report concluded in 2012.

The wealthy also took big hits when the stock market dropped. But they had the resources to hold on to their holdings and even buy more stocks when prices were low. That meant they more than made up for their losses when the market recovered. By 2012, it was estimated that just 1 percent of U.S. households controlled 18 percent of the country's wealth and 36 percent of its annual income.

But the defenders of the *1 percenters* were quick to point out that the very wealthy also paid 25 percent of all federal income taxes, contributed 30 percent of all charitable giving, and were three times as likely to work more than 50 hours a week as anyone else.

"If those people could camp out in the park all day," a wealthy businessman told *The New York Times* in 2012, referring to anti-rich protesters, "why aren't they out looking for a job? Why are they blaming others?"

The blame game

On September 17, 2011, a group of about 1,000 people showed up in New York City's financial district and set up camp in a park. The *Occupy Wall Street* movement, conceived and organized through the Internet and social media, was designed mainly to protest the social and economic inequities that had grown during the Great Recession. "We are the 99 percent" became the movement's rallying slogan, and allied demonstrations were held in more than 70 other cities around the country.

The occupiers' camp was cleared out by police in mid-November, and the movement rather quickly faded from the public eye. But if nothing else, Occupy Wall Street cemented the terms *1 percenters* and *the other 99 percent* in America's political lexicon and fostered debate about economic inequality.

"We can either settle for a country where a shrinking number of people do really well while a growing number of Americans barely get by," President Obama said in his January 2012 State of the Union address, "or we can restore an economy where everyone gets a fair shot, and everyone does their fair share, and everyone plays by the same set of rules."

Deciding who drew up the rules, however, became the country's biggest bone of contention in the new century.

Chapter 23

Reforming Healthcare Is No Tea Party

In This Chapter

▶ Electing — and reelecting — a new kind of president
▶ Boiling over with the Tea Party
▶ Getting sick over healthcare
▶ Battling over the budget

Although the Founding Fathers warned against them, political parties have been a prominent feature of American politics since the 1790s. Generally, two major parties have been all Americans can stomach at any one time. But every once in a while, a third party or political movement has risen temporarily to prominence, if not lasting influence.

In this chapter, I look at the rise of one such movement. I also detail an ambitious effort to improve America's health (or at least its healthcare) and chronicle the brief shutdown of the federal government. Oh, and I throw in a couple of presidential elections, no extra charge.

The Great Presidential Race of 2008

A U.S. presidential race with no incumbent chief executive or vice president running hadn't occurred since 1928, so when a wide-open field presented itself in the 2008 contest, it attracted a veritable herd of candidates.

In an effort to enhance their voters' clout in selecting the parties' nominees, a host of states raced to move their primaries to the front of the pack. As a result, 6 states held caucuses or primary elections before the end of January, and 30 more by mid-February. The earlier primaries meant an earlier start to serious campaigning. By the spring of 2008, Democratic presidential wannabes had participated in 26 debates or forums; Republicans in 21.

In early March, U.S. Sen. John McCain of Arizona sewed up the GOP nomination. It capped a startling comeback for McCain, whose campaign had been broken and almost done just a few months before.

In the Democratic race, Senators Barack Obama of Illinois and Hillary Clinton of New York (the former First Lady) ran away from the rest of the field by mid-February. That guaranteed the 2008 general election would be the first of its kind, with either the first woman presidential nominee by a major U.S. political party or the first African American. But if they outdistanced the rest of the field, they couldn't outdistance each other, trading primary victories in key states throughout the spring. Finally, Obama clinched the nomination in early June.

Obama selected Sen. Joe Biden of Delaware, a well-known political veteran, as his vice presidential running mate. But McCain surprised everyone by picking Sarah Palin, the obscure first-term governor of Alaska. At various times, Palin both energized the McCain campaign and acted as a distraction.

Obama versus McCain

The two top-of-the-ticket candidates offered Americans one of the most disparate choices in U.S. history. At 47, Obama would be the fourth-youngest president ever. At 72, McCain would be the oldest. McCain was a naval veteran of 22 years (5½ as a prisoner during the Vietnam War) and a fourth-term senator. Obama hadn't served in the military and was a first-term senator. Obama was the son of a white American woman and a black Kenyan man. McCain had an ancestor who had served on the staff of George Washington. Obama liked to deliver electrifying speeches before huge crowds. McCain preferred chatting with small groups in informal settings.

The two also had widely differing views on nearly every issue: the war in Iraq, healthcare, taxes, energy, and the environment. Obama fought charges that he was a socialist in progressive's clothing. McCain fought charges that he represented four more years of policies identical to those of the highly unpopular Bush.

Obama's historic victory

Obama held a narrow lead through most of the summer. But as Election Day grew closer, the country's staggering economy came to dominate the campaign, and voters decided Obama was better equipped to deal with it.

It was a convincing victory. Obama carried states no Democratic candidate had carried in 30 years. He also galvanized young voters and minorities to vote in record numbers. Obama's campaign leaned heavily on new technology and techniques, such as sending Election Day voting reminders to cellphones and using websites to raise money and organize grassroots efforts.

"If there is anyone out there who still doubts that America is a place where all things are possible, who still wonders if the dream of our founders is alive in our time, who still questions the power of our democracy, tonight is your answer," Obama said during an election night celebration in Chicago.

In 1858, buying and selling human beings was legal in America. In 1958, discrimination based on race was widespread. In 2008, an African American was elected 44th president of the United States. The country had come a long way. But as Obama would find out, it also had a long way to go.

Calling the president a liar

On September 9, 2009, 232 days after taking office, Obama was addressing a joint session of Congress about his proposed healthcare reform program. When the president said that despite claims to the contrary, the plan would not cover illegal immigrants, Rep. Joe Wilson of South Carolina pointed at Obama and shouted "you lie!" Twice.

Wilson, a former real estate attorney and judge who was in his fifth term in Congress, later apologized to Obama "for this lack of civility" but refused to make a formal apology on the floor of the House. (It didn't hurt his career: Wilson became a prolific fundraiser for the GOP and was easily reelected in 2010 and 2012, the second time unopposed.)

The incident showed just how nasty the partisan split in the nation's capital had become. It belied, however, just how busy Congress actually was during the first two years of Obama's administration. In that time, Congress lifted a ban on homosexuals serving in the military; approved a new arms control treaty with Russia; overhauled regulations for the financial industry; enacted a sweeping healthcare plan; called for pay equity for women; approved more regulation of the tobacco industry; confirmed the nominations to the U.S. Supreme Court of two women, one of them Hispanic; and approved a mammoth economic stimulus program and an even bigger tax-cut package.

It did so through Democratic dominance. Along with electing Obama, American voters in 2008 had increased the Democrats' control of the House of Representatives by 21 seats from 2006 and gave Democrats a 16-seat edge in the Senate. Simply put, the majority party did pretty much what it wanted. But American voters can be a fickle bunch, and not everyone was happy with all that congressional activity.

Going to a Tea Party

One of the things that stuck in the craws of many Americans in the Great Recession was the series of decisions by the Bush and Obama administrations, abetted by Congress, to provide hundreds of billions of taxpayer dollars to huge banks and corporations.

They weren't buying the rationale that temporary aid to the companies would provide economic stability and combat unemployment. The average guy was worried about losing his job, paying his mortgage, and sending his kids to college — and without any government "bailout." Moreover, many were weary of what they regarded as too much federal interference in matters they thought were best left to local or state decisions, such as education or voter registration.

"I worked hard and I went for the American dream and I did okay," an actor named John Ratzenberger told a crowd of 5,000 on the state capitol steps in Sacramento, California, on April 15, 2009. "But now I'm confused . . . why does the government want to take my money and give it to people who don't work?"

Ratzenberger, who was best known for his portrayal of an obnoxious mailman on the TV show *Cheers,* was taking part in one of about 750 rallies throughout the country. Although partly financed by Republican-affiliated groups and individuals and promoted by conservative media, the rallies' organizers insisted they were part of a nonpartisan, loosely organized, grassroots effort that became known as the *Tea Party movement.*

The movement took its name from the 1773 incident in Boston when American colonists dumped British tea into the harbor (see Chapter 4). It sprang up in February 2009, fueled by protests from Seattle to New York about various issues, and it was given national impetus after a Chicago TV reporter named Rick Santelli launched a tirade about the government bailing out people whose house mortgage deals had soured. Santelli suggested it was time for a "Chicago tea party," and the "tea party" name stuck.

The movement wasn't a formal political party, and members prided themselves that it had no formal central structure. Its message generally focused on economic issues more than social ones: Tea Partyers wanted to reduce the federal budget deficit, cut taxes, reduce government spending, and require strict faithfulness to the U.S. Constitution.

Through 2009, Tea Party devotees focused mostly on protest rallies and recruiting new members and were generally viewed as a minor ingredient in the country's political stew. That view changed considerably in 2010.

Taking over the House

In January 2010, a special election was held in Massachusetts to fill the U.S. Senate seat of Ted Kennedy, who had died in 2009. A relatively obscure Republican state legislator named Scott Brown squared off against the state's Democratic attorney general, Martha Coakley. With Democrats outnumbering Republicans by 3-to-1, Coakley was a big favorite. But Brown pulled off a huge upset, becoming the first GOP senator elected in the state in 38 years.

It was a harbinger of things to come. A perfect storm of elements converged on Democrats: Unemployment rates remained high, despite federal bailouts of banks and big businesses; many Americans found the new national healthcare plan confusing, and others just didn't like it; and Obama was the target of persistent (if ridiculous) rumors that he was born in Kenya and thus not eligible to be president. In addition, Democrats had won many congressional seats in 2006 and 2008 in districts that contained a lot of Republican and independent voters, who were ready for a change.

The hundreds of Tea Party groups that had formed in 2009 also played roles. The groups raised money and organized get-out-the-vote efforts. They also endorsed candidates in Republican primaries, often against "establishment" candidates who had the official blessings of GOP leaders. How much direct impact the movement had in the general election has been dissected and debated in various academic studies.

But it certainly galvanized the electorate. A November Gallup poll found that 73 percent of Americans thought the Tea Party energized more people into getting involved in the political process (although 55 percent also thought it deepened partisan divisions). Larger percentages of white, senior citizen, and self-described conservative voters turned out in 2010 than in 2008, and they tended to vote Republican. Worse for Democrats, 63 percent of voters describing themselves as independents voted for GOP candidates in 2010, as opposed to just 49 percent in 2008.

The result was a Republican landslide. The party gained 63 seats and a majority in the House, the biggest gain by either party in a midterm election since 1938. The GOP also picked up 6 seats in the Senate and captured a record 680 state legislative seats.

"Tonight there's a Tea Party tidal wave," said Rand Paul of Kentucky, one of the Tea Party–backed Senate winners, "and we're sending a message. . . ."

Cutting taxes by compromising

"Taxes," the noted American jurist Oliver Wendell Holmes Jr. noted in 1904, "are the price we pay for a civilized society." In 2010, however, American politicians were more interested in resuscitating the economy than in civilizing society.

So with a set of 10-year-old "temporary" federal tax cuts ready to expire on January 1, 2011 — and Republicans ready to take control of the House of Representatives two days after that — President Obama was ready to make a deal.

On December 6, the Democratic president and Republican lawmakers reached agreement on an $858 billion plan that gave each side some of what it wanted. In addition to extending the tax cuts for two years, the package continued lower tax rates on capital gains and dividends; expanded unemployment insurance benefits for up to 99 weeks; cut the percentage of Social Security taxes deducted from paychecks; and extended tax credits for college tuition and business investment in research and development.

Supporters said the plan would save jobs, give families more spending money, and generally goose the economy. The bill passed the Senate on a bipartisan 81–19 vote. But Democrats in the House balked, characterizing it as "a huge giveaway to the super-rich." First they tried to limit the tax cuts to households making less than $250,000, then to less than $1 million. The Senate rejected both efforts.

A Gulf full of oil

The oil spill seemed minimal — at first. The day after the April 20, 2010, explosion in the Gulf of Mexico of an oil rig owned by British Petroleum (BP), officials were keeping their fingers crossed that most of the leaking oil would burn up and that the 11 missing rig crew members would be found.

No such luck. The 11 men were never found. The well gushed oil — 210 million gallons — for nearly three months. Marine life died, the land and sea were polluted, and the Gulf Coast region's economy was walloped. All in all, it turned out to be the worst marine oil spill in history.

A federal investigation concluded that BP and two contractors, Halliburton and Transocean, had cut construction costs on the rig, and also that government officials had been too prone to accept assurances from the oil industry that things were being done safely. BP pleaded guilty to 11 felony counts related to the workers' deaths and paid a $4 billion fine. The company also paid out more than $25 billion in cleanup costs and damages through the end of 2013.

Eventually, the House approved the package on a 277–148 vote, with 139 Democrats joining 138 Republicans in the majority. Many of the Democrats who voted for it acknowledged the reality that Republicans would be taking over the House and feared any bill the Republicans proposed then would be unlikely to include jobless benefits or the payroll tax cut. "The choice is to pay the ransom now or watch it go up next month," said Rep. Brad Sherman, a California Democrat.

Obama signed the bill on December 17 at a ceremony attended by Republican, but not Democratic, congressional leaders. "I'm hopeful that we might refresh the American people's faith in the capability of their leaders to govern," he said.

Lurching Toward Healthcare

One of Obama's biggest first-term goals was to find a cure for America's healthcare system. The president, and many others, contended that soaring healthcare costs were bankrupting individuals, shutting down small businesses, and crippling corporations. Getting well, or trying not to get sick in the first place, was sucking up larger and larger percentages of the nation's economy, which as you recall wasn't feeling too good itself.

Revamping the healthcare system had been tried before by other presidents as far back as Theodore Roosevelt. The last Democratic president before Obama, Bill Clinton, had tried and failed in 1993. But Obama was buoyed by the relative success of a Massachusetts plan that had been signed into law in 2006 by a Republican governor named Mitt Romney. The system required everyone to have health insurance and provided aid for those who couldn't afford it.

With his public approval rating above 60 percent and comfortable Democratic majorities in both the House and Senate, Obama prodded and cajoled a sweeping healthcare reform bill through Congress, signing it into law on March 23, 2010. Not a single Republican in either house voted for it.

The 906-page "Patient Protection and Affordable Care Act of 2010" — commonly known as "Obamacare" — was humongous in size and excruciating in detail. Basically (and a bit simplistically), here's some of what it was supposed to do:

- Allow individuals to keep their current health plan if they chose to do so, and allowed parents to add children up to the age of 26 to their plans.
- Prohibit insurance companies from dropping customers who got sick and from denying them coverage because of preexisting conditions.

- Require healthcare providers to provide preventive services such as wellness exams and tests for specific problems such as prostate and breast cancer.
- Require everyone to buy some kind of health insurance — known as the "individual mandate" — by March 31, 2014, or face a financial penalty, and require employers with more than 49 employees to provide a health insurance plan.

At the heart of the plan was the idea that if everyone had to buy insurance, a lot of young healthy people wouldn't use the health system and thus would help defray the costs of those who did. States were allowed to set up their own insurance exchanges to match people up with plans. If they chose not to, their residents could use a federally run exchange.

The law also required states to expand their Medicaid programs (which provide healthcare for low-income and disabled people) to help those who needed financial assistance in buying insurance. The feds would pay for all the expanded Medicaid costs for three years, and 90 percent thereafter.

"It represents a major step forward toward giving Americans with insurance and those without a sense of security when it comes to their healthcare," Obama said while signing the act into law.

What it gave opponents was political heartburn. Critics said Obamacare would drive thousands of small companies out of business because they couldn't afford to provide health insurance for their workers. It was too complex, they said, would cost state governments millions of dollars in Medicaid payments, and was un-American in forcing people to buy something whether they wanted it or not.

"One thing all Republicans agree on is we think Obamacare is the worst piece of legislation in 50 years," said Senate GOP leader Mitch McConnell of Kentucky. "Every Republican thinks it was a huge mistake and would like to get rid of it."

Republicans tried. The GOP-controlled House of Representatives voted more than 40 times to strip the healthcare plan of funding, suspend major portions of it, or repeal it altogether. Each time they were blocked by the Democratic-controlled Senate. Meanwhile, other foes of the law took a different approach.

Courting the Supreme Court

In January 2011, the state of Florida sued to block the healthcare plan from taking effect, on the grounds the federal government didn't have the constitutional authority to require individuals to buy health insurance. Both a trial court judge and an appellate court sided with Florida (whose cause was eventually joined by 25 other states). Similar suits followed with varying degrees of success before various appeals courts. Finally, in December, the U.S. Supreme Court agreed to decide the issue.

In March 2012, justices listened to three days of argument over the act's constitutionality. The prevailing public opinion, both expert and novice, was that the five conservative justices on the nine-member court would overturn the law. That view was buttressed at one point in the proceedings when Justice Antonin Scalia sarcastically asked if Congress could force people to buy broccoli as well as health insurance.

But the prevailing opinion was proved wrong on June 26, when Chief Justice John Roberts joined the court's four liberal justices in a decision that gave Obamacare supporters most, but not all, of what they wanted. The majority ruled that mandating individuals to buy health insurance or face a financial penalty was essentially just a form of taxation, which Congress had the power to do.

States whose elected leaders opposed the law, however, did get a consolation prize: They could refuse to accept additional federal funds to expand their Medicaid programs to cover low-income people who weren't eligible for current Medicaid help but couldn't afford to buy health insurance.

And the decision is . . .

The fate of Obamacare wasn't the only big ruling to come from the closely divided Supreme Court during the first years of the 21st century. Among the others:

- On January 21, 2010, the court ruled on a 5–4 vote that the government couldn't prohibit corporations and labor unions from spending on political campaigns and causes. The ruling overturned not only federal election laws but also two earlier decisions by earlier Supreme Courts. The decision was a huge impetus to the blossoming of "Super PACS," which were huge political action committees that raised hundreds of millions of dollars for candidates but made it difficult if not impossible to trace precisely the sources of the contributions.

- On June 25, 2013, on a 5–4 vote, the court struck down a major part of the 1965 Voting Rights Act. The decision allowed states to make changes in their voting laws, such as requiring photo identification, without federal approval.

- On June 26, 2013, the court ruled that married couples of the same sex were entitled to federal benefits and cleared the way for same-sex marriages in California. Both decisions were on — surprise! — 5–4 votes, but different combinations of justices voted with the majority in each case.

A stumbling start

The court had ruled, but the Obamacare battles were far from over. For one thing, different states took far different approaches to implementing the plan, which began on October 1, 2013. Although the plan originally envisioned each state setting up its own exchange where its residents could buy insurance, only 14 did so. That left it up to the federal government to set up a national exchange.

While exchanges in some states, such as California and New York, performed reasonably well, others had technical glitches. And the launch of the federal exchange was little short of a disaster: People spent hours vainly trying to even sign in to the system, let alone navigate the labyrinthine application process. By mid-November, only 106,000 people had signed up, of the 7 million-plus the Obama administration estimated might eventually be covered.

In addition, 25 states decided not to accept additional federal money and extend their Medicaid programs to cover residents who made too much money to qualify for existing aid but too little to afford health insurance. The result was that many Americans faced the choice of going without coverage — or moving to another state.

To make matters worse, it turned out an Obama promise that people with existing policies could keep them wasn't so. Thousands of policies were canceled by insurance companies because their benefits didn't comply with Obamacare requirements. That resulted in many people facing higher premiums for new policies they didn't want in the first place.

All this delighted Obamacare opponents. In mid-November, House GOP leaders issued an 18-page memo that listed ways to exploit the plan's problems in the 2014 election. The suggested methods ranged from "digital fliers" and sample videos to anecdotes from individuals with horror stories to tell about the program.

And as it turned out, the legal battles weren't over after all. In late November, the Supreme Court agreed to hear arguments in 2014 as to whether the healthcare act could require employers to offer birth control coverage.

Reelecting Obama

The economy was still shaky. The war in Afghanistan was entering its second decade. Polls showed fewer than half of Americans liked his healthcare plan — and fewer than half liked the job he was doing.

Still, Barack Obama wanted to extend his lease on the White House. Even without all the problems, he was bucking the odds, if you believed in historical precedent: Only once had three consecutive presidents served two full terms (Jefferson, Madison, and Monroe), and that was nearly two centuries before.

The challenger

Mitt Romney had finished second to John McCain in the 2008 GOP presidential derby and had a yen to do better in 2012. The son of former Michigan Gov. Hugh Romney, who had also run for president, Mitt (that was his middle name; his first name was Willard) held both law and business degrees from Harvard. His career had included being governor of Massachusetts for a term, running the Winter Olympics in Salt Lake City in 2002, and operating Bain Capital, a private equity company that bought businesses, tried to increase their market value, and then sold them again.

Romney, 65, outlasted a small army of other GOP candidates in the primaries. By May, the last two challengers, former House Speaker Newt Gingrich and former Pennsylvania Sen. Rick Santorum, dropped out. Romney chose Paul Ryan, a Wisconsin congressman who was considered a whiz at economics and the federal budget, as his vice presidential running mate.

The race

The campaign centered mainly on domestic issues, such as how best to create jobs, Obama's healthcare plan, and how to balance the needs of programs such as Social Security and Medicare against the growing national debt. Obama and Romney spent a total of more than $2 billion, the overwhelming majority (as much as 80 percent according to some studies) of it going for ads that ripped into each other's characters and often exaggerated their stands on issues.

Obama led in most polls through the summer, albeit narrowly. But Romney briefly took the lead in early October, after a nationally televised debate in Denver, in which Obama appeared tired, whiny, and a bit bored. In two subsequent debates, however, the president acquitted himself much better.

The results

Obama won fairly easily. He took 332 of the 538 electoral votes and 51.4 percent of the popular vote. The president lost only two states — North Carolina and Indiana — that he had won in 2008. Obama crushed Romney among minority voters, winning 93 percent of African-American votes, 71 percent of Hispanic, and 73 percent of Asian Americans. He also won among voters under the age of 40 and those making less than $50,000 a year.

American Faces: Newtown, Connecticut

Founded in 1705, this quiet, white-collar Connecticut town of about 28,000 was best-known — if it was known at all — for being the birthplace of the popular board game Scrabble and the place where Olympic champion decathlete Bruce Jenner went to high school. Newtown was home to ten spots on the National Register of Historic Places. Many residents commuted to jobs in nearby Stamford or Hartford.

On the morning of December 12, 2012, a 20-year-old loner named Adam Lanza, who loved violent video games and apparently almost nothing else, shot and killed his mother. Armed with several guns, including a semi-automatic rifle, Lanza then went to the Sandy Hook Elementary School, smashed through the locked school entrance, and began shooting. Ten minutes and 154 rounds later, he had killed 26 children and school staff members, and himself. A year later, investigators had yet to come up with a specific motive for the massacre.

The shootings sparked national debates on mental health, gun control, and the depiction of violence in popular culture. Stricter national gun control measures were proposed, but none were enacted. The school was demolished, and a new school was being built in its place. And Newtown — like Littleton and Aurora, Colorado; San Ysidro, California; and Killeen, Texas — became another synonym for tragedy.

In Their Words

"Democracy in a nation of 300 million can be noisy and messy and complicated," Obama said on Election Night. "We have our own opinions . . . and when we go through tough times, when we make big decisions as a country, it necessarily stirs passions, stirs up controversy. That won't change after tonight. And it shouldn't."

And it didn't.

Meanwhile, Back at the Budget . . .

Despite all the warm-and-fuzzy talk about "bipartisan cooperation" after reaching a compromise on tax cuts at the end of 2010, America began a three-year pinball game of careening from one federal fiscal crisis to another.

At their essence, the fights boiled down to some deep ideological differences between Republican and Democratic lawmakers. Republicans generally favored cutting taxes — including those at the highest income levels — and limiting government spending. That approach, they reasoned, would leave more money in the hands of individuals and businesses, which in turn would create more jobs. Democrats argued that extending tax cuts to the wealthy was less important than having enough revenue to ensure aid to those Americans at the bottom of the economic ladder.

Add to that the fact that Republicans controlled the House and Democrats the Senate and White House. Then buckle your seat belt as we tour the Great Budget Battles of 2011–2013.

Hitting the debt ceiling

The federal debt ceiling is the highest amount the U.S. Treasury can borrow without congressional approval. Formalized by Congress in 1917, the ceiling has been repeatedly, and routinely, raised by Congress with little or no debate.

That changed, however, in 2011, when Republican lawmakers demanded federal spending cuts in return for raising the debt ceiling. The Treasury Department warned that if the ceiling wasn't raised by August 2, the United States would default on financial debts it had already incurred. (The only time in U.S. history that ever happened was in the War of 1812, when the British burned down the Treasury.) After weeks of arguing, the two parties reached a deal, and Obama signed it into law on August 2.

The deal raised the debt ceiling by $900 billion. But — and it was a big "but" — if the two sides failed to find a way to cut $1.2 trillion from the national debt, the agreement called for automatic across-the-board cuts to take place on January 1, 2013.

The looming cuts amounted to $1.2 trillion in reduced spending over ten years. That was relatively peanuts compared to the size of the national debt, which in late 2013 was more than $17 trillion — about 2½ times what it had been in 2003. But it was a fortune if you depended on the government programs that would be chopped.

Most members of both parties didn't favor across-the-board budget cuts (called *sequestration*) because it would include programs and projects each side supported. The hope was that sequestration would put burrs under both parties' saddles and get them to find some long-range solutions. But Congress turned out to have a pretty thick hide.

The deal did spur the credit rating agency Standard & Poor's to downgrade America's credit rating for the first time ever. S&P officials said they just didn't trust Obama and Congress to come up with a stable long-term plan. The downgrade triggered a hefty, if temporary, plunge in the stock market.

Driving off the fiscal cliff

In February 2012, Ben Bernanke, chairman of the Federal Reserve Board, warned that America faced "a massive fiscal cliff of large spending cuts and tax increases."

His reference was to the fact that the tax cuts Obama and Congress had compromised on in late 2010 were set to expire on January 1, 2013. At the same time, the budget cuts the two sides had agreed to postpone in August 2011 were poised to kick in. That was a surefire recipe for a giant economic stomachache.

So everyone sat down to squabble, er, negotiate. Democrats wanted to eliminate tax cuts for the wealthiest Americans. Republicans wanted to continue the cuts for everyone and pay for it by cutting deeper into social programs. After months of rhetorical battle, they reached a deal in the wee morning hours of January 1, 2013. The tax cuts were extended for Americans making less than $400,000 a year, and the budget cuts were kicked down the road again, until March 2013. But despite further negotiations, Congress failed to head off the budget cuts, which kicked in on schedule.

Shutting down the government

Meanwhile, Treasury officials warned that the country would hit its debt ceiling again in mid-October. And throughout the summer, Congress also failed to agree on a spending plan to keep the federal government running.

So on October 1, the government shut down. About 800,000 federal employees were told to stay home. National parks and monuments were closed. People relying on the approval of various federal agencies for loans, medical procedures, and other services were out of luck.

After 16 days of rhetorically rattling sabers and studying public opinion polls (Congress's approval rating dropped to an abysmal 9 percent), the two sides agreed to fund the government until January 2014 and suspend the debt ceiling until February. In mid-December, a shockingly subdued Congress approved a federal spending plan designed to last through September 2015. The plan eliminated some of the sequestration budget cuts and helped ensure against another embarrassing government shutdown in 2014, an election year.

The wheels of government began to turn once more.

Chapter 24
This New America

In This Chapter

- Blogging, tweeting, posting: the impact of the new technology
- Changing the faces of America
- Redefining families

Over the years, America's multicultural, multiethnic, multiracial populace has been described by playwrights, demographers, and other assorted deep thinkers as a "melting pot," a "mixed salad," a "fondue," and even "tomato soup." The common ingredient in all those descriptions is that the country has proved itself pretty adaptable, even when change hasn't come easy.

As the new century unfolded, continually evolving technology revolutionized the ways people got their information, talked to one another, and entertained themselves. At the same time, immigration, changing cultural mores, and just plain living longer were altering how they lived and with whom.

The Techno Revolution

In 1965, a California physicist named Gordon Moore made a prediction. Moore, who was helping to develop semiconductor microchips made of silicon (and three years later cofounded Intel, the world's largest microchip maker), had observed that the number of transistors that could be crammed onto a single chip had been doubling every two years. He thought they would probably continue to do so for some years into the future.

He was right — and then some. In 1975, 5,000 transistors per chip was a pretty good ratio. By 2013, it was 5 *billion*. The microchip had become the foundation for nearly every aspect of American life, from buying socks to falling in love. But first, the news.

Getting news from new news sources

Throughout most of U.S. history, Americans got most of their news from three kinds of media: first newspapers, then radio, then TV. In the first years of the 21st century, however, that began to change.

Newspapers nose dive

In 2000, 56 percent of Americans surveyed said they had watched TV news the day before, 47 percent had read newspapers, and 43 percent had listened to radio news. In 2012, the answers were 55 percent TV, 29 percent newspapers, 33 percent radio, and 39 percent online, a news source not even tabulated in the 2000 survey.

Hardest hit by the advent of online news was the print media. In 2013, only one major weekly news magazine, *Time,* was still publishing a print product. From 2000 to 2011, daily newspaper circulation dropped 20 percent. More ominous, newspaper advertising revenue dropped 52 percent between 2003 and 2012. Many papers tried to recover by launching their own websites as adjuncts to their print products. By 2007, more people read *The New York Times* online each day than read it in print.

But the rise of the web as a news medium also saw the rise of a host of new news competitors. Web-based "news aggregators" such as the Huffington Post (launched in 2005) or specialized news-gathering organizations such as Politico (launched in 2007) gave news seekers a cornucopia of choices. The bad news was that many websites focused as much on spreading rumors as on journalism. Readers had more choices, but not all of them were good ones.

TV troubles

While the web's impact wasn't as great on TV news as it was on newspapers, the traditional Big Three of TV — NBC, CBS, and ABC — found things getting a lot more crowded on America's airwaves. In 1996, Congress approved the first sweeping reform of U.S. telecommunications law since 1934.

One of the law's effects was to pave the way for hundreds of new TV channels and networks, delivered via satellite and through cable systems. By 2013, Americans seeking a dose of TV news could pick from the traditional three broadcast networks — or CNN, Fox News, MSNBC, CNBC, PBS, Univision, and others. As with web-based news sources, the variety was a big plus for consumers, but not always the quality of journalism.

"We've discovered many smart new voices out there," veteran TV journalist Bob Schieffer observed in late 2013, "and excuse me for being blunt, a lot of people who have absolutely no idea what they are talking about."

Calling all cells

On a clear, brisk day in April 1973, a 44-year-old engineer named Martin Cooper was crossing Sixth Avenue in New York City when he decided to call an engineer friend at a rival company and razz him about a device Cooper's company had just invented. So Cooper took out his cellphone. It measured 10 inches long, weighed 2.5 pounds, and, if it had been for sale, would have cost at least $3,500 ($18,410 in 2013 dollars).

As time passed, manufacturers made improvements. In fact, cellphones became pretty popular. There were 5.3 million of them in use in America by 1990, 109.5 million by 2000, and 300 million by 2010. A 2013 survey found that 91 percent of adult Americans owned cellphones (and 67 percent admitted to frequently checking them for calls and messages, even when they hadn't been prompted to do so). As cellphone use proliferated, the use of landline phones waned. A federal government study found that while 95 percent of American households had traditional phones in 2003, just 64 percent had them in 2012.

Cellphones — particularly smartphones that were basically mini-computers — had many uses. You could use them to navigate, take photos, check sports scores, read restaurant reviews, send text messages, and listen to music. They also came in handy in emergencies — more than 400,000 times in 2012 alone.

Americans not only were almost constantly in touch with one another and most of the rest of the world but also probably carried access to more information in their pockets than their grandparents had access to in their entire lifetimes. Nearly every aspect of daily life was made easier.

Of course, this development wasn't all good. In 2011, it was estimated that cellphone use was a factor in 23 percent of U.S. traffic accidents, resulting in more than 300,000 injuries. By 2013, 39 states had laws prohibiting texting while driving, and 10 banned the use of hand-held phones for any purpose while behind the wheel.

Cellphones also made for breaches of etiquette. In one survey, 82 percent of Americans said they had been irritated by "loud and annoying" cellphone users in public places. But only 8 percent admitted being scolded for making loud and annoying calls in public places.

Socializing on the web

If you got a busy signal on your cellphone, there was always e-mail. Like the cellphone, technology for sending electronic text improved considerably from the first attempt to send a message via the Internet in 1969, by scientists at UCLA and Stanford University. (The system crashed when the sender typed the "g" in "login.")

By 2012, an estimated 144 billion e-mails were being sent worldwide each day (about two-thirds of which were believed to be spam, the electronic version of junk mail). So ubiquitous was e-mail that perhaps the most surprising statistic by 2013 was that 15 percent of adult Americans still claimed they *didn't* use the Internet to stay in touch.

E-mails were both a boon and a bane to U.S. business. Though e-mail made staying in touch with customers, suppliers, information sources, and colleagues a snap, studies found that some workers spent up to 28 percent of their day sending electronic messages. That wasn't necessarily a good thing: A 2012 study by researchers at the University of California, Irvine, found that cutting workers off from e-mail access "significantly" reduced their stress and improved their focus and productivity.

E-mails and the web begat *blogging,* which emerged in the 1990s. Blogs (short for *web logs*) were essentially a discussion site usually focused on a particular subject or person and overseen by an individual, organization, or company. Most blogs allowed people to contribute commentary and information. And they fostered a panoply of *social media:*

- **Facebook:** Founded in 2004 and initially designed for college students, this social networking service let friends, relatives, and sometimes perfect strangers exchange messages; share photos, recipes, and favorite books; and join common-interest groups. By 2012, Facebook had more than a billion users worldwide and an annual income of $5.1 billion.

- **LinkedIn:** Launched in 2003, this site was designed for business people to find jobs and potential employees and keep track of other people in their industry or profession. It had 66 million U.S. users in 2013 (and more than 250 million globally). LinkedIn began selling stock in 2011 and had a market value in 2013 of about $24 billion.

- **Twitter:** Created in 2006, Twitter was envisioned as a "micro-blogging" service that let users send text messages — as long as they kept it to 140 characters or fewer. By 2012, it had 500 million users who posted 350 million "tweets" per day. In November 2013, the company began issuing stock, establishing a market value of more than $20 billion — despite never having made a profit.

So, by the end of 2013, Americans could "friend" one another on Facebook, "follow" one another on Twitter, and, uh, "link in" on LinkedIn. They could also find lots of ways to entertain themselves in ways that enabled them to escape commercial interruptions — and one another.

The rise of Silicon Valley

It was once a place devoted largely to growing fruits and nuts. But in 1938, two young guys named William Hewlett and David Packard took $500 in cash, a used drill press, and an unused garage and began building an electronics empire. Over the years, the surrounding Santa Clara Valley, just south of San Francisco, began shedding its orchards and replacing them with suburbs — and innovation.

Spurred by the presence of Stanford University, the area attracted or home-grew scientists and inventors who tinkered and toyed with all sorts of technology. In 1971, a series of articles in *Electronic News* magazine began using the term *Silicon Valley* to describe the enclave of electronics entrepreneurs that were clustered in the area. The innovators attracted investors, who in turn attracted more innovators to the region.

In 2013, it was estimated that more than one-third of all the money being invested in startup companies in America was in Silicon Valley. The area was home to dozens of tech giants: Apple, Google, Facebook, Netflix, Intel, HP, eBay, and Oracle. To which Silicon Valley's 250,000 tech industry workers might say "Yahoo!"

Entertaining ourselves, by ourselves

Once upon a time, say around 1995, Americans who had a yen to see a movie could visit their neighborhood video store, plunk down a few bucks, and rent a VHS tape for a day or two. Of course, if they brought it back late, they had to pay another buck or two.

Fast-forward to 2013. For less than $10 a month, Americans could click a button and watch all the movies they wanted without ever leaving the couch. (Which is the major reason most video stores, including the 9,000-store Blockbuster chain, were out of business by 2013.)

The shift was emblematic of Americans moving to the Internet for their entertainment. "Streaming video" companies such as Netflix and Hulu offered films and TV shows (sans commercials) on a monthly subscription basis. If you fancied something a bit less polished, there was the no-cost YouTube, a 2005-launched website on which people could post videos. The subjects ranged from an infant biting his brother's finger (500 million people around the world watched it) to a pudgy South Korean pop singer performing (this one topped 2 billion views).

There were also online games to play. Americans played tennis, killed zombies, and stole cars, all from their desks or easy chairs. Opponents, often complete strangers, could come from anywhere in the world. Just one game — World of Warcraft — had more than 11.5 million regular players.

Entertainment made up a good part of Americans' time online, and that was plenty of time. From 2010 to 2013, overall annual U.S. Internet use jumped from 451 billion minutes to 890 billion. A 2013 study found that the average American adult spent 5 hours a day online, compared to 4.5 hours watching TV and 30 minutes reading newspapers and magazines. A study by the National Bureau of Economic Research concluded those extra minutes online weren't just coming out of reading or TV time: Americans were spending less time sleeping, eating, cleaning the house, traveling, and hanging with the family.

Some academic studies suggested that all that Internet use was making many people unhappy and unsociable. On the other hand, other studies found that nearly 20 percent of newly married American couples met each other through Internet dating sites.

But one thing everyone agreed on was that all this Internet activity wasn't going unwatched.

Spying on web activities

In the wake of the September 11, 2001, terrorist attacks, the federal government had quietly ratcheted up its security and surveillance efforts. In 2013, Americans began finding out just how much.

On June 5, the London-based *Guardian* newspaper ran a story about a secret order issued in April by the U.S. Foreign Intelligence Surveillance Court (FISC), which was created by Congress in 1978 to oversee domestic surveillance by federal intelligence agencies in cases where criminal activity was suspected.

The court order required Verizon, one of America's largest cellphone service providers, to give the National Security Agency all the information the company had, on a daily basis, about calls made on its system. The order covered which phone numbers were involved and how long the call was for, but not what was said.

Almost simultaneously, the *Washington Post* reported that the NSA and FBI were gathering information from nine leading U.S. Internet companies that included e-mails, photos, documents, and audio and visual "chats." The information-gathering program was code-named PRISM. The agencies cited antiterrorism laws that had been passed in 2008 as their authority for the operation.

The 200,000-plus documents the newspaper stories were based on came from Edward Snowden, a 30-year-old former CIA employee who had also worked for the NSA as a contractor. Snowden said he leaked the information because he was appalled at the damage the spying programs were inflicting on Americans' civil liberties. But federal officials saw his acts as traitorous, and he was indicted for espionage shortly after the stories ran. His prosecution was problematic because he had fled the country and, at the end of 2013, was living under a grant of temporary asylum in Russia.

The revelations outraged civil liberties groups, who filed suit in federal courts, seeking to block some of the surveillance, or at the very least make the federal government disclose what it had been doing, how much it had learned, and what it intended to do with the information. The surveillance also worried U.S. tech industry companies, who feared that foreign governments and businesses wouldn't trust U.S. firms with sensitive data because the U.S. government might be sifting through it.

And the spying programs alarmed members of both parties in Congress, angered both at the spying and the fact that they didn't know about it. By the end of 2013, legislators had introduced more than 20 bills to curb the authority of the NSA to snoop into Americans' phone calls and e-mails.

"The government is stockpiling sensitive personal data on a grand scale," said Representative Ted Deutch, a Florida Democrat. "Intelligence officers, contractors, and personnel only need a rubber-stamp warrant from the court to then learn virtually everything there is to know about an American citizen."

But most Americans appeared to be ambivalent about the spying — and about Snowden. Opinion surveys variously concluded that the country was upset with both Snowden and the spying; that people thought Snowden was a hero; that they considered Snowden a rat; that they believed the spying was justified; or that they were chilled by the thought of someone monitoring their Internet and phone habits.

Going Gray — but with More Variety

There was no getting around it: Americans were getting older. In 2010, there were three times as many Americans over the age of 65 as there had been in 1910. The first of the 78-million-strong *baby boomer* generation (those born between 1946 and 1964; see Chapter 17) reached the ripe old age of 65 in 2011. And 65 wasn't as ripe as it once was. America's life expectancy rate had grown from about 70 in 1960 to 79 in 2013.

In addition to showing a little more silver around the temples, America was also growing more colorful when it came to its ethnic and racial composition. In 1960, nonwhite Americans made up about 15 percent of the population. By 2011, it was 37 percent. And by 2050, it was projected that minorities would be the new majority.

Surfing the "silver tsunami"

As the baby boomers crested normal retirement age, they picked up the collective nickname *silver tsunami* — and not because they looked good in bathing suits. Instead, the reference was to the impact the giant generation was having, or likely to have, on many aspects of American life.

Dealing with tough times

For one thing, living longer was not necessarily synonymous with living better. Many boomers who had counted on company pensions to pay for their retirement were knocked out of work prematurely in the Great Recession and saw their pensions shrink or disappear. Many were also hit by the housing bust and had a potentially large chunk of their retirement nest eggs melt away with the value of their home. Not only that, they were more likely to still be paying for those homes: According to a Federal Reserve study, just 8 percent of Americans age 70 and older had mortgages in 2001. In 2011, it was 30 percent.

The tough economic times meant many older Americans were staying on the job longer. A U.S. Census study found that 16.1 percent of American workers 65 and older were still working in 2012, a 33 percent increase from 1990. In turn, that meant fewer open jobs for younger people. From 2007 to 2011, the number of 55-plus workers grew 12 percent, while the 25–54 group shrank 7 percent.

Straining Social Security and Medicare

But even with a lot of older Americans staying at work, the sheer size of the boomer/tsunami generation helped put a severe strain on key federal social service programs such as Medicare and Social Security. In May 2013, federal officials said the Social Security system, which was already providing benefits to 57 million people, faced an additional 10,000 baby boomers becoming eligible *every* day. The number of Americans eligible for Medicare (the federal program that provided subsidized healthcare to those 65 and over) was expected to grow from 52 million in 2013 to 73 million by 2025.

Meanwhile, the number of working Americans whose payroll taxes supported the programs was shrinking. Officials estimated the trust fund that financed Medicare would be exhausted by 2026, and the Social Security fund by 2033.

"Neither Medicare nor Social Security can sustain projected long-run programs in full under currently scheduled financing," a 2013 federal report warned, "and legislative changes are necessary to avoid disruptive consequences for beneficiaries and taxpayers."

There were plenty of proposed fixes. Among them were "privatizing" Social Security by allowing workers to invest their payroll taxes individually; increasing payroll taxes for the two funds; delaying the age at which workers could become eligible for coverage; and lowering the annual increases in benefits.

All the possible solutions, however, were controversial and the subject of intense partisan debate in Congress. And that was rarely a good place to be a subject.

Stirring the melting pot

The idea of America as a melting pot — where new arrivals could, and should, blend into the existing culture — was popularized in 1908 by an otherwise forgettable play called, well, *The Melting Pot.* But the metaphor was challenged in the last part of the 20th century by those who thought a better image was America as a sort of recipe, where the ingredients kept their own identities but still worked together to produce something tasty.

One indisputable fact was that there were plenty of ingredients from which to choose. In 1980, about 6 percent of the U.S. population had been born in other countries. In 2010, it was more than 13 percent. Federal statistics showed that from 2010 to 2012, about 3 million people became legal permanent residents, or "got their green cards."

Many of the legal immigrants were here because they possessed special skills — in medicine, technology and other areas — that made them highly desirable to American employers. In 2011, 129,000 immigrants were admitted on H-1B visas, more than half of them from India.

But a whole lot of people — an estimated 11.7 million in 2012 — didn't come to the country legally. That number had actually dropped between 2007 and 2009, during the Great Recession, but appeared to begin climbing again by 2012.

Arguments raged continually among economists, demographers, politicians, and others about just what impact illegal immigration had. Heaps of studies were done, and the conclusions ranged from "illegal immigration is a horrid drain on America" to "we couldn't function without it." In between were studies suggesting that while illegal immigrants undeniably soaked up taxpayer-financed education and health and social services, their contributions to the overall economy balanced the scales.

Trying to fix the system

Still, they were here in violation of U.S. immigration laws, and for many Americans, that was enough. Frustrated that the federal government had failed to do anything meaningful on the question since 1986, lawmakers in 43 states passed state laws dealing with the issue. The laws ranged from the punitive, such as an Arizona law that required law enforcement officials to determine the immigration status of anyone they stopped if they suspected the person was in the country illegally, to the accommodating, such as a California law allowing illegal immigrants to obtain drivers licenses.

Polls showed that the overwhelming majority of Americans favored an overhaul of the federal immigration system and that most believed that immigrants already here illegally should be allowed to stay if they met certain requirements, such as learning to speak English.

In June 2013, the U.S. Senate passed a sweeping reform measure that included a 13-year path for illegal immigrants to obtain citizenship — and an extra $40 billion for adding 20,000 Border Patrol agents and 700 miles of fencing along the border with Mexico.

Despite the bipartisan 68–32 Senate vote, however, House Speaker John Boehner refused to take the bill up in 2013. Boehner's Republican caucus was divided between those who favored reform and those adamantly against any bill that included a citizenship path for people who were in the country illegally.

The country's changing face

The tug of war over immigration had political implications as well as legal ones. The issue was of heightened importance to Hispanic voters in particular — and along with other minority groups, Hispanic voters were a growing political force. A 2013 U.S. Census Bureau analysis found that while the numbers of minority voters grew considerably from 2004 to 2012, the number of white voters had shrunk. Minority groups voted overwhelmingly for Barack Obama in 2008 and 2012, providing his margin of victory both times.

Moreover, immigration and higher birth rates among minority groups suggested the voting patterns of 2008 and 2012 were likely to continue. A Pew Research Center study in 2012 projected that by 2050, the Hispanic share of the U.S. population would reach 29 percent. Coupled with projected 13 percent black and 9 percent Asian shares, that meant slightly more Americans would be nonwhite than white by the middle of the century.

There were also signs that minority groups were closing, albeit slowly, the economic gap. Between 1960 and 2008, for example, the number of African-American households with incomes considered below the poverty line ($22,000 in 2007 dollars) had dropped from 55 percent to 25 percent. The number of minority-owned businesses rose from about 10 percent in 1987 to nearly 25 percent in 2012.

And a lot of Americans just weren't interested anymore in being racially categorized: In the 2010 census, more than 19 million people chose the catch-all classification "some other race" in describing themselves.

Redefining the American Family

If an observer from outer space had tried to figure out the typical American family by watching TV in the 1950s, he would most probably have deduced that it consisted of an employed father, a stay-at-home mother, and two or three children who were the center of their parents' universe.

Had the same extraterrestrial come back in the 2010s, he would doubtless have been a bit more confused by the array of choices: a gay father raising a single child, an extended family so dysfunctional they sometimes forgot the children's names, and a cartoon family where the imbecile father routinely choked the incorrigible son. Clearly, there had been some changes.

"There no longer is any such thing," said Zhenchao Qian, chair of the Dept. of Sociology at Ohio State University, "as a typical American family."

Changing with the times

A raft of studies by Qian and others revealed seismic shifts and variations in American family life in the last decades of the 20th century and first decades of the 21st. More people got married later in life, or not at all. Fewer people had children. There were more mixed-race marriages, more people getting divorced and then remarrying, and more families composed of nonrelated friends or combinations of friends and relatives. And there were fewer families of any kind. Some numbers help illustrate the shifting patterns:

- In 1970, 81 percent of U.S. households contained families of some kind. In 2012, it was down to 66 percent.
- In 1970, 40 percent of U.S. households were comprised of a married couple with children. In 2012, it was 20 percent.
- In 1980, about 18 percent of all births in America were to unmarried women. In 2010, it was 41 percent. A quarter of all American children lived in one-parent households.

Oh, and the U.S. birthrate in 2012 was half what it had been at the peak of the baby boom in 1957.

Legalizing gay marriage

Perhaps nothing marked the shifting landscape of family life as much as the issue of same-sex marriage. It came to the forefront in 1993, when the Hawaii Supreme Court ruled that state officials couldn't bar gay marriages unless they could show that doing so was for the public good. Alarmed by the ruling, more than 40 states quickly passed laws expressly prohibiting same-sex marriages.

In 1996, Congress passed and President Clinton signed into law the Defense of Marriage Act, which defined marriage as a union between a man and a woman and asserted that no state could be forced to recognize a same-sex marriage ratified in another state.

The issue simmered for a few years. Then in 2003, the Massachusetts Supreme Court ruled that a gay marriage ban was unconstitutional in that state. The ruling led to another reaction by lawmakers, when conservative members of Congress tried vainly in 2004 and 2006 to amend the U.S. Constitution to ban gay marriages throughout the country. More than two dozen states acted on their own, banning the unions.

But in two landmark decisions in June 2013, the U.S. Supreme Court ruled that the federal Defense of Marriage Act unconstitutionally denied same-sex married partners federal benefits to which they were entitled, and refused to overturn a lower court's ruling that effectively allowed gay marriages in California.

Supporters of gay marriage were cheered by the two decisions and by polls that showed Americans were changing their mind about same-sex unions: In 2001, gay marriage was opposed by a 57–35 margin. In mid-2013, it was supported by a 50–43 margin.

But neither the court's decisions nor the polls decided the issue or ended the controversy. At the end of 2013, 17 states and the District of Columbia allowed gay marriage, while 33 states had bans or restrictions.

Part VI
The Part of Tens

Enjoy an additional Part of Tens chapter online at www.dummies.com/extras/ushistory.

In this part...

- Ten events that had a lasting impact on American culture.
- Ten things that U.S. presidents said that were sort of dumb (or at least dumber than most of the other things they said).

Chapter 25

Ten Events That Defined American Culture

In This Chapter

- Looking at some important works of art and literature
- Describing some projects and inventions that caused societal change

*I*nvention isn't the only important word to begin with the letter *i*. *Innovation* and *inspiration* also fit the bill. And, of course, *important*. Here's a list of ten important innovations or inspirations in various cultural fields that have made a major impact on American life.

The Publication of "Poor Richard's Almanack" (1732)

Benjamin Franklin was 26 years old when he began *Poor Richard's Almanack* in 1732, under the name Richard Saunders. He would continue it every year until 1758, liberally borrowing maxims and proverbs from lots of other people. No matter. It became a huge bestseller and the first American book besides the Bible to give Americans something in common from a literary standpoint.

The Performance of "The Black Crook" (1866)

Americans had been singing and dancing on stage in comic operas since the 1780s. But it wasn't until the opening of *The Black Crook* at Niblo's Garden in New York City that song and dance were married to melodrama, giving birth to the American musical. The cast included a chorus and dancing girls who showed their legs.

The Opening of the Home Insurance Building (1884)

A whole lot of construction took place in Chicago following the great fire of 1871, including the first big building to be erected on a skeleton of steel girders, which gave it more strength and allowed it to be ten stories high. Designed by architect William L. Jenney, the Home Insurance building opened the door, with the invention of the elevator brake, to the skyscrapers of the 20th century.

The Advent of the Copyright Act (1909)

The Copyright Act gave authors, publishers, and composers control over their work and the rights to compensation if others wanted to use it. Over the rest of the century, the law was extended to other creations, including paintings, movies, and computer programs. It helped make the arts a more attractive way to make a living.

The Rise of Jazz (1920s)

Born from the slave songs of the South, jazz hit its stride in the 1920s and has influenced nearly every form of music to come along since: swing, bop, rock, fusion, and even classical. Jazz also influenced the culture in other ways, such as clothing styles and language.

The Birth of Talking Pictures (1927)

On October 6, 1927, American movie patrons were thrilled to hear a popular singer named Al Jolson say, "Wait a minute, wait a minute, you ain't heard nothin' yet." Grammar aside, Jolson was right. The opening of *The Jazz Singer* heralded the birth of "the talkies," an entertainment medium that would have a huge impact on American speech patterns, manners, and cultural mores.

The Jazz Singer, which was a smash hit, wasn't the first feature-length movie to have sound. In 1926, *Don Juan* had been accompanied by sound effects and music synchronized to action on the screen, but no dialogue. *The Jazz Singer* not only had six songs but also 350 spoken words. Movie actors haven't shut up since.

The Abstract Expressionism Movement (1950s)

Abstract expressionism was the first major art movement to begin in the United States. It featured violent color patterns and motion over subject. Its leader was Jackson Pollock, who discarded easel and palette, laid his canvas on the floor, and dripped or poured paint on it.

The Establishment of the NEA (1965)

Though other countries had long histories of government support of the arts, America didn't get into the act until the establishment of the National Endowment for the Arts (NEA) in 1965. Since then, the NEA has provided support for a wide range of artistic efforts, some of them intensely controversial. It has also sponsored exhibits from around the world.

The Acceptance of "Deep Throat" (1972)

It was pretty much like every other porn movie: inane plot, bad puns, and wooden acting. But *Deep Throat* somehow was seen as chic by Middle America. It played in "legitimate" theaters, attracted couples instead of just men, and paved the way for greater acceptance of sex in the cinema and society in general.

The Opening of Facebook (2004)

Born from a web-based photo directory of college students, Facebook became nothing less than a global cultural force. It was launched by a Harvard sophomore named Mark Zuckerberg (along with others) and at first was limited to college students. But in 2006, the site was opened to everyone. Good idea. By 2013, 67 percent of all adult Americans who used the Internet were Facebook users. And users they were: It has been estimated that the data on Facebook grows by half a petabyte a day — and a *petabyte* is one quadrillion bytes.

All those bytes consist of 1 billion people sharing nearly every facet of their personal lives every day. All that sharing, in turn, has affected American politics, fashion, music, and the economy. "It wasn't until I saw Facebook," noted veteran tech journalist David Kirkpatrick, "that I saw a company that was going to change the way we lived."

Chapter 26

Ten Unfortunate Statements by U.S. Presidents

In This Chapter
▶ Recounting some outright lies
▶ Remembering some funny misstatements

*E*veryone occasionally stretches the truth or just plain says something stupid. But when you're the Leader of the Free World (or are going to be), a lot of people hear what you say — and repeat it.

Here are ten statements that U.S. presidents made before taking office or while they were in office. They didn't always backtrack or recant, but you gotta think they would've just as soon kept quiet.

I'm No Physicist, but . . .

> *Railroad carriages are pulled at the enormous speed of 15 miles per hour . . . the Almighty certainly never intended that people should travel at such breakneck speed.*
>
> —New York Governor Martin Van Buren in a January 31, 1829, letter to President Andrew Jackson

Van Buren was fearful that the advent of railroads was threatening the nation's system of canals, much of which was located in the state of New York. Van Buren succeeded Jackson in the White House in 1837 but was unable to do much about slowing down those trains.

Uh, Are You Sure, Mr. President?

Gentlemen, you have come 60 days too late. The Depression is over.

—President Herbert Hoover to a visiting group of clergymen, June 1930

Actually, Hoover was about ten years early in declaring an end to America's darkest economic era.

Yup, It'll Sure Come in Handy Some Day

I've always wondered about that taping equipment, but I'm damn glad we have it. Aren't you?

—President Richard Nixon to his chief of staff, April 25, 1973

The taping equipment to which Nixon referred was used to secretly record White House conversations, including some that incriminated the president and his top aides in the Watergate coverup.

Geography Was Not My Best Class

There is no Soviet domination of Eastern Europe, and there never will be under a Ford Administration.

—President Gerald R. Ford, during an October 6, 1976, presidential election debate with Jimmy Carter

Of course, the truth was that the Soviet Union controlled most of Eastern Europe. Ford compounded his mistake by refusing to correct himself when the debate moderator gave him a chance to do so. Then he went on to lose the election to Carter.

Well, Keep It in Your Pants

I've looked on a lot of women with lust. I've committed adultery in my heart many times.

—Democratic presidential candidate Jimmy Carter in a *Playboy* magazine interview just before the 1976 general election

During the aforementioned debate with Gerald Ford, Carter admitted that "in retrospect, I would not have given that interview if I had it to do over again." He won the election anyway.

Uh, This Is Only a Test

My fellow Americans, I am pleased to tell you I just signed legislation which outlaws Russia forever. The bombing will begin in five minutes.

—President Ronald Reagan during a radio microphone check before a speech, August 11, 1984

Reagan's joke wasn't broadcast but leaked out anyway — far enough that Soviet military forces briefly went on alert.

Go Ahead and Read, but Don't Listen

Read my lips: No new taxes.

—Republican presidential candidate George H. W. Bush at the GOP national convention, August 18, 1988

Bush won the White House, beating Democrat foe Michael Dukakis, and true to his word, he didn't approve any new taxes. But he did agree with Congress to increase some old ones, and doing so helped dash his reelection hopes in 1992.

I Shall Not Tell a Lie . . . .

I want you to listen to me. I'm going to say this again. I did not have sexual relations with that woman, Miss Lewinsky. I never told anybody to lie a single time. Never. These allegations are false, and I need to go back to work for the American people.

—President Bill Clinton, January 21, 1998

If this wasn't an outright lie, it was first cousin to one. On August 17, Clinton told the nation that his relationship with White House intern Monica Lewinsky was "not appropriate. In fact, it was wrong." But he also insisted there had been no coverup, and he was later acquitted by the Senate of impeachment charges brought by the House of Representatives.

They Were under Saddam's Bed

We found the weapons of mass destruction. We found biological laboratories . . . and we'll find more weapons as time goes on. But for those who say we haven't found the banned manufacturing devices or banned weapons, they're wrong, we found them.

—President George W. Bush to a Polish TV interviewer, May 29, 2003, in justifying the U.S. invasion of Iraq

The existence of weapons of mass destruction, also known as WMDs, was Bush's chief justification for the invasion of Iraq. Trouble was, none were ever found. As a consolation prize, U.S. forces did find Iraqi dictator Saddam Hussein, who was eventually hanged by the Iraqi people.

Geography Was Not My Best Class, Either

I've now been in 57 states? I think one left to go.

—Democratic presidential candidate Barack Obama, campaigning in Oregon, May 9, 2008

Obama meant to say 47 because he wasn't going to Hawaii or Alaska. But because no misstatement is so innocent that it can't be parsed by conspiracy theorists, a rumor spread that Obama was showing his allegiance to Islam by inadvertently referring to the Organization of the Islamic Conference, which has 57 member countries. He wasn't.

Part VII
The Appendixes

Visit www.dummies.com for more great Dummies content online.

In this part...

- The Bill of Rights.
- The Declaration of Independence.

Appendix A

The Bill of Rights: Amendments 1–10 of the Constitution

The Conventions of a number of the States having, at the time of adopting the Constitution, expressed a desire, in order to prevent misconstruction or abuse of its powers, that further declaratory and restrictive clauses should be added, and as extending the ground of public confidence in the Government will best insure the beneficent ends of its institution;

Resolved, by the Senate and House of Representatives of the United States of America, in Congress assembled, two-thirds of both Houses concurring, that the following articles be proposed to the Legislatures of the several States, as amendments to the Constitution of the United States; all or any of which articles, when ratified by three-fourths of the said Legislatures, to be valid to all intents and purposes as part of the said Constitution, namely:

Amendment I

Congress shall make no law respecting an establishment of religion, or prohibiting the free exercise thereof; or abridging the freedom of speech, or of the press; or the right of the people peaceably to assemble, and to petition the government for a redress of grievances.

Amendment II

A well-regulated militia, being necessary to the security of a free state, the right of the people to keep and bear arms, shall not be infringed.

Amendment III

No soldier shall, in time of peace be quartered in any house, without the consent of the owner, nor in time of war, but in a manner to be prescribed by law.

Amendment IV

The right of the people to be secure in their persons, houses, papers, and effects, against unreasonable searches and seizures, shall not be violated, and no warrants shall issue, but upon probable cause, supported by oath or affirmation, and particularly describing the place to be searched, and the persons or things to be seized.

Amendment V

No person shall be held to answer for a capital, or otherwise infamous crime, unless on a presentment or indictment of a grand jury, except in cases arising in the land or naval forces, or in the militia, when in actual service in time of war or public danger; nor shall any person be subject for the same offense to be twice put in jeopardy of life or limb; nor shall be compelled in any criminal case to be a witness against himself, nor be deprived of life, liberty, or property, without due process of law; nor shall private property be taken for public use, without just compensation.

Amendment VI

In all criminal prosecutions, the accused shall enjoy the right to a speedy and public trial, by an impartial jury of the state and district wherein the crime shall have been committed, which district shall have been previously ascertained by law, and to be informed of the nature and cause of the accusation; to be confronted with the witnesses against him; to have compulsory process for obtaining witnesses in his favor, and to have the assistance of counsel for his defense.

Amendment VII

In suits at common law, where the value in controversy shall exceed twenty dollars, the right of trial by jury shall be preserved, and no fact tried by a jury, shall be otherwise reexamined in any court of the United States, than according to the rules of the common law.

Amendment VIII

Excessive bail shall not be required, nor excessive fines imposed, nor cruel and unusual punishments inflicted.

Amendment IX

The enumeration in the Constitution, of certain rights, shall not be construed to deny or disparage others retained by the people.

Amendment X

The powers not delegated to the United States by the Constitution, nor prohibited by it to the states, are reserved to the states respectively, or to the people.

Appendix B

The Declaration of Independence

IN CONGRESS, July 4, 1776.

The unanimous Declaration of the thirteen united States of America,

When in the Course of human events, it becomes necessary for one people to dissolve the political bands which have connected them with another, and to assume among the powers of the earth, the separate and equal station to which the Laws of Nature and of Nature's God entitle them, a decent respect to the opinions of mankind requires that they should declare the causes which impel them to the separation.

We hold these truths to be self-evident, that all men are created equal, that they are endowed by their Creator with certain unalienable Rights, that among these are Life, Liberty and the pursuit of Happiness. —That to secure these rights, Governments are instituted among Men, deriving their just powers from the consent of the governed, —That whenever any Form of Government becomes destructive of these ends, it is the Right of the People to alter or to abolish it, and to institute new Government, laying its foundation on such principles and organizing its powers in such form, as to them shall seem most likely to effect their Safety and Happiness. Prudence, indeed, will dictate that Governments long established should not be changed for light and transient causes; and accordingly all experience hath shewn, that mankind are more disposed to suffer, while evils are sufferable, than to right themselves by abolishing the forms to which they are accustomed. But when a long train of abuses and usurpations, pursuing invariably the same Object evinces a design to reduce them under absolute Despotism, it is their right, it is their duty, to throw off such Government, and to provide new Guards for their future security. —Such has been the patient sufferance of these Colonies; and such is now the necessity which constrains them to alter their former Systems of Government. The history of the present King of Great Britain is a history of repeated injuries and usurpations, all having in direct object the establishment of an absolute Tyranny over these States. To prove this, let Facts be submitted to a candid world.

He has refused his Assent to Laws, the most wholesome and necessary for the public good. He has forbidden his Governors to pass Laws of immediate and pressing importance, unless suspended in their operation till his Assent should be obtained; and when so suspended, he has utterly neglected to attend to them. He has refused to pass other Laws for the accommodation of large districts of people, unless those people would relinquish the right of Representation in the Legislature, a right inestimable to them and formidable to tyrants only. He has called together legislative bodies at places unusual, uncomfortable, and distant from the depository of their public Records, for the sole purpose of fatiguing them into compliance with his measures. He has dissolved Representative Houses repeatedly, for opposing with manly firmness his invasions on the rights of the people. He has refused for a long time, after such dissolutions, to cause others to be elected; whereby the Legislative powers, incapable of Annihilation, have returned to the People at large for their exercise; the State remaining in the mean time exposed to all the dangers of invasion from without, and convulsions within.

He has endeavoured to prevent the population of these States; for that purpose obstructing the Laws for Naturalization of Foreigners; refusing to pass others to encourage their migrations hither, and raising the conditions of new Appropriations of Lands. He has obstructed the Administration of Justice, by refusing his Assent to Laws for establishing Judiciary powers. He has made Judges dependent on his Will alone, for the tenure of their offices, and the amount and payment of their salaries.

He has erected a multitude of New Offices, and sent hither swarms of Officers to harrass our people, and eat out their substance. He has kept among us, in times of peace, Standing Armies without the Consent of our legislatures. He has affected to render the Military independent of and superior to the Civil power. He has combined with others to subject us to a jurisdiction foreign to our constitution, and unacknowledged by our laws; giving his Assent to their Acts of pretended Legislation:

For Quartering large bodies of armed troops among us: For protecting them, by a mock Trial, from punishment for any Murders which they should commit on the Inhabitants of these States: For cutting off our Trade with all parts of the world: For imposing Taxes on us without our Consent: For depriving us in many cases, of the benefits of Trial by Jury: For transporting us beyond Seas to be tried for pretended offences: For abolishing the free System of English Laws in a neighbouring Province, establishing therein an Arbitrary government, and enlarging its Boundaries so as to render it at once an example and fit instrument for introducing the same absolute rule into these Colonies: For taking away our Charters, abolishing our most valuable Laws, and altering fundamentally the Forms of our Governments: For suspending our own Legislatures, and declaring themselves invested with power to legislate for us in all cases whatsoever.

He has abdicated Government here, by declaring us out of his Protection and waging War against us. He has plundered our seas, ravaged our Coasts, burnt our towns, and destroyed the lives of our people. He is at this time transporting large Armies of foreign Mercenaries to compleat the works of death, desolation and tyranny, already begun with circumstances of Cruelty & perfidy scarcely paralleled in the most barbarous ages, and totally unworthy the Head of a civilized nation.

He has constrained our fellow Citizens taken Captive on the high Seas to bear Arms against their Country, to become the executioners of their friends and Brethren, or to fall themselves by their Hands. He has excited domestic insurrections amongst us, and has endeavoured to bring on the inhabitants of our frontiers, the merciless Indian Savages, whose known rule of warfare, is an undistinguished destruction of all ages, sexes and conditions.

In every stage of these Oppressions We have Petitioned for Redress in the most humble terms: Our repeated Petitions have been answered only by repeated injury. A Prince whose character is thus marked by every act which may define a Tyrant, is unfit to be the ruler of a free people.

Nor have We been wanting in attentions to our Brittish brethren. We have warned them from time to time of attempts by their legislature to extend an unwarrantable jurisdiction over us. We have reminded them of the circumstances of our emigration and settlement here. We have appealed to their native justice and magnanimity, and we have conjured them by the ties of our common kindred to disavow these usurpations, which, would inevitably interrupt our connections and correspondence. They too have been deaf to the voice of justice and of consanguinity. We must, therefore, acquiesce in the necessity, which denounces our Separation, and hold them, as we hold the rest of mankind, Enemies in War, in Peace Friends.

We, therefore, the Representatives of the united States of America, in General Congress, Assembled, appealing to the Supreme Judge of the world for the rectitude of our intentions, do, in the Name, and by Authority of the good People of these Colonies, solemnly publish and declare, That these United Colonies are, and of Right ought to be Free and Independent States; that they are Absolved from all Allegiance to the British Crown, and that all political connection between them and the State of Great Britain, is and ought to be totally dissolved; and that as Free and Independent States, they have full Power to levy War, conclude Peace, contract Alliances, establish Commerce, and to do all other Acts and Things which Independent States may of right do. And for the support of this Declaration, with a firm reliance on the protection of divine Providence, we mutually pledge to each other our Lives, our Fortunes and our sacred Honor.

(Signed) John Hancock, Button Gwinnett, Lyman Hall, George Walton, William Hooper, Joseph Hewes, John Penn, Edward Rutledge, Thomas Heyward, Jr., Thomas Lynch, Jr., Arthur Middleton, Samuel Chase, William Paca, Thomas Stone, Charles Carroll of Carrollton, George Wythe, Richard Henry Lee, Thomas Jefferson, Benjamin Harrison, Thomas Nelson, Jr., Francis Lightfoot Lee, Carter Braxton, Robert Morris, Benjamin Rush, Benjamin Franklin, John Morton, George Clymer, James Smith, George Taylor, James Wilson, George Ross, Caesar Rodney, George Read, Thomas McKean, William Floyd, Philip Livingston, Francis Lewis, Lewis Morris, Richard Stockton, John Witherspoon, Francis Hopkinson, John Hart, Abraham Clark, Josiah Bartlett, William Whipple, Samuel Adams, John Adams, Robert Treat Paine, Elbridge Gerry, Stephen Hopkins, William Ellery, Roger Sherman, Samuel Huntington, William Williams, Oliver Wolcott, Matthew Thornton

Index

• A •

AAA (Agricultural Adjustment Act), 240
Abstract Expression movement, 383
AC (alternating current), 192
Adams, John, 65, 67, 74, 87, 89, 94, 99, 123–124
Adams, John Quincy, 114, 117, 123
Adams, Samuel, 64, 66
advertising and installment buying, 222
AEF (American Expeditionary Force), 213–214
Afghanistan, 314, 336
AFL (American Federation of Labor), 193–194, 207, 237
African American History For Dummies (Penrice), 211
African Americans. *See also* slavery
  civil rights, 290–292
  first school, 169
  Great Migration movement, 211
  Jim Crow laws, 187–188, 211
  lynchings, 211
  NAACP, 212
  race riots, 291
  racial discrimination, 186–188
  segregation, 235
Agnew, Spiro T., 299–300
Agricultural Adjustment Act (AAA), 240
agriculture
  colonial, 61
  early Native American, 22
Aguinaldo, Emilio, 200
AIDS, 18, 320–321
AIG (American International Group), 345, 351
Alamo, Battle of, 134–135
alcohol
  Prohibition, 14, 205, 226–227
  whiskey taxation, 90–91, 99

Aldrin, Buzz, 298
Alfred P. Murrah Building, 319
Algonquin tribe, 25
Ali, Muhammad, 288
al-Qaida, 314, 331–332, 335
alternating current (AC), 192
America
  in 21st century, 18–19
  100th birthday, 184
  national identity establishment, 9–13
  reconstruction struggles, 13–15
  roots, 7–9
American Birth Control League, 210
American Expeditionary Force (AEF), 213–214
American Federation of Labor (AFL), 193–194, 207, 237
American Indian Movement, 293
American International Group (AIG), 345, 351
American Recovery and Reinvestment Act of 2009, 346
American Revolution
  America's roots, 9
  battles, 78
  population, 61
Amherst, Jeffrey, 59
anaconda plan, 156
Anasazi, 23
Andrew, Johnson, 172–174
animal resources, 182–183
Anthony, Susan B., 145
anthrax, 333
Antietam, Battle of, 162
Anti-Imperialist League, 200
Apple computer, 311
Appomattox Courthouse, 163
Argonauts, 141
Armstrong, Neil, 298
Army and National Guard, 213
Arnold, Benedict, 79

Arthur, Chester A., 195
Articles of Confederation, 83–84
assassination
  Kennedy, 16
  Lincoln, 13, 165
Astor, John Jacob, 100
Austin, Moses, 134
automobile industry, 208
Axis of Evil, 337

• B •

Babe Ruth, 14
baby boomers, 276
Bacon, Nathaniel, 51
Bakker, Jim, 306
Balboa, Vasco Nunez de, 32
banks
  Bank of the United States, 116, 118, 128
  during Great Depression, 232
  nationally chartered, 90, 128–129
  state-chartered, 116
Barrow, Clyde, 245
Barton, Bruce, 223
baseball, 203, 229, 281, 330
Basket Makers, 23
basketball, 191
Battle of Antietam, 162
Battle of Bunker Hill, 79
Battle of Chancellorsville, 162
Battle of Charleston, 80
Battle of Chattanooga, 163
Battle of Chickamauga, 163
Battle of Gettysburg, 155, 162
Battle of Guilford Courthouse, 80–81
Battle of Princeton, 79
Battle of Saratoga, 76, 80
Battle of Shiloh, 162
Battle of Thames River, 111
Battle of the Alamo, 134–135
Battle of the Wilderness, 163
Battle of Tippecanoe Creek, 136
Battle of Trenton, 79
Battle of Vicksburg, 163
Bay of Pigs, 284
Beckley, John James, 106
Begin, Menachim, 303
Bell, Alexander Graham, 184, 192
Benz, Daimler, 324
Bering Straight passage theory, 21–22
Berlin Airlift, 269
Bernanke, Ben, 366
Biden, Joe, 354
Bill of Rights, 86–87, 391–392
bin Laden, Osama, 331–332
bipartisan plan opposition, 339
birth control, 210
The Birth of a Nation movie, 211
Black Codes, 170–171
The Black Crook, 381
Black Gold, 182
blacks. *See* African Americans; slavery
blogging, 370
blood types, 22
bombings, 18
Bonaparte, Napoleon (emperor of France), 102–103
bonds, 222
Bonhomme Richard ship, 80
Bonus Army, 234
Booth, John Wilkes, 165
Bore, Jean Etienne, 119
Boston, 54
Boston Massacre (1770), 65
Boston Red Sox, 2, 203, 330
Boston Tea Party, 64–65
Bow, Clara, 225
Bowie brothers, 134
boycott, 281–282
BP (British Petroleum), 358
Braddock, Edward, 58
Branch Davidian compound, 318
Britain
  army, 69–70
  British and American disagreement, 62
  colonial, 70–71
  colonial policies, 62–63
  debt, 62
  disadvantages in Revolutionary Ward, 77–78
  impressments, 107
  invasion of D.C., 112–113

British Petroleum (BP), 358
Brown, John, 149
Brown, Pat, 304
Brown, Scott, 357
Brown v. Board of Education of Topeka, Kansas, 280–281
Bruce, Blanche Kelso, 169
Bryan, William Jennings, 196, 218–219
buffalo, 185
Bull Run, 162
Bunker Hill, Battle of, 79
Burnside, Ambrose, 160
Burr, Aaron, 98, 104
Bush, George H. W.
  Gulf War, 309–311
  Los Angeles riots, 311–312
  Pentagon terrorism, 330
  savings and loan regulations, 311
  statement, 387
Bush, George W.
  Axis of Evil, 337
  bipartisan plan opposition, 339
  butterfly ballots, 328
  controversial tactic defense, 334
  election, 327–328
  hanging chads, 328
  Medicare reform, 338
  No Child Left Behind Act, 338
  NSA authorization, 334
  post-election scrutiny, 329
  speech on economy, 345
  stance against Iraq, 335
  statement, 388
  Taliban terrorism, 332
  U.S. invasion, 336–337
  USA Patriot Act, 333
  World Trade Center terrorism, 330–331
butterfly ballots, 328

• **C** •

Cabot, John, 32
Cahokia, 24
Calhoun, John C., 108, 118, 123, 126–127
California, 138–140
California Gold Rush, 140–142

Calley, William, 289
Calvert, George, 48
Cambodia, 289
Canada, 79, 110–111
Cape of Good Hope, 29
Capone, Al, 227
Carnegie, Andrew, 157, 191–192, 200
carpetbaggers, 171
Carson, Rachel, 285
Carter, James Earl, 301–304
Carter, Jimmy, 17, 386–387
Cartier, Jacques, 32
casinos, 3
Castro, Fidel, 284
Catholics, 48–49
cattle industry, 182–183
CCC (Civilian Conservation Corps), 240
cellphones, 369
Central America, 60
Central Intelligence Agency (CIA), 271
Challenger shuttle, 308
Chambers, Whittaker, 273
Champlain, Samuel de, 33
Chancellorsville, Battle of, 162
Charbonneau, Toussaint, 104
Charleston, 54, 80
Chase, Samuel, 101
Chattanooga, Battle of, 163
Chavez, Cesar, 292–293
Cheney, Dick, 334
Cherokee Strip, 184
Chesapeake incident, 107
Chicago, 194
Chicanos, 292
Chickamauga, Battle of, 163
child labor, 207–208
Chinese immigration, 188–189
Chivington, John, 185
Christian Coalition, 306
Christianity, 48–49, 306
Church of Jesus Christ of Latter Day Saints, 144
Churchill, Winston, 268
CIA (Central Intelligence Agency), 271
cigars, 30

CIO (Congress of Industrial Organizations), 237
Civil Rights Act, 291
civil rights, 16, 279–281, 290–292
Civil War. *See also* Reconstruction
  anti-draft troubles, 157
  Antietam, 162
  Appomattox Courthouse, 163
  armies, 159
  Bull Run, 162
  casualties, 159–161
  Chancellorsville, 162
  Chattanooga, 163
  Chickamauga, 163
  Fort Sumter, 162
  Gettysburg, 162
  ground war, 161
  Northern economy, 164
  North's advantages, 155
  at sea, 161
  Sherman's march, 161
  Shiloh, 162
  slavery during, 157–159
  Southern economy, 164
  South's advantages, 156
  Vicksburg, 163
  Wilderness, 163
The Civil War For Dummies (Dickson), 151
Civil Works Administration (CWA), 240
Civilian Conservation Corps (CCC), 240
Clark, William, 104–105
Clay, Henry, 108, 118, 121, 123, 142
Clemens, Samuel L., 194
Clevelend, Grover, 157, 195–196
Clinton, Bill
  budgetary success, 18
  Contract with America, 315–316
  Defense of Marriage Act, 378
  domestic policies, 314–315
  election, 313
  federal budget deficit, 18
  healthcare reform failure, 315
  impeachment charges, 316
  Lewinsky affair, 316
  missile attacks in Sudan and Afghanistan, 314
  Republican resurgence, 315
  sexual harassment, 316
  statement, 387
  Welfare Reform Act, 315
Clinton, Hillary, 314–315, 354
Clovis points (spearheads), 23
Coakley, Martha, 357
Cobbett, William, 92
Coca-Cola, 193
Cold War
  Berlin Airlift, 269
  foundations, 267
  Korean War, 270, 272
  Truman Doctrine, 269
  Vietnam, 272
college admission, women's right, 145
Collins, Michael, 298
Colorado Fuel & Iron Company, 207
Columbia, 308
Columbus, Bartholomew, 29
Columbus, Christopher, 8, 29–31, 34
common school movement, 130
"Common Sense" pamphlet, 74
communism, 15–16, 217, 268–269, 272
Compromise of 1850, 142
Comstock silver, 182
Confederate States of America, 153
Congress
  Articles of Confederation, 83–84
  Library of Congress, 106
  United States Constitution, 85
Congress of Industrial Organizations (CIO), 237
Connecticut, 47, 364
Constitution, United States
  Bill of Rights, 86–87, 391–392
  Eighteenth Amendment, 205
  Eighth Amendment, 392
  Fifteenth Amendment, 173
  Fifth Amendment, 392
  First Amendment, 391
  Fourteenth Amendment, 171
  Fourth Amendment, 391
  Nineteenth Amendment, 209
  Ninth Amendment, 392
  ratification, 86

Second Amendment, 391
Seventh Amendment, 392
Sixteenth Amendment, 205
Sixth Amendment, 392
Tenth Amendment, 392
Third Amendment, 391
Thirteenth Amendment, 170
writing, 85
continentals, 71
Contract with America, 315–316
Cooke, Jay, 176–177
Coolidge, Calvin, 219–220, 223–224
Cooper, Martin, 369
Copperheads, 154
Copyright Act, 382
Coronado, Francisco, 32–33
cotton
  cotton gin, 119
  industry growth, 118
  production after Civil War, 168
Coughlin, Charles, 244
courers de bois (runners of the woods), 54
cowboy, 183
crank (drugs), 321
Crawford, William, 123
Crazy Horse, 187
credit default swap, 342
Credit Mobilier Construction Company, 191
Crittenden, John, 159
Croatoan, 37
Crockett, Davy, 134
Cuba, 197, 284
Cuban missile crisis, 286
Custer, George Armstrong, 186
CWA (Civil Works Administration), 240

• D •

dambargo, 107
Darrow, Charles B., 236
Darrow, Clarence, 218
Darwin's theory of evolution, 218–219
Davis, Jefferson, 153, 156
Dawes, William, 68
DC (direct current), 192
Deadwood, 183
debt ceiling, 365
Declaration of Independence, 74–75, 393–396
declaration of sentiments, 145
Deep Throat, 383
Deere, John, 131
default and foreclosure, 343–344
Defense of Marriage Act, 378
Democratic National Convention, 294
demonstrations, 294
Dempsey, Jack, 229
depression, 344. *See also* Great Depression
desegregation, 281–282
Detroit, 349
Dewey, George, 197
Diaz, Bartelmo, 29
Dickson, Keith D.
  The Civil War For Dummies, 151
Dillinger, John, 245
diners, 178
direct current (DC), 192
direct primary election, social reform, 204
discrimination, racial, 186–188
disease, 35–36
District of Columbia, 116
domestic surveillance, 372–373
dot-com boom, 342
Douglas, Frederick, 158
Douglas, Helen Gahagan, 273
Douglas, Stephen, 142, 147–150
Dow Jones Industrial Average, 351
draft cards, 294–295
Drake, Francis, 33, 37
drugs, 294, 321
DuBois, William Edward Burghart, 211–212
Dukakis, Michael, 309
Dust Bowl, 232
Dutch colonies, 49–50

• E •

Eastman, Crystal, 210
Eaton, John, 126
Eaton, Peggy, 126
Eaton, William, 106
Ederle, Gertrude, 229

Edinburgh Journal of Science, 132
Edwards, Jonathan, 57
Egypt and Israel peace agreement, 303
Ehrlichman, John, 300
Eighteenth Amendment, 205
Eighth Amendment, 392
Eisenhower, Dwight, 16
Ellsberg, Daniel, 289
e-mail, 322–323, 369–370
Emancipation Proclamation, 157–158
Emergency Banking Act, 240
Emergency Quota Act of 1921, 217
England, 37
English colonies
   Dutch, 49–50
   economic incentive, 39
   institutionalized slavery, 42–43
   original 13 colonies, 47
   overpopulation, 40
   Pilgrims, 43–45
   Puritans, 45–47
   religious dissent, 40
   settlement of Jamestown, 40–42
   wool industry, 40
English settlement, 8
Equal Rights Amendment (ERA), 295
Eric the Red, 27
Ericsson, Leif (Leif the Lucky), 27–28
Ericsson, Thorvald, 28
Eriksdottir, Freydis, 28
evangelicalism, 306
exploration
   15th-century, 31–33
   Columbus voyages, 29–31
   England, 37
   France, 37
   Native American slavery, 34
   Spain, 36
Exxon Valdez, 310

• F •

Facebook, 370, 383
factories, industry growth, 118
Fallen Timbers, 91
Falwell, Jerry, 306
family life variation, 377–378
Fannie Mae finance firm, 345
farm failure, 232
Faye, Tammy, 306
Federal Emergency Management Agency
   (FEMA), 340
Federal Emergency Relief Act (FERA), 240
federal funds rate, 346–347
Federal Reserve Act of 1913, 206
Federal Reserve Board, 221
Federal Reserve System, 232
Federalists, 88, 99
Feingold, Russell, 333
FEMA (Federal Emergency Management
   Agency), 340
Fenway Park, 330
FERA (Federal Emergency Relief Act), 240
Ferdinand of Castile, 29
Fifteenth Amendment, 173
Fifth Amendment, 392
Filipino revolution, 200
First Amendment, 391
First Continental Congress, 67
Fisher, Irving, 230
Five Civilized Tribes, 26
flappers, 228–229
flipping houses, 343
Flowers, Gennifer, 316
Floyd, Charles "Pretty Boy," 245
flu, Spanish, 213
Ford, Gerald R., 17, 299–300, 386
Ford, Henry, 208
foreclosure, 343–344
Foreman, George, 288
Fort Sumter, 163
Fort Ticonderogo, 78
Four Point Program, 269
Fourteenth Amendment, 171
Fourth Amendment, 391
France, 37
Franklin, Benjamin, 58, 61, 74–75, 85–86
Freddie Mac finance firm, 345
Freed, Alan, 279
Freedman's Bureau, 168
freedom rides, 290
French and Indian War, 57–59

French Revolution, 76, 93–94
Freneau, Phillip, 92
Friedman, Milton, 307
fuel inflation, 302
Fugitive Slave Law, 142, 147–148
fundamentalism, 218–219
fur trading, 54

• G •

Gage, Thomas, 68
gambling, 317
games, 226
gangsters, 227
Garfield, James A., 195
Garvey, Marcus, 221
gay marriage, 361, 378
gay rights, 295
GDP (gross domestic product), 344
generation gap, 294
George III (king of England), 63, 66
German immigrants, 143–144
Germany, 214, 216
Gettysburg Address, 155
Gettysburg, Battle of, 155, 162
G.I. Bill of Rights, 275
The Gilded Age (Twain), 13
Gingrich, Newt, 315–316, 363
Glass-Stagall Banking Act, 240
global economy, 324
G-men, 245
gold, 12
Gold Rush, 140–142, 181
Goldman, Ronald, 318
golf, 226
Gompers, Samuel, 200
Gonzales, Rodolfo, 292
Goodrich, Benjamin Franklin, 178
Goodyear, Charles, 178
Gorbachev, Mikhail, 309
Gore, Al, 18, 327–329
Gould, Jay, 191
government bonds, 222
government shutdown, 366
Grange, Red, 229

Grant, Ulysses S., 13
The Grapes of Wrath (Steinbeck), 239
Great Awakening, 57
Great Depression, 14–15, 231–236
Great Five-Cent Store, 195
Great Migration movement, 211
Great Plains, 25
Great Recession, 19, 341–352
Great Society programs, 291
Greeley, Horace, 176
Greenspan, Alan, 342
Greenwich Village, 295
Grenville, George, 63
Griswold, Roger, 92–93
gross domestic product (GDP), 344
gross national product, 276, 307
Guam, 199–200
Guantanamo Bay, 334
Guatemala, 271–272
guerilla fighting, 55
Guilford Courthouse, Battle of, 80–81
Gulf War, 309–311
gun control, 364
gunboat diplomacy, 202
Gustav, Hurricane, 340

• H •

Haiti, 103
Haldeman, Bob, 300
Hamilton, Alexander, 87–90
Hancock, John, 62
Handler, Ruth, 278
hanging chads, 328
Hanna, Mark, 201
hard bread, 161
Harding, Warren G., 219–220, 223
hardtrack, 161
Harlem Renaissance, 226
Harrison, Benjamin, 196
Harrison, William Henry, 101, 111, 135–136
Hawaii, 197
Hawkins, John, 37, 42
Hayes, Rutherford B., 195
Haymarket Square, 194

Hayne, Robert, 127
Hazelwood, Joseph, 310
healthcare reform, 315, 355
healthcare system, Obamacare, 359–360, 362–363
Hemmings, Sally, 99
Henry, Patrick, 66
Herjolfsson, Bjarni, 27
Hesse-Kassal principality, 73
Hewlett, William, 371
Hill, James J., 191
HIV virus, 320
Hobart, Garret, 201
Holly, Charles Hardin, 280
Home Insurance building, 382
Homeowners Loan Act, 240
Hooker, Joseph, 2, 160
hookers, 160
Hoover, Herbert, 219–220, 223, 233–234, 246, 386
Hoover, J. Edgar, 217
Hoovervilles, 233
Hopkins, Harry, 241
Houdini, Harry, 229
House of Burgesses, 41
House of Representatives, 85
housing market, 342–345
Houston, Sam, 134
Howell, Vernon Wayne, 318
Hudson, Henry, 33
Hulu company, 371
Huntington, Colis P., 176
Hurricane Gustav, 340
Hurricane Ike, 340
Hurricane Katrina, 339–340
Hussein, Saddam, 310, 314, 335

• I •

Ice Age, 22–23
ice box, 184
Ike, Hurricane, 340
illegal immigration, 375–376
immigration
 Chinese, 188–189
 German, 143–144
 illegal, 375–376
 Irish, 143–144
 mid-19th century, 142–143
 as population explosion factor, 61
imperialism, 14, 200–201
impressments, 94, 107
income tax, 205
Indian Civil Rights Act, 293
Indian Removal Act, 132–133
Indians. *See* Native Americans
Industrial Workers of the World (IWW), 207
industry growth, 118–119
infant mortality rate, 61
inflation rate, 302
installments, 222
interest rates, 221
International Labor Defense, 235
Internet, 322–323
Intolerable Acts, 66
invasion of Cambodia, 289
Iraq, 335
Irish immigrants, 143–144
Iroquois League, 25
Iroquois tribe, 25
Isabella (queen of Spain), 29–30
Israel and Egypt peace agreement, 303
Ivins, Bruce, 333
IWW (Industrial Workers of the World), 207

• J •

Jackson, Andrew, 11, 113, 123–126, 385
Jackson, Jesse, 303
James I (King of England), 43
Jamestown settlement, 40–42
Jarvis, Howard, 307
Jay, John, 66, 94
Jay treaty, 94
jazz, 225–226, 382
The Jazz Singer, 382
Jefferson, Thomas
 character traits, 97–98
 Declaration of Independence, 74–75, 98
 as president, 97–99
 reelection, 105
 Republicans, 88–89

Sally Hemmings affair, 99
as secretary of state, 88
as vice president, 89
Jenkins, Robert, 56
Jenney, William L., 382
Jennings, Ken, 323
Jim Crow laws, 13, 187–188, 211
Jobs, Steve, 311
Johnson, Byron Bancroft, 203
Johnson, Hiram, 204, 216
Johnson, Lyndon B., 16
Johnson, Tom, 204
Jolson, Al, 382
Jones, Bobby, 229
Jones, Jim, 305
Jones, Paula, 316
Jones, Sam, 178
Jong-un, Kim, 337
The Jungle (Sinclair), 204–205

• K •

Kaczynski, Theodore, 319
Kansas, 146–147, 184
Karlsefni, Thorfinn, 28
Kasparov, Garry, 323
Katrina, Hurricane, 339–340
KDKA radio station, 225
Kelly, George, 245
Kennedy, John F., 16, 97, 283, 286
Kent State massacre, 289
Kerry, John, 336
Key, Francis Scott, 113
A Key to Uncle Tom's Cabin (Stowe), 147
Keynes, John Maynard, 346
Khomeini, Ayatollah Ruhollah, 303
Khrushchev, Nikita, 270, 285
King George's War, 56
King, Martin Luther, Jr., 290–292, 294, 303
King, Rodney, 311
King William's War, 55
Kirkpatrick, David, 384
Kissinger, Henry, 288
KKK (Ku Klux Klan), 171, 218
Knights of Labor, 193
Knights of the White Camelia, 171

Know, Henry, 88
Know-Nothing party, 144
Korean War, 270, 272
Koresh, David, 318
Ku Klux Klan (KKK), 171, 218

• L •

labor union, 193, 200, 206–208
Ladies' Home Journal magazine, 204
LaFollette, Robert, 204
Land Ordinance of 1785, 84
Lanz, Adam, 364
Latin Americans, 292
League of Nations, 215–216
Lee, Richard Henry, 74
Lee, Robert E., 138, 160
Lessons from the Great Depression For Dummies (Wiegand), 230
Levitt, William, 276
Lewinsky, Monica, 316
Lewis and Clark expedition, 104–105
Lewis, John L., 237
Lewis, Meriwether, 104–105
Library of Congress, 106
life expectancy, 373
light bulb invention, 192
Lincoln, Abraham
assassination, 13, 165
begins presidency, 151–152
character traits, 152
Douglas debates, 149–150
election, 149–150
Emancipation Proclamation, 157–158
Gettysburg Address, 155
reelection, 154
Thanksgiving holiday, 45
Thirteenth Amendment, 170
view on slavery, 12, 146, 153–154
view on Union, 153–154
Lindbergh, Charles, 14, 230, 234
Lindbergh Law, 234
LinkedIn, 370
literature, 226
Livingston, Robert, 74
lobsterbacks, 65

Lodge, Henry Cabot, 216
Long, Huey, 243
Los Angeles riots, 311–312
Louganis, Greg, 320
Louisiana Purchase, 3, 102–103
Lowell, James Russell, 140
Loyalists, 76–77
lunch wagons, 178
Lusitania ship, 212
lynchings, 211
Lyon, Matthew, 92–93

• M •

MacArthur, Douglas, 234, 271
MacDonough, Thomas, 113
Madison, Dolley, 109
Madison, James, 10, 84, 87, 108–109
Magellan, Ferdinand, 32
Mah Jong game, 227
Maine, 47
Maine (battleship), 197
maize, 22
Malcolm X, 290–291
Manifest Destiny, 11–12, 137
Mann, Horace, 130
Marbury v. Madison case, 9, 100
Marbury, William, 99–100
Marines, 106
Marshall, George C., 269
Marshall, James, 140
Marshall, John, 100, 118
Marshall Plan, 269
Maryland, 48–49
Mason-Dixon line, 10
Massachusetts, 47, 53
Massachusetts Bay colony, 45–47
Mayflower, 44
Mayflower Compact, 44–45
McAuliffe, Christa, 308
McCain, John, 328, 354, 363
McCarthy, Joseph, 16, 274–275
McClure's magazine, 204
McCord, James, 297
McCormick, Cyrus, 131
McDonald, Maurice, 277

McDonald, Richard, 277
McKinley, William, 196, 200–201
McPherson, Aimee Semple, 219
McVeigh, Timothy, 318–319
measles, 35
Meat Inspection Act, 205
median household income, 351–352
Medicare, 374–375
Medicare reform, 338
medicine, 126
Mellon, Andrew, 222
The Melting Pot, 375
Memorial Day Massacre, 237
Mennonites, 43
mental health, 364
Merrimac vessel, 161
Mexico, 137–140, 235
microchips, 367
Milk, Harvey, 296
mineral resources, 181–182
Minnesota, 184
minutemen, 64, 68
misery index, 302
Missouri Compromise, 121–122
Mitchell, John, 300
Model T. automobile, 208
molasses, 34
Mondale, Walter, 304
monopolies, 193, 205
Monopoly board game, 236
Monroe Doctrine, 10, 122
Monroe, James, 10, 122–123
Montgomery, Richard, 79
Moore, Gordon, 367
moral behavior, 227–228
Moral Majority, 306
Moran, George, 227
Morgan, J. P., 157, 217
Mormons, 144–145
Morrison, Toni, 322
Morse, Samuel F.B., 131
Moscone, George, 296
Moscow, 270
Mott, Lucretia, 145
Mound Builders, 23–24
movies, 224, 371

muckrakers, 204
Muhammad, Elijah, 290
music, 225–226
My Lai village, 289

• N •

NAACP (National Association for the Advancement of Colored People), 212
Nader, Ralph, 329
NAFTA (North American Free Trade Agreement), 314
Naismith, James, 191
NASA (National Aeronautics and Space Administration), 308
National American Woman Suffrage Association, 209
National Association for the Advancement of Colored People (NAACP), 212
National Baseball League, 203
National Broadcasting Company (NBC), 225
National Endowment for the Arts (NEA), 383
National Indian Youth Council, 293
National Industrial Recovery Act (NIRA), 240
National Organization of Women (NOW), 295
National Rainbow Coalition, 303
National Security Agency (NSA), 334
National Union for Social Justice, 244
nationalism
  Bank of the United States, 116
  industry growth, 118–119
  land prices, 116–117
  national pride, 115–116
  Panic of 1819, 116
  Supreme Court, 118
  tariffs, 116–117
Native Americans
  agriculture, 22
  America's roots, 9
  Anasazi, 23
  Bering Strait passage theory, 21–22
  colonial relations with, 50–51
  disease, 35
  early civilizations, 22–24
  Five Civilized Tribes, 26
  gifts, 26
  Great Plains, 25
  Indian Removal Act, 132–133
  Iroquois League, 25
  migration to America, 21–22
  Mound Builders, 23–24
  Northeast, 25
  Northwest, 24–25
  slavery, 34
  smallpox, 59
  Southeast, 26
  Southwest, 25
  stereotypes, 26–27
  Tecumseh battle with, 109
  tribal groups, 24–26
  Vikings, 27–28
Nativists, 144
NATO (North Atlantic Treaty Organization), 269
Navidad trading post, 29
Navy Seals, 332
NBC (National Broadcasting Company), 225
NEA (National Endowment for the Arts), 383
Nebraska, 184
Netflix company, 371
New Amsterdam colony, 49–50
New Deal, 239–240, 242
New England, 114
New France, 54
New Hampshire, 47
New Orleans, 339–340
New Sweden, 48
the New World, 31
New York City, 54, 79
New York Stock Exchange, 177
New York Times, 368
newspapers, 92–93, 368
Newton, Connecticut, 364
Nichols, Terry, 319
Nicot, Jean, 30
nicotine, 30
Nineteenth Amendment, 209
Ninth Amendment, 392
NIRA (National Industrial Recovery Act), 240
Nixon, Richard, 16–17, 270, 272, 288–289, 294, 296–298, 300, 386
No Child Left Behind Act, 338
nodes, 322–323
no-fly zone, 310

Norsemen, 27
North America, 60
North Atlantic Treaty Organization
    (NATO), 269
North Carolina, 47
North Korea, 337
North, Oliver, 308
North Vietnam, 289
North Vietnamese Army (NVA), 287
Northwest Indians, 24–25
Northwest Ordinance, 84
NOW (National Organization of Women), 295
NSA (National Security Agency), 334
nuclear power, 302
nuclear war, 285–286
nullification, 11, 127
NVA (North Vietnamese Army), 287

• O •

Obama, Barack, 19, 332–334, 337, 346,
    352–364, 388
Obamacare, 359–363
Occupy Wall Street movement, 352
oil, 182, 192, 302, 310
oil spill, 358
Oklahoma City, 18, 319
Olympic Games, 18
Omar, Mullah Mohammad, 332
Onate, Juan de, 33
Operation PUSH (People United to Save
    Humanity) program, 303
Oregon Territory, 145
organized labor, 237
Oswald, Lee Harvey, 286
Otis, James, 62
outlaws, 244–245
outsourced jobs, 350

• P •

Packard, David, 371
Paine, Thomas, 73–74
Pale Faces group, 171
Palin, Sarah, 354
Palmer, A. Mitchell, 217

Panama, 202
Panama Canal, 202–203, 303
Pan-American Exposition, 201
Panetta, Leon, 337
Panic of 1819, 116
Panic of 1837, 135
Parker, Bonnie, 245
Parks, Rosa, 281
Parliament, 62–63, 66
Patient Protection and Affordable Care Act
    of 2010, 359
Paul, Marie Joseph, 75
Paul, Rand, 357
Paulson, Henry, 345
Peace Corps, 284
Peace Democrats, 154
Pearl Harbor, 197
Pemberton, John, 193
Penn, William, 49
Pennsylvania, 49
Penrice, Ronda Racha
    African American History For Dummies, 211
Pentagon Papers, 289
Pequot tribe, 50–51
Perot, Ross, 312
Perry, Oliver, 111
Perry, Rick, 340
Pershing, John, 203, 213
petabyte, 383–384
Philadelphia, 54, 84–85
Philip (king of England), 51
Philippines, 199
Pilgrims, 43–45
pirates, 105–107
Pitt, William, 59, 64, 67
Plains Indians, 185
Planned Parenthood, 210
Plessy v. Ferguson, 187
police action, 16
political and social reform, 204–206
Polk, James K., 11–12, 136–138, 140
polygamy, 145
Pontiac, 59
poor farmers, 223
Poor Richard's Alamac, 381
popular sovereignty, 147

population
  American Revolution, 61
  census of 1800, 101
  census of 1810, 117
  census of 1820, 117
  census of 1860, 142
  Civil War era, 155
  fast growth of, 60–61
  immigration as factor of, 61
  infant mortality rate, 61
  slaves, 61
Populism, 196
potlatches, 24
poverty, 232
Powell, Colin, 335
Prescott, Samuel, 68
Presley, Elvis, 279
Princeton, Battle of, 79
printing process, 184
PRISM program, 372
privateer, 37
Proclamation of 1763, 63
Progressive Era
  improved working conditions, 205–206
  muckrakers, 204
  social reform, 204–205
progressivism, 14
Prohibition, 14, 205, 226–227
Proposition 13, 307
Puerto Rico, 199–200
Pullman strike, 194
punitive expedition, 203
Pure Food and Drug Act (1906), 205
Puritans, 45–47

• Q •

Qian, Zhenchao, 377
Quakers, 49
Quebec Act, 66
Queen Anne's War, 56

• R •

race riots, 291
racial discrimination, 186–188

Radical Republicans, 170
radio, 225
Radio Corporation of America (RCA), 225
railroad
  business expansion, 190–191
  labor strikes, 194
  post-Civil War economy, 176–177
  steam locomotive engine development, 130–131
Raleigh, Walter, 33, 37
Randolph, Edmund, 88
Rankin, Jeanette Pickering, 209
Ratzenberger, John, 356
Ray, James Earl, 291
RCA (Radio Corporation of America), 225
Reagan, Ronald
  election, 304
  foreign affairs, 307–308
  health problems, 304
  Reagan Revolution, 305–307
  Reaganomics, 307
  reelection, 304
  statement, 387
  Strategic Defense Initiative, 307–308
  as "Teflon president," 305
recall, social reform, 204
recession, 135. *See also* Great Recession
Reconstruction. *See also* Civil War
  Black Codes issue, 170–171
  carpetbaggers, 171
  corrupt politics, 175–178
  Freedman's Bureau, 168
  Johnson presidency, 172–174
  Ku Klux Klan (KKK), 171
  readmission to Union, 169–171
  scalawags, 171
  sharecropping, 168–169
  Southern life, 167–169
Red Scare, 217
Red Sox baseball, 2, 203, 330
referendum, social reform, 204
religious freedom
  dissidents, Catholics, and Quakers, 47–49
  Great Awakening, 57
  shifting of attitude, 56–57
Remus, George, 228

Repressive Acts, 66
Republicans, 88–89, 99
retail stores, 195
Revenue Acts (1764), 63
Revere, Paul, 67–68
Revolution of 1800, 97
Revolutionary War
  Battle of Bunker Hill, 79
  Battle of Charleston, 80
  Battle of Guilford Courthouse, 80–81
  Battle of Princeton, 79
  Battle of Saratoga, 80
  Battle of Trenton, 79
  British disadvantages, 77–78
  invasion of Canada, 79
  naval battles, 80
  slavery in, 77
  surrender of Yorktown, 81
Rhode Island, 48
Rickey, Branch, 281
Roaring Twenties
  game play, 226
  moral behavior, 227–228
  movies, 224
  music and literature, 225–226
  radio, 225
robber barons, 175
Roberts, Dave, 330
Robertson, Pat, 306
Robinson, Jackie, 281
rock 'n' roll, 279
Rockefeller, John D., 176, 192, 217
Rockne, Knute, 229
Roe v. Wade, 295
Rogers, Will, 222, 229
Rolfe, John, 41
Romney, Hugh, 363
Romney, Mitt, 363
Roosevelt, Eleanor, 239
Roosevelt, Franklin D., 15, 238–242
Roosevelt, Theodore, 14, 201–203, 212
Rosenberg, Ethel, 273
rubber, 178
Ruby, Jack, 286
Ruby Ridge, 317
rum, 34
Rush, Benjamin, 126
Russian Revolution, 217
Ruth, George Herman (Babe), 229
Ryan, Leo, 305
Ryan, Paul, 363

• S •

Sadat, Anwar, 303
Sagebrush Rebellion, 306
Salk, Jonas, 274
same-sex marriage, 361, 378
Sandy Hook Elementary school, 364
Sanger, Margaret, 210
Santa Anna, Antonio Lopéz de, 134, 139
Santorum, Rick, 363
Saratoga, Battle of, 76, 80
satellite and cable systems, 368
The Saturday Evening Post magazine, 204
savings and loan regulations, 311
scalawags, 171
scarlet fever, 35
Schieffer, Bob, 368
school
  African American, 169
  common school movement, 130
  No Child Left Behind Act, 338
  Sandy Hook Elementary, 364
Scopes, John, 218
Scott, Dred, 148
Scott, Thomas A., 191
Scott, Walter, 178
Scott, Winfield, 156
SDI (Strategic Defense Initiative), 307–308
Seabees battalion, 276
Second Amendment, 391
Sedition Act, 92–93
segregation, 235, 281–282
Seminoles, 133
Seneca Falls, 145
Separatists, 43–44
September 11 attacks, 330–331, 333
sequestration, 365
Sequoyah, 133
settlement of Jamestown, 40–42
Seven Years' War, 57–59

Seventeenth Amendment of 1913, 206
Seventh Amendment, 392
Sewall, Samuel, 43
sharecropping, 168–169, 234
Shays, Daniel, 90–91
Shays's Rebellion, 90–91
Sheridan, Philip, 185
Sherman, Brad, 359
Sherman, Roger, 74
Sherman, William T., 161
Shiite militia, 336
Shiloh, Battle of, 162
Shuster, Joe, 242
sideburns, 160
Siegel, Jerry, 242
Silicon Valley, 371
silver, 182
silver tsunami, 374–375
Simpson, Nicole Brown, 318
Simpson, Orenthal James, 318
Sinclair, Upton
   The Jungle, 204–205
Sioux tribe, 185
Sixteenth Amendment, 205
Sixth Amendment, 392
skraelings, 28
slavery
   America's roots, 8
   Black Codes, 170–171
   Civil War era, 157–159
   compromise of, 141–142
   conditions of, 146
   cotton gin, 119
   Emancipation Proclamation, 157–158
   Franklin's view on, 61
   Freedman's Bureau, 168
   Fugitive Slave Law, 142, 147–148
   institutionalized, 42–43
   Lincoln's view on, 153–154
   Mason-Dixon line, 10
   Missouri Compromise, 121
   Nat Turner's rebellion, 129
   Native American, 34
   opposition, 120
   population explosion, 61
   Revolutionary War period, 77
   rise of cotton and sugar, 119–120
   Underground Railroad network, 148
smallpox, 35, 59
Smith, John, 41
Smith, Joseph, 144
social media, 370, 383
social reform, 204–206
Social Security, 374–375
The Souls of Black Folk (DuBois), 212
Somalia, 314
Sons of Liberty, 64
Soto, Hernando de, 33
Soule, John B., 145
South Carolina, 47
South Korea, 337
Southeast Native American culture, 26
Southern Christian Leadership
   Conference, 290
Southwest Native Americans, 25
Spain, 8, 36, 199–201
Spam, 2
Spanish flu, 213
Spanish-American war, 199–201
spearhead, 23
Speedwell, 44
spending habits, increasing, 222
spices, 29–30
Spinks, Leon, 288
"a splendid little war," 197
spoils system, 125
sports, 229
Sputnik, 282
spying programs, 372–373
Squanto, 44
St. Clair, Arthur, 92
Stamp Act (1765), 63–64
standard of living, colonial, 61–62
Standard Oil Company, 176, 192–193
Stanton, Edwin, 152, 165, 174
Stanton, Elizabeth Cady, 145
Starr, Kenneth, 316
The Star-Spangled Banner, 113
steam locomotive engine development,
   130–131
steamboat development, 119
steel manufacturing, 191–192

steel plow, 131
Steinbeck, John
   The Grapes of Wrath, 239
Stephens, Alexander, 170
Stevens, Thaddeus, 173–174
stimulus package, 346
stock market crash, 232
Stonewall, 295
Stowe, Harriet Beecher, 147
Strategic Defense Initiative (SDI), 307–308
streaming video, 371
strikes, labor, 194, 207
suburban growth, 276
suffrage, 208–210
sugar, 34, 119–120
Sumner, Charles, 148
Sun newspaper, 132
Sunbelt, 305–306
Super PACS, 361
Superman, 242
Supreme Court, U.S.
   Brown v. Board of Education of Topeka, Kansas, 280–281
   International Labor Defense, 235
   Marbury v. Madison, 9, 100
   nationalism, 118
   Plessy v. Ferguson, 187
   Roe v. Wade, 295
   Roosevelt packing attempt, 241
surveillance, 372–373
syphilis, 36

• T •

Taft, William Howard, 200, 202, 212
Taft-Hartley Act, 276
Taliban, 332
tariffs, 90, 116–117, 128
TARP (Troubled Asset Relief Program), 345
taxation
   colonial, 62–63
   income, 205
   Stamp Act (1765), 63–64
   tariffs, 90
   tea, 65
   on wealthy citizens, 221–222
   whiskey, 90–91, 99
Taylor, Zachary, 138, 141–142
tea, 65–66
Tea Party movement, 356–357
Teapot Dome scandal, 220
technological innovation
   blogging, 370
   cellphones, 369
   domestic surveillance, 372–373
   e-mail, 369–370
   Facebook, 370
   LinkedIn, 370
   newspaper circulation decrease, 368
   Silicon Valley, 371
   social media, 370
   spying programs, 372–373
   streaming video capability, 371
   Twitter, 370
Tecumseh, 109–110
telegraph, 131–132
telephone invention, 184, 192
television, 277–278, 368
Temple, Shirley, 245
Tennessee Valley Authority Act (TVA), 240
tennis, 226
Tenth Amendment, 392
terrorism
   anthrax, 333
   on Pentagon, 330
   Ruby Ridge, 317
   September 11 attacks, 330–331, 333
   Unabomber, 319
   Waco, Texas, 318
   on World Trade Center, 18, 319, 330–331
Tet Offensive, 287
Tet (Vietnamese New Year), 287
Texas, 134–135
Thames River, Battle of, 111
Thanksgiving, 45
Third Amendment, 391
Thirteenth Amendment, 170
Thoreau, Henry David, 131, 139
Three Mile Island, 302
Tijerina, Reies Lopez, 292

Index

Tilden, Bill, 229
Tilden, Samuel B., 177
Tippecanoe Creek, Battle of, 136
tobacco, 30, 41, 101
Tories, 76–77
Townsend, Francis, 243–244
Townshend Act (1767), 64–65
Townshend, Charles, 64–65
Trail of Tears term, 133
train system, 130–131
transportation, industry growth, 118–119
Treaty of Guadeloupe Hidalgo, 139
Treaty of Versailles, 216
Trenton, Battle of, 79
tribes. *See* Native Americans
Tripoli, 106
Troubled Asset Relief Program (TARP), 345
Truman Doctrine, 269
Truman, Harry, 268–269, 271
trusts, 193–194
Truth in Securities Act, 240
Turner, Nat, 129
Tunney, Gene, 229
Turkey, 285
Turkish Empire, 29
Tuskegee Institute, 188
TVA (Tennessee Valley Authority Act), 240
Twain, Mark, 13, 194, 200
Twitter, 370
Tyler, John, 136
typhus, 35

• U •

UAW (United Auto Workers), 237
UFW (United Farm Workers), 293
UN (United Nations), 268
Unabomber, 319
Uncle Sam, 111
Uncle Tom's Cabin (Stowe), 147
Underground Railroad network, 148
unemployment, 233, 344–345, 348–350
Union of Soviet Socialist Republics (USSR), 267
Union Pacific railroad, 191
Union Party, 142, 153–154
United Auto Workers (UAW), 237
United Farm Workers (UFW), 293
United Nations (UN), 268
United States Constitution. *See* Constitution
Universal Negro Improvement Association, 221
upside down mortgage, 344
U.S. invasion, 336–337
U.S. presidential race of 2008, 353–355
USA Patriot Act, 333
USSR (Union of Soviet Socialist Republics), 267

• V •

Valentino, Rudolph, 229
Van Buren, Martin, 135–136
Vanderbilt, Cornelius, 191
Verrazano, Giovanni, 32
Versailles, Treaty of, 216
Vespucci, Amerigo, 31
Vicksburg, Battle of, 163
Vietnam, 272, 286–289
vigilantes, 182
Vikings, 8, 27–28
Villa, Pancho, 203
Virginia, 47, 53, 161
voting, 209
Voting Rights Act, 361
vulcanization, 178

• W •

Waco, Texas, 318
Wallace, George, 292
war
  French and Indian, 57–59
  Kind William's, 55
  King George's, 56
  Queen Anne's, 56
  Seven Years', 57–59
  with Tripoli, 106
War Hawks, 108–109
War of 1812, 10, 110–111, 116–117
Washington, Booker T., 188, 212

Washington, D.C., 112–113
Washington, George
  appointed to commander in chief, 71–72
  character traits, 72–73
  election of, 9, 87
  faults, 72
  French and Indian War, 57–58
waterboarding, 334
Watergate scandal, 17, 297–298, 300
wealth
  advertising and installment buying, 222
  efficiency and productivity, 221–222
  Federal Reserve Board, 221
  federal tax cuts, 222
  interest rates, 221
  minimum wage laws, 223
  poor farmers, 223
weapons of mass destruction (WMD), 335
Weaver, Randy, 317
web logs (blogs), 370
Webster, Daniel, 127, 142
Weissmuller, Johnny, 229
Welch, Joseph, 275
Welfare Reform Act, 315
Welles, Orson, 246
Westinghouse, George, 192
Westward expansion
  animal resources, 182–183
  mineral resources, 181–182
  vegetable industry, 184
whale oil, 192
Whigs, 136
whip inflation now (WIN), 301
whiskey, 90–91, 99
Whiskey Rebellion, 91
White House, 112–113
Whitefield, George, 57
Whitewater Development Corporation, 314–315
Whitney, Eli, 119
whooping cough, 35
Wiegand, Steve
  Lessons from the Great Depression For Dummies, 230
Wilderness, Battle of, 163
Williams, Roger, 48
Wilson, Joe, 355
Wilson, Sam, 111
Wilson, Woodrow, 202, 209, 211, 215–216
WIN (whip inflation now), 301
Winfrey, Oprah, 338
Winthrod, John, 46
witch hunting, 46
WMD (weapons of mass destruction), 335
Wolfe, James, 59
women's liberation movement, 295
women's rights
  admission to college, 145
  birth control, 210
  Seneca Falls, 145
  suffrage, 208–210
  voting, 209
Woodland Culture group, 24
Woolworth, Frank W., 195
Work Projects Administration (WPA), 240
working conditions, 205–207
World Trade Center, 18, 319, 330–331
World War I, 215, 217, 222–223
World Wide Web, 323
Wozniak, Steve, 311
WPA (Work Projects Administration), 240
Wright, Orville, 208
Wright, Wilbur, 208

• Y •

Yankee Doodle, 77, 81
Yellen, Janet, 347
Yorktown, 81
Young, Brigham, 144
YouTube, 371
Yugoslavia, 314

• Z •

Zuckerburg, Mark, 383

About the Author

Steve Wiegand has been around for 26.1 percent of America's history as a nation — and he's gaining ground.

An award-winning political journalist and history writer for more than three decades, he's worked as a reporter and columnist for the *San Diego Evening Tribune, San Francisco Chronicle,* and *Sacramento Bee.*

Wiegand is a graduate of Santa Clara University, where he majored in American literature and U.S. history. He also holds a Master of Science degree in Mass Communications from California State University, San Jose.

In addition to *U.S. History For Dummies,* Wiegand is the author of *Lessons from the Great Depression For Dummies* (Wiley), *Sacramento Tapestry* (Towery Books), and *Papers of Permanence* (McClatchy). He coauthored *The Mental Floss History of the World* (Harper Collins) and was a contributing author to *mental floss presents: Forbidden Knowledge* (Harper Collins).

He lives in Northern California.

Dedication

To Ceil, for all my pasts, and to Erin, for all our futures.

Author's Acknowledgments

Thanks first to my friends and colleagues: John D. Cox for launching me on the path to authorship, and Bill Enfield, for his interest and encouragement.

For this third edition, thanks to Project Editor Tim Gallan, Copy Editor Todd Lothery, Technical Editor Troy Guthrie, and Acquisitions Editor Erin Calligan Mooney. All the good stuff is mostly their doing; any mistakes are mine.

Finally, thanks to my mom for having given me the inspiration to read books, so I could someday write them, and to my dad for giving me the sense of humor not to take it too seriously along the way.

Publisher's Acknowledgments

Acquisitions Editor: Erin Calligan Mooney
Senior Project Editor: Tim Gallan
  (Previous Edition: Natalie Faye Harris)
Copy Editor: Todd Lothery
  (Previous Edition: Christy Pingleton)
Technical Editor: Troy Guthrie
Art Coordinator: Alicia B. South

Project Coordinator: Erin Zeltner
Cover Image: ©iStockphoto.com/erick4x4